OB-5

THE
WORLD IS FLAT

*Also by Thomas L. Friedman
in Large Print:*

Longitudes and Attitudes: Exploring the
    World After September 11
The Lexus and the Olive Tree

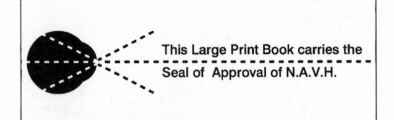

This Large Print Book carries the
Seal of Approval of N.A.V.H.

THE WORLD IS FLAT

A Brief History of the Twenty-first Century

THOMAS L. FRIEDMAN

Thorndike Press • Waterville, Maine

Grateful acknowledgment is made to the following for permission to reprint excerpts of their work: *Business Monthly*; *Business Week*; *City Journal*; Discovery Channel / Discovery Times Channel; *Education Week*, Editorial Projects in Education; *Forbes*; *New Perspectives Quarterly*; The International Finance Corporation / World Bank; *YaleGlobal Online Magazine* (http://yaleglobal.yale.edu/). Excerpts from articles from *The Washington Post* are © 2004. Reprinted with permission.

Published in 2005 by arrangement with Farrar, Straus and Giroux, LLC.

Thorndike Press® Large Print Core.

The tree indicium is a trademark of Thorndike Press.

The text of this Large Print edition is unabridged.
Other aspects of the book may vary from the original edition.

Set in 16 pt. Plantin.

Printed in the United States on permanent paper.

Library of Congress Cataloging-in-Publication Data

Friedman, Thomas L.
    The world is flat : a brief history of the twenty-first century / by Thomas L. Friedman.
      p. cm.
    Originally published: New York : Farrar, Straus and Giroux, 2005.
    ISBN 0-7862-7722-X (lg. print : hc : alk. paper)
    1. Diffusion of innovations.   2. Information society.
3. Globalization — Economic aspects.   4. Globalization — Social aspects.   5. Large type books.   I. Title.
HM846.F75 2005b
   303.48′33—dc22   2005008444

To Matt and Kay
and to Ron

As the Founder/CEO of NAVH, the only national health agency solely devoted to those who, although not totally blind, have an eye disease which could lead to serious visual impairment, I am pleased to recognize Thorndike Press* as one of the leading publishers in the large print field.

Founded in 1954 in San Francisco to prepare large print textbooks for partially seeing children, NAVH became the pioneer and standard setting agency in the preparation of large type.

Today, those publishers who meet our standards carry the prestigious "Seal of Approval" indicating high quality large print. We are delighted that Thorndike Press is one of the publishers whose titles meet these standards. We are also pleased to recognize the significant contribution Thorndike Press is making in this important and growing field.

Lorraine H. Marchi, L.H.D.
Founder/CEO
NAVH

* Thorndike Press encompasses the following imprints: Thorndike, Wheeler, Walker and Large Print Press.

Contents

How the World Became Flat

America and the Flat World

How
the World Became Flat

ONE

While I Was Sleeping

Your Highnesses, as Catholic Christians, and princes who love and promote the holy Christian faith, and are enemies of the doctrine of Mahomet, and of all idolatry and heresy, determined to send me, Christopher Columbus, to the above-mentioned countries of India, to see the said princes, people, and territories, and to learn their disposition and the proper method of converting them to our holy faith; and furthermore directed that I should not proceed by land to the East, as is customary, but by a Westerly route, in which direction we have hitherto no certain evidence that anyone has gone.

— Entry from the journal of Christopher
Columbus on his voyage of 1492

No one ever gave me directions like this on a golf course before: "Aim at either Microsoft or IBM." I was standing on the first tee at the KGA Golf Club in downtown Bangalore, in southern India, when my playing partner

11

pointed at two shiny glass-and-steel buildings off in the distance, just behind the first green. The Goldman Sachs building wasn't done yet; otherwise he could have pointed that out as well and made it a threesome. HP and Texas Instruments had their offices on the back nine, along the tenth hole. That wasn't all. The tee markers were from Epson, the printer company, and one of our caddies was wearing a hat from 3M. Outside, some of the traffic signs were also sponsored by Texas Instruments, and the Pizza Hut billboard on the way over showed a steaming pizza, under the headline "Gigabites of Taste!"

No, this definitely wasn't Kansas. It didn't even seem like India. Was this the New World, the Old World, or the Next World?

I had come to Bangalore, India's Silicon Valley, on my own Columbus-like journey of exploration. Columbus sailed with the *Niña*, the *Pinta*, and the *Santa María* in an effort to discover a shorter, more direct route to India by heading west, across the Atlantic, on what he presumed to be an open sea route to the East Indies — rather than going south and east around Africa, as Portuguese explorers of his day were trying to do. India and the magical Spice Islands of the East were famed at the time for their gold, pearls, gems, and silk — a source of untold riches. Finding this shortcut by sea to India, at a time when the Muslim powers of the day had blocked the overland routes from Europe, was a way for both Columbus and the Spanish monarchy to become wealthy and powerful. When Columbus set sail, he apparently assumed the Earth was round, which was why he was convinced that he could get to India by going west. He miscalculated the distance, though. He thought the Earth was a smaller sphere than it is. He also did not anticipate running into a landmass before he reached the East Indies. Nevertheless, he called the aboriginal peoples he encountered in the new world "Indians." Returning home, though, Columbus was able to tell his patrons, King Ferdinand and Queen Isabella, that although he never did find India, he could confirm that the world was indeed round.

I set out for India by going due east, via Frankfurt. I had Lufthansa business class. I knew exactly which direction I was going thanks to the GPS map displayed on the screen that popped out of the armrest of my airline seat. I landed safely and on schedule. I too encountered people called Indians. I too was searching for the source of India's riches. Columbus was searching for hardware — precious metals, silk, and spices — the source of wealth in his day. I was searching for software, brainpower, complex algorithms, knowledge workers, call centers, transmission protocols, break-throughs in optical engineering — the sources of wealth in our day. Columbus was happy to make the Indians he met his slaves, a pool of free manual labor.

I just wanted to understand why the Indians I met were taking our work, why they had become such an important pool for the outsourcing of service and information technology work from America and other industrialized countries. Columbus had more than one hundred men on his three ships; I had a small crew from the Discovery Times channel that fit comfortably into two banged-up vans, with Indian drivers who drove barefoot. When I set sail, so to speak, I too assumed that the world was round, but what I encountered in the real India profoundly shook my faith in that notion. Columbus accidentally ran into America but thought he had discovered part of India. I actually found India and thought many of the people I met there were Americans. Some had actually taken American names, and others were doing great imitations of American accents at call centers and American business techniques at software labs.

Columbus reported to his king and queen that the world was round, and he went down in history as the man who first made this discovery. I returned home and shared my discovery only with my wife, and only in a whisper.

"Honey," I confided, "I think the world is flat."

How did I come to this conclusion? I guess you could say it all started in Nandan Nilekani's conference room at Infosys Technologies Limited. Infosys is one of the jewels of the Indian information technology world, and Nilekani, the company's CEO, is one of the most thoughtful and respected captains of Indian industry. I drove with the Discovery Times crew out to the Infosys campus, about forty minutes from the heart of Bangalore, to tour the facility and interview Nilekani. The Infosys campus is reached by a pockmarked road, with sacred cows, horse-drawn carts, and motorized rickshaws all jostling alongside our vans. Once you enter the gates of Infosys, though, you are in a different world. A massive resort-size swimming pool nestles amid boulders and manicured lawns, adjacent to a huge putting green. There are multiple restaurants and a fabulous health club. Glass-and-steel buildings seem to sprout up like weeds each week. In some of those buildings, Infosys employees are writing specific software programs for American or European companies; in others, they are running the back rooms of major American- and European-based multinationals — everything from computer maintenance to specific research projects to answering customer calls routed there from all over the world. Security is tight, cameras monitor the doors, and if you are working for American Express, you cannot get into the building that is managing services and research for General Electric. Young Indian engineers, men and women, walk briskly from building to building, dangling ID badges. One looked like he could do my taxes. Another looked like she could take my computer apart. And a third looked like she designed it!

After sitting for an interview, Nilekani gave our TV crew a tour of Infosys's global conferencing center — ground zero of the Indian outsourcing industry. It was a cavernous wood-paneled room that looked like a tiered classroom from an Ivy League law school. On one end was a massive wall-size screen and overhead there were cameras in the ceiling for teleconferencing. "So this is our conference room, probably the largest screen in Asia — this is forty digital screens [put together]," Nilekani explained proudly, pointing to the biggest flat-screen TV I had ever seen. Infosys, he said, can hold a virtual meeting of the key players from its entire global supply chain for any project at any time on that supersize screen. So their American designers could be on the screen speaking with their Indian software writers and their Asian manufacturers all at once. "We could be sitting here, somebody from New York, London, Boston, San Francisco, all live. And maybe the implementation is in Singapore, so the Singapore person could also be live here . . . That's globalization," said Nilekani. Above the screen there were eight clocks that pretty well summed up the Infosys workday: 24/7/365. The clocks were labeled US West, US East, GMT, India, Singapore, Hong Kong, Japan, Australia.

"Outsourcing is just one dimension of a much more fundamental thing happening today in the world," Nilekani explained. "What happened over the last [few] years is that there was a massive investment in technology, especially in the bubble era, when hundreds of millions of dollars were invested in putting broadband connectivity around the world, undersea cables, all those things." At the same time, he added, computers became cheaper and dispersed all over the world, and there was an explosion of software — e-mail, search engines like Google, and proprietary software that can chop up any piece of work and send one part to Boston, one part to Bangalore, and one part to Beijing, making it easy for anyone to do remote development. When all of these things suddenly came together around 2000, added Nilekani, they "created a platform where intellectual work, intellectual capital, could be delivered from anywhere. It could be disaggregated, delivered, distributed, produced, and put back together again — and this gave a whole new degree of freedom to the way we do work, especially work of an intellectual nature . . . And what you are seeing in Bangalore today is really the culmination of all these things coming together."

We were sitting on the couch outside of Nilekani's office, waiting for the TV crew to set up its cameras. At one point, summing up the implications of all this, Nilekani uttered a phrase that rang in my ear. He said to me, "Tom, the playing field is being leveled." He meant that countries like India are now able to compete for global knowledge work as never before — and that America had better get ready for this. America was going to be challenged, but, he insisted, the challenge would be good for America because we are always at our best when we are being challenged. As I left the Infosys campus that evening and bounced along the road back to Bangalore, I kept chewing on that phrase: "The playing field is being leveled."

What Nandan is saying, I thought, is that the playing field is being flattened . . .

Flattened? Flattened? My God, he's telling me the world is flat!

Here I was in Bangalore — more than five hundred years after Columbus sailed over the horizon, using the rudimentary navigational technologies of his day, and returned safely to prove definitively that the world was round — and one of India's smartest engineers, trained at his country's top technical institute and backed by the most modern technologies of his day, was essentially telling me that the world was *flat* — as flat as that screen on which he can host a meeting of his whole global supply chain. Even more interesting, he was citing this development as a good thing, as a new milestone in human progress and a great opportunity for India and the world — the fact that we had made our world flat!

In the back of that van, I scribbled down four words in my notebook: "The world is flat." As soon as I wrote them, I realized that this was the underlying message of everything that I had seen and heard in Bangalore in two weeks of filming. The global competitive playing field was being leveled. The world was being flattened.

As I came to this realization, I was filled with both excitement and dread. The journalist in me was excited at having found a framework to better understand the morning headlines and to explain what was happening in the world today. Clearly, it is now possible for more people than ever to collaborate and compete in real time with more other people on more different kinds of work from more different corners of the planet and on a more equal footing than at any previous time in the history of the world — using computers, e-mail, networks, teleconferencing, and dynamic new software. That is what Nandan was telling me. That was what I discovered on my journey to India and beyond. And that is what this book is about. When you start to think of the world as flat, a lot of things make sense in ways they did not before. But I was also excited personally, because what the flattening of the world means is that we are now connecting all the knowledge centers on the planet together into a single global network, which — if politics and terrorism do not get in the way — could usher in an amazing era of prosperity and innovation.

But contemplating the flat world also left me filled with dread, professional and personal. My personal dread derived from the obvious fact that it's not only the software writers and computer geeks who get empowered to collaborate on work in a flat world. It's also al-Qaeda and other terrorist networks. The playing field is not being leveled only in ways that draw in and superempower a whole new group of innovators. It's being leveled in a way that draws in and superempowers a whole new group of angry, frustrated, and humiliated men and women.

Professionally, the recognition that the world was flat was unnerving because I realized that this flattening had been taking place while I was sleeping, and I had missed it. I wasn't really sleeping, but I was otherwise engaged. Before 9/11, I was focused on tracking globalization and exploring the tension between the "Lexus" forces of economic integration and the "Olive Tree" forces of identity and nationalism — hence my 1999 book, *The Lexus and the Olive Tree*. But after 9/11, the olive tree wars became all-consuming for me. I spent almost all my time traveling in the Arab and Muslim worlds. During those years I lost the trail of globalization.

I found that trail again on my journey to Bangalore in February 2004. Once I did, I realized that something really important had happened while I was fixated on the olive groves of Kabul and Baghdad. Globalization had gone to a whole new level. If you put *The Lexus and the Olive Tree* and this book together, the broad historical argument you end up with is that that there have been three great eras of globalization.

The first lasted from 1492 — when Columbus set sail, opening trade between the Old World and the New World — until around 1800. I would call this era Globalization 1.0. It shrank the world from a size large to a size medium. Globalization 1.0 was about countries and muscles. That is, in Globalization 1.0 the key agent of change, the dynamic force driving the process of global integration was how much brawn — how much muscle, how much horsepower, wind power, or, later, steam power — your country had and how creatively you could deploy it. In this era, countries and governments (often inspired by religion or imperialism or a combination of both) led the way in breaking down walls and knitting the world together, driving global integration. In Globalization 1.0, the primary questions were: Where does my country fit into global competition and opportunities? How can I go global and collaborate with others through my country?

The second great era, Globalization 2.0, lasted roughly from 1800 to 2000, interrupted by the Great Depression and World Wars I and II. This era shrank the world from a size medium to a size small. In Globalization 2.0, the key agent of change, the dynamic force driving global integration, was multinational companies. These multinationals went global for markets and labor, spearheaded first by the expansion of the Dutch and English joint-stock companies and the Industrial Revolution. In the first half of this era, global integration was powered by falling transportation costs, thanks to the steam engine and the railroad, and in the second half by falling telecommunication costs — thanks to the diffusion of the telegraph, telephones, the PC, satellites, fiber-optic cable, and the early version of the World Wide Web. It was during this era that we really saw the birth and maturation of a global economy, in the sense that there was enough movement of goods and information from continent to continent for there to be a global market, with global arbitrage in products and labor. The dynamic forces behind this era of globalization were breakthroughs in hardware — from steamships and railroads in the beginning to telephones and mainframe computers toward the end. And the big questions in this era were: Where does my company fit into the global economy? How does it take advantage of the opportunities? How can I go global and collaborate with others through my company? *The Lexus and the Olive Tree* was primarily about the climax of this era, an era when the walls started falling all around the world, and integration, and the backlash to it, went to a whole new level. But even as the walls fell, there were still a lot of barriers to seamless global integration. Remember, when Bill Clinton was elected president in 1992, virtually no one outside of government and the academy had e-mail, and when I was writing *The Lexus and the Olive Tree* in 1998, the Internet and e-commerce were just taking off.

Well, they took off — along with a lot of other things that came together while I was sleeping. And that is why I argue in this book that around the year 2000 we entered a whole new era: Globalization 3.0. Globalization 3.0 is shrinking the world from a size small to a size tiny and flattening the playing field at the same time. And while the dynamic force in Globalization 1.0 was countries globalizing and the dynamic force in Globalization 2.0 was companies globalizing, the dynamic force in Globalization 3.0 — the thing that gives it its unique character — is the newfound power for *individuals* to collaborate and compete globally. And the lever that is enabling individuals and groups to go global so easily and so seamlessly is not horsepower, and not hardware, but software — all sorts of new applications — in conjunction with the creation of a global fiber-optic network that has made us all next-door neighbors. Individuals must, and can, now ask, Where do *I* fit into the global competition and opportunities of the day, and how can *I*, on my own, collaborate with others globally?

But Globalization 3.0 not only differs from the previous eras in how it is shrinking and flattening the world and in how it is empowering individuals. It is different in that Globalization 1.0 and 2.0 were driven primarily by European and American individuals and businesses. Even though China actually had the biggest economy in the world in the eighteenth century, it was Western countries, companies, and explorers who were doing most of the globalizing and shaping of the system. But going forward, this will be less and less true. Because it is flattening and shrinking the world, Globalization 3.0 is going to be more and more driven not only by individuals but also by a much more diverse — non-Western, non-white — group of individuals. Individuals from every corner of the flat world are being empowered. Globalization 3.0 makes it possible for so many more people to plug and play, and you are going to see every color of the human rainbow take part.

(While this empowerment of individuals to act globally is the most important new feature of Globalization 3.0, companies — large and small — have been newly empowered in this era as well. I discuss both in detail later in the book.)

Needless to say, I had only the vaguest appreciation of all this as I left Nandan's office that day in Bangalore. But as I sat contemplating these changes on the balcony of my hotel room that evening, I did know one thing: I wanted to drop everything and write a book that would enable me to understand how this flattening process happened and what its implications might be for countries, companies, and individuals. So I picked up the phone and called my wife, Ann, and told her, "I am going to write a book called *The World Is Flat.*" She was both amused and curious — well, maybe *more* amused than curious! Eventually, I was able to bring her around, and I hope I will be able to do the same with you, dear reader. Let me start by taking you back to the beginning of my journey to India, and other points east, and share with you some of the encounters that led me to conclude the world was no longer round — but flat.

Jaithirth "Jerry" Rao was one of the first people I met in Bangalore — and I hadn't been with him for more than a few minutes at the Leela Palace hotel before he told me that he could handle my tax returns and any other accounting needs I had — from Bangalore. No thanks, I demurred, I already have an accountant in Chicago. Jerry just

26

smiled. He was too polite to say it — that he may already be my accountant, or rather my accountant's accountant, thanks to the explosion in the outsourcing of tax preparation.

"This is happening as we speak," said Rao, a native of Mumbai, formerly Bombay, whose Indian firm, MphasiS, has a team of Indian accountants able to do outsourced accounting work from any state in America and the federal government. "We have tied up with several small and medium-sized CPA firms in America."

"You mean like my accountant?" I asked. "Yes, like your accountant," said Rao with a smile. Rao's company has pioneered a work flow software program with a standardized format that makes the outsourcing of tax returns cheap and easy. The whole process starts, Jerry explained, with an accountant in the United States scanning my last year's tax returns, plus my W-2, W-4, 1099, bonuses, and stock statements — everything — into a computer server, which is physically located in California or Texas. "Now your accountant, if he is going to have your taxes done overseas, knows that you would prefer not to have your surname be known or your Social Security number known [to someone outside the country], so he can choose to suppress that information," said Rao. "The accountants in India call up all the raw information directly from the server in America [using a password], and they complete your tax returns, with you remaining anonymous. All the data stays in the U.S. to comply with privacy regulations . . . We take data protection and privacy very seriously. The accountant in India can see the data on his screen, but he cannot take a download of it or print it out — our program does not allow it. The most he could do would be to try to memorize it, if he had some ill intention. The accountants are not allowed to even take a paper and pen into the room when they are working on the returns."

I was intrigued at just how advanced this form of service outsourcing had become. "We are doing several thousand returns," said Rao. What's more, "Your CPA in America need not even be in their office. They can be sitting on a beach in California and e-mail us and say, 'Jerry, you are really good at doing New York State returns, so you do Tom's returns. And Sonia, you and your team in Delhi do the Washington and Florida returns.' Sonia, by the way, is working out of her house in India, with no overhead [for the company to pay]. 'And these others, they are really complicated, so I will do them myself.' "

In 2003, some 25,000 U.S. tax returns

were done in India. In 2004, the number was 100,000. In 2005, it is expected to be 400,000. In a decade, you will assume that your accountant has outsourced the basic preparation of your tax returns — if not more.

"How did you get into this?" I asked Rao.

"My friend Jeroen Tas, a Dutchman, and I were both working in California for Citigroup," Rao explained. "I was his boss and we were coming back from New York one day together on a flight and I said that I was planning to quit and he said, 'So am I.' We both said, 'Why don't we start our own business?' So in 1997–98, we put together a business plan to provide high-end Internet solutions for big companies . . . Two years ago, though, I went to a technology convention in Las Vegas and was approached by some medium-size [American] accounting firms, and they said they could not afford to set up big tax outsourcing operations to India, but the big guys could, and [the medium guys] wanted to get ahead of them. So we developed a software product called VTR — Virtual Tax Room — to enable these medium-size accounting firms to easily outsource tax returns."

These midsize firms "are getting a more level playing field, which they were denied before," said Jerry. "Suddenly they can get access to the same advantages of scale that the bigger guys always had."

Is the message to Americans, "Mama, don't let your kids grow up to be accountants"? I asked.

Not really, said Rao. "What we have done is taken the grunt work. You know what is needed to prepare a tax return? Very little creative work. This is what will move overseas."

"What will stay in America?" I asked.

"The accountant who wants to stay in business in America will be the one who focuses on designing creative complex strategies, like tax avoidance or tax sheltering, managing customer relationships," he said. "He or she will say to his clients, 'I am getting the grunt work done efficiently far away. Now let's talk about how we manage your estate and what you are going to do about your kids. Do you want to leave some money in your trusts?' It means having the quality-time discussions with clients rather than running around like chickens with their heads cut off from February to April, and often filing for extensions into August, because they have not had the quality time with clients."

Judging from an essay in the journal *Accounting Today* (June 7, 2004), this does, indeed, seem to be the future. L. Gary Boomer, a CPA and CEO of Boomer Consulting in Manhattan, Kansas, wrote, "This past [tax] season produced over 100,000 [outsourced] returns and has now expanded beyond individual returns to trusts, partnerships and corporations . . . The primary reason that the industry has been able to scale up as rapidly as it has over the past three years is due to the investment that these [foreign-based] companies have made in systems, processes and training." There are about seventy thousand accounting grads in India each year, he added, many of whom go to work for local Indian firms starting at $100 a month. With the help of high-speed communications, stringent training, and standardized forms, these young Indians can fairly rapidly be converted into basic Western accountants at a fraction of the cost. Some of the Indian accounting firms even go about marketing themselves to American firms through teleconferencing and skip the travel. Concluded Boomer, "The accounting profession is currently in transformation. Those who get caught in the past and resist change will be forced deeper into commoditization. Those who can create value through leadership, relationships and creativity will transform the industry, as well as strengthen relationships with their existing clients."

What you're telling me, I said to Rao, is that no matter what your profession —

doctor, lawyer, architect, accountant — if you are an American, you better be good at the touchy-feely service stuff, because anything that can be digitized can be outsourced to either the smartest or the cheapest producer, or both. Rao answered, "Everyone has to focus on what exactly is their value-add."

But what if I am just an average accountant? I went to a state university. I had a B+ average. Eventually I got my CPA. I work in a big accounting firm, doing a lot of standard work. I rarely meet with clients. They keep me in the back. But it is a decent living and the firm is basically happy with me. What is going to happen to me in this system?

"It is a good question," said Rao. "We must be honest about it. We are in the middle of a big technological change, and when you live in a society that is at the cutting edge of that change [like America], it is hard to predict. It's easy to predict for someone living in India. In ten years we are going to be doing a lot of the stuff that is being done in America today. We can predict our future. But we are behind you. You are defining the future. America is always on the edge of the next creative wave . . . So it is difficult to look into the eyes of that accountant and say this is what is going to be. We should not trivialize that. We must deal with it and talk about it honestly . . . Any activity where we can digitize and decompose the value chain, and move the work around, will get moved around. Some people will say, 'Yes, but you can't serve me a steak.' True, but I can take the reservation for your table sitting anywhere in the world, if the restaurant does not have an operator. We can say, 'Yes, Mr. Friedman, we can give you a table by the window.' In other words, there are parts of the whole dining-out experience that we can decompose and outsource. If you go back and read the basic economics textbooks, they will tell you: Goods are traded, but services are consumed and produced in the same place. And you cannot export a haircut. But we are coming close to exporting a haircut, the appointment part. What kind of haircut do you want? Which barber do you want? All those things can and will be done by a call center far away."

As we ended our conversation, I asked Rao what he is up to next. He was full of energy. He told me he'd been talking to an Israeli company that is making some big advances in compression technology to allow for easier, better transfers of CAT scans via the Internet so you can quickly get a second opinion from a doctor half a world away.

A few weeks after I spoke with Rao, the following e-mail arrived from Bill Brody, the president of Johns Hopkins University, whom I had just interviewed for this book:

Dear Tom, I am speaking at a Hopkins continuing education medical meeting for radiologists (I used to be a radiologist) . . . I came upon a very fascinating situation that I thought might interest you. I have just learned that in many small and some medium-size hospitals in the US, radiologists are outsourcing reading of CAT scans to doctors in India and Australia!!! Most of this evidently occurs at night (and maybe weekends) when the radiologists do not have sufficient staffing to provide in-hospital coverage. While some radiology groups will use teleradiology to ship images from the hospital to their home (or to Vail or Cape Cod, I suppose) so that they can interpret images and provide a diagnosis 24/7, apparently the smaller hospitals are shipping CAT scan images to radiologists abroad. The advantage is that it is daytime in Australia or India when it is nighttime here — so after-hours coverage becomes more readily done by shipping the images across the globe. Since CAT (and MRI) images are already in digital format and available on a network with a standardized protocol, it is no problem to view the images anywhere in the world . . . I assume that the radiologists on the other end . . . must have trained in [the] US and acquired the appropriate licenses and credentials . . . The groups abroad that provide these after-hours readings are called "Nighthawks" by the American radiologists that employ them.

Best,
Bill

Thank goodness I'm a journalist and not an accountant or a radiologist. There will be no outsourcing for me — even if some of my readers wish my column could be shipped off to North Korea. At least that's what I thought. Then I heard about the Reuters operation in India. I didn't have time to visit the Reuters office in Bangalore, but I was able to get hold of Tom Glocer, the CEO of Reuters, to hear what he was doing. Glocer is a pioneer in the outsourcing of elements of the news supply chain.

With 2,300 journalists around the world, in 197 bureaus, serving a market including investment bankers, derivatives traders, stockbrokers, newspapers, radio, television, and Internet outlets, Reuters has always had a very complex audience to satisfy.

After the dot-com bust, though, when many of its customers became very cost-conscious, Reuters started asking itself, for reasons of both cost and efficiency: Where do we actually need our people to be located to feed our global news supply chain? And can we actually disaggregate the work of a journalist and keep part in London and New York and shift part to India?

Glocer started by looking at the most basic bread-and-butter function Reuters provides, which is breaking news about company earnings and related business developments, every second of every day. "Exxon comes out with its earnings and we need to get that as fast possible up on screens around the world: 'Exxon earned thirty-nine cents this quarter as opposed to thirty-six cents last quarter.' The core competency there is speed and accuracy," explained Glocer. "You don't need a lot of analysis. We just need to get the basic news up as fast as possible. The flash should be out in seconds after the company releases, and the table [showing the recent history of quarterly earnings] a few seconds later."

Those sorts of earnings flashes are to the news business what vanilla is to the ice cream business — a basic commodity that actually can be made anywhere in the flat world. The real value-added knowledge work happens in the next five minutes.

That is when you need a real journalist who knows how to get a comment from the company, a comment from the top two analysts in the field, and even some word from competitors to put the earnings report in perspective. "That needs a higher journalistic skill set — someone in the market with contacts, who knows who the best industry analysts are and has taken the right people to lunch," said Glocer.

The dot-com bust and the flattening of the world forced Glocer to rethink how Reuters delivered news — whether it could disaggregate the functions of a journalist and ship the low-value-added functions to India. His primary goal was to reduce the overlap Reuters payroll, while preserving as many good journalism jobs as possible. "So the first thing we did," said Glocer, "was hire six reporters in Bangalore as an experiment. We said, 'Let's let them just do the flash headlines and the tables and whatever else we can get them to do in Bangalore.' "

These new Indian hires had accounting backgrounds and were trained by Reuters, but they were paid standard local wages and vacation and health benefits. "India is an unbelievably rich place for recruiting people, not only with technical skills but also financial skills," said Glocer. When a company puts out its earnings, one of the first things it does is hand it to the wires —

Reuters, Dow Jones, and Bloomberg — for distribution. "We will get that raw data," he said, "and then it's a race to see how fast we can turn it around. Bangalore is one of the most wired places in the world, and although there's a slight delay — one second or less — in getting the information over there, it turns out you can just as easily sit in Bangalore and get the electronic version of a press release and turn it into a story as you can in London or New York."

The difference, however, is that wages and rents in Bangalore are less than one-fifth what they are in those Western capitals.

While economics and the flattening of the world have pushed Reuters down this path, Glocer has tried to make a virtue of necessity. "We think we can off-load commoditized reporting and get that done efficiently somewhere else in the world," he said, and then give the conventional Reuters journalists, whom the company is able to retain, a chance to focus on doing much higher-value-added and personally fulfilling journalism and analysis. "Let's say you were a Reuters journalist in New York. Do you reach your life's fulfillment by turning press releases into boxes on the screen, or by doing the analysis?" asked Glocer. Obviously, it is the latter. Outsourcing news bulletins to India also allows Reuters to extend the breadth of its reporting to more small-cap companies, companies it was not cost-efficient for Reuters to follow before with higher-paid journalists in New York. But with lower-wage Indian reporters, who can be hired in large numbers for the cost of one reporter in New York, it can now do that from Bangalore. By the summer of 2004, Reuters had grown its Bangalore content operation to three hundred staff, aiming eventually for a total of fifteen hundred. Some of those are Reuters veterans sent out to train the Indian teams, some are reporters filing earnings flashes, but most are journalists doing slightly more specialized data analysis — number crunching — for securities offerings.

"A lot of our clients are doing the same thing," said Glocer. "Investment research has had to have huge amounts of cost ripped out of it, so a lot of firms are using shift work in Bangalore to do bread-and-butter company analysis." Until recently the big Wall Street firms had conducted investment research by spending millions of dollars on star analysts and then charging part of their salaries to their stockbrokerage departments, which shared the analysis with their best customers, and part to their investment banking business, which sometimes used glowing analyses of a company to lure its banking business. In the wake of

New York State Attorney General Eliot Spitzer's investigations into Wall Street practices, following several scandals, investment banking and stockbrokerage have had to be distinctly separated — so that analysts will stop hyping companies in order to get their investment banking. But as a result, the big Wall Street investment firms have had to sharply reduce the cost of their market research, all of which has to be paid for now by their brokerage departments alone. And this created a great incentive for them to outsource some of this analytical work to places like Bangalore. In addition to being able to pay an analyst in Bangalore about $15,000 in total compensation, as opposed to $80,000 in New York or London, Reuters has found that its India employees tend to be financially literate and highly motivated as well. Reuters also recently opened a software development center in Bangkok because it turned out to be a good place to recruit developers who had been overlooked by all the Western companies vying for talent in Bangalore.

I find myself torn by this trend. Having started my career as a wire service reporter with United Press International, I have enormous sympathy with wire service reporters and the pressures, both professional and financial, under which they toil. But UPI might still be thriving today as a wire service, which it is not, if it had been able to outsource some of its lower-end business when I started as a reporter in London twenty-five years ago.

"It is delicate with the staff," said Glocer, who has cut the entire Reuters staff by roughly a quarter, without deep cuts among the reporters. The Reuters staff, he said, understand that this is being done so that the company can survive and then thrive again. At the same time, said Glocer, "these are sophisticated people out reporting. They see that our clients are doing the exact same things. They get the plot of the story . . . What is vital is to be honest with people about what we are doing and why and not sugarcoat the message. I firmly believe in the lesson of classical economists about moving work to where it can be done best. However, we must not ignore that in some cases, individual workers will not easily find new work. For them, retraining and an adequate social safety net are needed."

In an effort to deal straight with the Reuters staff, David Schlesinger, who heads Reuters America, sent all editorial employees a memo, which included the following excerpt:

OFF-SHORING WITH OBLIGATION
I grew up in New London, Connecticut, which in the 19th century was a major

whaling center. In the 1960's and 70's the whales were long gone and the major employers in the region were connected with the military — not a surprise during the Vietnam era. My classmates' parents worked at Electric Boat, the Navy and the Coast Guard. The peace dividend changed the region once again, and now it is best known for the great gambling casinos of Mohegan Sun and Foxwoods and for the pharmaceutical researchers of Pfizer. Jobs went; jobs were created. Skills went out of use; new skills were required. The region changed; people changed. New London, of course, was not unique. How many mill towns saw their mills close; how many shoe towns saw the shoe industry move elsewhere; how many towns that were once textile powerhouses now buy all their linens from China? Change is hard. Change is hardest on those caught by surprise. Change is hardest on those who have difficulty changing too. But change is natural; change is not new; change is important. The current debate about off-shoring is dangerously hot. But the debate about work going to India, China and Mexico is actually no different from the debate once held about submarine work leaving New London or shoe work leaving Massachusetts or textile work leaving North Carolina. Work gets done where it can be done most effectively and efficiently. That ultimately helps the New Londons, New Bedfords and New Yorks of this world even more than it helps the Bangalores and Shenzhens. It helps because it frees up people and capital to do different, more sophisticated work, and it helps because it gives an opportunity to produce the end product more cheaply, benefiting customers even as it helps the corporation. It's certainly difficult for individuals to think about "their" work going away, being done thousands of miles away by someone earning thousands of dollars less per year. But it's time to think about the opportunity as well as the pain, just as it's time to think about the obligations of off-shoring as well as the opportunities . . . Every person, just as every corporation, must tend to his or her own economic destiny, just as our parents and grandparents in the mills, shoe shops and factories did.

"The Monitor Is Burning?"

Do you know what an Indian call center sounds like?

While filming the documentary about outsourcing, the TV crew and I spent an evening at the Indian-owned "24/7 Customer" call center in Bangalore. The call center is a cross between a co-ed college frat house and a phone bank raising money for the local public TV station. There are several floors with rooms full of twenty-somethings — some twenty-five hundred in all — working the phones. Some are known as "outbound" operators, selling everything from credit cards to phone minutes. Others deal with "inbound" calls — everything from tracing lost luggage for U.S. and European airline passengers to solving computer problems for confused American consumers. The calls are transferred here by satellite and undersea fiber-optic cable. Each vast floor of a call center consists of clusters of cubicles. The young people work in little teams under the banner of the company whose phone support they are providing. So one corner might be the Dell group, another might be flying the flag of Microsoft. Their working conditions look like those at your average insurance company. Although I am sure that there are call centers that are operated like sweatshops, 24/7 is not one of them.

Most of the young people I interviewed give all or part of their salary to their parents. In fact, many of them have starting salaries that are higher than their parents' retiring salaries. For entry-level jobs into the global economy, these are about as good as it gets.

I was wandering around the Microsoft section around six p.m. Bangalore time, when most of these young people start their workday to coincide with the dawn in America, when I asked a young Indian computer expert there a simple question: What was the record on the floor for the longest phone call to help some American who got lost in the maze of his or her own software?

Without missing a beat he answered, "Eleven hours."

"Eleven hours?" I exclaimed.

"Eleven hours," he said.

I have no way of checking whether this is true, but you do hear snippets of some oddly familiar conversations as you walk the floor at 24/7 and just listen over the shoulders of different call center operators doing their things. Here is a small sample of what we heard that night while filming for Discovery Times. It should be read, if you can imagine this, in the voice of someone with an Indian accent trying to imitate an American or a Brit. Also imagine that no matter how rude, unhappy, irritated, or ornery the voices are on the other end of the line, these young Indians are incessantly and unfailingly polite.

Woman call center operator: "Good afternoon, may I speak with . . . ?" (Someone on the other end just slammed down the phone.)

Male call center operator: "Merchant services, this is Jerry, may I help you?" (The Indian call center operators adopt Western names of their own choosing. The idea, of course, is to make their American or European customers feel more comfortable. Most of the young Indians I talked to about this were not offended but took it as an opportunity to have some fun. While a few just opt for Susan or Bob, some really get creative.)

Woman operator in Bangalore speaking to an American: "My name is Ivy Timberwoods and I am calling you . . ."

Woman operator in Bangalore getting an American's identity number: "May I have the last four digits of your Social Security?"

Woman operator in Bangalore giving directions as though she were in Manhattan and looking out her window: "Yes, we have a branch on Seventy-fourth and Second Avenue, a branch at Fifty-fourth and Lexington . . ."

Male operator in Bangalore selling a credit card he could never afford himself: "This card comes to you with one of the lowest APR . . ."

Woman operator in Bangalore explaining to an American how she screwed up her checking account: "Check number six-six-five for eighty-one dollars and fifty-five cents. You will still be hit by the thirty-dollar charge. Am I clear?"

Woman operator in Bangalore after walking an American through a computer glitch: "Not a problem, Mr. Jassup. Thank you for your time. Take care. Bye-bye."

Woman operator in Bangalore after someone has just slammed down the phone on her: "Hello? Hello?"

Woman operator in Bangalore apologizing for calling someone in America too early: "This is just a courtesy call, I'll call back later in the evening . . ."

Male operator in Bangalore trying desperately to sell an airline credit card to someone in America who doesn't seem to want one: "Is that because you have too many credit cards, or you don't like flying, Mrs. Bell?"

Woman operator in Bangalore trying to talk an American out of her computer crash: "Start switching between memory okay and memory test . . ."

Male operator in Bangalore doing the same thing: "All right, then, let's just punch in three and press Enter . . ."

Woman operator in Bangalore trying to help an American who cannot stand being on the help line another second: "Yes, ma'am, I do understand that you are in a hurry right now. I am just trying to help you out . . ."

Woman operator in Bangalore getting another phone slammed down on her: "Yes, well, so what time would be goo . . ."

Same woman operator in Bangalore getting another phone slammed down on her: "Why, Mrs. Kent, it's not a . . ."

Same woman operator in Bangalore getting another phone slammed down on her: "As a safety back . . . Hello?"

Same woman operator in Bangalore looking up from her phone: "I definitely have a bad day!"

Woman operator in Bangalore trying to help an American woman with a computer problem that she has never heard before: "What is the problem with this machine, ma'am? The monitor is burning?"

There are currently about 245,000 Indians answering phones from all over the world or dialing out to solicit people for credit cards or cell phone bargains or overdue bills. These call center jobs are low-wage, low-prestige jobs in America, but when shifted to India they become high-wage, high-prestige jobs. The esprit de corps at 24/7 and other call centers I visited seemed quite high, and the young people were all eager to share some of the bizarre phone conversations they've had with Americans who dialed 1-800-HELP, thinking they would wind up talking to someone around the block, not around the world.

C. M. Meghna, a 24/7 call center female operator, told me, "I've had lots of customers who call in [with questions] not even connected to the product that we're dealing with. They would call in because they had lost their wallet or just to talk to somebody. I'm like, 'Okay, all right, maybe you should look under the bed [for your wallet] or where do you normally keep it,' and she's like, 'Okay, thank you so much for helping.'"

Nitu Somaiah: "One of the customers asked me to marry him."

Sophie Sunder worked for Delta's lost-baggage department: "I remember this lady called from Texas," she said, "and she was, like, weeping on the phone. She had traveled two connecting flights and she lost her bag and in the bag was her daughter's wedding gown and wedding ring and I felt so sad for her and there was nothing I could do. I had no information.

"Most of the customers were irate," said Sunder. "The first thing they say is, 'Where's my bag? I want my bag now!' We were like supposed to say, 'Excuse me, can I have your first name and last name?' 'But where's my bag!' Some would ask which country am I from? We are supposed to

49

tell the truth, [so] we tell them India. Some thought it was Indiana, not India! Some did not know where India is. I said it is the country next to Pakistan."

Although the great majority of the calls are rather routine and dull, competition for these jobs is fierce — not only because they pay well, but because you can work at night and go to school during part of the day, so they are stepping-stones toward a higher standard of living. P. V. Kannan, CEO and cofounder of 24/7, explained to me how it all worked: "Today we have over four thousand associates spread out in Bangalore, Hyderabad, and Chennai. Our associates start out with a take-home pay of roughly $200 a month, which grows to $300 to $400 per month in six months. We also provide transportation, lunch, and dinner at no extra cost. We provide life insurance, medical insurance for the entire family — and other benefits."

Therefore, the total cost of each call center operator is actually around $500 per month when they start out and closer to $600 to $700 per month after six months. Everyone is also entitled to performance bonuses that allow them to earn, in certain cases, the equivalent of 100 percent of their base salary. "Around 10 to 20 percent of our associates pursue a degree in business or computer science during the day hours," said Kannan, adding that more than one-third are taking some kind of extra computer or business training, even if it is not toward a degree. "It is quite common in India for people to pursue education through their twenties — self-improvement is a big theme and actively encouraged by parents and companies. We sponsor an MBA program for consistent performers [with] full-day classes over the weekend. Everyone works eight hours a day, five days a week, with two fifteen-minute breaks and an hour off for lunch or dinner."

Not surprisingly, the 24/7 customer call center gets about seven hundred applications a day, but only 6 percent of applicants are hired. Here is a snippet from a recruiting session for call center operators at a women's college in Bangalore:

Recruiter 1: "Good morning, girls."

Class in unison: "Good morning, ma'am."

Recruiter 1: "We have been retained by some of the multinationals here to do the recruitment for them. The primary clients that we are recruiting [for] today are Honeywell. And also for America Online."

The young women — dozens of them — then all lined up with their application forms and waited to be interviewed by a recruiter at a wooden table. Here is what some of the interviews sounded like:

Recruiter 1: "What kind of job are you looking at?"

Applicant 1: "It should be based on accounts, then, where I can grow, I can grow in my career."

Recruiter 1: "You have to be more confident about yourself when you're speaking. You're very nervous. I want you to work a little on that and then get in touch with us."

Recruiter 2 to another applicant: "Tell me something about yourself."

Applicant 2: "I have passed my SSC with distinction. Second P also with distinction. And I also hold a 70 percent aggregate in previous two years." (This is Indian lingo for their equivalents of GPA and SAT scores.)

Recruiter 2: "Go a little slow. Don't be nervous. Be cool."

The next step for those applicants who are hired at a call center is the training program, which they are paid to attend. It combines learning how to handle the specific processes for the company whose calls they will be taking or making, and attending something called "accent neutralization class." These are daylong sessions with a language teacher who prepares the new Indian hires to disguise their pronounced Indian accents when speaking English and replace them with American, Canadian, or

British ones — depending on which part of the world they will be speaking with. It's pretty bizarre to watch. The class I sat in on was being trained to speak in a neutral middle-American accent. The students were asked to read over and over a single phonetic paragraph designed to teach them how to soften their *t*'s and to roll their *r*'s.

Their teacher, a charming eight-months-pregnant young woman dressed in a traditional Indian sari, moved seamlessly among British, American, and Canadian accents as she demonstrated reading a paragraph designed to highlight phonetics. She said to the class, "Remember the first day I told you that the Americans flap the 'tuh' sound? You know, it sounds like an almost 'duh' sound — not crisp and clear like the British. So I would not say" — here she was crisp and sharp — " 'Betty bought a bit of better butter' or 'Insert a quarter in the meter.' But I would say" — her voice very flat — " 'Insert a quarter in the meter' or 'Betty bought a bit of better butter.' So I'm just going to read it out for you once, and then we'll read it together. All right? 'Thirty little turtles in a bottle of bottled water. A bottle of bottled water held thirty little turtles. It didn't matter that each turtle had to rattle a metal ladle in order to get a little bit of noodles.'

"All right, who's going to read first?" the

instructor asked. Each member of the class then took a turn trying to say this tongue twister in an American accent. Some of them got it on the first try, and others, well, let's just say that you wouldn't think they were in Kansas City if they answered your call to Delta's lost-luggage number.

After listening to them stumble through this phonetics lesson for half an hour, I asked the teacher if she would like me to give them an authentic version — since I'm originally from Minnesota, smack in the Midwest, and still speak like someone out of the movie *Fargo*. Absolutely, she said. So I read the following paragraph: "A bottle of bottled water held thirty little turtles. It didn't matter that each turtle had to rattle a metal ladle in order to get a little bit of noodles, a total turtle delicacy . . . The problem was that there were many turtle battles for less than oodles of noodles. Every time they thought about grappling with the haggler turtles their little turtle minds boggled and they only caught a little bit of noodles."

The class responded enthusiastically. It was the first time I ever got an ovation for speaking Minnesotan. On the surface, there is something unappealing about the idea of inducing other people to flatten their accents in order to compete in a flatter world. But before you disparage it, you have to taste just how hungry these kids are to escape the lower end of the middle class and move up. If a little accent modification is the price they have to pay to jump a rung of the ladder, then so be it — they say.

"This is a high-stress environment," said Nilekani, the CEO of Infosys, which also runs a big call center. "It is twenty-four by seven. You work in the day, and then the night, and then the next morning." But the working environment, he insisted, "is not the tension of alienation. It is the tension of success. They are dealing with the challenges of success, of high-pressure living. It is not the challenge of worrying about whether they would have a challenge."

That was certainly the sense I got from talking to a lot of the call center operators on the floor. Like any explosion of modernity, outsourcing is challenging traditional norms and ways of life. But educated Indians have been held back so many years by both poverty and a socialist bureaucracy that many of them seem more than ready to put up with the hours. And needless to say, it is much easier and more satisfying for them to work hard in Bangalore than to pack up and try to make a new start in America. In the flat world they can stay in India, make a decent salary, and not have to be away from families, friends, food, and culture. At the end of the day, these new jobs actually allow them to be more Indian. Said Anney Unnikrishnan, a personnel manager at 24/7, "I finished my MBA and I remember writing the GMAT and getting into Purdue University. But I couldn't go because I couldn't afford it. I didn't have the money for it. Now I can, [but] I see a whole lot of American industry has come into Bangalore and I don't really need to go there. I can work for a multinational sitting right here. So I still get my rice and sambar [a traditional Indian dish], which I eat. I don't need to, you know, learn to eat coleslaw and cold beef. I still continue with my Indian food and I still work for a multinational. Why should I go to America?"

The relatively high standard of living that she can now enjoy — enough for a small apartment and car in Bangalore — is good for America as well. When you look around at 24/7's call center, you see that all the computers are running Microsoft Windows. The chips are designed by Intel. The phones are from Lucent. The air-conditioning is by Carrier, and even the bottled water is by Coke. In addition, 90 percent of the shares in 24/7 are owned by U.S. investors. This explains why, although the United States has lost some service jobs to India in recent years, total exports from American-based companies — merchandise and services —

to India have grown from $2.5 billion in 1990 to $5 billion in 2003. So even with the outsourcing of some service jobs from the United States to India, India's growing economy is creating a demand for many more American goods and services.

What goes around, comes around.

Nine years ago, when Japan was beating America's brains out in the auto industry, I wrote a column about playing the computer geography game Where in the World is Carmen Sandiego? with my nine-year-old daughter, Orly. I was trying to help her by giving her a clue suggesting that Carmen had gone to Detroit, so I asked her, "Where are cars made?" And without missing a beat she answered, "Japan."

Ouch!

Well, I was reminded of that story while visiting Global Edge, an Indian software design firm in Bangalore. The company's marketing manager, Rajesh Rao, told me that he had just made a cold call to the VP for engineering of a U.S. company, trying to drum up business. As soon as Mr. Rao introduced himself as calling from an Indian software firm, the U.S. executive said to him, *"Namaste,"* a common Hindi greeting. Said Mr. Rao, "A few years ago nobody in America wanted to talk to us. Now they are eager." And a few even know how to say hello in proper Hindu fashion. So now I wonder: If I have a grand-daughter one day, and I tell her I'm going to India, will she say, "Grandpa, is that where software comes from?"

No, not yet, honey. Every new product — from software to widgets — goes through a cycle that begins with basic research, then applied research, then incubation, then development, then testing, then manufacturing, then deployment, then support, then continuation engineering in order to add improvements. Each of these phases is specialized and unique, and neither India nor China nor Russia has a critical mass of talent that can handle the whole product cycle for a big American multinational. But these countries are steadily developing their research and development capabilities to handle more and more of these phases. As that continues, we really will see the beginning of what Satyam Cherukuri, of Sarnoff, an American research and development firm, has called "the globalization of innovation" and an end to the old model of a single American or European multinational handling all the elements of the development product cycle from its own resources. More and more American and European companies are outsourcing significant research and development tasks to India, Russia, and China.

According to the information technology office of the state government in Karnataka, where Bangalore is located, Indian units of Cisco Systems, Intel, IBM, Texas Instruments, and GE have already filed 1,000 patent applications with the U.S. Patent Office. Texas Instruments alone has had 225 U.S. patents awarded to its Indian operation. "The Intel team in Bangalore is developing microprocessor chips for high-speed broadband wireless technology, to be launched in 2006," the Karnataka IT office said, in a statement issued at the end of 2004, and "at GE's John F. Welch Technology Centre in Bangalore, engineers are developing new ideas for aircraft engines, transport systems and plastics." Indeed, GE over the years has frequently transferred Indian engineers who worked for it in the United States back to India to integrate its whole global research effort. GE now even sends non-Indians to Bangalore. Vivek Paul is the president of Wipro Technologies, another of the elite Indian technology companies, but he is based in Silicon Valley to be close to Wipro's American customers. Before coming to Wipro, Paul managed GE's CT scanner business out of Milwaukee. At the time he had a French colleague who managed GE's power generator business for the scanners out of France.

"I ran into him on an airplane recently," said Paul, "and he told me he had moved to India to head up GE's high-energy research there."

I told Vivek that I love hearing an Indian who used to head up GE's CT business in Milwaukee but now runs Wipro's consulting business in Silicon Valley tell me about his former French colleague who has moved to Bangalore to work for GE. That is a flat world.

Every time I think I have found the last, most obscure job that could be outsourced to Bangalore, I discover a new one. My friend Vivek Kulkarni used to head the government office in Bangalore responsible for attracting high technology global investment. After stepping down from that post in 2003, he started a company called B2K, with a division called Brickwork, which offers busy global executives their own personal assistant in India. Say you are running a company and you have been asked to give a speech and a PowerPoint presentation in two days. Your "remote executive assistant" in India, provided by Brickwork, will do all the research for you, create the PowerPoint presentation, and e-mail the whole thing to you overnight so that it is on your desk the day you have to deliver it.

"You can give your personal remote executive assistant their assignment when you are leaving work at the end of the day in New York City, and it will be ready for you the next morning," explained Kulkarni. "Because of the time difference with India, they can work on it while you sleep and have it back in your morning." Kulkarni suggested I hire a remote assistant in India to do all the research for this book. "He or she could also help you keep pace with what you want to read. When you wake up, you will find the completed summary in your in-box." (I told him no one could be better than my longtime assistant, Maya Gorman, who sits ten feet away!)

Having your own personal remote executive assistant costs around $1,500 to $2,000 a month, and given the pool of Indian college grads from which Brickwork can recruit, the brainpower you can hire dollar-for-dollar is substantial. As Brickwork's promotional material says, "India's talent pool provides companies access to a broad spectrum of highly qualified people. In addition to fresh graduates, which are around 2.5 million per year, many qualified homemakers are entering the job market." India's business schools, it adds, produce around eighty-nine thousand MBAs per year.

"We've had a wonderful response," said Kulkarni, with clients coming from two main areas. One is American health-care consultants, who often need lots of numbers crunched and PowerPoint presentations drawn up. The other, he said, are American investment banks and financial services companies, which often need to prepare glossy pamphlets with graphs to illustrate the benefits of an IPO or a proposed merger. In the case of a merger, Brickwork will prepare those sections of the report dealing with general market conditions and trends, where most of the research can be gleaned off the Web and summarized in a standard format. "The judgment of how to price the deal will come from the investment bankers themselves," said Kulkarni. "We will do the lower-end work, and they will do the things that require critical judgment and experience, close to the market." The more projects his team of remote executive assistants engages in, the more knowledge they build up. They are full of ambition to do their higher problem solving as well, said Kulkarni. "The idea is to constantly learn. You are always taking an examination. There is no end to learning . . . There is no real end to what can be done by whom."

Unlike Columbus, I didn't stop with India. After I got home, I decided to keep exploring the East for more signs that the world was flat. So after India, I was soon off to Tokyo, where I had a chance to interview Kenichi Ohmae, the legendary former McKinsey & Company consultant in Japan. Ohmae has left McKinsey and struck out on his own in business, Ohmae & Associates. And what do they do? Not consulting anymore, explained Ohmae. He is now spearheading a drive to outsource low-end Japanese jobs to Japanese-speaking call centers and service providers in China. "Say what?" I asked. "To China? Didn't the Japanese once colonize China, leaving a very bad taste in the mouths of the Chinese?"

Well, yes, said Ohmae, but he explained that the Japanese also left behind a large number of Japanese speakers who have maintained a slice of Japanese culture, from sushi to karaoke, in northeastern China, particularly around the northeastern port city of Dalian. Dalian has become for Japan what Bangalore has become for America and the other English-speaking countries: outsourcing central. The Chinese may never forgive Japan for what it did to China in the last century, but the Chinese are so focused on leading the world in the next century that they are ready to brush up on their Japanese and take all the work Japan can outsource.

"The recruiting is quite easy," said

Ohmae in early 2004. "About one-third of the people in this region [around Dalian] have taken Japanese as a second language in high school. So all of these Japanese companies are coming in." Ohmae's company is doing primarily data-entry work in China, where Chinese workers take handwritten Japanese documents, which are scanned, faxed, or e-mailed over from Japan to Dalian, and then type them into a digital database in Japanese characters. Ohmae's company has developed a software program that takes the data to be entered and breaks it down into packets. These packets can then be sent around China or Japan for typing, depending on the specialty required, and then reassembled at the company's database in its Tokyo headquarters. "We have the ability to allocate the job to the person who knows the area best." Ohmae's company even has contracts with more than seventy thousand housewives, some of them specialists in medical or legal terminologies, to do data-entry work at home. The firm has recently expanded into computer-aided designs for a Japanese housing company. "When you negotiate with the customer in Japan for building a house," he explained, "you would sketch out a floor plan — most of these companies don't use computers." So the hand-drawn plans are sent electronically to China, where they are converted into digital designs, which then are e-mailed back to the Japanese building firm, which turns them into manufacturing blueprints. "We took the best-performing Chinese data operators," said Ohmae, "and now they are processing seventy houses a day."

Chinese doing computer drawings for Japanese homes, nearly seventy years after a rapacious Japanese army occupied China, razing many homes in the process. Maybe there is hope for this flat world . . .

I needed to see Dalian, this Bangalore of China, firsthand, so I kept moving around the East. Dalian is impressive not just for a Chinese city. With its wide boulevards, beautiful green spaces, and nexus of universities, technical colleges, and massive software park, Dalian would stand out in Silicon Valley. I had been here in 1998, but there had been so much new building since then that I did not recognize the place. Dalian, which is located about an hour's flight northeast of Beijing, symbolizes how rapidly China's most modern cities — and there are still plenty of miserable, backward ones — are grabbing business as knowledge centers, not just as manufacturing hubs. The signs on the buildings tell the whole story: GE,

Microsoft, Dell, SAP, HP, Sony, and Accenture — to name but a few — all are having backroom work done here to support their Asian operations, as well as new software research and development.

Because of its proximity to Japan and Korea, each only about an hour away by air, its large number of Japanese speakers, its abundance of Internet bandwidth, and many parks and a world-class golf course (all of which appeal to knowledge workers), Dalian has become an attractive locus for Japanese outsourcing. Japanese firms can hire three Chinese software engineers for the price of one in Japan and still have change to pay a roomful of call center operators ($90 a month starting salary). No wonder some twenty-eight hundred Japanese companies have set up operations here or teamed up with Chinese partners.

"I've taken a lot of American people to Dalian, and they are amazed at how fast the China economy is growing in this high-tech area," said Win Liu, director of U.S./EU projects for DHC, one of Dalian's biggest homegrown software firms, which has expanded from thirty to twelve hundred employees in six years. "Americans don't realize the challenge to the extent that they should."

Dalian's dynamic mayor, Xia Deren, forty-nine, is a former college president.

(For a Communist authoritarian system, China does a pretty good job of promoting people on merit. The Mandarin meritocratic culture here still runs very deep.) Over a traditional ten-course Chinese dinner at a local hotel, the mayor told me how far Dalian has come and just where he intends to take it. "We have twenty-two universities and colleges with over two hundred thousand students in Dalian," he explained. More than half those students graduate with engineering or science degrees, and even those who don't, those who study history or literature, are still being directed to spend a year studying Japanese or English, plus computer science, so that they will be employable. The mayor estimated that more than half the residents of Dalian had access to the Internet at the office, home, or school.

"The Japanese enterprises originally started some data processing industries here," the mayor added, "and with this as a base they have now moved to R & D and software development . . . In the past one or two years, the software companies of the U.S. are also making some attempts to move outsourcing of software from the U.S. to our city . . . We are approaching and we are catching up with the Indians. Exports of software products [from Dalian] have been increasing by 50 percent annually. And China is now becoming the country that develops the largest number of university graduates. Though in general our English is not as competent as that of the Indian people, we have a bigger population, [so] we can pick out the most intelligent students who can speak the best English."

Are Dalian residents bothered by working for the Japanese, whose government has still never formally apologized for what the wartime Japanese government did to China?

"We will never forget that a historical war occurred between the two nations," he answered, "but when it comes to the field of economy, we only focus on the economic problems — especially if we talk about the software outsourcing business. If the U.S. and Japanese companies make their products in our city, we consider that to be a good thing. Our youngsters are trying to learn Japanese, to master this tool so they can compete with their Japanese counterparts to successfully land high-salary positions for themselves in the future."

The mayor then added for good measure, "My personal feeling is that Chinese youngsters are more ambitious than Japanese or American youngsters in recent years, but I don't think they are ambitious enough, because they are not as ambitious as my generation. Because our generation, before they got into university and colleges, were sent to distant rural areas and factories and military teams, and went through a very hard time, so in terms of the spirit to overcome and face the hardships, [our generation had to have more ambition] than youngsters nowadays."

Mayor Xia had a charmingly direct way of describing the world, and although some of what he had to say gets lost in translation, he gets it — and Americans should too: "The rule of the market economy," this Communist official explained to me, "is that if somewhere has the richest human resources and the cheapest labor, of course the enterprises and the businesses will naturally go there." In manufacturing, he pointed out, "Chinese people first were the employees and working for the big foreign manufacturers, and after several years, after we have learned all the processes and steps, we can start our own firms. Software will go down the same road . . . First we will have our young people employed by the foreigners, and then we will start our own companies. It is like building a building. Today, the U.S., you are the designers, the architects, and the developing countries are the bricklayers for the buildings. But one day I hope we will be the architects."

I just kept exploring — east and west. By the summer of 2004, I was in Colorado on vacation. I had heard about this new low-fare airline called JetBlue, which was launched in 1999. I had no idea where they operated, but I needed to fly between Washington and Atlanta, and couldn't quite get the times I wanted, so I decided to call JetBlue and see where exactly they flew. I confess I did have another motive. I had heard that JetBlue had outsourced its entire reservation system to housewives in Utah, and I wanted to check this out. So I dialed JetBlue reservations and had the following conversation with the agent:

"Hello, this is Dolly. Can I help you?" answered a grandmotherly voice.

"Yes, I would like to fly from Washington to Atlanta," I said. "Do you fly that route?"

"No, I'm sorry we don't. We fly from Washington to Ft. Lauderdale," said Dolly.

"How about Washington to New York City?" I asked.

"I'm sorry, we don't fly that route. We do fly from Washington to Oakland and Long Beach," said Dolly.

"Say, can I ask you something? Are you really at home? I read that JetBlue agents just work at home."

"Yes, I am," said Dolly in the most cheerful voice. (I later confirmed with JetBlue that her full name is Dolly Baker.) "I am sitting in my office upstairs in my house, looking out the window at a beautiful sunny day. Just five minutes ago someone called and asked me that same question and I told them and they said, 'Good, I thought you were going to tell me you were in New Delhi.' "

"Where do you live?" I asked.

"Salt Lake City, Utah," said Dolly. "We have a two-story home, and I love working here, especially in the winter when the snow is swirling and I am up here in the office at home."

"How do you get such a job?" I asked.

"You know, they don't advertise," said Dolly in the sweetest possible voice. "It's all by word of mouth. I worked for the state government and I retired, and [after a little while] I thought I have to do something else and I just love it."

David Neeleman, the founder and CEO of JetBlue Airways Corp., has a name for all this. He calls it "homesourcing." JetBlue now has four hundred reservation agents, like Dolly, working at home in the Salt Lake City area, taking reservations — in between babysitting, exercising, writing novels, and cooking dinner.

A few months later I visited Neeleman at JetBlue's headquarters in New York, and he explained to me the virtues of homesourcing, which he actually started at Morris Air, his first venture in the airline business. (It was bought by Southwest.) "We had 250 people in their homes doing reservations at Morris Air," said Neeleman. "They were 30 percent more productive — they take 30 percent more bookings, by just being happier. They were more loyal and there was less attrition. So when I started JetBlue, I said, 'We are going to have 100 percent reservation at home.'"

Neeleman has a personal reason for wanting to do this. He is a Mormon and believes that society will be better off if more mothers are able to stay at home with their young children but are given a chance to be wage earners at the same time. So he based his home reservations system in Salt Lake City, where the vast majority of the women are Mormons and many are stay-at-home mothers. Home reservationists work twenty-five hours a week and have to come into the JetBlue regional office in Salt Lake City for four hours a month to learn new skills and be brought up to date on what is going on inside the company.

"We will never outsource to India," said Neeleman. "The quality we can get here is far superior . . . [Employers] are more willing to outsource to India than to their own homes, and I can't understand that. Somehow they think that people need to be sitting in front of them or some boss they have designated. The productivity we get here more than makes up for the India [wage] factor."

A *Los Angeles Times* story about JetBlue (May 9, 2004) noted that "in 1997, 11.6 million employees of U.S. companies worked from home at least part of the time. Today, that number has soared to 23.5 million — 16% of the American labor force. (Meanwhile, the ranks of the self-employed, who often work from home, have swelled during the same period — to 23.4 million from 18 million.) In some eyes, homesourcing and outsourcing aren't so much competing strategies as they are different manifestations of the same thing: a relentless push by corporate America to lower costs and increase efficiency, wherever that may lead."

That is exactly what I was learning on my own travels: Homesourcing to Salt Lake City and outsourcing to Bangalore were just flip sides of the same coin — sourcing. And the new, new thing, I was also learning, is the degree to which it is now possible for companies and individuals to source work anywhere.

I just kept moving. In the fall of 2004, I accompanied the chairman of the Joint Chiefs of Staff, General Richard Myers, on a tour of hot spots in Iraq. We visited Baghdad, the U.S. military headquarters in

Fallujah, and the 24th Marine Expeditionary Unit encampment outside Babil, in the heart of Iraq's so-called Sunni Triangle. The makeshift 24th MEU base is a sort of Fort Apache, in the middle of a pretty hostile Iraqi Sunni Muslim population. While General Myers was meeting with officers and enlisted men there, I was free to walk around the base, and eventually I wandered into the command center, where my eye was immediately caught by a large flat-screen TV. On the screen was a live TV feed that looked to be coming from some kind of overhead camera. It showed some people moving around behind a house. Also on the screen, along the right side, was an active instant-messaging chat room, which seemed to be discussing the scene on the TV.

"What is that?" I asked the soldier who was carefully monitoring all the images from a laptop. He explained that a U.S. Predator drone — a small pilotless aircraft with a high-power television camera — was flying over an Iraqi village, in the 24th MEU's area of operation, and feeding real-time intelligence images back to his laptop and this flat screen. This drone was actually being "flown" and manipulated by an expert who was sitting back at Nellis Air Force Base in Las Vegas, Nevada. That's right, the drone over Iraq was actually being remotely directed from Las Vegas. Meanwhile, the video images it was beaming back were being watched simultaneously by the 24th MEU, United States Central Command headquarters in Tampa, CentCom regional headquarters in Qatar, in the Pentagon, and probably also at the CIA. The different analysts around the world were conducting an online chat about how to interpret what was going on and what to do about it. It was their conversation that was scrolling down the right side of the screen.

Before I could even express my amazement, another officer traveling with us took me aback by saying that this technology had "flattened" the military hierarchy — by giving so much information to the low-level officer, or even enlisted man, who was operating the computer, and empowering him to make decisions about the information he was gathering. While I'm sure that no first lieutenant is going to be allowed to start a firefight without consulting superiors, the days when only senior officers had the big picture are over. The military playing field is being leveled.

I told this story to my friend Nick Burns, the U.S. ambassador to NATO and a loyal member of the Red Sox Nation. Nick told me he was at CentCom headquarters in Qatar in April 2004, being briefed by

General John Abizaid and his staff. Abizaid's team was seated across the table from Nick with four flat-screen TVs behind them. The first three had overhead images being relayed in real time from different sectors of Iraq by Predator drones. The last one, which Nick was focused on, was showing a Yankees–Red Sox game.

On one screen it was Pedro Martinez versus Derek Jeter, and on the other three it was Jihadists versus the First Cavalry.

Flatburgers and Fries

I kept moving — all the way back to my home in Bethesda, Maryland. By the time I settled back into my house from this journey to the edges of the earth, my head was spinning. But no sooner was I home than more signs of the flattening came knocking at my door. Some came in the form of headlines that would unnerve any parent concerned about where his college-age children are going to fit in. For instance, Forrester Research, Inc., was projecting that more than 3 million service and professional jobs would move out of the country by 2015. But my jaw really dropped when I read a July 19, 2004, article from the *International Herald Tribune* headlined: "Want Fries With Outsourcing?"

"Pull off U.S. Interstate Highway 55 near Cape Girardeau, Missouri, and into the drive-through lane of a McDonald's next to the highway and you'll get fast, friendly service, even though the person taking your order is not in the restaurant — or even in Missouri," the article said. "The order taker is in a call center in Colorado Springs, more than 900 miles, or 1,450 kilometers, away, connected to the customer and to the workers preparing the food by high-speed data lines. Even some restaurant jobs, it seems, are not immune to outsourcing.

"The man who owns the Cape Girardeau restaurant, Shannon Davis, has linked it and three other of his 12 McDonald's franchises to the Colorado call center, which is run by another McDonald's franchisee, Steven Bigari. And he did it for the same reasons that other business owners have embraced call centers: lower costs, greater speed and fewer mistakes.

"Cheap, quick and reliable telecommunications lines let the order takers in Colorado Springs converse with customers in Missouri, take an electronic snapshot of them, display their order on a screen to make sure it is right, then forward the order and the photo to the restaurant kitchen. The photo is destroyed as soon as the order is completed, Bigari said. People picking up their burgers never know that their order traverses two states and bounces back before they can even start driving to the pickup window.

"Davis said that he had dreamed of doing something like this for more than a decade. 'We could not wait to go with it,' he added. Bigari, who created the call center for his own restaurants, was happy to oblige — for a small fee per transaction."

The article noted that McDonald's Corp. said it found the call center idea interesting enough to start a test with three stores near its headquarters in Oak Brook, Illinois, with different software from that used by Bigari. "Jim Sappington, a McDonald's vice president for information technology, said that it was 'way, way too early' to tell if the call center idea would work across the thirteen thousand McDonald's restaurants in the United States . . . Still, franchisees of two other McDonald's restaurants, beyond Davis's, have outsourced their drive-through ordering to Bigari in Colorado Springs. (The other restaurants are in Brainerd, Minnesota, and Norwood, Massachusetts.) Central to the system's success, Bigari said, is the way it pairs customers' photos with their orders; by increasing accuracy, the system cuts down on the number of complaints and therefore makes the service faster. In the fast-food business, time is truly money: shaving even five seconds off the processing time of an order is significant," the article noted. "Bigari said he had cut order time in his dual-lane drive-throughs by slightly more than 30 seconds, to about 1 minute, 5 seconds, on average. That's less than half the average of 2 minutes, 36 seconds, for all McDonald's, and among the fastest of any franchise in the country, according to QSRweb.com, which tracks such things. His drive-throughs now handle 260 cars an hour, Bigari said, 30 more than they did before he started the call center . . . Though his operators earn, on average, 40 cents an hour more than his line employees, he has cut his overall labor costs by a percentage point, even as drive-through sales have increased . . . Tests conducted by outside companies found that Bigari's drive-throughs now make mistakes on fewer than 2 percent of all orders, down from about 4 percent before he started using the call centers, Bigari said."

Bigari "is so enthusiastic about the call center idea," the article noted, "that he has expanded it beyond the drive-through window at his seven restaurants that use the system. While he still offers counter service at those restaurants, most customers now order through the call center, using phones with credit card readers on tables in the seating area."

Some of the signs of flattening I encountered back home, though, had nothing to do with economics. On October 3, 2004, I appeared on the CBS News Sunday morning show *Face the Nation*, hosted by veteran CBS correspondent Bob Schieffer. CBS had been in the news a lot in previous weeks because of Dan Rather's *60 Minutes* report about President George W. Bush's Air National Guard service that turned out to be based on bogus documents. After the show that Sunday, Schieffer mentioned that the oddest thing had happened to him the week before. When he walked out of the CBS studio, a young reporter was waiting for him on the sidewalk. This isn't all that unusual, because as with all the Sunday-morning shows, the major networks — CBS, NBC, ABC, CNN, and Fox — always send crews to one another's studios to grab exit interviews with the guests. But this young man, Schieffer explained, was not from a major network. He politely introduced himself as a reporter for a Web site called InDC Journal and asked whether he could ask Schieffer a few questions. Schieffer, being a polite fellow, said sure. The young man interviewed him on a device Schieffer did not recognize and then asked if he could take his picture. A picture?

Schieffer noticed that the young man had no camera. He didn't need one. He turned his cell phone around and snapped Schieffer's picture.

"So I came in the next morning and looked up this Web site and there was my picture and the interview and there were already three hundred comments about it," said Schieffer, who, though keenly aware of online journalism, was nevertheless taken aback at the incredibly fast, low-cost, and solo manner in which this young man had put him up in lights.

I was intrigued by this story, so I tracked down the young man from InDC Journal. His name is Bill Ardolino, and he is a very thoughtful guy. I conducted my own interview with him online — how else? — and began by asking about what equipment he was using as a one-man network/newspaper.

"I used a minuscule MP3 player/digital recorder (three and a half inches by two inches) to get the recording, and a separate small digital camera phone to snap his picture," said Ardolino. "Not quite as sexy as an all-in-one phone/camera/recorder (which does exist), but a statement on the ubiquity and miniaturization of technology nonetheless. I carry this equipment around D.C. at all times because, hey, you never know. What's perhaps more startling is how well Mr. Schieffer thought on his feet, after being jumped on by some stranger with interview questions. He blew me away."

Ardolino said the MP3 player cost him about $125. It is "primarily designed to play music," he explained, but it also "comes prepackaged as a digital recorder that creates a WAV sound file that can be uploaded back to a computer . . . Basically, I'd say that the barrier to entry to do journalism that requires portable, ad hoc recording equipment, is [now] about $100 — $200 to $300 if you add a camera, $400 to $500 for a pretty nice recorder and a pretty nice camera. [But] $200 is all that you need to get the job done."

What prompted him to become his own news network?

"Being an independent journalist is a hobby that sprang from my frustration about biased, incomplete, selective, and/or incompetent information gathering by the mainstream media," explained Ardolino, who describes himself as a "center-right libertarian." "Independent journalism and its relative, blogging, are expressions of market forces — a need is not being met by current information sources. I started taking pictures and doing interviews of the antiwar rallies in D.C., because the media was grossly misrepresenting the nature of the groups that were organizing the gatherings — unrepentant Marxists, explicit and implicit supporters of terror, etc. I originally chose to use humor as a device, but I've since branched out. Do I have more power, power to get my message out, yes. The Schieffer interview actually brought in about twenty-five thousand visits in twenty-four hours. My peak day since I've started was fifty-five thousand when I helped break 'Rathergate' . . . I interviewed the first forensics expert in the Dan Rather National Guard story, and he was then specifically picked up by *The Washington Post*, *Chicago Sun-Times*, *Globe*, *NYT*, etc., within forty-eight hours.

"The pace of information gathering and correction in the CBS fake memo story was astounding," he continued. "It wasn't just that CBS News 'stonewalled' after the fact, it was arguably that they couldn't keep up with an army of dedicated fact-checkers. The speed and openness of the medium is something that runs rings around the old process . . . I'm a twenty-nine-year-old marketing manager [who] always wanted to write for a living but hated the AP style book. As überblogger Glenn Reynolds likes to say, blogs have given the people a chance to stop yelling at their TV and have a say in the process. I think that they serve as sort of a 'fifth estate' that works in conjunction with the mainstream media (often by keeping an eye on them or feeding them raw info) and potentially function as a journalism and commentary farm system that provides a new means to establish success.

"Like many facets of the topic that you're talking about in your book, there are good and bad aspects of the development. The splintering of media makes for a lot of incoherence or selective cognition (look at our country's polarization), but it also decentralizes power and provides a better guarantee that the *complete* truth *is* out there . . . somewhere . . . in pieces."

On any given day one can come across any number of stories, like the encounter between Bob Schieffer and Bill Ardolino, that tell you that old hierarchies are being flattened and the playing field is being leveled. As Micah L. Sifry nicely put it in *The Nation* magazine (November 22, 2004): "The era of top-down politics — where campaigns, institutions and journalism were cloistered communities powered by hard-to-amass capital — is over. Something wilder, more engaging and infinitely more satisfying to individual participants is arising alongside the old order."

I offer the Schieffer-Ardolino encounter as just one example of how the flattening of the world has happened faster and changed rules, roles, and relationships more quickly than we could have imagined. And, though I know it is a cliché, I have to say it nevertheless: *You ain't seen nothin' yet.* As I detail in the next chapter, we are entering a phase where we are going to see the digitization, virtualization, and automation of almost everything. The gains in productivity will be staggering for those countries, companies, and individuals who can absorb the new technological tools. And we are entering a phase where more people than ever before in the history of the world are going to have access to these tools — as innovators, as collaborators, and, alas, even as terrorists. You say you want a revolution? Well, the real information revolution is about to begin. I call this new phase Globalization 3.0 because it followed Globalization 2.0, but I think this new era of globalization will prove to be such a difference of degree that it will be seen, in time, as a difference in kind. That is why I introduced the idea that the world has gone from round to flat. Everywhere you turn, hierarchies are being challenged from below or transforming themselves from top-down structures into more horizontal and collaborative ones.

"Globalization is the word we came up with to describe the changing relationships between governments and big businesses," said David Rothkopf, a former senior Department of Commerce official in the Clinton administration and now a private strategic consultant. "But what is going on today is a much broader, much more profound phenomenon." It is not simply about how governments, business, and people communicate, not just about how organizations interact, but is about the emergence of completely new social, political, and business models. "It is about things that impact some of the deepest, most ingrained aspects of society right down to the nature of the social contract," added Rothkopf. "What happens if the political entity in which you are located no longer corresponds to a job that takes place in cyberspace, or no longer really encompasses workers collaborating with other workers in different corners of the globe, or no longer really captures products produced in multiple places simultaneously? Who regulates the work? Who taxes it? Who should benefit from those taxes?"

If I am right about the flattening of the world, it will be remembered as one of those fundamental changes — like the rise of the nation-state or the Industrial Revolution — each of which, in its day, noted Rothkopf, produced changes in the role of individuals, the role and form of governments, the way we innovated, the way we conducted business, the role of women, the way we fought wars, the way we educated ourselves, the way religion responded, the way art was expressed, the way science and research were conducted, not to mention the political labels we assigned to ourselves and to our opponents. "There are certain pivot points or watersheds in history that are greater than others because the changes they produced were so sweeping, multifaceted, and hard to predict at the time," Rothkopf said.

If the prospect of this flattening — and all of the pressures, dislocations, and opportunities accompanying it — causes you unease about the future, you are neither alone nor wrong. Whenever civilization has gone through one of these disruptive, dislocating technological revolutions — like Gutenberg's introduction of the printing press — the whole world has changed in profound ways. But there is something about the flattening of the world that is going to be qualitatively different from other such profound changes: the speed and breadth with which it is taking hold. The introduction of printing happened over a period of decades and for a long time affected only a relatively small part of the planet. Same with the Industrial Revolution. This flattening process is happening at warp speed and directly or indirectly touching a lot more people on the planet at once. The faster and broader this transition to a new era, the more likely is the potential for disruption, as opposed to an orderly transfer of power from the old winners to the new winners.

To put it another way, the experiences of the high-tech companies in the last few decades who failed to navigate the rapid changes brought about in their marketplace by these types of forces may be a warning to all the businesses, institutions, and nation-states that are now facing these inevitable, even predictable, changes but lack the leadership, flexibility, and imagination to adapt — not because they are not smart or aware, but because the speed of change is simply overwhelming them.

And that is why the great challenge for our time will be to absorb these changes in ways that do not overwhelm people but also do not leave them behind. None of this will be easy. But this is our task. It is inevitable and unavoidable. It is the ambition of this book to offer a framework for how to think about it and manage it to our maximum benefit.

I have shared with you in this chapter how I personally discovered that the world is flat. The next chapter details how it got that way.

TWO

The Ten Forces
That Flattened the World

The Bible tells us that God created the world in six days and on the seventh day he rested. Flattening the world took a little longer. The world has been flattened by the convergence of ten major political events, innovations, and companies. None of us has rested since, or maybe ever will again. This chapter is about the forces that flattened the world and the multiple new forms and tools for collaboration that this flattening has created.

Flattener #1
11/9/89
When the Walls Came Down
and the Windows Went Up

The first time I saw the Berlin Wall, it already had a hole in it.

It was December 1990, and I was traveling to Berlin with the reporters covering Secretary of State James A. Baker III. The Berlin Wall had been breached a year earlier, on

November 9, 1989. Yes, in a wonderful kabbalistic accident of dates, the Berlin Wall fell on 11/9. The wall, even in its punctured and broken state, was still an ugly scar across Berlin. Secretary Baker was making his first visit to see this crumbled monument to Soviet communism. I was standing next to him with a small group of reporters. "It was a foggy, overcast day," Baker recalled in his memoir, *The Politics of Diplomacy*, "and in my raincoat, I felt like a character in a John le Carré novel. But as I peered through a crack in the Wall [near the Reichstag] and saw the high-resolution drabness that characterizes East Berlin, I realized that the ordinary men and women of East Germany, peacefully and persistently, had taken matters into their own hands. This was their revolution." After Baker finished looking through the wall and moved along, we reporters took turns peering through the same jagged concrete hole. I brought a couple of chunks of the wall home for my daughters. I remember thinking how unnatural it looked — indeed, what a bizarre thing it was, this cement wall snaking across a modern city for the sole purpose of preventing the people on the other side from enjoying, even glimpsing, freedom.

The fall of the Berlin Wall on 11/9/89 unleashed forces that ultimately liberated all the captive peoples of the Soviet Empire. But it actually did so much more. It tipped the balance of power across the world toward those advocating democratic, consensual, free-market-oriented governance, and away from those advocating authoritarian rule with centrally planned economies. The Cold War had been a struggle between two economic systems — capitalism and communism — and with the fall of the wall, there was only one system left and everyone had to orient himself or herself to it one way or another. Henceforth, more and more economies would be governed from the ground up, by the interests, demands, and aspirations of the people, rather than from the top down, by the interests of some narrow ruling clique. Within two years, there was no Soviet Empire to hide behind anymore or to prop up autocratic regimes in Asia, the Middle East, Africa, or Latin America. If you were not a democracy or a democratizing society, if you continued to hold fast to highly regulated or centrally planned economics, you were seen as being on the wrong side of history.

For some, particularly among the older generations, this was an unwelcome transformation. Communism was a great system for making people equally poor. In fact, there was no better system in the world for that than communism. Capitalism made people unequally rich, and for some who were used to the plodding, limited, but secure Socialist lifestyle — where a job, a house, an education, and a pension were all guaranteed, even if they were meager — the fall of the Berlin Wall was deeply unsettling. But for many others, it was a get-out-of-jail-free card. That is why the fall of the Berlin Wall was felt in so many more places than just Berlin, and why its fall was such a world-flattening event.

Indeed, to appreciate the far-reaching flattening effects of the fall of the Berlin Wall, it's always best to talk to non-Germans or non-Russians. Tarun Das was heading the Confederation of Indian Industry when the wall fell in Berlin, and he saw its ripple effect felt all the way to India. "We had this huge mass of regulation and controls and bureaucracy," he recalled. "Nehru had come to power [after the end of British colonial rule] and had a huge country to manage, and no experience of running a country. The U.S. was busy with Europe and Japan and the Marshall Plan. So Nehru looked north, across the Himalayas, and sent his team of economists to Moscow. They came back and said that this country [the Soviet Union] was amazing. They allocate resources, they give licenses, there is a planning commission that decides everything, and the country moves. So we took that model and forgot that we had a private sector . . . That private sector got put under this wall of regulation. By 1991, the private sector was there, but under wraps, and there was mistrust about business. They made profits! The entire infrastructure from 1947 to 1991 was government-owned . . . [The burden of state ownership] almost bankrupted the country. We were not able to pay our debts. As a people, we did not have self-confidence. Sure, we might have won a couple of wars with Pakistan, but that did not give the nation confidence."

In 1991, with India running out of hard currency, Manmohan Singh, the finance minister at that time (and now the prime minister), decided that India had to open its economy. "Our Berlin Wall fell," said Das, "and it was like unleashing a caged tiger. Trade controls were abolished. We were always at 3 percent growth, the so-called Hindu rate of growth — slow, cautious, and conservative. To make [better returns], you had to go to America. Well, three years later [after the 1991 reforms] we were at 7 percent rate of growth. To hell with poverty! Now to make it you could stay in India and become one of *Forbes*'s richest people in the world . . . All the years of socialism and controls had taken us downhill to the point where we had only $1 billion in foreign currency. Today we have $118 billion . . . We went from quiet self-confidence to outrageous ambition in a decade."

The fall of the Berlin Wall didn't just help flatten the alternatives to free-market capitalism and unlock enormous pent-up energies for hundreds of millions of people in places like India, Brazil, China, and the former Soviet Empire. It also allowed us to think about the world differently — to see it as more of a seamless whole. Because the Berlin Wall was not only blocking our way; it was blocking our sight — our ability to think about the world as a single market, a single ecosystem, and a single community. Before 1989, you could have an Eastern policy or a Western policy, but it was hard to think about having a "global" policy. Amartya Sen, the Nobel Prize–winning Indian economist now teaching at Harvard, once remarked to me that "the Berlin Wall was not only a symbol of keeping people inside East Germany — it was a way of preventing a kind of global view of our future. We could not think globally about the world when the Berlin Wall was there. We could not think about the world as a whole." There is a lovely story in Sanskrit, Sen added, about a frog that is born in a well and stays in the well and lives its entire life in the well. "It has a worldview that consists of the well," he said. "That was what the world was like for many people on the planet before the fall of the wall. When it fell, it was like the frog in the well was suddenly able to communicate with frogs in all the other wells . . . If I celebrate the fall of the wall, it is because I am convinced of how much we can learn from each other. Most knowledge is learning from the other across the border."

Yes, the world became a better place to live in after 11/9, because each outbreak of freedom stimulated another outbreak, and that process in and of itself had a flattening effect across societies, strengthening those below and weakening those above. "Women's freedom," noted Sen, citing just one example, "which promotes women's literacy, tends to reduce fertility and child mortality and increase the employment opportunities for women, which then affects the political dialogue and gives women the opportunity for a greater role in local self-government."

Finally, the fall of the wall did not just open the way for more people to tap into one another's knowledge pools. It also paved the way for the adoption of common standards — standards on how economies should be run, on how accounting should be done, on how banking should be conducted, on how PCs should be made, and on how economics papers should be written. I discuss this more later, but suffice it to say here that common standards create a flatter, more level playing field. To put it another way, the fall of the wall enhanced the free movement of best practices. When an economic or technological standard emerged and proved itself on the world stage, it was much more quickly adopted after the wall was out of the way. In Europe alone, the fall of the wall opened the way for the formation of the European Union and its expansion from fifteen to twenty-five countries. That, in combination with the advent of the euro as a common currency, has created a single economic zone out of a region once divided by an Iron Curtain.

While the positive effects of the wall coming down were immediately apparent, the cause of the wall's fall was not so clear. There *was* no single cause. To some degree the termites just ate away at the foundations of the Soviet Union, which were already weakened by the system's own internal contradictions and inefficiencies; to some degree the Reagan administration's military buildup in Europe forced the Kremlin to bankrupt itself paying for warheads; and to some degree Mikhail Gorbachev's hapless efforts to reform something that was unreformable brought communism to an end. But if I had to point to one factor as first among equals, it was the information revolution that began in the early- to mid-1980s. Totalitarian systems depend on a monopoly of information and force, and too much information started to slip through the Iron Curtain, thanks to the spread of fax machines, telephones, and other modern tools of communication.

A critical mass of IBM PCs, and the Windows operating system that brought them to life, came together in roughly this same time period that the wall fell, and their diffusion put the nail in the coffin of communism, because they vastly improved horizontal communication — to the detriment of the exclusively top-down form that communism was based upon. They also greatly enhanced personal information gathering and personal empowerment. (Each component of this information revolution was brought about by separate evolutions: The phone network evolved from the desire of people to talk to each other over long distances. The fax machine evolved as a way to transmit written communication over the phone network. The PC was diffused by the original killer apps — spreadsheets and word processing. And Windows evolved out of the need to make all of this usable, and programmable, by the masses.)

The first IBM PC hit the markets in 1981. At the same time, many computer scientists around the world had started using these things called the Internet and e-mail. The first version of the Windows operating system shipped in 1985, and the real breakthrough version that made PCs truly user-friendly — Windows 3.0 — shipped on May 22, 1990, only six months after the wall went down. In this same time period, some people other than scientists started to discover that if they bought a PC and a dial-up modem, they could connect their PCs to their telephones and send e-mails through private Internet service providers — like CompuServe and America Online.

"The diffusion of personal computers, fax machines, Windows, and dial-up modems connected to a global telephone network all came together in the late 1980s and early 1990s to create the basic platform that started the global information revolution," argued Craig J. Mundie, the chief technology officer for Microsoft. The key was the melding of them all together into a single interoperable system. That happened, said Mundie, once we had in crude form a standardized computing platform — the IBM PC — along with a standardized graphical user interface for word processing and spreadsheets — Windows — along with a standardized tool for communication — dial-up modems and the global phone network. Once we had that basic interoperable platform, then the killer applications drove its diffusion far and wide.

"People found that they really liked doing all these things on a computer, and they really improved productivity," said Mundie. "They all had broad individual appeal and made individual people get up and buy a Windows-enabled PC and put it on their desk, and that forced the diffusion of this new platform into the world of corporate computing even more. People said, 'Wow, there is an asset here, and we should take advantage of it.'"

The more established Windows became as the primary operating system, added Mundie, "the more programmers went out and wrote applications for rich-world businesses to put on their computers, so they could do lots of new and different business tasks, which started to enhance productivity even more. Tens of millions of people around the world became programmers to make the PC do whatever they wanted in their own languages. Windows was eventually translated into thirty-eight languages. People were able to become familiar with the PC in their own languages."

This was all new and exciting, but we shouldn't forget how constricted this early PC-Windows-modem platform was. "This platform was constrained by too many architectural limits," said Mundie. "There was missing infrastructure." The Internet as we know it today — with seemingly magical transmission protocols that can connect everyone and everything — had not yet emerged. Back then, networks had only very basic protocols for exchanging files and e-mail messages. So people who were using computers with the same type of operating systems and software could exchange documents through e-mail or file transfers, but even doing this was tricky enough that only the computing elite took the trouble. You couldn't just sit down and zap an e-mail or a file to anyone anywhere — especially outside your own company or outside your own Internet service — the way you can today. Yes, AOL users could communicate with CompuServe users, but it was neither simple nor reliable. As a result, said Mundie, a huge amount of data and creativity was accumulating in all those computers, but there was no easy, interoperable way to share it and mold it. People could write new applications that allowed selected systems to work together, but in general this was limited to planned exchanges between PCs within the network of a single company.

This period from 11/9 to the mid-1990s still led to a huge advance in personal empowerment, even if networks were limited.

It was the age of "Me and my machine can now talk to each other better and faster, so that I personally can do more tasks" and the age of "Me and my machine can now talk to a few friends and some other people in my company better and faster, so we can become more productive." The walls had fallen and the Windows had opened, making the world much flatter than it had ever been — but the age of seamless global communication had not dawned.

Though we didn't notice it, there was a discordant note in this exciting new era. It wasn't only Americans and Europeans who joined the people of the Soviet Empire in celebrating the fall of the wall — and claiming credit for it. Someone else was raising a glass — not of champagne but of thick Turkish coffee. His name was Osama bin Laden and he had a different narrative. His view was that it was the jihadi fighters in Afghanistan, of which he was one, who had brought down the Soviet Empire by forcing the Red Army to withdraw from Afghanistan (with some help from U.S. and Pakistani forces). And once that mission had been accomplished — the Soviets completed their pullout from Afghanistan on February 15, 1989, just nine months before the fall of the Berlin Wall — bin Laden looked around and found that the other superpower, the United States, had a huge presence in his own native land, Saudi Arabia, the home of the two holiest cities in Islam. And he did not like it.

So, while we were dancing on the wall and opening up our Windows and proclaiming that there was no ideological alternative left to free-market capitalism, bin Laden was turning his gun sights on America. Both bin Laden and Ronald Reagan saw the Soviet Union as the "evil empire," but bin Laden came to see America as evil too. He did have an ideological alternative to free-market capitalism — political Islam. He did not feel defeated by the end of the Soviet Union; he felt emboldened by it. He did not feel attracted to the widened playing field; he felt repelled by it. And he was not alone. Some thought that Ronald Reagan brought down the wall by bankrupting the Soviet Union through an arms race; others thought IBM, Steve Jobs, and Bill Gates brought down the wall by empowering individuals to download the future. But a world away, in Muslim lands, many thought bin Laden and his comrades brought down the Soviet Empire and the wall with religious zeal, and millions of them were inspired to upload the past.

In short, while we were celebrating 11/9, the seeds of another memorable date — 9/11 — were being sown. But more about that later in the book. For now, let the flattening continue.

Flattener #2
8/9/95
When Netscape Went Public

By the mid-1990s, the PC-Windows network revolution had reached its limits. If the world was going to become really intercon-nected, and really start to flatten out, the revolution needed to go to the next phase. And the next phase, notes Microsoft's Mundie, "was to go from a PC-based com-puting platform to an Internet-based plat-form." The killer applications that drove this new phase were e-mail and Internet browsing. E-mail was being driven by the rapidly expanding consumer portals like AOL, CompuServe, and eventually MSN. But it was the new killer app, the Web browser — which could retrieve documents or Web pages stored on Internet Web sites and display them on any computer screen — that really captured the imagination. The actual concept of the World Wide Web — a system for creating, organizing, and linking documents so they could be easily browsed — was created by British computer scientist Tim Berners-Lee. He put up the first Web site in 1991, in an effort to foster a computer network that would enable scientists to easily share their research. Other scientists and academics had created a number of browsers to surf this early Web, but the first mainstream browser — and the whole culture of Web browsing for the general public — was created by a tiny start-up company in Mountain View, California, called Netscape. Netscape went public on August 9, 1995, and the world has not been the same since.

As John Doerr, the legendary venture capitalist whose firm Kleiner Perkins Caulfield & Byers had backed Netscape, put it, "The Netscape IPO was a clarion call to the world to wake up to the Internet. Until then, it had been the province of the early adopters and geeks."

This Netscape-triggered phase drove the flattening process in several key ways: It gave us the first broadly popular commercial browser to surf the Internet. The Netscape browser not only brought the Internet alive but also made the Internet accessible to everyone from five-year-olds to eighty-five-year-olds. The more alive the Internet became, the more consumers wanted to do different things on the Web, so the more they demanded computers, software, and telecommunications networks that could easily digitize words, music, data, and photos and transport them on the Internet to anyone else's computer. This demand was satisfied by another catalytic event: the rollout of Windows 95, which shipped the week after Netscape took its stock public. Windows 95 would soon become the operating system used by most people worldwide, and unlike previous versions of Windows, it was equipped with built-in Internet support, so that not just browsers but all PC applications could "know about the Internet" and interact with it.

Looking back, what enabled Netscape to take off was the existence, from the earlier phase, of millions of PCs, many already equipped with modems. Those are the shoulders Netscape stood on. What Netscape did was bring a new killer app — the browser — to this installed base of PCs, making the computer and its connectivity inherently more useful for millions of people. This in turn set off an explosion in demand for all things digital and sparked the Internet boom, because every investor looked at the Internet and concluded that if everything was going to be digitized — data, inventories, commerce, books, music, photos, and entertainment — and transported and sold on the Internet, then the demand for Internet-based products and services would be infinite. This led to the dot-com stock bubble and a massive overinvestment in the fiber-optic cable needed to carry all the new digital information. This development, in turn, wired the whole world together, and, without anyone really planning it, made Bangalore a suburb of Boston.

Let's look at each one of these developments.

When I sat down with Jim Barksdale, the former Netscape CEO, to interview him for this book, I explained to him that one of the early chapters was about the ten innovations, events, and trends that had flattened the world. The first event, I told him, was 11/9, and I explained the significance of that date. Then I said, "Let me see if you can guess the significance of the second date, 8/9." That was all I told him: 8/9. It took Barksdale only a second to ponder that before shooting back with the right answer: "The day Netscape went public!"

Few would argue that Barksdale is one of the great American entrepreneurs. He helped Federal Express develop its package tracking and tracing system, then moved over to McCaw Cellular, the mobile phone company, built that up, and oversaw its merger with AT&T in 1994. Just before the sale closed, he was approached by a headhunter to become the CEO of a new company called Mosaic Communications, forged by two now-legendary innovators — Jim Clark and Marc Andreessen. In mid-1994, Clark, the founder of Silicon Graphics, had joined forces with Andreessen to found Mosaic, which would quickly be renamed Netscape Communications. Andreessen, a brilliant young computer scientist, had just spearheaded a small software project at the National Center for Supercomputing Applications (NCSA), based at the University of Illinois, that developed the first really effective Web browser, also called Mosaic. Clark and Andreessen quickly understood the huge potential for Web-browsing software and decided to partner up to commercialize it. As Netscape began to grow, they reached out to Barksdale for guidance and insight into how best to go public.

Today we take this browser technology for granted, but it was actually one of the most important inventions in modern history. When Andreessen was back at the University of Illinois NCSA lab, he found that he had PCs, workstations, and the basic network connectivity to move files around the Internet, but it was still not very exciting — because there was nothing to browse with, no user interface to pull up and display the contents of other people's Web sites. So Andreessen and his team developed the Mosaic browser, making Web sites viewable for any idiot, scientist, student, or grandma. Marc Andreessen did not invent the Internet, but he did as much as any single person to bring it alive and popularize it.

"The Mosaic browser started out in 1993 with twelve users, and I knew all twelve," said Andreessen. There were only about fifty Web sites at the time and they were mostly just single Web pages. "Mosaic," he explained, "was funded by the National Science Foundation. The money wasn't actually allocated to build Mosaic. Our specific group was to build software that would enable scientists to use supercomputers that were in remote locations, and to connect to them by the NSF network. So we built [the first browsers as] software tools to enable researchers to 'browse' each other's research. I looked at it as a positive feedback loop: The more people had the browser, the more people would want to be interconnected, and the more incentive there would be to create content and applications and tools. Once that kind of thing gets started, it just takes off and virtually nothing can stop it. When you are developing it, you are not sure anyone is going to use it, but once it started we realized that if anyone is going to use it *everyone is going to use it*, and the only question then was how fast it would spread and what would be the barriers along the way."

Indeed, everyone who tried the browser, including Barksdale, had the same initial reaction: *Wow!* "Every summer, *Fortune* magazine had an article about the twenty-five coolest companies around," Barksdale recalled. "That year [1994] Mosaic was one of them. I not only had read about Clark and Andreessen but had turned to my wife and said, 'Honey, this a great idea.' And then just a few weeks later I get this call from the headhunter. So I went down and spoke to Doerr and Jim Clark, and I began using the beta version of the Mosaic browser. I became more and more intrigued the more I used it." Since the late 1980s, people had been putting up databases with Internet access. Barksdale said that after speaking to Doerr and Clark, he went home, gathered his three children around his computer, and asked them each to suggest a topic he could browse the Internet for — and wowed them by coming up with something for each of them. "That convinced me," said Barksdale. "So I called back the headhunter and said, 'I'm your man.' "

Netscape's first commercial browser — which could work on an IBM PC, an Apple Macintosh, or a Unix computer — was released in December 1994, and within a year it completely dominated the market. You could download Netscape for free if you were in education or a non-profit. If you were an individual, you could evaluate the software for free to your heart's content and buy it on disk if you wanted it. If you were a company, you could evaluate the software for ninety days. "The underlying rationale," said Andreessen, "was: If you can afford to pay for it, please do so. If not, use it anyway." Why? Because all the free usage stimulated a massive growth in the network, which was valuable to all the paying customers. It worked.

"We put up the Netscape browser," said Barksdale, "and people were downloading it for three-month trials. I've never seen volume like this. For big businesses and government it was allowing them to connect and unlock all their information, and the point-and-click system that Marc Andreessen invented allowed mere mortals to use it, not just scientists. And that made it a true revolution. And we said, 'This thing will just grow and grow and grow.'"

Nothing did stop it, and that is why Netscape played another hugely important flattening role: It helped make the Internet truly interoperable. You will recall that in the Berlin Wall–PC–Windows phase, individuals who had e-mail and companies that had internal e-mail could not connect very far. The first Cisco Internet router, in fact, was built by a husband and wife at Stanford who wanted to exchange e-mail; one was working off a mainframe and the other on a PC, and they couldn't connect. "The corporate networks at the time were proprietary and disconnected from each other," said Andreessen. "Each one had its own formats, data protocols, and different ways of doing content. So there were all these islands of information out there that were disconnected. And as the Internet emerged as a public, commercial venture, there was a real danger that it would emerge in the same disconnected way."

Joe in the accounting department would get on his office PC and try to get the latest sales numbers for 1995, but he couldn't do that because the sales department was on a different system from the one accounting was using. It was as if one was speaking German and the other French. And then Joe would say, "Get me the latest shipment information from Goodyear on what tires they have sent us," and he would find that Goodyear was using a different system altogether, and the dealer in Topeka was running yet another system. Then Joe would go home and find his seventh-grader on the World Wide Web researching a term paper, using open protocols, and looking at the holdings of some art museum in France. And Joe would say, "This is crazy. There has to be one totally interconnected network."

In the years before the Internet became commercial, explained Andreessen, scientists developed a series of "open protocols" meant to make everyone's e-mail system or university computer network connect seamlessly with everyone else's — to ensure that no one had some special advantage. These mathematical-based protocols, which enable digital devices to talk to each other, were like magical pipes that, once you adopted them for your network, made you compatible with everyone else, no matter what kind of computer they were running. These protocols were (and still are) known by their alphabet soup names: mainly FTP, HTTP, SSL, SMTP, POP, and TCP/IP. Together, they form a system for transporting data around the Internet in a relatively secure manner, no matter what network your company or household has or what computer or cell phone or handheld device you are using. Each protocol had a different function: TCP/IP was the basic plumbing of the Internet, or the basic railroad tracks, on which everything else above it was built and moved around. FTP moved files; SMTP and POP moved e-mail messages, which became standardized, so that they could be written and read on different e-mail systems. HTML was a language that allowed even ordinary people to author Web pages that anyone with a Web browser could display. But it was the introduction of HTTP to move HTML documents around that gave birth to the World Wide Web as we know it. Finally, as people began to use these Web pages for electronic commerce, SSL was created to provide security for Web-based transactions.

As browsing and the Internet in general grew, Netscape wanted to make sure that Microsoft, with its huge market dominance, would not be able to shift these Web protocols from open to proprietary standards that only Microsoft's servers would be able to handle. "Netscape helped to guarantee that these open protocols would not be proprietary by commercializing them for the public," said Andreessen. "Netscape came along not only with the browser but with a family of software products that implemented all these open standards so that the scientists could communicate with each other no matter what system they were on — a Cray supercomputer, a Macintosh, or a PC. Netscape was able to provide a real reason for everyone to say, 'I want to be on open standards for everything I do and for all the systems I work on.' Once we created a way to browse the Internet, people wanted a universal way to access what was out there. So anyone who wanted to work on open standards went to Netscape, where we supported them, or they went to the open-source world and got the same standards for free but unsupported, or they went to their private vendors and said, 'I am not going to buy your proprietary stuff anymore . . . I am not going to sign up to your walled garden anymore. I am only going to stay with you if you interconnect to the Internet with these open protocols.' "

Netscape began pushing these open standards through the sale of its browsers, and the public responded enthusiastically. Sun started to do the same with its servers, and Microsoft started to do the same with Windows 95, considering browsing so critical that it famously built its own browser directly into Windows with the addition of Internet Explorer. Each realized that the public, which suddenly could not get enough of e-mail and browsing, wanted the Internet companies to work together and create one interoperable network. They wanted companies to compete with each other over different applications, that is, over what consumers could do *once they were on* the Internet — not over *how they got on* the Internet in the first place. As a result, after quite a few "format wars" among the big companies, by the late

1990s the Internet computing platform became seamlessly integrated. Soon anyone was able to connect with anyone else anywhere on any machine. It turned out that the value of compatibility was much higher for everyone than the value of trying to maintain your own little walled network. This integration was a huge flattener, because it enabled so many more people to get connected with so many more other people.

There was no shortage of skeptics at the time, who said that none of this would work because it was all too complicated, recalled Andreessen. "You had to go out and get a PC and a dial-up modem. The skeptics all said, 'It takes people a long time to change their habits and learn a new technology.' [But] people did it very quickly, and ten years later there were eight hundred million people on the Internet." The reason? "People will change their habits quickly when they have a strong reason to do so, and people have an innate urge to connect with other people," said Andreessen. "And when you give people a new way to connect with other people, they will punch through any technical barrier, they will learn new languages — people are wired to want to connect with other people and they find it objectionable not to be able to. That is what Netscape unlocked." As Joel Cawley,

IBM's vice president of corporate strategy, put it, "Netscape created a standard around how data would be transported and rendered on the screen that was so simple and compelling that anyone and everyone could innovate on top of it. It quickly scaled around the world and to everyone from kids to corporations."

In the summer of 1995, Barksdale and his Netscape colleagues went on an old-fashioned road show with their investment bankers from Morgan Stanley to try to entice investors around the country to buy Netscape stock once it went public. "When we went out on the road," said Barksdale, "Morgan Stanley said the stock could sell for as high as $14. But after the road show got going, they were getting such demand for the stock, they decided to double the opening price to $28. The last afternoon before the offering, we were all in Maryland. It was our last stop. We had this caravan of black limousines. We looked like some kind of Mafia group. We needed to be in touch with Morgan Stanley [headquarters], but we were somewhere where our cell phones didn't work. So we pulled into these two filling stations across from each other, all these black limos, to use the phones. We called up Morgan Stanley, and they said, 'We're thinking of bringing it out at $31.' I said, 'No, let's keep it at $28,' because I wanted people to remember it as a $20 stock, not a $30 stock, just in case it didn't go so well. So then the next morning I get on the conference call and the thing opened at $71. It closed the day at $56, exactly twice the price I set."

Netscape eventually fell victim to overwhelming (and, the courts decided, monopolistic) competitive pressure from Microsoft. Microsoft's decision to give away its browser, Internet Explorer, as part of its dominant Windows operating system, combined with its ability to throw more programmers at Web browsing than Netscape, led to the increasing slippage of Netscape's market share. In the end, Netscape was sold for $10 billion to AOL, which never did much with it. But though Netscape may have been only a shooting star in commercial terms, what a star it was, and what a trail it left.

"We were profitable almost from the start," said Barksdale. "Netscape was not a dot-com. We did not participate in the dot-com bubble. We *started* the dot-com bubble."

And what a bubble it was.

"Netscape going public stimulated a lot of things," said Barksdale. "The technologists loved the new technology things it could do, and the businesspeople and regular folks got excited about how much money they could make. People saw all those young kids making money out of this and said, 'If those young kids can do this and make all that money, I can too.' Greed can be a bad thing — folks thought they could make a lot of money without a lot of work. It certainly led to a degree of overinvestment, putting it mildly. Every sillier and sillier idea got funded."

What was it that stimulated investors to believe that demand for Internet usage and Internet-related products would be infinite? The short answer is digitization. Once the PC-Windows revolution demonstrated to everyone the value of being able to digitize information and manipulate it on computers and word processors, and once the browser brought the Internet alive and made Web pages sing and dance and display, everyone wanted everything digitized as much as possible so they could send it to someone else down the Internet pipes. Thus began the digitization revolution. Digitization is that magic process by which words, music, data, films, files, and pictures are turned into bits and bytes — combinations of 1s and 0s — that can be manipulated on a computer screen, stored on a microprocessor, or transmitted over satellites and fiber-optic lines. It used to be the post office was where I went to send my mail, but once the Internet came alive,

I wanted my mail digitized so I could e-mail it. Photography used to be a cumbersome process involving film coated with silver dug up from mines halfway across the world. I used to take some pictures with my camera, then bring the film to the drugstore to be sent off to a big plant somewhere for processing. But once the Internet made it possible to send pictures around the world, attached to or in e-mails, I didn't want to use silver film anymore. I wanted to take pictures in the digital format, which could be uploaded, not developed. (And by the way, I didn't want to be confined to using a camera to take them. I wanted to be able to use my cell phone to do it.) I used to have to go to Barnes & Noble to buy and browse books, but once the Internet came alive, I wanted to browse for books digitally on Amazon.com as well. I used to go to the library to do research, but now I wanted to do it digitally through Google or Yahoo!, not just by roaming the stacks. I used to buy a CD to listen to Simon and Garfunkel — CDs had already replaced albums as a form of digitized music — but once the Internet came alive, I wanted those music bits to be even more malleable and mobile. I wanted to be able to download them into an iPod. In recent years the digitization technology evolved so I could do just that.

Well, as investors watched this mad rush to digitize everything, they said to themselves, "Holy cow. If everyone wants all this stuff digitized and turned into bits and transmitted over the Internet, the demand for Web service companies and the demand for fiber-optic cables to handle all this digitized stuff around the world is going to be limitless! You cannot lose if you invest in this!"

And thus was the bubble born.

Overinvestment is not necessarily a bad thing — provided that it is eventually corrected. I'll always remember a news conference that Microsoft chairman Bill Gates held at the 1999 World Economic Forum in Davos, at the height of the tech bubble. Over and over again, Gates was bombarded by reporters with versions of the question, "Mr. Gates, these Internet stocks, they're a bubble, right? Surely they're a bubble. They must be a bubble?" Finally an exasperated Gates said to the reporters something to the effect of, "Look, you bozos, of course they're a bubble, but you're all missing the point. This bubble is attracting so much new capital to this Internet industry, it is going to drive innovation faster and faster." Gates compared the Internet to the gold rush, the idea being that more money was made selling Levi's, picks, shovels, and hotel rooms to

120

the gold diggers than from digging up gold from the earth. Gates was right: Booms and bubbles may be economically dangerous; they may end up with many people losing money and a lot of companies going bankrupt. But they also often do drive innovation faster and faster, and the sheer overcapacity that they spur — whether it is in railroad lines or automobiles — can create its own unintended positive consequences.

That is what happened with the Internet stock boom. It sparked a huge overinvestment in fiber-optic cable companies, which then laid massive amounts of fiber-optic cable on land and under the oceans, which dramatically drove down the cost of making a phone call or transmitting data anywhere in the world.

The first commercial installation of a fiber-optic system was in 1977, after which fiber slowly began to replace copper telephone wires, because it could carry data and digitized voices much farther and faster in larger quantities. According to Howstuffworks.com, fiber optics are made up of strands of optically pure glass each "as thin as a human hair," which are arranged in bundles, called "optical cables," to carry digitized packets of information over long distances. Because these optical fibers are so much thinner than copper wires, more fibers can be bundled into a given diameter of cable than can copper wires, which means that much more data or many more voices can be sent over the same cable at a lower cost. The most important benefit of fiber, though, derives from the dramatically higher bandwidth of the signals it can transport over long distances. Copper wires can carry very high frequencies too, but only for a few feet before the signal starts to degrade in strength due to certain parasitic effects. Optical fibers, by contrast, can carry very high-frequency optical pulses on the same individual fiber without substantial signal degradation for many, many miles.

The way fiber-optic cables work, explains one of the manufacturers, ARC Electronics, on its Web site, is by converting data or voices into light pulses and then transmitting them down fiber lines, instead of using electronic pulses to transmit information down copper lines. At one end of the fiber-optic system is a transmitter. The transmitter accepts coded electronic pulse information — words or data — coming from copper wire out of your home telephone or office computer. The transmitter then processes and translates those digitized, electronically coded words or data into equivalently coded light pulses. A light-emitting diode (LED) or an injection-laser diode (ILD) can be used to generate the light pulses, which are then funneled down the fiber-optic cable. The cable functions as a kind of light guide, guiding the light pulses introduced at one end of the cable through to the other end, where a light-sensitive receiver converts the pulses back into the electronic digital 1s and 0s of the original signal, so they can then show up on your computer screen as e-mail or in your cell phone as a voice. Fiber-optic cable is also ideal for secure communications, because it is very difficult to tap.

It was actually the coincidence of the dot-com boom and the Telecommunications Act of 1996 that launched the fiber-optic bubble. The act allowed local and long-distance companies to get into each other's businesses, and enabled all sorts of new local exchange carriers to compete head-to-head with the Baby Bells and AT&T in providing both phone services and infrastructure. As these new phone companies came online, offering their own local, long-distance, international, data, and Internet services, each sought to have its own infrastructure. And why not? The Internet boom led everyone to assume that the demand for bandwidth to carry all that Internet traffic would double every three months — *indefinitely*. For about two years that was true. But then the law of large numbers started to kick in, and the pace of doubling slowed. Unfortunately, the telecom companies weren't paying close attention to the developing mismatch between demand and reality. The market was in the grip of an Internet fever, and companies just kept building more and more capacity. And the stock market boom meant *money was free! It was a party!* So every one of these incredibly optimistic scenarios from every one of these new telecom companies got funded. In a period of about five or six years, these telecom companies invested about $1 trillion in wiring the world. And virtually no one questioned the demand projections.

Few companies got crazier than Global Crossing, one of the companies hired by all these new telecoms to lay fiber-optic cable for them around the world. Global Crossing was founded in 1997 by Gary Winnick and went public the next year. Robert Annunziata, who lasted only a year as CEO, had a contract that the Corporate Library's Nell Minow once picked as the worst (from the point of view of shareholders) in the United States. Among other things, it included Annunziata's mother's first-class airfare to visit him once a month. It also included a signing bonus of 2 million shares of stock at $10 a share below market.

Henry Schacht, a veteran industrialist now with E. M. Warburg, Pincus & Co., was brought in by Lucent, the successor of Western Electric, to help manage it through this crazy period. He recalled the atmosphere: "The telecom deregulation of 1996 was hugely important. It allowed competitive local exchange carriers to build their own capacities and sell in competition with each other and with the Baby Bells. These new telecoms went to companies like Global Crossing and had them install fiber networks for them so they could compete at the transport level with AT&T and MCI, particularly on overseas traffic . . . Everyone thought this was a new world, and it would never stop. [You had] competitive firms using free capital, and everyone thought the pie would expand infinitely. So [each company said,] 'I will put my fiber down before you do, and I will get a bigger share than you.' It was supposed to be just a vertical growth line, straight up, and we each thought we would get our share, so everybody built to the max projections and assumed that they would get their share."

It turned out that while business-to-business and e-commerce developed as projected, and a lot of Web sites that no one anticipated exploded — like eBay, Amazon, and Google — they still devoured only a fraction of the capacity that was being made available. So when the dot-com bust came along, there was just way too much fiber-optic cable out there. Long-distance phone rates went from $2 a minute to 10¢. And the transmission of data was virtually free. "The telecom industry has invested itself right out of a business," Mike McCue, chief operations officer of Tellme Networks, a voice-activated Internet service, told CNET News.com in June 2001. "They've laid so much fiber in the ground that they've basically commoditized themselves. They are going to get into massive price wars with everyone and it's going to be a disaster."

It was a disaster for many of the companies and their investors (Global Crossing filed for bankruptcy in January 2002, with $12.4 billion in debt), but it turned out to be a great boon for consumers. Just as the national highway system that was built in the 1950s flattened the United States, broke down regional differences, and made it so much easier for companies to relocate in lower-wage regions, like the South, because it had become so much easier to move people and goods long distances, so the laying of global fiber highways flattened the developed world. It helped to break down global regionalism, create a more seamless global commercial network, and made it simple and almost free to move digitized labor — service jobs and knowledge work

— to lower-cost countries.

(It should be noted, though, that those fiber highways in America tended to stop at the last mile — before connecting to households. While a huge amount of long-distance fiber cable was laid to connect India and America, virtually none of these new U.S. telecom companies laid any substantial new local loop infrastructure, due to a failure of the 1996 telecom deregulation act to permit real competition in the local loop between the cable companies and the telephone companies. Where the local broadband did get installed was in office buildings, which were already pretty well served by the old companies. So this pushed prices down for businesses — and for Indians who wanted to get online from Bangalore to do business with those businesses — but it didn't create the sort of competition that could bring cheap broadband capability to the American masses in their homes. That has started happening only more recently.)

The broad overinvestment in fiber cable is a gift that keeps on giving, thanks to the unique nature of fiber optics. Unlike other forms of Internet overinvestment, it was permanent: Once the fiber cables were laid, no one was going to dig them up and thereby eliminate the overcapacity. So when the telecom companies went bankrupt, the banks took them over and then sold their fiber cables for ten cents on the dollar to new companies, which continued to operate them, which they could do profitably, having bought them in a fire sale. But the way fiber cable works is that each cable has multiple strands of fiber in it with a potential capacity to transmit many terabits of data per second on each strand. When these fiber cables were originally laid, the optical switches — the transmitters and receivers — at each end of them could not take full advantage of the fiber's full capacity. But every year since then, the optical switches at each end of that fiber cable have gotten better and better, meaning that more and more voices and data can be transmitted down each fiber. So as the switches keep improving, the capacity of all the already installed fiber cables just keeps growing, making it cheaper and easier to transmit voices and data every year to any part of the world. It is as though we laid down a national highway system where people were first allowed to drive 50 mph, then 60 mph, then 70 mph, then 80 mph, then eventually 150 mph on the same highways without any fear of accidents. Only this highway wasn't just national. It was international.

"Every layer of innovation gets built on the next," said Andreessen, who went on from Netscape to start another high-tech firm, Opsware Inc. "And today the most profound thing to me is the fact that a fourteen-year-old in Romania or Bangalore or the Soviet Union or Vietnam has all the information, all the tools, all the software easily available to apply knowledge however they want. That is why I am sure the next Napster is going to come out of left field. As bioscience becomes more computational and less about wet labs, and as all the genomic data becomes easily available on the Internet, at some point you will be able to design vaccines on your laptop."

I think Andreessen touches on what is unique about the flat world and the era of Globalization 3.0. It is going to be driven by groups and individuals, but of a much more diverse background than those twelve scientists who made up Andreessen's world when he created Mosaic. Now we are going to see the real human mosaic emerge — from all over the world, from left field and right field, from West and East and North and South — to drive the next generation of innovation. Indeed, a few days after Andreessen and I talked, the following headline appeared on the front page of *The New York Times* (July 15, 2004): "U.S. Permits 3 Cancer Drugs from Cuba." The story went on to say, "The federal government is permitting a California biotechnology company to license three experimental cancer drugs from Cuba — making an exception to the policy of tightly restricting trade with that country." Executives of the company, CancerVex, said that "it was the first time an American biotechnology company had obtained permission to license a drug from Cuba, a country that some industry executives and scientists say is surprisingly strong in biotechnology for a developing nation . . . More than $1 billion was spent over the years to build and operate research institutes on the west side of Havana staffed by Cuban scientists, many of them educated in Europe."

Just to summarize again: The PC-Windows flattening phase was about me interacting with my computer and me interacting with my own limited network inside my own company. Then came along this Internet–e-mail–browser phase, and it flattened the earth a little bit more. It was about me and my computer interacting with anyone anywhere on any machine, which is what e-mail is all about, and me and my computer interacting with anybody's Web site on the Internet, which is what browsing is all about. In short, the PC-Windows phase begat the Netscape browsing–e-mail phase and the two together enabled more people to communicate and interact with more other people anywhere on the planet than ever before.

But the fun was just beginning. This phase was just the foundation for the next step in flattening the flat world.

Flattener #3
Work Flow Software
Let's Do Lunch: Have Your
Application Talk to My Application

I met Scott Hyten, the CEO of Wild Brain, a cutting-edge animation studio in San Francisco that produces films and cartoons for Disney and other major studios, at a meeting in Silicon Valley in the winter of 2004. I had been invited by John Doerr, the venture capitalist, to test out the ideas in this book to a few of the companies that he was backing. Hyten and I really hit it off, maybe because after hearing my arguments he wrote me an e-mail that said, "I am sure in Magellan's time there were plenty of theologians, geographers, and pundits who wanted to make the world flat again. I know the world is flat, and thank you for your support."

A man after my own heart.

When I asked him to elaborate, Hyten sketched out for me how animated films are produced today through a global supply chain. I understood immediately why he too had concluded that the world is flat.

"At Wild Brain," he said, "we make something out of nothing. We learn how to take advantage of the flat world. We are not fighting it. We are taking advantage of it."

Hyten invited me to come and watch them produce a cartoon segment to really appreciate how flat the world is, which I did. The series they were working on when I showed up was for the Disney Channel and called *Higglytown Heroes*. It was inspired by all the ordinary people who rose to the challenge of 9/11. Higglytown "is the typical 1950s small town," said Hyten. "It is Pleasantville. And we are exporting the production of this American small town around the world — literally and figuratively. The foundation of the story is that every person, all the ordinary people living their lives, are the heroes in this small town — from the schoolteacher to the pizza delivery man."

This all-American show is being produced by an all-world supply chain. "The recording session," explained Hyten, "is located near the artist, usually in New York or L.A., the design and direction is done in San Francisco, the writers network in from their homes (Florida, London, New York, Chicago, L.A., and San Francisco), and the animation of the characters is done in Bangalore with edits from San Francisco. For this show we have eight teams in Bangalore working in parallel with eight different writers. This efficiency has allowed us to contract with fifty 'stars' for the twenty-six episodes. These interactive recording/writing/animation sessions allow us to record an artist for an entire show in less than half a day, including unlimited takes and rewrites. We record two actors per week. For example, last week we recorded Anne Heche and Smokey Robinson. Technically, we do this over the Internet. We have a VPN [virtual private network] configured on computers in our offices and on what we call writers' 'footballs,' or special laptop computers that can connect over any cat-5 Ethernet connection or wireless broadband connection in the 'field.' This VPN allows us to share the feed from the microphone, images from the session, the real-time script, and all the animation designs amongst all the locations with a simple log-in. Therefore, one way for you to observe is for us to ship you a football. You connect at home, the office, most hotel rooms, or go down to your local Starbucks [which has wireless broadband Internet access], log on, put on a pair of Bose noise-reduction headphones, and listen, watch, read, and comment. 'Sharon, can you sell that line a little more?' Then, over the eleven-week production schedule for the show, you can log in twenty-four hours a day and check the progress of the production as it follows the sun around the world. Technically, you need the 'football' only for the session. You can use your regular laptop to follow the 'dailies' and 'edits' over the production cycle."

I needed to see Wild Brain firsthand, because it is a graphic example of the next layer of innovation, and the next flattener, that broadly followed on the Berlin Wall–Windows and Netscape phases. I call this the "work flow phase." When the walls went down, and the PC, Windows, and Netscape browser enabled people to connect with other people as never before, it did not take long before all these people who were connecting wanted to do more than just browse and send e-mail, instant messages, pictures, and music over this Internet platform. They wanted to shape things, design things, create things, sell things, buy things, keep track of inventories, do somebody else's taxes, and read somebody else's X-rays from half a world away. And they wanted to be able to do any of these things from anywhere to anywhere and from any computer to any computer — seamlessly. The wall-Windows-Netscape phases paved the way for that by standardizing the ways words, music, pictures, and data would be digitized and transported on the Internet — so e-mail and browsing became a very rich experience.

But for all of us to go to the next stage, to get more out of the Internet, the flattening process had to go another notch. We needed two things. We needed programmers to come along and write new applications — new software — that would enable us really to get the maximum from our computers as we worked with these digitized data, words, music, and pictures and shaped them into products. We also needed more magic pipes, more transmissions protocols, that would ensure that everyone's software applications could connect with everyone else's software applications. In short, we had to go from an Internet that just connected people to people, and people to their own applications, to an Internet that could connect any of my software programs to any of your software programs. Only then could we really work together.

Think of it this way: In the beginning, work flow consisted of your sales department taking an order on paper, walking it over to your shipping department, which shipped the product, and then someone from shipping walking over to billing with a piece of paper and instructing them to churn out an invoice to the customer. As a result of the Berlin Wall–Windows–Netscape phases, work flow took a huge leap forward. Now your sales department could electronically take that order, e-mail it to the shipping department within your own company, and then have the shipping department send out the product to the customer and automatically spit out a bill at the same time. The fact that all the departments within your company were seamlessly interoperable and that work could flow between them was a great boost to productivity — but this could happen only if all your company's departments were using the same software and hardware systems. More often than not, back in the 1980s and early 1990s, a company's sales department was running Microsoft and the inventory department was running Novell, and they could not communicate with each other. So work did not flow as easily as it should.

We often forget that the software industry started out like a bad fire department. Imagine a city where every neighborhood had a different interface for connecting the fire hose to the hydrant. Everything was fine as long as your neighborhood fire department could handle your fire. But when a fire became too big, and the fire engines from the next neighborhood had to be called in, they were useless because they could not connect their hoses to your hydrants.

For the world to get flat, all your internal departments — sales, marketing, manufacturing, billing, and inventory — had to become interoperable, no matter what machines or software each of them was running. And for the world to get *really flat,* all your systems had to be interoperable with all the systems of any other company. That is, your sales department had to be connected to your supplier's inventory department and your supplier's inventory department had to be seamlessly connected to its supplier's supplier, which was a factory in China. That way, when you made a sale, an item was automatically shipped from your supplier's warehouse, and another item was automatically manufactured by your supplier's supplier, and a bill was generated from your billing department. The disparate computer systems and software applications of three distinctly different companies had to be seamlessly interoperable so that work could flow between them.

In the late 1990s, the software industry began to respond to what its consumers wanted. Technology companies, through much backroom wrangling and trial and error, started to forge more common Web-based standards, more integrated digital plumbing and protocols, so that anyone could fit his hose — his software applications — onto anyone else's hydrant.

This was a quiet revolution. Technically, what made it possible was the development of a new data description language, called XML, and its related transport protocol, called SOAP. IBM, Microsoft, and a host of other companies contributed to the development of both XML and SOAP, and both were subsequently ratified and popularized as the Internet standards. XML and SOAP created the technical foundation for software program–to–software program interaction, which was the foundation for Web-enabled work flow. They enabled digitized data, words, music, and photos to be exchanged between diverse software programs so that they could be shaped, designed, manipulated, edited, reedited, stored, published, and transported — without any regard to where people are physically sitting or what computing devices they are connecting through.

Once this technical foundation was in place, more and more people started writing work flow software programs for more and more different tasks. Wild Brain wanted programs to make animated films with a production team spread out around the world. Boeing wanted them so that its airplane factories in America could constantly resupply different airline customers with parts, through its computer ordering systems, no matter what country those orders came from. Doctors wanted them so that an X-ray taken in Bangor could be read in a hospital in Bangalore, without the doctor in Maine ever having to think about what computers that Indian hospital had. And Mom and Dad wanted them because they wanted their e-banking software, e-brokerage software, office e-mail, and spreadsheet software to all work off their home laptop and be able to interface with their office desktop. And once everyone's applications started to connect to everyone else's applications — which took several years and a lot of technology and brainpower to make happen — work could not only flow like never before, but it could be chopped up and disaggregated like never before and sent to the four corners of the world. This meant that work could flow anywhere. Indeed, it was the ability to enable applications to speak to applications, not just people to speak to people, that would soon make outsourcing possible. Thanks to different kinds of Web services–work flow, said Craig Mundie, Microsoft's chief technology officer, "the industry created a global platform for a global workforce of people and computers."

The vast network of underground plumbing that made it possible for all this work to flow has become quite extensive. It includes all the Internet protocols of the previous era, like TCP/IP and others, which made browsing and e-mail and Web sites possible. It includes newer tools, like XML and SOAP, which enabled Web applications to communicate with each other more seamlessly, and it includes software agents known as middleware, which serves as an intermediary between wildly diverse applications. The nexus of these technologies has been a huge boon to innovation and a huge reducer of friction between companies and applications. Instead of everyone trying to control the fire hydrant nozzle, they made all the nozzles and hoses the same, creating a much bigger market that stretched across every neighborhood of the world. Then companies started to compete instead over the quality of the hose, the pump, and the fire truck. That is, they competed over who could make the most useful and nifty applications. Said Joel Cawley, the head of IBM's strategic planning unit, "Standards don't eliminate innovation, they just allow you to focus it. They allow you to focus on where the real value lies, which is usually everything you can add above and around the standard."

I found this out writing my last book. Once Microsoft Word got established as the global standard, work could flow between people on different continents much more easily, because we were all writing off the same screen with the same basic toolbar. When I was working on my first book, *From Beirut to Jerusalem*, in 1988, I spent part of my year's leave in the Middle East and had to take notes with pen and paper, as it was the pre-laptop and pre–Microsoft Word era. When I wrote my second book, *The Lexus and the Olive Tree*, in 1998, I had to do some of the last-minute editing from the computer behind the front desk at a Swiss hotel in Davos on a German version of Microsoft Word. I could not understand a single word, a single command function, on the toolbar of the German version of Word. But by 1998, I was so familiar with the Word for Windows writing program, and where the various on-screen icons were, that I was able to point and click my way through the editing on the German version and type my corrections with the English letters on the German keyboard. Shared standards are a huge flattener, because they both force and empower more people to communicate and innovate over much wider platforms.

Another of my favorite examples of this is PayPal, which enabled eBay's e-commerce bazaar to become what it is today. PayPal is a money transfer system founded in 1998 to facilitate C2C (customer-to-customer) transactions, like a buyer and seller brought together by eBay. According to the

Web site ecommerce-guide.com, using PayPal, anyone with an e-mail address can send money to anyone else with an e-mail address, whether the recipient has a PayPal account or not. PayPal doesn't even care whether a commercial transaction is taking place. If someone in the office is organizing a party for someone else and everyone needs to chip in, they can all do it using PayPal. In fact, the organizer can send everyone PayPal reminders by e-mail with clear instructions as to how to pay up. PayPal can accept money from the purchaser in one of three ways, notes ecommerce-guide.com: charging the purchaser's credit card for any transactions (payments), debiting a checking account for any payments, or deducting payments from a PayPal account established with a personal check. Payment recipients can use the money in their account for online purchases or payments, can receive the payment from PayPal by check, or can have PayPal directly deposit the money into a checking account. Setting up a PayPal account is simple. As a payer, all you have to do is to provide your name, your e-mail address, your credit card information, and your billing address for your credit card.

All of these interoperable banking and e-commerce functions flattened the Internet marketplace so radically that even eBay was taken by surprise. Before PayPal, explained eBay CEO Meg Whitman, "If I did business on eBay in 1999, the only way I could pay you as a buyer was with a check or money order, a paper-based system. There was no electronic way to send money, and you were too small a merchant to qualify for a credit card account. What PayPal did was enable people, *individuals,* to accept credit cards. I could pay you as an *individual* seller on eBay with a credit card. This really leveled the playing field and made commerce more frictionless." In fact, it was so good that eBay bought PayPal, but not on the recommendation of its Wall Street investment bankers — on the recommendation of its users.

"We woke up one day," said Whitman, "and found out that 20 percent of the people on eBay were saying, 'I accept PayPal, please pay me that way.' And we said, 'Who are these people and what are they doing?' At first we tried to fight them and launched our own service, called Billpoint. Finally, in July 2002, we were at [an] eBay Live [convention] and the drum-beat through the hall was deafening. Our community was telling us, "Would you guys stop fighting? We want a standard — and by the way, *we have picked the standard* and it's called PayPal, and we know you guys at eBay would like it to be your [standard], but it's theirs.' And that is when we knew we had to buy the company, because it was the standard and it was not ours . . . It is the best acquisition we ever made."

Here's how I just wrote the above section: I transferred my notes from the Meg Whitman phone interview from my Dell laptop to my Dell desktop, then fired up my DSL connection and double-clicked on AOL, where I used Google to find a Web site that could explain PayPal, which directed me to ecommerce-guide.com. I downloaded the definition from the ecommerce-guide.com Web site, which was written in some Internet font as a text file, and then called it up on Microsoft Word, which automatically transformed it into a Word document, which I could then use to write this section on my desktop. That is also work flow! And what is most important about it is not that I have these work flow tools; it is how many people in India, Russia, China, Brazil, and Timbuktu now have them as well — along with all the transmission pipes and protocols so they too can plug and play from anywhere.

Where is all this going? More and more work flow will be automated. In the coming phase of Web services–work flow, here is how you will make a dentist appointment: You will instruct your computer by voice to make an appointment.

Your computer will automatically translate your voice into a digital instruction. It will automatically check your calendar against the available dates on your dentist's calendar and offer you three choices. You will click on the preferred date and hour. The week before your appointment, your dentist's calendar will automatically send you an e-mail reminding you of the appointment. The night before, you will get a computer-generated voice message by phone, also reminding of your appointment.

For work flow to reach this next stage, and the productivity enhancements it will deliver, "we need more and more common standards," said IBM's strategic planner Cawley. "The first round of standards to emerge with the Internet were around basic data — how do you represent a number, how do you organize files, how do you display and store content, and how do you share and exchange information. That was the Netscape phase. Now a whole new set of standards is emerging to enable work flow. These are standards about how we do business work together. For example, when you apply for a mortgage, go to your closing, or buy a house, there are literally dozens of processes and data flows among many different companies. One bank may handle securing your approval, checking your credit, establishing your interest rates, and handling the closing — after which the loan almost immediately is sold to a different bank."

The next level of standards, added Cawley, will be about automating all these processes, so they flow even more seamlessly together and can stimulate even more standards. We are already seeing standards emerging around payroll, e-commerce payment, and risk profiling, around how music and photos are digitally edited, and, most important, around how supply chains are connected. All of these standards, on top of the work flow software, help enable work to be broken apart, reassembled, and made to flow, without friction, back and forth between the most efficient producers. The diversity of applications that will automatically be able to interact with each other will be limited only by our imaginations. The gains in productivity from this could be bigger than anything we have ever seen before.

"Work flow platforms are enabling us to do for the service industry what Henry Ford did for manufacturing," said Jerry Rao, the entrepreneur doing accounting work for Americans from India. "We are taking apart each task and sending it around to whomever can do it best, and because we are doing it in a virtual environment, people need not be physically adjacent to each other, and then we are reassembling all the pieces back together at headquarters [or some other remote site]. This is not a trivial revolution. This is a major one. It allows for a boss to be somewhere and his employees to be someplace else." These work flow software platforms, Jerry added, "enable you to create virtual global offices — not limited by either the boundaries of your office or your country — and to access talent sitting in different parts of the world and have them complete tasks that you need completed in real time. And so 24/7/365 we are all working. And all this has happened in the twinkling of an eye — the span of the last two or three years."

Genesis:
The Flat World Platform Emerges

We need to stop here and take stock, because at this point — the mid-1990s — the platform for the flattening of the world has started to emerge. First, the falling walls, the opening of Windows, the digitization of content, and the spreading of the Internet browser seamlessly connected people with people as never before. Then work flow software seamlessly connected applications to applications, so that people could manipulate all their digitized content, using computers and the Internet, as never before.

When you add this unprecedented new level of people-to-people communication to all these Web-based application-to-application work flow programs, you end up with a whole new global platform for multiple forms of collaboration. This is the Genesis moment for the flattening of the world. This is when it started to take shape. It would take more time to converge and really become flat, but this is the moment when people started to feel that something was changing. Suddenly more people from more different places found that they could collaborate with more other people on more different kinds of work and share more different kinds of knowledge than ever before. "It is the creation of this platform, with these unique attributes, that is the truly important sustainable breakthrough that made what you call the flattening of the world possible," said Microsoft's Craig Mundie.

Indeed, thanks to this platform that emerged from the first three flatteners, we were not just able to talk to each other more, we were able to do more things together. This is the key point, argued Joel Cawley, the IBM strategist. "We were not just communicating with each other more than ever, we were now able to collaborate

— to build coalitions, projects, and products together — more than ever."

The next six flatteners represent the new forms of collaboration which this new platform empowered. As I show, some people will use this platform for open-sourcing, some for outsourcing, some for offshoring, some for supply-chaining, some for insourcing, and some for in-forming. Each of these forms of collaboration was either made possible by the new platform or greatly enhanced by it. And as more and more of us learn how to collaborate in these different ways, we are flattening the world even more.

Flattener #4
Open-Sourcing
Self-Organizing Collaborative
Communities

Alan Cohen still remembers the first time he heard the word "Apache" as an adult, and it wasn't while watching a cowboys-and-Indians movie. It was the 1990s, the dot-com market was booming, and he was a senior manager for IBM, helping to oversee its emerging e-commerce business. "I had a whole team with me and a budget of about $8 million," Cohen recalled. "We were competing head-to-head with Microsoft, Netscape, Oracle, Sun — all the big boys.

And we were playing this very big-stakes game for e-commerce. IBM had a huge sales force selling all this e-commerce software. One day I asked the development director who worked for me, 'Say, Jeff, walk me through the development process for these e-commerce systems. What is the underlying Web server?' And he says to me, 'It's built on top of Apache.' The first thing I think of is John Wayne. 'What is Apache?' I ask. And he says it is a shareware program for Web server technology. He said it was produced for free by a bunch of geeks just working online in some kind of open-source chat room. I was floored. I said, 'How do you buy it?' And he says, 'You download it off a Web site for free.' And I said, 'Well, who supports it if something goes wrong?' And he says, 'I don't know — it just works!' And that was my first exposure to Apache . . .

"Now you have to remember, back then Microsoft, IBM, Oracle, Netscape were all trying to build commercial Web servers. These were huge companies. And suddenly my development guy is telling me that he's getting ours off the Internet for free! It's like you had all these big corporate executives plotting strategies, and then suddenly the guys in the mail room are in charge. I kept asking, 'Who runs Apache? I mean, who are these guys?' "

Yes, the geeks in the mail room are deciding what software they will be using and what you will be using too. It's called the open-source movement, and it involves thousands of people around the world coming together online to collaborate in writing everything from their own software to their own operating systems to their own dictionary to their own recipe for cola — building always from the bottom up rather than accepting formats or content imposed by corporate hierarchies from the top down. The word "open-source" comes from the notion that companies or ad hoc groups would make available online the source code — the underlying program-ming instructions that make a piece of soft-ware work — and then let anyone who has something to contribute improve it and let millions of others just download it for their own use for free. While commercial software is copyrighted and sold, and companies guard the source code as they would their crown jewels so they can charge money to anyone who wants to use it and thereby gen-erate income to develop new versions, open-source software is shared, constantly im-proved by its users, and made available for free to anyone. In return, every user who comes up with an improvement — a patch that makes this software sing or dance better — is encouraged to make that patch avail-able to every other user for free.

Not being a computer geek, I had never focused much on the open-source movement, but when I did, I discovered it was an amazing universe of its own, with communities of online, come-as-you-are volunteers who share their insights with one another and then offer it to the public for nothing. They do it because they want something the market doesn't offer them; they do it for the psychic buzz that comes from creating a collective product that can beat something produced by giants like Microsoft or IBM, and — even more important — to earn the respect of their intellectual peers. Indeed, these guys and gals are one of the most interesting and controversial new forms of collaboration that have been facilitated by the flat world and are flattening it even more.

In order to explain how this form of collaboration works, why it is a flattener and why, by the way, it has stirred so many controversies and will be stirring even more in the future, I am going to focus on just two basic varieties of open-sourcing: the intellectual commons movement and the free software movement.

The intellectual commons form of open-sourcing has its roots in the academic and scientific communities, where for a long time self-organized collaborative communities of scientists have come together through private networks and later the Internet to pool their brainpower or share insights around a particular science or math problem. The Apache Web server had its roots in this form of open-sourcing. When I asked a friend of mine, Mike Arguello, an IT systems architect, to explain to me why people share knowledge or work in this way, he said, "IT people tend to be very bright people and they want everybody to know just how brilliant they are." Marc Andreessen, who invented the first Web browser, agreed: "Open-source is nothing more than peer-reviewed science. Sometimes people contribute to these things because they make science, and they discover things, and the reward is reputation. Sometimes you can build a business out of it, sometimes they just want to increase the store of knowledge in the world. And the peer review part is critical — and open-source is peer review. Every bug or security hole or deviation from standards is reviewed."

I found this intellectual commons form of open-sourcing fascinating, so I went exploring to find out who were those guys and girls in the mail room. Eventually, I found my way to one of their pioneers, Brian Behlendorf. If Apache — the open-source Web server community — were an Indian tribe, Behlendorf would be the tribal elder. I caught up with him one day in his glass-and-steel office near the San Francisco airport, where he is now founder and chief technology officer of CollabNet, a start-up focused on creating software for companies that want to use an open-source approach to innovation. I started with two simple questions: Where did you come from? and: How did you manage to pull together an open-source community of on-line geeks that could go toe-to-toe with IBM?

"My parents met at IBM in Southern California, and I grew up in a town just north of Pasadena, La Canada," Behlendorf recalled. "The public school was very competitive academically, because a lot of the kids' parents worked at the Jet Propulsion Laboratory that was run by Caltech there. So from a very early age I was around a lot of science in a place where it was okay to be kind of geeky. We always had computers around the house. We used to use punch cards from the original IBM mainframes for making shopping lists. In grade school, I started doing some basic programming, and by high school I was pretty into computers . . . I graduated in 1991, but in 1989, in the early days of the Internet, a friend gave me a copy of a program he had downloaded onto a floppy disk, called 'Fractint.' It was not pirated, but was freeware, produced by a group of programmers, and was a program for drawing fractals. [Fractals are beautiful images produced at the intersection of art and math.] When the program started up, the screen would show this scrolling list of e-mail addresses for all the scientists and mathematicians who contributed to it. I noticed that the source code was included with the program. This was my first exposure to the concept of open-source. Here was this program that you just downloaded for free, and they even gave you the source code with it, and it was done by a community of people. It started to paint a different picture of programming in my mind. I started to think that there were some interesting social dynamics to the way certain kinds of software were written or could be written — as opposed to the kind of image I had of the professional software developer in the back office tending to the mainframe, feeding info in and taking it out for the business. That seemed to me to be just one step above accounting and not very exciting."

After graduating in 1991, Behlendorf went to Berkeley to study physics, but he quickly became frustrated by the disconnect between the abstractions he was learning in the classroom and the excitement that was starting to emerge on the Internet.

"When you entered college back then, every student was given an e-mail address, and I started using it to talk to students and explore discussion boards that were starting to appear around music," said Behlendorf. "In 1992, I started my own Internet mailing list focused on the local electronic music scene in the Bay Area. People could just post onto the discussion board, and it started to grow, and we started to discuss different music events and DJs. Then we said, 'Hey, why don't we invite our own DJs and throw our own events?' It became a collective thing. Someone would say, 'I have some records,' and someone else would say, 'I have a sound system,' and someone else would say, 'I know the beach and if we showed up at midnight we could have a party.' By 1993, the Internet was still just mailing lists and e-mail and FTP sites [file transfer protocol repositories where you could store things]. So I started collecting an archive of electronic music and was interested in how we could put this online and make it available to a larger audience. That was when I heard about Mosaic [the Web browser developed by Marc Andreessen.] So I got a job at the computer lab in the Berkeley business school, and I spent my spare time researching Mosaic and other Web technologies. That led me to a discussion board with a lot of the people who were writing the first generation of Web browsers and Web servers."

(A Web server is a software program that enables anyone to use his or her home or office computer to host a Web site on the World Wide Web. Amazon.com, for instance, has long run its Web site on Apache software. When your Web browser goes to www.amazon.com, the very first piece of software it talks to is Apache. The browser asks Apache for the Amazon Web page and Apache sends back to the browser the content of the Amazon Web page. Surfing the Web is really your Web browser interacting with different Web servers.)

"I found myself sitting in on this forum watching Tim Berners-Lee and Marc Andreessen debating how all these things should work," recalled Behlendorf. "It was pretty exciting, and it seemed radically inclusive. I didn't need a Ph.D. or any special credentials, and I started to see some parallels between my music group and these scientists, who had a common interest in building the first Web software. I followed that [discussion] for a while and then I told a friend of mine about it. He was one of the first employees at *Wired* magazine, and he said *Wired* would be interested in having me set up a Web site for them. So I joined there at $10 an hour, setting up their e-mail and their first Web site — HotWired . . . It was one of the first ad-supported online magazines."

HotWired decided it wanted to start by having a registration system that required passwords — a controversial concept at that time. "In those days," noted Andrew Leonard, who wrote a history of Apache for Salon.com in 1997, "most Webmasters depended on a Web server program developed at the University of Illinois's National Center for Supercomputing Applications (also the birthplace of the groundbreaking Mosaic Web browser). But the NCSA Web server couldn't handle password authentication on the scale that HotWired needed. Luckily, the NCSA server was in the public domain, which meant that the source code was free to all comers. So Behlendorf exercised the hacker prerogative: He wrote some new code, a 'patch' to the NCSA Web server, that took care of the problem." Leonard commented, "He wasn't the only clever programmer rummaging through the NCSA code that winter. All across the exploding Web, other Webmasters were finding it necessary to take matters into their own keyboards. The original code had been left to gather virtual dust when its primary programmer, University of Illinois student Rob McCool, had been scooped up (along with Marc Andreessen and Lynx author Eric Bina) by a little-known company in Silicon Valley named Netscape. Meanwhile, the Web refused to stop growing — and kept creating new problems for Web servers to cope with." So patches of one kind or another proliferated like Band-Aids on bandwidth, plugging one hole here and breaching another gap there.

Meanwhile, all these patches were slowly, in an ad hoc open-source manner, building a new modern Web server. But everyone had his or her own version, trading patches here and there, because the NCSA lab couldn't keep up with it all.

"I was just this near-dropout," explained Behlendorf. "I was having a lot of fun building this Web site for *Wired* and learning more than I was learning at Berkeley. So a discussion started in our little working group that the NCSA people were not answering our e-mails. We were sending in patches for the system and they weren't responding. And we said, 'If NCSA would not respond to our patches, what's going to happen in the future?' We were happy to continue improving this thing, yet we were worried when we were not getting any feedback and seeing our patches integrated. So I started to contact the other people I knew trading patches

. . . Most of them were on the standards working groups [the Internet Engineering Task Force] that were setting the first standards for the interconnectivity between machines and applications on the Internet . . . And we said, 'Why don't we take our future into our own hands and release our own [Web server] version that incorporated all our patches?'

"We looked up the copyright for the NCSA code, and it basically just said give us credit at Illinois for what we invented if you improve it — and don't blame us if it breaks," recalled Behlendorf. "So we started building our own version from all our patches. None of us had time to be a full-time Web server developer, but we thought if we could combine our time and do it in a public way, we could create something better than we could buy off the shelf — and nothing was available then, anyway. This was all before Netscape had shipped its first commercial Web server. That was the beginning of the Apache project."

By February 1999, they had completely rewritten the original NCSA program and formalized their cooperation under the name "Apache."

"I picked the name because I wanted it to have a positive connotation of being assertive," said Behlendorf. "The Apache tribe was the last tribe to surrender to the oncoming U.S. government, and at the time we worried that the big companies would come in and 'civilize' the landscape that the early Internet engineers built. So 'Apache' made sense to me as a good code name, and others said it also would make a good pun" — as in the APAtCHy server, because they were patching all these fixes together.

So in many ways, Behlendorf and his open-source colleagues — most of whom he had never met but knew only by e-mail through their open-source chat room — had created a virtual, online, bottom-up software factory, which no one owned and no one supervised. "We had a software project, but the coordination and direction were an emergent behavior based on who-ever showed up and wanted to write code," he said.

But how does it actually work? I asked Behlendorf. You can't just have a bunch of people, unmonitored, throwing code to-gether, can you?

"Most software development involves a source code repository and is managed by tools such as the Concurrent Versions System," he explained. "So there is a CVS server out there, and I have a CVS pro-gram on my computer. It allows me to connect to the server and pull down a copy of the code, so I can start working with it and making modifications. If I think my patch is something I want to share with others, I run a program called Patch, which allows me to create a new file, a compact collection of all the changes. That is called a patch file, and I can give that file to someone else, and they can apply it to their copy of the code to see what impact that patch has. If I have the right privileges to the server [which is restricted to a tightly controlled oversight board], I can then take my patch and commit it to the repository and it will become part of the source code. The CVS server keeps track of everything and who sent in what . . . So you might have 'read access' to the repository but not 'commit access' to change things. When someone makes a commit to the repository, that patch file gets e-mailed out to all the other developers, and so you get this peer review system after the fact, and if there is something wrong, you fix the bug."

So how does this community decide who are trusted members?

"For Apache," said Behlendorf, "we started with eight people who really trusted each other, and as new people showed up at the discussion forum and offered patch files posted to the discussion form, we would gain trust in others, and that eight grew to over one thousand. We were the first open-source project to get attention from the business community and get the backing from IBM."

Because of Apache's proficiency at allowing a single-server machine to host thousands of different virtual Web sites — music, data, text, pornography — it began to have "a commanding share of the Internet Service Provider market," noted Salon's Leonard. IBM was trying to sell its own proprietary Web server, called GO, but it gained only a tiny sliver of the market. Apache proved to be both a better technology and free. So IBM eventually decided that if it could not beat Apache, it should join Apache. You have to stop here and imagine this. The world's biggest computer company decided that its engineers could not best the work of an ad hoc opensource collection of geeks, so they threw out their own technology and decided to go with the geeks!

IBM "initiated contact with me, as I had a somewhat public speaker role for Apache," said Behlendorf. "IBM said, 'We would like to figure out how we can use [Apache] and not get flamed by the Internet community, [how we can] make it sustainable and not just be ripping people off but contributing to the process . . .' IBM was saying that this new model for software development was trustworthy and valuable, so let's invest in it and get rid of the one that we are trying to make on our own, which isn't as good."

John Swainson was the senior IBM executive who led the team that approached Apache (he's now chairman of Computer Associates). He picked up the story: "There was a whole debate going on at the time about open-source, but it was all over the place. We decided we could deal with the Apache guys because they answered our questions. We could hold a meaningful conversation with these guys, and we were able to create the [nonprofit] Apache Software Foundation and work out all the issues."

At IBM's expense, its lawyers worked with the Apache group to create a legal framework around it so that there would be no copyright or liability problems for companies, like IBM, that wanted to build applications on top of Apache and charge money for them. IBM saw the value in having a standard vanilla Web server architecture — which allowed heterogeneous computer systems and devices to talk to each other, displaying e-mail and Web pages in a standard format — that was constantly being improved for free by an open-source community. The Apache collaborators did not set out to make free software. They set out to solve a common problem — Web serving — and found that collaborating for free in this open-source manner was the best way to assemble the best brains for the job they needed done.

"When we started working with Apache, there was an apache.org Web site but no formal legal structure, and businesses and informal structures don't coexist well," said Swainson. "You need to be able to vet the code, sign an agreement, and deal with liability issues. [Today] anybody can download the Apache code. The only obligation is that they acknowledge that it came from the site, and if they make any changes that they share them back." There is an Apache development process that manages the traffic, and you earn your way into that process, added Swainson. It is something like a pure meritocracy. When IBM started using Apache, it became part of the community and started making contributions.

Indeed, the one thing the Apache people demanded in return for their collaboration with IBM was that IBM assign its best engineers to join the Apache open-source group and contribute, like everyone else, for free. "The Apache people were not interested in payment of cash," said Swainson. "They wanted *contribution* to the base. Our engineers came to us and said, 'These guys who do Apache are good and they are insisting that we contribute good people.' At first they rejected some of what we contributed.

They said it wasn't up to their standards! The compensation that the community expected was our best contribution."

On June 22, 1998, IBM announced plans to incorporate Apache into its own new Web server product, named WebSphere. The way the Apache collaborative community organized itself, whatever you took out of Apache's code and improved on, you had to give back to the whole community. But you were also free to go out and build a patented commercial product on top of the Apache code, as IBM did, provided that you included a copyright citation to Apache in your own patent. In other words, this intellectual commons approach to open-sourcing encouraged people to build commercial products on top of it. While it wanted the foundation to be free and open to all, it recognized that it would remain strong and fresh if both commercial and noncommercial engineers had an incentive to participate.

Today Apache is one of the most successful open-source tools, powering about two-thirds of the Web sites in the world. And because Apache can be downloaded for free anywhere in the world, people from Russia to South Africa to Vietnam use it to create Web sites. Those individuals who need or want added capabilities for their Web servers can buy products like

WebSphere, which attach right on top of Apache.

At the time, selling a product built on top of an open-source program was a risky move on IBM's part. To its credit, IBM was confident in its ability to keep producing differentiated software applications on top of the Apache vanilla. This model has since been widely adopted, after everyone saw how it propelled IBM's Web server business to commercial leadership in that category of software, generating huge amounts of revenue.

As I will repeat often in this book: There is no future in vanilla for most companies in a flat world. A lot of vanilla making in software and other areas is going to shift to open-source communities. For most companies, the commercial future belongs to those who know how to make the richest chocolate sauce, the sweetest, lightest whipped cream, and the juiciest cherries to sit on top, or how to put them all together into a sundae. Jack Messman, chairman of the Novell software company, which has now become a big distributor of Linux, the open-source operating system, atop which Novell attaches gizmos to make it sing and dance just for your company, put it best: "Commercial software companies have to start operating further up the [software] stack to differentiate themselves. The open source community is basically focusing on infrastructure" (*Financial Times*, June 14, 2004).

The IBM deal was a real watershed. Big Blue was saying that it believed in the open-source model and that with the Apache Web server, this open-source community of engineers had created something that was not just useful and valuable but "best in its class." That's why the open-source movement has become a powerful flattener, the effects of which we are just beginning to see. "It is incredibly empowering of individuals," Brian Behlendorf said. "It doesn't matter where you come from or where you are — someone in India and South America can be just as effective using this software or contributing to it as someone in Silicon Valley." The old model is winner take all: I wrote it, I own it — the standard software license model. "The only way to compete against that," concluded Behlendorf, "is to all become winners."

Behlendorf, for his part, is betting his career that more and more people and companies will want to take advantage of the new flat-world platform to do open-source innovation. In 2004, he started a new company called CollabNet to promote the use of open-sourcing as a tool to drive software innovation within companies. "Our premise is that software is not gold, it is lettuce — it is a perishable good," explained Behlendorf. "If the software is not in a place where it is getting improved over time, it will rot." What the open-source community has been doing, said Behlendorf, is globally coordinated distributed software development, where it is constantly freshening the lettuce so that it never goes rotten. Behlendorf's premise is that the open-source community developed a better method for creating and constantly updating software. CollabNet is a company created to bring the best open-source techniques to a closed community, i.e., a commercial software company.

"CollabNet is an arms dealer to the forces flattening the world," said Behlendorf. "Our role in this world is to build the tools and infrastructure so that an individual — in India, China, or wherever — as a consultant, an employee, or just someone sitting at home can collaborate. We are giving them the toolkit for decentralized collaborative development. We are enabling bottom-up development, and not just in cyberspace . . . We have large corporations who are now interested in creating a bottom-up environment for writing software. The old top-down, silo software model is broken. That system said, 'I develop something and then I throw it over the wall to you. You find the bugs and then throw it back. I patch it and then sell a new version.' There is constant frustration with getting software that is buggy — maybe it will get fixed or maybe not. So we said, 'Wouldn't it be interesting if we could take the open-source benefits of speed of innovation and higher-quality software, and that feeling of partnership with all these stakeholders, and turn that into a business model for corporations to be more collaborative both within and without?' "

I like the way Irving Wladawsky-Berger, IBM's Cuban-born vice president for technical strategy and innovation, summed open-sourcing up: "This emerging era is characterized by the collaborative innovation of many people working in gifted communities, just as innovation in the industrial era was characterized by individual genius."

The striking thing about the intellectual commons form of open-sourcing is how quickly it has morphed into other spheres and spawned other self-organizing collaborative communities, which are flattening hierarchies in their areas. I see this most vividly in the news profession, where bloggers, one-person online commentators, who often link to one another depending on their ideology, have created a kind of open-source newsroom. I now read bloggers (the term comes from the word "Weblog") as part of my daily information-gathering routine. In an article about how a tiny group of relatively obscure news bloggers were able to blow the whistle that exposed the bogus documents used by CBS News's Dan Rather in his infamous report about President George W. Bush's Air National Guard service, Howard Kurtz of *The Washington Post* wrote (September 20, 2004), "It was like throwing a match on kerosene-soaked wood. The ensuing blaze ripped through the media establishment as previously obscure bloggers managed to put the network of Murrow and Cronkite firmly on the defensive. The secret, says Charles Johnson, is 'open-source intelligence gathering.' Meaning: 'We've got a huge pool of highly motivated people who go out there and use tools to find stuff. We've got an army of citizen journalists out there.' "

That army is often armed with nothing more than a tape recorder, a camera-enabled cell phone, and a Web site, but in a flat world it can collectively get its voice heard as far and wide as CBS or *The New York Times*. These bloggers have created their own online commons, with no barriers to entry. That open commons often has many rumors and wild allegations swirling in it. Because no one is in charge, standards of practice vary wildly, and some of it is downright irresponsible. But because no one is in charge, information flows with total freedom. And when this community is on to something real, like the Rather episode, it can create as much energy, buzz, and hard news as any network or major newspaper.

Another intellectual commons collaboration that I used regularly in writing this book is Wikipedia, the user-contributed online encyclopedia, also known as "the people's encyclopedia." The word "wikis" is taken from the Hawaiian word for "quick." Wikis are Web sites that allow users to directly edit any Web page on their own from their home computer. In a May 5, 2004, essay on YaleGlobal online, Andrew Lih, an assistant professor at the Journalism and Media Studies Centre at the University of Hong Kong, explained how Wikipedia works and why it is such a breakthrough.

"The Wikipedia project was started by Jimmy Wales, head of Internet startup Bomis.com, after his original project for a volunteer, but strictly controlled, free encyclopedia ran out of money and resources after two years," wrote Lih. "Editors with PhD degrees were at the helm of the project then, but it produced only a few hundred articles. Not wanting the content to languish,

Wales placed the pages on a wiki Website in January 2001 and invited any Internet visitors to edit or add to the collection. The site became a runaway success in the first year and gained a loyal following, generating over 20,000 articles and spawning over a dozen language translations. After two years, it had 100,000 articles, and in April 2004, it exceeded 250,000 articles in English and 600,000 articles in 50 other languages. And according to Website rankings at Alexa.com, it has become more popular than traditional online encyclopedias such as Britannica.com."

How, you might ask, does one produce a credible, balanced encyclopedia by way of an ad hoc open-source, open-editing movement? After all, every article in the Wikipedia has an "Edit this page" button, allowing anyone who surfs along to add or delete content on that page.

It starts with the fact, Lih explained, that "because wikis provide the ability to track the status of articles, review individual changes, and discuss issues, they function as social software. Wiki Websites also track and store every modification made to an article, so no operation is ever permanently destructive. Wikipedia works by consensus, with users adding and modifying content while trying to reach common ground along the way.

"However, the technology is not enough on its own," wrote Lih. "Wales created an editorial policy of maintaining a neutral point of view (NPOV) as the guiding principle . . . According to Wikipedia's guidelines, 'The neutral point of view attempts to present ideas and facts in such a fashion that both supporters and opponents can agree . . .' As a result, articles on contentious issues such as globalization have benefited from the cooperative and global nature of Wikipedia. Over the last two years, the entry has had more than 90 edits by contributors from the Netherlands, Belgium, Sweden, United Kingdom, Australia, Brazil, United States, Malaysia, Japan and China. It provides a manifold view of issues from the World Trade Organization and multinational corporations to the anti-globalization movement and threats to cultural diversity. At the same time malicious contributors are kept in check because vandalism is easily undone. Users dedicated to fixing vandalism watch the list of recent changes, fixing problems within minutes, if not seconds. A defaced article can quickly be returned to an acceptable version with just one click of a button. This crucial asymmetry tips the balance in favor of productive and cooperative members of the wiki community, allowing quality content to prevail." A *Newsweek* piece on Wikipedia

(November 1, 2004) quoted Angela Beesley, a volunteer contributor from Essex, England, and self-confessed Wikipedia addict who monitors the accuracy of more than one thousand entries: "A collaborative encyclopedia sounds like a crazy idea, but it naturally controls itself."

Meanwhile, Jimmy Wales is just getting started. He told *Newsweek* that he is expanding into Wiktionary, a dictionary and thesaurus; Wikibooks, textbooks and manuals; and Wikiquote, a book of quotations. He said he has one simple goal: to give "every single person free access to the sum of all human knowledge."

Wales's ethic that everyone should have free access to all human knowledge is undoubtedly heartfelt, but it also brings us to the controversial side of open-source: If everyone contributes his or her intellectual capital for free, where will the resources for new innovation come from? And won't we end up in endless legal wrangles over which part of any innovation was made by the community for free, and meant to stay that way, and which part was added on by some company for profit and has to be paid for so that the company can make money to drive further innovation? These questions are all triggered by the other increasingly popular form of self-organized collaboration — the free software move-ment. According to the openknowledge.org Web site, "The free/open source software movement began in the 'hacker' culture of U.S. computer science laboratories (Stanford, Berkeley, Carnegie Mellon, and MIT) in the 1960's and 1970's. The community of programmers was small, and close-knit. Code passed back and forth between the members of the community — if you made an improvement you were expected to submit your code to the community of developers. To withhold code was considered gauche — after all, you benefited from the work of your friends, you should return the favor."

The free software movement, however, was and remains inspired by the ethical ideal that software should be free and available to all, and it relies on open-source collaboration to help produce the best software possible to be distributed for free. This a bit different from the approach of the intellectual commons folks, like Apache. They saw open-sourcing as a technically superior means of creating software and other innovations, and while Apache was made available to all for free, it had no problem with commercial software being built on top of it. The Apache group allowed anyone who created a derivative work to own it himself, provided he acknowledge the Apache contribution.

The primary goal of the free software movement, however, is to get as many people as possible writing, improving, and distributing software for free, out of a conviction that this will empower everyone and free individuals from the grip of global corporations. Generally speaking, the free software movement structures its licenses so that if your commercial software draws directly from their free software copyright, they want your software to be free too.

In 1984, according to Wikipedia, an MIT researcher and one of these ex-hackers, Richard Stallman, launched the "free software movement" along with an effort to build a free operating system called GNU. To promote free software, and to ensure that its code would always be freely modifiable and available to all, Stallman founded the Free Software Foundation and something called the GNU General Public License (GPL). The GPL specified that users of the source code could copy, change, or upgrade the code, provided that they made their changes available under the same license as the original code. In 1991, a student at the University of Helsinki named Linus Torvalds, building off of Stallman's initiative, posted his Linux operating system to compete with the Microsoft Windows operating system and invited other engineers and geeks online to try to improve it — for free. Since Torvalds's initial post, programmers all over the world have manipulated, added to, expanded, patched, and improved the GNU/Linux operating system, whose license says anyone can download the source code and improve upon it but then must make the upgraded version freely available to everybody else. Torvalds insists that Linux must always be free. Companies that sell software improvements that enhance Linux or adapt it to certain functions have to be very careful not to touch its copyright in their commercial products.

Much like Microsoft Windows, Linux offers a family of operating systems that can be adapted to run on the smallest desktop computers, laptops, PalmPilots, and even wristwatches, all the way up to the largest supercomputers and mainframes. So a kid in India with a cheap PC can learn the inner workings of the same operating system that is running in some of the largest data centers of corporate America. Linux has an army of developers across the globe working to make it better. As I was working on this segment of the book, I went to a picnic one afternoon at the Virginia country home of Pamela and Malcolm Baldwin, whom my wife came to know through her membership on the board of World Learning, an educational NGO. I mentioned in the course of lunch that I was thinking of going to Mali to see just how flat the world looked from its outermost edge — the town of Timbuktu. The Baldwins' son Peter happened to be working in Mali as part of something called the GeekCorps, which helps to bring technology to developing countries. A few days after the lunch, I received an e-mail from Pamela telling me that she had consulted with Peter about accompanying me to Timbuktu, and then she added the following, which told me everything I needed to know and saved me the whole trip: "Peter says that his project is creating wireless networks via satellite, making antennas out of plastic soda bottles and mesh from window screens! Apparently everyone in Mali uses Linux . . ."

"Everyone in Mali uses Linux." That is no doubt a bit of an exaggeration, but it's a phrase that you'd hear only in a flat world.

The free software movement has become a serious challenge to Microsoft and some other big global software players. As *Fortune* magazine reported on February 23, 2004, "The availability of this basic, powerful software, which works on Intel's ubiquitous microprocessors, coincided with the explosive growth of the Internet. Linux soon began to gain a global following among programmers and business users . . . The revolution goes far beyond little Linux . . . Just about any kind of software [now] can be found in open-source form. The SourceForge.net website, a meeting place for programmers, lists an astounding 86,000 programs in progress. Most are minor projects by and for geeks, but hundreds pack real value . . . If you hate shelling out $350 for Microsoft Office or $600 for Adobe Photoshop, OpenOffice.org and the Gimp are surprisingly high-quality free alternatives." Big companies like Google, E*Trade, and Amazon, by combining Intel-based commodity server components and the Linux operating system, have been able dramatically to cut their technology spending — and get more control over their software.

Why would so many people be ready to write software that would be given away for free? Partly it is out of the pure scientific challenge, which should never be underestimated. Partly it is because they all hate Microsoft for the way it has so dominated the market and, in the view of many techies, bullied everyone else. Partly it is because they believe that open-source software can be kept more fresh and bugfree than any commercial software, because of the way it is constantly updated by an army of unpaid programmers. And partly it is because some big tech companies are paying engineers to work on Linux and other software, hoping it will cut into Microsoft's market share and make it a weaker competitor all around. There are a lot of motives at work here, and not all of them altruistic. When you put them all together, though, they make for a very powerful movement that will continue to present a major challenge to the whole commercial software model of buying a program and then downloading its fixes and buying its updates.

Until now, the Linux operating system was the best-known success among open-source free software projects challenging Microsoft. But Linux is largely used by big corporate data centers, not individuals. However, in November 2004, the Mozilla Foundation, a nonprofit group supporting open-source software, released Firefox, a free Web browser that *New York Times* technology writer Randall Stross (December 19, 2004) described as very fast and filled with features that Microsoft's Internet Explorer lacks. Firefox 1.0, which is easily installed, was released on November 9. "Just over a month later," Stross reported, "the foundation celebrated a remarkable milestone: 10 million downloads." Donations from Firefox's appreciative fans paid for a two-page advertisement in *The New York Times*. "With Firefox," Stross added, "open-source software moves from back-office obscurity to your home, and to your parents', too. (Your children in college are already using it.) It is polished, as easy to use as Internet Explorer and, most compelling, much better defended against viruses, worms and snoops. Microsoft has always viewed Internet Explorer's tight integration with Windows to be an attractive feature. That, however, was before security became the unmet need of the day. Firefox sits lightly on top of Windows, in a separation from the underlying operating system that the Mozilla Foundation's president, Mitchell Baker, calls a 'natural defense.' For the first time, Internet Explorer has been losing market share. According to a worldwide survey conducted in late November by OneStat.com, a company in Amsterdam that analyzes the Web, Internet Explorer's share dropped to less than 89 percent, 5 percentage points less than in May. Firefox now has almost 5 percent of the market, and it is growing."

It will come as no surprise that Microsoft officials are not believers in the viability or virtues of the free software form of open-source. Of all the issues I dealt with in this book, none evoked more passion from proponents and opponents than open-source. After spending time with the open-source community, I wanted to hear what Microsoft had to say, since this is going to be an important debate that will determine just how much of a flattener open-source becomes.

Microsoft's first point is, How do you push innovation forward if everyone is working for free and giving away their work? Yes, says Microsoft, it all sounds nice and chummy that we all just get together online and write free software by the people and for the people. But if innovators are not going to be rewarded for their innovations, the incentive for path-breaking innovation will dry up and so will the money for the really deep R & D that is required to drive progress in this increasingly complex field. The fact that Microsoft created the standard PC operating system that won out in the marketplace, it argues, produced the bankroll that allowed Microsoft to spend billions of dollars on R & D to develop Microsoft Office, a whole suite of applications that it can now sell for a little over $100.

"Microsoft would admit that there are number of aspects of the open-source movement that are intriguing, particularly around the scale, community collaboration, and communication aspects," said Craig Mundie, the Microsoft chief technology officer. "But we fundamentally believe in a commercial software industry, and some variants of the open-source model attack the economic model that allows companies to build businesses in software. The virtuous cycle of innovation, reward, reinvestment, and more innovation is what has driven all big breakthroughs in our industry. The software business as we have known it is a scale economic business. You spend a ton of money up front to develop a software product, and then the marginal cost of producing each one is very small, but if you sell a lot of them, you make back your investment and then plow profits back into developing the next generation. But when you insist that you cannot charge for software, you can only give it away, you take the software business away from being a scale economic business."

Added Bill Gates, "You need capitalism [to drive innovation.] To have [a movement] that says innovation does not deserve an economic reward is contrary to where the world is going. When I talk to the Chinese, they dream of starting a company. They are not thinking, 'I will be a barber during the day and do free software at night.' . . . When you have a security crisis in your [software] system, you don't want to say, 'Where is the guy at the barbershop?' "

As we move into this flat world, and you have this massive Web-enabled global workforce, with all these collaborative tools, there will be no project too small for some members of this workforce to take on, or copy, or modify — for free. Someone out there will be trying to produce the free versions of every kind of software or drug or music. "So how will products retain their value?" asked Mundie. "And if companies cannot derive fair value from their products, will innovation move forward in this area, or others, at the speed that it could or should?" Can we always count on a self-organizing open-source movement to come together to drive things forward for free?

It seems to me that we are too early in the history of the flattening of the world to answer these questions. But they will need answers, and not just for Microsoft. So far — and maybe this is part of the long-term answer — Microsoft has been able to count on the fact that the only thing more expensive than commercial software is free software. Few big companies can simply download Linux off the Web and expect it to work for all their tasks. A lot of design and systems engineering needs to go around it and on top of it to tailor it to a company's specific needs, especially for sophisticated, large-scale, mission-critical operations. So when you add up all the costs of adapting the Linux operating system to the needs of your company and its specific hardware platform and applications, Microsoft argues, it can end up costing as much as or more than Windows.

The second issue Microsoft raises about this whole open-source movement has to do with how we keep track of who owns which piece of any innovation in a flat world, where some is generated for free and others build on it for profit. Will Chinese programmers really respect the rules of the Free Software Foundation? Who will govern all this?

"Once you start to socialize the global population on the idea that software or any other innovation is supposed to be free, a lot of people will not distinguish between free software, free pharmaceuticals, free music, or free patents on car designs," argued Mundie. There is some truth to this. I work for a newspaper, that is where my paycheck comes from. But I believe that all online newspapers should be free, and on principle I refuse to pay for an online subscription to *The Wall Street Journal*. I have not read the paper copy of *The New York Times* regularly for two years. I read it only online. But what if my daughters' generation, which is being raised to think that newspapers are something to be accessed online for free, grows up and refuses to pay for the paper editions? Hmmm. I loved Amazon.com until it started providing a global platform that wasn't selling only my new books but also used versions. And I am still not sure how I feel about Amazon offering sections of this book to be browsed online for free.

Mundie noted that a major American auto company recently discovered that some Chinese firms were using new digital-scanning technology to scan an entire car and churn out computer-aided design models of every part within a very short period of time. They can then feed those designs to industrial robots and in short order produce a perfect copy of a GM car — without having to spend any money on R & D. American automakers never thought they had anything to worry about from wholesale cloning of their cars, but in the flat world, given the technologies that are out there, that is no longer the case.

My bottom line is this: Open-source is an important flattener because it makes available for free many tools, from software to encyclopedias, that millions of people around the world would have had to buy in order to use, and because open-source network associations — with their open borders and come-one-come-all approach — can challenge hierarchical structures with a horizontal model of innovation that is clearly working in a growing number of areas. Apache and Linux have each helped to drive down costs of computing and Internet usage in ways that are profoundly flattening. This movement is not going away. Indeed, it may just be getting started — with a huge, growing appetite that could apply to many industries. As *The Economist* mused (June 10, 2004), "some zealots even argue that the open-source approach represents a new, post-capitalist model of production."

That may prove true. But if it does, then we have some huge global governance issues to sort out over who owns what and how individuals and companies will profit from their creations.

Flattener #5
Outsourcing
Y2K

India has had its ups and downs since it achieved independence on August 15, 1947, but in some ways it might be remembered as the luckiest country in the history of the late twentieth century.

Until recently, India was what is known

in the banking world as "the second buyer." You always want to be the second buyer in business — the person who buys the hotel or the golf course or the shopping mall after the first owner has gone bankrupt and its assets are being sold by the bank at ten cents on the dollar. Well, the first buyers of all the cable laid by all those fiber-optic cable companies — which thought they were going to get endlessly rich in an endlessly expanding digital universe — were their American shareholders. When the bubble burst, they were left holding either worthless or much diminished stock. The Indians, in effect, got to be the second buyers of the fiber-optics companies.

They didn't actually purchase the shares, they just benefited from the overcapacity in fiber optics, which meant that they and their American clients got to use all that cable practically for free. This was a huge stroke of luck for India (and to a lesser degree for China, the former Soviet Union, and Eastern Europe), because what is the history of modern India? In short, India is a country with virtually no natural resources that got very good at doing one thing — mining the brains of its own people by educating a relatively large slice of its elites in the sciences, engineering, and medicine. In 1951, to his enduring credit, Jawaharlal Nehru, India's first prime minister, set up the first of India's seven Indian Institutes of Technology (IIT) in the eastern city of Kharagpur. In the fifty years since then, hundreds of thousands of Indians have competed to gain entry and then graduate from these IITs and their private-sector equivalents (as well as the six Indian Institutes of Management, which teach business administration). Given India's 1 billion–plus population, this competition produces a phenomenal knowledge meritocracy. It's like a factory, churning out and exporting some of the most gifted engineering, computer science, and software talent on the globe.

This, alas, was one of the few things India did right. Because its often dysfunctional political system, coupled with Nehru's preference for pro-Soviet, Socialist economics, ensured that up until the mid-1990s India could not provide good jobs for most of those talented engineers. So America got to be the second buyer of India's brainpower! If you were a smart, educated Indian, the only way you could fulfill your potential was by leaving the country and, ideally, going to America, where some twenty-five thousand graduates of India's top engineering schools have settled since 1953, greatly enriching America's knowledge pool thanks to their education, which was subsidized by Indian taxpayers.

"The IITs became islands of excellence by not allowing the general debasement of the Indian system to lower their exacting standards," noted *The Wall Street Journal* (April 16, 2003). "You couldn't bribe your way to get into an IIT . . . Candidates are accepted only if they pass a grueling entrance exam. The government does not interfere with the curriculum, and the workload is demanding . . . Arguably, it is harder to get into an IIT than into Harvard or the Massachusetts Institute of Technology . . . IIT alumnus Vinod Khosla, who co-founded Sun Microsystems, said: 'When I finished IIT Delhi and went to Carnegie Mellon for my Masters, I thought I was cruising all the way because it was so easy relative to the education I got at IIT.' "

For most of their first fifty years, these IITs were one of the greatest bargains America ever had. It was as if someone installed a brain drain that filled up in New Delhi and emptied in Palo Alto.

And then along came Netscape, the 1996 telecom deregulation, and Global Crossing and its fiber-optic friends. The world got flattened and that whole deal got turned on its head. "India had no resources and no infrastructure," said Dinakar Singh, one of the most respected young hedge fund managers on Wall Street, whose parents graduated from an IIT and then immigrated to America, where he was born. "It produced people with quality and by quantity. But many of them rotted on the docks of India like vegetables. Only a relative few could get on ships and get out. Not anymore, because we built this ocean crosser, called fiber-optic cable . . . For decades you had to leave India to be a professional . . . Now you can plug into the world from India. You don't have to go to Yale and go to work for Goldman Sachs [as I did.]"

India could never have afforded to pay for the bandwidth to connect brainy India with high-tech America, so American shareholders paid for it. Sure, overinvestment can be good. The overinvestment in railroads turned out to be a great boon for the American economy. "But the railroad overinvestment was confined to your own country and so too were the benefits," said Singh. In the case of the digital railroads, "it was the foreigners who benefited." India got to ride for free.

It is fun to talk to Indians who were around at precisely the moment when American companies started to discover they could draw on India's brainpower in India. One of them is Vivek Paul, now the president of Wipro, the Indian software giant. "In many ways the Indian information technology [outsourcing] revolution began with General Electric coming over. We're talking the late 1980s and early '90s. At the time, Texas Instruments was doing some chip design in India. Some of their key designers [in America] were Indians, and they basically let them go back home and work from there [using the rather crude communications networks that existed then to stay in touch.] At that time, I was heading up the operations for GE Medical Systems in Bangalore. [GE's chairman] Jack Welch came to India in 1989 and was completely taken by India as a source of intellectual advantage for GE. Jack would say, 'India is a developing country with a developed intellectual capability.' He saw a talent pool that could be leveraged. So he said, 'We spend a lot of money doing software. Couldn't we do some work for our IT department here?' " Because India had closed its market to foreign technology companies, like IBM, Indian companies had started their own factories to make PCs and servers, and Welch felt that if they could do it for themselves, they could do it for GE.

To pursue the project, Welch sent a team headed by GE's chief information officer over to India to check out the possibilities. Paul was also filling in as GE's business development manager for India at the time. "So it was my job to escort the corporate CIO, in early 1990, on his first trip," he recalled. "They had come with some pilot projects to get the ball rolling. I remember in the middle of the night going to pick them up at the Delhi airport with a caravan of Indian cars, Ambassadors, based on a very dated 1950s Morris Minor design. Everyone in the government drove one. So we had a five-car caravan and we were driving back from the airport to town. I was in the back car, and at one point we heard this loud bang, and I thought, What happened? I shot to the front, and the lead car's hood had flown off and smashed the windshield — with these GE people inside! So this whole caravan of GE execs pulls over to the side of the road, and I could just hear them saying to themselves, 'This is the place we're going to get software from?'"

Fortunately for India, the GE team was not discouraged by the poor quality of Indian cars. GE decided to sink roots, starting a joint development project with Wipro. Other companies were trying different models. But this was still pre-fiber-optic days. Simon & Schuster, the book publisher, for instance, would ship its books over to India and pay Indians $50 a month (compared to $1,000 a month in the United States) to type them by hand into computers, converting the books into digitized electronic files that could be edited or amended easily in the future — particularly dictionaries, which constantly need updating. In 1991, Manmohan Singh, then India's finance minister, began opening the Indian economy for foreign investment and introducing competition into the Indian telecom industry to bring down prices. To attract more foreign investment, Singh made it much easier for companies to set up satellite downlink stations in Bangalore, so they could skip over the Indian phone system and connect with their home bases in America, Europe, or Asia. Before then, only Texas Instruments had been willing to brave the Indian bureaucracy, becoming the first multinational to establish a circuit design and development center in India in 1985. TI's center in Bangalore had its own satellite downlink but had to suffer through having an Indian government official to oversee it — with the right to examine any piece of data going in or out. Singh loosened all those reins post-1991. A short time later, in 1994, HealthScribe India, a company originally funded in part by Indian-American doctors, was set up in Bangalore to do outsourced medical transcription for American doctors and hospitals. Those doctors at the time were taking handwritten notes and then dictating them into a Dictaphone for a secretary or someone else to transcribe, which would usually take days or weeks. HealthScribe set up a system that turned a doctor's touch-tone phone into a dictation machine. The doctor would punch in a number and simply dictate his notes to a PC with a voice card in it, which would digitize his voice. He could be sitting anywhere when he did it. Thanks to the satellite, a housewife or student in Bangalore could go into a computer and download that doctor's digitized voice and transcribe it — not in two weeks but in two hours. Then this person would zip it right back by satellite as a text file that could be put into the hospital's computer system and become part of the billing file. Because of the twelve-hour time difference with India, Indians could do the transcription while the American doctors were sleeping, and the file would be ready and waiting the next morning. This was an important breakthrough for companies, because if you could safely, legally, and securely transcribe from Bangalore medical records, lab reports, and doctors' diagnoses — in one of the most litigious industries in the world — a lot of other industries could think about sending some of their backroom work to be done in India as well.

And they did. But it remained limited by what could be handled by satellite, where there was a voice delay. (Ironically, said Gurujot Singh Khalsa, one of the founders of HealthScribe, they initially explored having Indians in Maine — that is, American Indians — do this work, using some of the federal money earmarked for the tribes to get started, but they could never get them interested enough to put the deal together.) The cost of doing the transcription in India was about one-fifth the cost per line of doing it the United States, a difference that got a lot of people's attention.

By the late 1990s, though, Lady Luck was starting to shine on India from two directions: The fiber-optic bubble was starting to inflate, linking India with the United States, and the Y2K computer crisis — the so-called millennium bug — started gathering on the horizon. As you'll remember, the Y2K bug was a result of the fact that when computers were built, they came with internal clocks. In order to save memory space, these clocks rendered dates with just six digits — two for the day, two for the month, and, you guessed it, two for the year. That meant they could go up to only 12/31/99. So when the calendar hit January 1, 2000, many older computers were poised to register that not as 01/01/2000 but as 01/01/00, and they would think it was 1900 all over again. It meant that a huge number of existing computers (newer ones were being made with better clocks) needed to have their internal clocks and related systems adjusted; otherwise, it was feared, they would shut down, creating a global crisis, given how many different management systems — from water to air traffic control — were computerized.

This computer remediation work was a huge, tedious job. Who in the world had enough software engineers to do it all? Answer: India, with all the techies from all those IITs and private technical colleges and computer schools.

And so with Y2K bearing down on us, America and India started dating, and that relationship became a huge flattener, because it demonstrated to so many different businesses that the combination of the PC, the Internet, and fiber-optic cable had created the possibility of a whole new form of collaboration and horizontal value creation: outsourcing. Any service, call center, business support operation, or knowledge work that could be digitized could be sourced globally to the cheapest, smartest, or most efficient provider. Using fiber-optic cable-connected workstations, Indian techies could get under the hood of your company's computers and do all the adjustments, even though they were located halfway around the world.

"[Y2K upgrading] was tedious work that was not going to give them an enormous competitive advantage," said Vivek Paul, the Wipro executive whose company did some outsourced Y2K drudge work. "So all these Western companies were incredibly challenged to find someone else who would do it and do it for as little money as possible. They said, 'We just want to get past the damn year 2000!' So they started to work with Indian [technology] companies who they might not have worked with otherwise."

To use my parlance, they were ready to go on a blind date with India. They were ready to get "fixed up." Added Jerry Rao, "Y2K means different things to different people. For Indian industry, it represented the biggest opportunity. India was considered as a place of backward people. Y2K suddenly required that every single computer in the world needed to be reviewed. And the sheer number of people needed to review line-by-line code existed in India. The Indian IT industry got its footprint across the globe because of Y2K. Y2K became our engine of growth, our engine of being known around the world. We never looked back after Y2K."

By early 2000, the Y2K work started to wind down, but then a whole new driver of business emerged — e-commerce. The dot-com bubble had not yet burst, engineering talent was scarce, and demand from dot-coms was enormous. Said Paul, "People wanted what they felt were mission-critical applications, key to their very existence, to be done and they could go nowhere else. So they turned to the Indian companies, and as they turned to the Indian companies they found that they were getting delivery of complex systems, with great quality, sometimes better than what they were getting from others. That created an enormous respect for Indian IT providers[.] And if [Y2K work] was the acquaintanceship process, this was the falling-in-love process."

Outsourcing from America to India, as a new form of collaboration, exploded. By just stringing a fiber-optic line from a workstation in Bangalore to my company's mainframe, I could have Indian IT firms like Wipro, Infosys, and Tata Consulting Services managing my e-commerce and mainframe applications.

"Once we're in the mainframe business and once we're in e-commerce — now we're married," said Paul. But again, India was lucky that it could exploit all that undersea fiber-optic cable. "I had an office very close to the Leela Palace hotel in Bangalore," Paul added. "I was working with a factory located in the information technology park in Whitefield, a suburb of Bangalore, and I *could not get a local telephone line between our office and the factory.* Unless you paid a bribe, you could not get a line, and we wouldn't pay. So my phone call to Whitefield would go from my office in Bangalore to Kentucky, where there was a GE mainframe computer we were working with, and then from Kentucky to Whitefield. We used our own fiber-optic lease line that ran across the ocean — but the one across town required a bribe."

India didn't benefit only from the dot-com boom; it benefited even more from the dot-com bust! That is the real irony. The boom laid the cable that connected India to the world, and the bust made the cost of using it virtually free and also vastly increased the number of American companies that would want to use that fiber-optic cable to outsource knowledge work to India.

Y2K led to this mad rush for Indian brainpower to get the programming work done. The Indian companies were good and cheap, but price wasn't first on customers' minds — getting the work done was, and India was the only place with the volume of workers to do it. Then the dot-com boom comes along right in the wake of Y2K, and India is one of the few places where you can find surplus English-speaking engineers, at any price, because all of those in America have been scooped up by e-commerce companies. Then the dot-com bubble bursts, the stock market tanks, and the pool of investment capital dries up. American IT companies that survived the boom and venture capital firms that still wanted to fund start-ups had much less cash to spend. Now they needed those Indian engineers not just because there were a lot of them, but precisely because they were low-cost. So the relationship between India and the American business community intensified another notch.

One of the great mistakes made by many analysts in the early 2000s was conflating the dot-com boom with globalization, suggesting that both were just fads and hot air. When the dot-com bust came along, these same wrongheaded analysts assumed that globalization was over as well. Exactly the opposite was true. The dot-com bubble was only one aspect of globalization, and when it imploded, rather than imploding globalization, it actually turbocharged it.

Promod Haque, an Indian-American and one of the most prominent venture capitalists in Silicon Valley with his firm Norwest Venture Partners, was in the middle of this transition. "When the bust took place, a lot of these Indian engineers in the U.S. [on temporary work visas] got laid off, so they went back to India," explained Haque. But as a result of the bust, the IT budgets of virtually every major U.S. firm got slashed. "Every IT manager was told to get the same amount of work or more done with less money. So guess what he does? He says, 'You remember Vijay from India who used to work here during the boom and then went back home? Let me call him over in Bangalore and see if he will do the work for us for less money than what we would pay an engineer here in the U.S.' " And thanks to all that fiber cable laid during the boom, it was easy to find Vijay and put him to work.

The Y2K computer readjustment work was done largely by low-skilled Indian programmers right out of tech schools, said Haque, "but the guys on visas who were coming to America were not trade school guys. They were guys with advanced engineering degrees. So a lot of our companies saw that these guys were good at Java and C++ and architectural design work for computers, and then they got laid off and went back home, and the IT manager back here who is told, 'I don't care how you get the job done, just get it done for less money,' calls Vijay." Once America and India were dating, the burgeoning Indian

IT companies in Bangalore started coming up with their own proposals. The Y2K work had allowed them to interact with some pretty large companies in the United States, and as a result they began to understand the pain points and how to do business-process implementation and improvement. So the Indians, who were doing a lot of very specific custom code maintenance to higher-value-add companies, started to develop their own products and transform themselves from maintenance to product companies, offering a range of software services and consulting. This took Indian companies much deeper inside American ones, and business-process outsourcing — letting Indians run your back room — went to a whole new level. "I have an accounts payable department and I could move this whole thing to India under Wipro or Infosys and cut my costs in half," said Haque. All across America, CEOs were saying, " 'Make it work for less,' " said Haque. "And the Indian companies were saying, 'I have taken a look under your hood and I will provide you with a total solution for the lowest price.' " In other words, the Indian outsourcing companies said, "Do you remember how I fixed your tires and your pistons during Y2K? Well, I could actually give you a whole lube job if you like. And now that you know me and trust me, you know I can do it." To their credit, the Indians were not just cheap, they were also hungry and ready to learn anything.

The scarcity of capital after the dot-com bust made venture capital firms see to it that the companies they were investing in were finding the most efficient, high-quality, low-price way to innovate. In the boom times, said Haque, it was not uncommon for a $50 million investment in a start-up to return $500 million once the company went public. After the bust, that same company's public offering might bring in only $100 million. Therefore, venture firms wanted to risk only $20 million to get that company from start-up to IPO.

"For venture firms," said Haque, "the big question became, How do I get my entrepreneurs and their new companies to a point where they were breaking even or profitable sooner, so they can stop being a draw on my capital and be sold so our firm can *generate good liquidity and returns?* The answer many firms came up with was: I better start outsourcing as many functions as I can from the beginning. I have to make money for my investors faster, so what can be outsourced must be outsourced."

Henry Schacht, who, as noted, was heading Lucent during part of this period, saw the whole process from the side of corporate management. The business economics, he told me, became "very ugly" for everyone. Everyone found prices flat to declining and markets stagnant, yet they were still spending huge amounts of money running the backroom operations of their companies, which they could no longer afford. "Cost pressures were enormous," he recalled, "and the flat world was available, [so] economics were forcing people to do things they never thought they would do or could do . . . Globalization got supercharged" — for both knowledge work and manufacturing. Companies found that they could go to MIT and find four incredibly smart Chinese engineers who were ready to go back to China and work for them from there for the same amount that it would cost them to hire one engineer in America. Bell Labs had a research facility at Tsingdao that could connect to Lucent's computers in America. "They would use our computers overnight," said Schacht. "Not only was the incremental computing cost close to zero, but so too was the transmission cost, and the computer was idle [at night]."

For all these reasons I believe that Y2K should be a national holiday in India, a second Indian Independence Day, in addition to August 15. As Johns Hopkins foreign policy expert Michael Mandelbaum, who spent part of his youth in India, put it, "Y2K should be called Indian Interdepedence

Day," because it was India's ability to collaborate with Western companies, thanks to the interdependence created by fiber-optic networks, that really vaulted it forward and gave more Indians than ever some real freedom of choice in how, for whom, and where they worked.

To put it another way, August 15 commemorates freedom at midnight. Y2K made possible *employment* at midnight — but not any employment, employment for India's best knowledge workers. August 15 gave independence to *India*. But Y2K gave independence to *Indians* — not all, by any stretch of the imagination, but a lot more than fifty years ago, and many of them from the most productive segment of the population. In that sense, yes, India was lucky, but it also reaped what it had sowed through hard work and education and the wisdom of its elders who built all those IITs.

Louis Pasteur said it a long time ago: "Fortune favors the prepared mind."

Flattener #6
Offshoring
Running with Gazelles,
Eating with Lions

On December 11, 2001, China formally joined the World Trade Organization, which meant Beijing agreed to follow the same global rules governing imports, exports, and foreign investments that most countries in the world were following. It meant China was agreeing, in principle, to make its own competitive playing field as level as the rest of the world. A few days later, the American-trained Chinese manager of a fuel pump factory in Beijing, which was owned by a friend of mine, Jack Perkowski, the chairman and CEO of ASIMCO Technologies, an American auto parts manufacturer in China, posted the following African proverb, translated into Mandarin, on his factory floor:

Every morning in Africa, a gazelle wakes up.
It knows it must run faster than the fastest
*   lion or it will be killed.*
Every morning a lion wakes up.
It knows it must outrun the slowest gazelle
*   or it will starve to death.*
It doesn't matter whether you are a lion or a
*   gazelle.*
When the sun comes up, you better start
*   running.*

I don't know who is the lion and who is the gazelle, but I do know this: Ever since the Chinese joined the WTO, both they and the rest of the world have had to run faster and faster. This is because China's joining the WTO gave a huge boost to another form of collaboration — offshoring. Offshoring, which has been around for decades, is different from outsourcing. Outsourcing means taking some specific, but limited, function that your company was doing in-house — such as research, call centers, or accounts receivable — and having another company perform that exact same function for you and then reintegrating their work back into your overall operation. Offshoring, by contrast, is when a company takes one of its factories that it is operating in Canton, Ohio, and moves the whole factory offshore to Canton, China. There, it produces the very same product in the very same way, only with cheaper labor, lower taxes, subsidized energy, and lower health-care costs. Just as Y2K took India and the world to a whole new level of outsourcing, China's joining the WTO took Beijing and the world to a whole new level of offshoring — with more companies shifting production offshore and then integrating it into their global supply chains.

In 1977, Chinese leader Deng Xiaoping put China on the road to capitalism, declaring later that "to get rich is glorious." When China first opened its tightly closed economy, companies in industrialized countries saw it as an incredible new market for exports. Every Western or Asian manufacturer dreamed of selling its equivalent of 1 billion pairs of underwear to a single market. Some foreign companies set up shop in China to do just that. But because China was not subject to world trade rules, it was able to restrict the penetration into its market by these Western companies through various trade and investment barriers. And when it was not doing that deliberately, the sheer bureaucratic and cultural difficulties of doing business in China had the same effect. Many of the pioneer investors in China lost their shirts and pants *and underwear* — and with China's Wild West legal system there was not much recourse.

Beginning in the 1980s, many investors, particularly overseas Chinese who knew how to operate in China, started to say, "Well, if we can't sell that many things to the Chinese right now, why don't we use China's disciplined labor pool to make things there and sell them abroad?" This dovetailed with the interests of China's leaders. China wanted to attract foreign manufacturers and their technologies — not simply to manufacture 1 billion pairs of underwear for sale in China but to use low-wage Chinese labor to also sell 6 billion pairs of underwear to everyone else in the world, and at prices that were a fraction of what the underwear companies in Europe or America or even Mexico were charging.

Once that offshoring process began in a range of industries — from textiles to consumer electronics to furniture to eyeglass frames to auto parts — the only way other companies could compete was by offshoring to China as well (taking advantage of its low-cost, high-quality platform), or by looking for alternative manufacturing centers in Eastern Europe, the Caribbean, or somewhere else in the developing world.

By joining the World Trade Organization in 2001, China assured foreign companies that if they shifted factories offshore to China, they would be protected by international law and standard business practices. This greatly enhanced China's attractiveness as a manufacturing platform. Under WTO rules, Beijing agreed — with some time for phase-in — to treat non-Chinese citizens or firms as if they were Chinese in terms of their economic rights and obligations under Chinese law. This meant that foreign companies could sell virtually anything anywhere in China. WTO membership status also meant that Beijing agreed to treat all WTO member nations equally, meaning that the same tariffs and the same regulations had to apply equally for everyone. And it agreed to submit itself to international arbitration in the event of a trade dispute with another country or a foreign company. At the same time, government bureaucrats became more customer-friendly, procedures for investments were streamlined, and Web sites proliferated in different ministries to help foreigners navigate China's business regulations. I don't know how many Chinese actually ever bought a copy of Mao's Little Red Book, but U.S. embassy officials in China told me that 2 million copies of the Chinese-language edition of the WTO rule book were sold in the weeks immediately after China signed on to the WTO. To put it another way, China under Mao was closed and isolated from the other flattening forces of his day, and as a result Mao was really a challenge only to his own people. Deng Xiaoping made China open to absorbing many of the ten flatteners, and, in so doing, made China a challenge to the whole world.

Before China signed on to the WTO, there was a sense that, while China had opened up to get the advantages of trade with the West, the government and the banks would protect Chinese businesses from any crushing foreign competition, said Jack Perkowski of ASIMCO. "China's entry into the WTO was a signal to the community outside of China that it was now on the capitalist track for good," he added. "Before, you had the thought in the back of your mind that there could be a turning back to state communism. With WTO, China said, 'We are on one course.' "

Because China can amass so many low-wage workers at the unskilled, semiskilled, and skilled levels, because it has such a voracious appetite for factory, equipment, and knowledge jobs to keep its people employed, and because it has such a massive and burgeoning consumer market, it has become an unparalleled zone for offshoring. China has more than 160 cities with a population of 1 million or more. You can go to towns on the east coast of China today that you have never heard of and discover that this one town manufactures most of the eyeglass frames in the world, while the town next door manufactures most of the portable cigarette lighters in the world, and the one next to that is doing most of the computer screens for Dell, and another is specializing in mobile phones. Kenichi Ohmae, the Japanese business consultant, estimates in his book *The United States of China* that in the Zhu Jiang Delta area alone, north of Hong Kong, there are fifty thousand Chinese electronics component suppliers.

"China is a threat, China is a customer, and China is an opportunity," Ohmae remarked to me one day in Tokyo. "You have to internalize China to succeed. You cannot ignore it." Instead of competing with China as an enemy, argues Ohmae, you break down your business and think about which part of the business you would like to do in China, which part you would like to sell to China, and which part you want to buy from China.

Here we get to the real flattening aspect of China's opening to the world market. The more attractive China makes itself as a base for offshoring, the more attractive other developed and developing countries competing with it, like Malaysia, Thailand, Ireland, Mexico, Brazil, and Vietnam, have to make themselves. They all look at what is going on in China and the jobs moving there and say to themselves, "Holy catfish, we had better start offering these same incentives." This has created a process of competitive flattening, in which countries scramble to see who can give companies the best tax breaks, education incentives, and subsidies, on top of their cheap labor, to encourage offshoring to their shores.

Ohio State University business professor Oded Shenkar, author of the book *The Chinese Century*, told *BusinessWeek* (December 6, 2004) that he gives it to American companies straight: "If you still make anything labor intensive, get out now rather than bleed to death. Shaving 5% here and there won't work." Chinese producers can make the same adjustments. "You need an entirely new business model to compete," he said. China's flattening power is also fueled by the fact that it is developing a huge domestic market of its own. The same *BusinessWeek* article noted that this brings economies of scale, intense local rivalries that keep prices low, an army of engineers that is growing by 350,000 annually, young workers and managers willing to put in twelve-hour days, an unparalleled component base in electronics and light industry, "and an entrepreneurial zeal to do whatever it takes to please big retailers such as Wal-Mart Stores, Target, Best Buy and JCPenney."

Critics of China's business practices say that its size and economic power mean that it will soon be setting the global floor not only for low wages but also for lax labor laws and workplace standards. This is known in the business as "the China price."

But what is really scary is that China is not attracting so much global investment by simply racing everyone to the bottom. That is just a short-term strategy. The biggest mistake any business can make when it comes to China is thinking that it is only winning on wages and not improving quality and productivity. In the private, non-state-owned sector of Chinese industry, productivity increased 17 percent annually — I repeat, 17 percent annually — between 1995 and 2002, according to a study by the U.S. Conference Board. This is due to China's absorption of both new technologies and modern business practices, starting from a very low base. Incidentally, the Conference Board study noted, China lost 15 million manufacturing jobs during this period, compared with 2 million in the United States. "As its manufacturing productivity accelerates, China is losing jobs in manufacturing — many more than the United States is — and gaining them in services, a pattern that has been playing out in the developed world for many years," the study said.

China's real long-term strategy is to outrace America and the E.U. countries to the top, and the Chinese are off to a good start. China's leaders are much more focused than many of their Western counterparts on how to train their young people in the math, science, and computer skills required for success in the flat world, how to build a physical and telecom infrastructure that will allow Chinese people to plug and play faster and easier than others, and how to create incentives that will attract global investors. What China's leaders really want is the next generation of underwear or airplane wings to be *designed* in China as well. That is where things are heading in another decade. So in thirty years we will have gone from "sold in China" to "made in China" to "designed in China" to "dreamed up in China" — or from China as collaborator with the worldwide manufacturers on nothing to China as a low-cost, high-quality, hyperefficient collaborator with worldwide manufacturers on *everything*. This should allow China to maintain its role as a major flattening force, provided that political instability does not disrupt the process. Indeed, while researching this chapter, I came across an online Silicon Valley newsletter called the *Inquirer*, which follows the semiconductor industry. What caught my eye was its November 5, 2001, article headlined, "China to Become Center of Everything." It quoted a *China People's Daily* article that claimed that four hundred out of the Forbes 500 companies have invested in more than two thousand projects in mainland China. And that was four years ago.

Japan, being right next door to China, has taken a very aggressive approach to internalizing the China challenge. Osamu Watanabe, chairman of the Japan External Trade Organization (JETRO), Japan's official organ for promoting exports, told me in Tokyo, "China is developing very rapidly and making the shift from low-grade products to high-grade, high-tech ones." As a result, added Watanabe, Japanese companies, to remain globally competitive, have had to shift some production and a lot of assembly of middle-range products to China, while shifting at home to making "even higher value-added products." So China and Japan "are becoming part of the same supply chain." After a prolonged recession, Japan's economy started to bounce back in 2003, due to the sale of thousands of tons of machinery, assembly robots, and other critical components in China. In 2003, China replaced the United States as the biggest importer of Japanese products. Still, the Japanese government is urging its companies to be careful not to overinvest in China. It encourages them to practice what Watanabe called a "China plus one" strategy: to keep one production leg in China but the other in a different Asian country — just in case political turmoil unflattens China one day.

This China flattener has been wrenching for certain manufacturing workers around the world, but a godsend for all consumers. *Fortune* magazine (October 4, 2004) quoted a study by Morgan Stanley estimating that since the mid-1990s alone, cheap imports from China have saved U.S. consumers roughly $600 billion and have saved U.S. manufacturers untold billions in cheaper parts for their products. This savings, in turn, *Fortune* noted, has helped the Federal Reserve to hold down interest rates longer, giving more Americans a chance to buy homes or refinance the ones they have, and giving businesses more capital to invest in new innovations.

In an effort to better understand how offshoring to China works, I sat down in Beijing with Jack Perkowski of ASIMCO, a pioneer in this form of collaboration. If they ever have a category in the Olympics called "extreme capitalism," bet on Perkowski to win the gold. In 1988 he stepped down as a top investment banker at Paine Webber and went to a leverage buyout firm, but two years later, at age forty-two, decided it was time for a new challenge. With some partners, he raised $150 million to buy companies in China and headed off for the adventure of his life. Since then he has lost and remade millions of dollars, learned every lesson the hard way, but survived to become a powerful example of what offshoring to China is all about and what a powerful collaborative tool it can become.

"When I first started back in 1992–1993, everyone thought the hard part was to actually find and gain access to opportunities in China," recalled Perkowski. It turned out that there were opportunities aplenty but a critical shortage of Chinese managers who understood how to run an auto parts factory along capitalist lines, with an emphasis on exports and making world-class products for the Chinese market. As Perkowski put it, the easy part was setting up shop in China. The hard part was getting the right local managers who could run the store. So when he initially started buying majority ownership in Chinese auto parts companies, Perkowski began by importing managers from abroad. Bad idea. It was too expensive, and operating in China was just too foreign for foreigners. Scratch plan A.

"So we sent all the expats home, which gave me problems with my investor base, and went to plan B," he said. "We then tried to convert the 'Old China' managers who typically came along with the plants we bought, but that didn't work either. They were simply too used to working in a planned economy where they never had to deal with the marketplace, just deliver their quotas. Those managers who did have an entrepreneurial flair got drunk on their first sip of capitalism and were ready to try anything.

"The Chinese are very entrepreneurial," said Perkowski, "but back then, before China joined the WTO, there was no rule of law and no bond or stock market to restrain this entrepreneurialism. Your only choices were managers from the state-owned sector, who were very bureaucratic, or managers from the first wave of private companies, who were practicing cowboy capitalism. Neither is where you want to be. If your managers are too bureaucratic, you can't get anything done — they just give excuses about how China is different — and if they are too entrepreneurial, you can't sleep at night, because you have no idea what they are going to do." Perkowski had a lot of sleepless nights.

One of his first purchases in China was an interest in a company making rubber parts. When he subsequently reached an agreement with his Chinese partner to purchase his shares in the company, the Chinese partner signed a noncompete clause as part of the transaction. As soon as the deal closed, however, the Chinese partner went out and opened a new factory. "Noncompete" did not quite translate into Mandarin. Scratch plan B.

Meanwhile, Perkowski's partnership was hemorrhaging money — Perkowski's tuition for learning how to do business in China — and he found himself owning a string of Chinese auto parts factories. "Around 1997 was the low point," he said. "Our company as a whole was shrinking and we were not profitable. While some of our companies were doing okay, we were generally in tough shape. Although we had majority ownership and could theoretically put anyone on the field that we wanted, I looked at my [managerial] bench and I had no one to put in the game." Time for plan C.

"We essentially concluded that, while we liked China, we wanted no part of 'Old China,' and instead wanted to place our bets on 'New China' managers," said Perkowski. "We began looking for a new breed of Chinese managers who were open-minded and had gotten some form of management training. We were looking for individuals who were experienced at operating in China and yet were familiar with how the rest of the world operated and knew where China had to go. So between 1997 and 1999, we recruited a whole team of 'New China' managers, typically mainland Chinese who had worked for multinationals, and as these managers came on board, we began one by one to replace the 'Old China' managers at our companies."

Once the new generation of Chinese managers, who understood global markets and customers and could be united around a shared company vision — *and knew China* — was in place, ASIMCO started making a profit. Today ASIMCO has sales of about $350 million a year in auto parts from thirteen Chinese factories in nine provinces. The company sells to customers in the United States, and it also has thirty-six sales offices throughout China servicing automakers in that country too.

From this base, Perkowski made his next big move — taking the profits from offshoring back onshore in America. "In April of 2003, we bought the North American camshaft operations of Federal-Mogul Corporation, an old-line components company that is now in bankruptcy," said Perkowski. "We bought the business first to get access to its customers, which were primarily the Big Three automakers, plus Caterpillar and Cummins. While we have had long-standing relationships with Cat and Cummins — and this acquisition enhanced our position with them — the camshaft sales to the Big Three were our first. The second reason to make the acquisition was to obtain technology which we could bring back to China. Like most of the technology that goes into modern passenger cars and trucks, people take camshaft technology for granted. However, camshafts [the part of the engine that controls how the pistons go up and down] are highly engineered products which are critical to the performance of the engine. The acquisition of this business essentially gave us the know-how and technology that we could use to become the camshaft leader in

China. As a result, we now have the best camshaft technology and a customer base both in China and the U.S."

This is a very important point, because the general impression is that offshoring is a lose-lose proposition for American workers — something that was here went over there, and that is the end of the story. The reality is more complicated.

Most companies build offshore factories not simply to obtain cheaper labor for products they want to sell in America or Europe. Another motivation is to serve that foreign market without having to worry about trade barriers and to gain a dominant foothold there — particularly a giant market like China's. According to the U.S. Commerce Department, nearly 90 percent of the output from U.S.-owned offshore factories is sold to foreign consumers. But this actually stimulates American exports. There is a variety of studies indicating that every dollar a company invests overseas in an offshore factory yields additional exports for its home country, because roughly one-third of global trade today is within multinational companies. It works the other way as well. Even when production is moved offshore to save on wages, it is usually not all moved offshore. According to a January 26, 2004, study by the Heritage Foundation, *Job Creation and the Taxation of For-*

eign-Source Income, American companies that produce at home and abroad, for both the American market and China's, generate more than 21 percent of U.S. economic output, produce 56 percent of U.S. exports, and employ three-fifths of all manufacturing employees, about 9 million workers. So if General Motors builds a factory offshore in Shanghai, it also ends up creating jobs in America by exporting a lot of goods and services to its own factory in China and benefiting from lower parts costs in China for its factories in America. Finally, America is a beneficiary of the same phenomenon. While much attention is paid to American companies going offshore to China, little attention is paid to the huge amount of offshore investment coming into America every year, because foreigners want access to American markets and labor just like we want access to theirs. On September 25, 2003, DaimlerChrysler celebrated the tenth anniversary of its decision to build the first Mercedes-Benz passenger car factory outside Germany, in Tuscaloosa, Alabama, by announcing a $600 million plant expansion. "In Tuscaloosa we have impressively shown that we can produce a new production series with a new workforce in a new factory, and we have also demonstrated that it is possible to have vehicles successfully

'Made by Mercedes' outside of Germany," Professor Jürgen Hubbert, the DaimlerChrysler Board of Management member responsible for the Mercedes Car Group, announced on the anniversary.

Not surprisingly, ASIMCO will use its new camshaft operation in China to handle the raw material and rough machining operations, exporting semifinished products to its camshaft plant in America, where more skilled American workers can do the finished machining operations, which are most critical to quality. In this way, ASIMCO's American customers receive the benefit of a China supply chain and at the same time have the comfort of dealing with a known, American supplier.

The average wage of a high-skilled machinist in America is $3,000 to $4,000 a month. The average wage for a factory worker in China is about $150 a month. In addition, ASIMCO is required to participate in a Chinese government–sponsored pension plan covering heath care, housing, and retirement benefits. Between 35 and 45 percent of a Chinese worker's monthly wage goes directly to the local labor bureau to cover these benefits. The fact that health insurance in China is so much cheaper — because of lower wages, much more limited health service offerings, and no malpractice suits — "certainly makes China an attractive place to expand and add employees," explained Perkowski. "Anything which can be done to reduce a U.S. company's liability for medical coverage would be a plus in keeping jobs in the U.S."

By taking advantage of the flat world to collaborate this way — between onshore and offshore factories, and between high-wage, high-skilled American workers close to their market and low-wage Chinese workers close to theirs — said Perkowski, "we make our American company more competitive, so it is getting more orders and we are actually growing the business. And that is what many in the U.S. are missing when they talk about offshoring. Since the acquisition, for example, we have doubled our business with Cummins, and our business with Caterpillar has grown significantly. All of our customers are exposed to global competition and really need their supply base to the do the right thing as far as cost competitiveness. They want to work with suppliers who understand the flat world. When I went to visit our U.S. customers to explain our strategy for the camshaft business, they were very positive about what we were doing, because they could see that we were aligning our business in a way that was going to enable them to be more competitive."

This degree of collaboration has been

possible only in the last couple of years. "We could not have done what we have done in China in 1983 or 1993," said Perkowski. "Since 1993, a number of things have come together. For example, people always talk about how much the Internet has benefited the U.S. The point I always make is that China has benefited even more. What has held China back in the past was the inability of people outside China to get information about the country, and the inability of people inside China to get information about the rest of the world. Prior to the Internet, the only way to close that information gap was travel. Now you can stay home and do it with the Internet. You could not operate our global supply chain without it. We now just e-mail blueprints over the Internet — we don't even need FedEx."

The advantages for manufacturing in China, for certain industries, are becoming overwhelming, added Perkowski, and cannot be ignored. Either you get flat or you'll be flattened by China. "If you are sitting in the U.S. and don't figure out how to get into China," he said, "in ten or fifteen years from now you will not be a global leader."

Now that China is in the WTO, a lot of traditional, slow, inefficient, and protected sectors of the Chinese economy are being exposed to some withering global competition — something received as warmly in Canton, China, as in Canton, Ohio. Had the Chinese government put WTO membership to a popular vote, "it never would have passed," said Pat Powers, who headed the U.S.-China Business Council office in Beijing during the WTO accession. A key reason why China's leadership sought WTO membership was to use it as a club to force China's bureaucracy to modernize and take down internal regulatory walls and pockets for arbitrary decision making. China's leadership "knew that China had to integrate globally and that many of their existing institutions would simply not change and reform, and so they used the WTO as leverage against their own bureaucracy. And for the last two and half years they've been slugging it out."

Over time, adherence to WTO standards will make China's economy even flatter and more of a flattener globally. But this transition will not be easy, and the chances of a political or economic crackup that disrupts or slows this process are not insignificant. But even if China implements all the WTO reforms, it won't be able to rest. It will soon be reaching a point where its ambitions for economic growth will require more political reform. China will never root out corruption without a free press and active civil society institutions. It can never really become efficient without a more codified rule of law. It will never be able to deal with the inevitable downturns in its economy without a more open political system that allows people to vent their grievances. To put it another way, China will never be truly flat until it gets over that huge speed bump called "political reform."

It seems to be heading in that direction, but it still has a long way to go. I like the way a U.S. diplomat in China put it to me in the spring of 2004: "China right now is doing titillation, not privatization. Reform here is translucent — and sometimes it is quite titillating, because you can see the shapes moving behind the screen — but it is not transparent. [The government still just gives] the information [about the economy] to a few companies and designated interest groups." Why only translucent? I asked. He answered, "Because if you are fully transparent, what do you do with the feedback? They don't know how to deal with that question. They cannot deal [yet] with the results of transparency."

If and when China gets over that political bump in the road, I think it could become not only a bigger platform for offshoring but another free-market version of the United States. While that may seem threatening to some, I think it would be an incredibly positive development for the world. Think about how many new products, ideas, jobs, and consumers arose from Western Europe's and Japan's efforts to become free-market democracies after World War II. The process unleashed an unprecedented period of global prosperity — and the world wasn't even flat then. It had a wall in the middle. If India and China move in that direction, the world will not only become flatter than ever but also, I am convinced, more prosperous than ever. Three United States are better than one, and five would be better than three.

But even as a free-trader, I am worried about the challenge this will pose to wages and benefits of certain workers in the United States, at least in the short run. It is too late for protectionism when it comes to China. Its economy is totally interlinked with those of the developed world, and trying to delink it would cause economic and geopolitical chaos that could devastate the global economy. Americans and Europeans will have to develop new business models that will enable them to get the best out of China and cushion themselves against some of the worst. As *BusinessWeek*, in its dramatic December 6, 2004, cover story on "The China Price," put it, "Can China dominate everything? Of course not.

America remains the world's biggest manufacturer, producing 75% of what it consumes, though that's down from 90% in the mid-'90s. Industries requiring huge R&D budgets and capital investment, such as aerospace, pharmaceuticals, and cars, still have strong bases in the U.S. . . . America will surely continue to benefit from China's expansion." That said, unless America can deal with the long-term industrial challenge posed by the China price in so many areas, "it will suffer a loss of economic power and influence."

Or, to put it another way, if Americans and Europeans want to benefit from the flattening of the world and the interconnecting of all the markets and knowledge centers, they will all have to run at least as fast as the fastest lion — and I suspect that lion will be China, and I suspect that will be pretty darn fast.

Flattener #7
Supply-Chaining
Eating Sushi in Arkansas

I had never seen what a supply chain looked like in action until I visited Wal-Mart headquarters in Bentonville, Arkansas. My Wal-Mart hosts took me over to the 1.2-million-square-foot distribution center, where we climbed up to a viewing perch and watched the show. On one side of the building, scores of white Wal-Mart trailer trucks were dropping off boxes of merchandise from thousands of different suppliers. Boxes large and small were fed up a conveyor belt at each loading dock. These little conveyor belts fed into a bigger belt, like streams feeding into a powerful river. Twenty-four hours a day, seven days a week, the suppliers' trucks feed the twelve miles of conveyor streams, and the conveyor streams feed into a huge Wal-Mart river of boxed products. But that is just half the show. As the Wal-Mart river flows along, an electric eye reads the bar codes on each box on its way to the other side of the building. There, the river parts again into a hundred streams. Electric arms from each stream reach out and guide the boxes — ordered by particular Wal-Mart stores — off the main river and down its stream, where another conveyor belt sweeps them into a waiting Wal-Mart truck, which will rush these particular products onto the shelves of a particular Wal-Mart store somewhere in the country. There, a consumer will lift one of these products off the shelf, and the cashier will scan it in, and the moment that happens, a signal will be generated. That signal will go out across the Wal-Mart network to the supplier of that product — whether that supplier's factory is in coastal China or coastal Maine. That signal will pop up on the supplier's computer screen and prompt him to make another of that item and ship it via the Wal-Mart supply chain, and the whole cycle will start anew. So no sooner does your arm lift a product off the local Wal-Mart's shelf and onto the checkout counter than another mechanical arm starts making another one somewhere in the world. Call it "the Wal-Mart Symphony" in multiple movements — with no finale. It just plays over and over 24/7/365: delivery, sorting, packing, distribution, buying, manufacturing, reordering, delivery, sorting, packing . . .

Just one company, Hewlett-Packard, will sell four hundred thousand computers through the four thousand Wal-Mart stores worldwide in *one day* during the Christmas season, which will require HP to adjust its supply chain, to make sure that all of its standards interface with Wal-Mart's, so that these computers flow smoothly into the Wal-Mart river, into the Wal-Mart streams, into the Wal-Mart stores.

Wal-Mart's ability to bring off this symphony on a global scale — moving 2.3 billion general merchandise cartons a year down its supply chain into its stores — has made it the most important example of the next great flattener I want to discuss, which I call supply-chaining. Supply-chaining is a method of collaborating horizontally — among suppliers, retailers, and customers — to create value. Supply-chaining is both enabled by the flattening of the world and a hugely important flattener itself, because the more these supply chains grow and proliferate, the more they force the adoption of common standards between companies (so that every link of every supply chain can interface with the next), the more they eliminate points of friction at borders, the more the efficiencies of one company get adopted by the others, and the more they encourage global collaboration.

As consumers, we love supply chains, because they deliver us all sorts of goods — from tennis shoes to laptop computers — at lower and lower prices. That is how Wal-Mart became the world's biggest retailer. But as workers, we are sometimes ambivalent or hostile to these supply chains, because they expose us to higher and higher pressures to compete, cut costs, and also, at times, cut wages and benefits. That is how Wal-Mart became one of the world's most controversial companies. No company has been more efficient at improving its supply chain (and thereby flattening the world) than Wal-Mart; and no company epitomizes the tension that supply chains evoke between the consumer in us and the worker in us than Wal-Mart. A September 30, 2002, article in *Computerworld* summed up Wal-Mart's pivotal role: " 'Being a supplier to Wal-Mart is a two-edged sword,' says Joseph R. Eckroth Jr., CIO at Mattel Inc. 'They're a phenomenal channel but a tough customer. They demand excellence.' It's a lesson that the El Segundo, Calif.–based toy manufacturer and thousands of other suppliers learned as the world's largest retailer, Wal-Mart Stores Inc., built an inventory and supply chain management system that changed the face of business. By investing early and heavily in cutting-edge technology to identify and track sales on the individual item level, the Bentonville, Ark.–based retail giant made its IT infrastructure a key competitive advantage that has been studied and copied by companies around the world. 'We view Wal-Mart as the best supply chain operator of all time,' says Pete Abell, retail research director at high-tech consultancy AMR Research Inc. in Boston."

In pursuit of the world's most efficient supply chain, Wal-Mart has piled up a list of business offenses over the years that has given the company several deserved black eyes and that it is belatedly starting to address in a meaningful way. But its role as one of the ten forces that flattened the world is undeniable, and it was to get a handle on this that I decided to make my own pilgrimage to Bentonville. I don't know why, but on the flight in from La Guardia, I was thinking, Boy, I would really like some sushi tonight. But where am I going to find sushi in northwest Arkansas? And even if I found it, would I want to eat it? Could you really trust the eel in Arkansas?

When I arrived at the Hilton near Wal-Mart's headquarters, I was stunned to see, like a mirage, a huge Japanese steak house–sushi restaurant right next door. When I remarked to the desk clerk who was checking me in that I never expected to get my sushi fix in Bentonville, he told me, "We've got three more Japanese restaurants opening up soon."

Multiple Japanese restaurants in Bentonville?

The demand for sushi in Arkansas is not an accident. It has to do with the fact that all around Wal-Mart's offices, vendors have set up their own operations to be close to the mother ship. Indeed, the area is known as "Vendorville." The amazing thing about Wal-Mart's headquarters is that it is so, well, Wal-Mart. The corporate offices are crammed into a reconfigured warehouse. As we passed a large building made of corrugated metal, I figured it was the maintenance shed. "Those are our international offices," said my host, spokesman William Wertz. The corporate suites are housed in offices that are one notch below those of the principal, vice principal, and head counselor at my daughter's public junior high school — *before it was remodeled.* When you pass through the lobby, you see these little cubicles where potential suppliers are pitching their products to Wal-Mart buyers. One has sewing machines all over the table, another has dolls, another has women's shirts. It feels like a cross between Sam's Club and the covered bazaar of Damascus. Attention Wal-Mart shareholders: The company is definitely not wasting your money on frills.

But how did so much innovative thinking — thinking that has reshaped the world's business landscape in many ways — come out of such a Li'l Abner backwater? It is actually a classic example of a phenomenon I point to often in this book: the coefficient of flatness. The fewer natural resources your country or company has, the more you will dig inside yourself for innovations in order to survive. Wal-Mart became the biggest retailer in the world because it drove a hard bargain with everyone it came in contact with. But make no mistake about one thing: Wal-Mart also became number one because this little hick company from northwest Arkansas was smarter and faster about adopting new technology than any of its competitors. And it still is.

David Glass, the company's CEO from 1988 to 2000, oversaw many of the innovations that made Wal-Mart the biggest and most profitable retailer on the planet. *Fortune* magazine once dubbed him "the most underrated CEO ever" for the quiet way he built on Sam Walton's vision. David Glass is to supply-chaining what Bill Gates is to word processing. When Wal-Mart was just getting started in northern Arkansas in the 1960s, explained Glass, it wanted to be a discounter. But in those days, every five-and-dime got its goods from the same wholesalers, so there was no way to get an edge on your competitors. The only way Wal-Mart could see to get an edge, he said, was for it to buy its goods in volume *directly from the manufacturers*. But it wasn't efficient for manufacturers to ship to multiple Wal-Mart stores spread all over, so Wal-Mart set up a distribution center to which all the manufacturers could ship their merchandise, and then Wal-Mart got its own trucks to distribute these goods itself to its stores. The math worked like this: It cost roughly 3 percent more on average for Wal-Mart to maintain its own distribution center. But it turned out, said Glass, that cutting out the wholesalers and buying direct from the manufacturers saved on average 5 percent, so that allowed Wal-Mart to cut costs on average 2 percent and then make it up on volume.

Once it established that basic method of buying directly from manufacturers to get the deepest discounts possible, Wal-Mart focused relentlessly on three things. The first was working with the manufacturers to get them to cut their costs as much as possible. The second was working on its supply chain from those manufacturers, wherever they were in the world, to Wal-Mart's distribution centers, to make it as low-cost and frictionless as possible. The third was constantly improving Wal-Mart's information systems, so it knew exactly what its customers were buying and could feed that information to all the manufacturers, so the shelves would always be stocked with the right items at the right time.

Wal-Mart quickly realized that if it could save money by buying directly from the manufacturers, by constantly innovating to cut the cost of running its supply chain, and by keeping its inventories low by learning more about its customers, it could beat its competitors on price every time. Sitting in Bentonville, Arkansas, it didn't have much choice.

"The reason we built all our own logistics and systems is because we are in the middle of nowhere," said Jay Allen, Wal-Mart's senior vice president of corporate affairs. "It really was a small town. If you wanted to go to a third party for logistics, it was impossible. It was pure survival. Now with all the attention we are getting there is an assumption that our low prices derive from our size or because we're getting stuff from China or being able to dictate to suppliers. The fact is the low prices are derived from efficiencies Wal-Mart has invested in — the system and the culture. It is a very low-cost culture." Added Glass, "I wish that I could say we were brilliant and visionary, [but] it was all born out of necessity."

The more that supply chain grew, the more Walton and Glass understood that scale and efficiency were the keys to their whole business. Put simply, the more scale and scope their supply chain had, the more things they sold for less to more customers, the more leverage they had with suppliers to drive prices down even more, the more they sold to more customers, the more scale and scope their supply chain had, the more profit they reaped for their shareholders . . .

Sam Walton was the father of that culture, but necessity was its mother, and its offspring has turned out to be a lean, mean supply-chain machine. In 2004, Wal-Mart purchased roughly $260 billion worth of merchandise and ran it through a supply chain consisting of 108 distribution centers around the United States, serving the some 3,000 Wal-Mart stores in America.

In the early years, "we were small — we were 4 or 5 percent of Sears and Kmart," said Glass. "If you are that small, you are vulnerable, so what we wanted to do more than anything else was grow market share. We had to undersell others. If I could reduce from 3 percent to 2 percent the cost of running my distribution centers, I could reduce retail prices and grow my market share and then not be vulnerable to anyone. So any efficiency we generated we passed on to the consumer."

For instance, after the manufacturers dropped off their goods at the Wal-Mart distribution center, Wal-Mart needed to deliver those goods in small bunches to each of its stores. It meant that Wal-Mart had trucks going all over America. Walton quickly realized if he connected his drivers by radios and satellites, after they dropped off at a certain Wal-Mart store, they could go a few miles down the road and pick up goods from a manufacturer so they wouldn't come back empty and so Wal-Mart could save the delivery charges from that manufacturer. A few pennies here, a few pennies there, and the result is more volume, scope, and scale.

In improving its supply chain, Wal-Mart leaves no link untouched. While I was touring the Wal-Mart distribution center in Bentonville, I noticed that some boxes were too big to go on the conveyor belts and were being moved around on pallets by Wal-Mart employees driving special minilift trucks with headphones on. A computer tracks how many pallets each employee is plucking every hour to put onto trucks for different stores, and a computerized voice tells each of them whether he is ahead of schedule or behind schedule. "You can choose whether you want your computer voice to be a man or a woman, and you can choose English or Spanish," explained Rollin Ford, Wal-Mart's executive vice president, who oversees the supply chain and was giving me my tour.

A few years ago, these pallet drivers would get written instructions for where to pluck a certain pallet and what truck to take it to, but Wal-Mart discovered that by giving them headphones with a soothing computer voice to instruct them, drivers could use both hands and not have to carry pieces of paper. And by having the voice constantly reminding them whether they were behind or ahead of expectations, "we got a boost in productivity," said Ford. It is a million tiny operational innovations like this that differentiate Wal-Mart's supply chain.

But the real breakthrough, said Glass, was when Wal-Mart realized that while it had to be a tough bargainer with its manufacturers on price, at the same time the two had to collaborate to create value for each other horizontally if Wal-Mart was going to keep driving down costs. Wal-Mart was one of the first companies to introduce computers to track store sales and inventory and was the first to develop a computerized network in order to share this information with suppliers. Wal-Mart's theory was that the more information everyone had about what customers were pulling off the shelves, the more efficient Wal-Mart's buying would be, the quicker its suppliers could adapt to changing market demand.

In 1983, Wal-Mart invested in point-of-sale terminals, which simultaneously rang up sales and tracked inventory deductions for rapid resupply. Four years later, it installed a large-scale satellite system linking all of the stores to company headquarters, giving Wal-Mart's central computer system real-time inventory data and paving the way for a supply chain greased by information and humming down to the last atom of efficiency. A major supplier can now tap into Wal-Mart's Retail Link private extranet system to see exactly how its products are selling and when it might need to up its production.

"Opening its sales and inventory databases to suppliers is what made Wal-Mart the powerhouse it is today, says Rena Granofsky, a senior partner at J. C. Williams Group Ltd., a Toronto-based retail consulting firm," in the 2002 *Computerworld* article on Wal-Mart. "While its competition guarded sales information, Wal-Mart approached its suppliers as if they were partners, not adversaries, says Granofsky. By implementing a collaborative planning, forecasting, and replenishment (CPFR) program, Wal-Mart began a just-in-time inventory program that reduced carrying costs for both the retailer and its suppliers. 'There's a lot less excess inventory in the supply chain because of it,' Granofsky says." Thanks to the efficiency of its supply chain alone, Wal-Mart's cost of goods is estimated to be 5 to 10 percent less than that of most of its competitors.

Now Wal-Mart, in its latest supply-chain innovation, has introduced RFID — radio frequency identification microchips, attached to each pallet and merchandise box that comes into Wal-Mart, to replace bar codes, which have to be scanned individually and can get ripped or soiled. In June 2003, Wal-Mart informed its top one hundred suppliers that by January 1, 2005, all pallets and boxes that they ship to Wal-Mart distribution centers have to come equipped with RFID tags. (According to the *RFID Journal*, "RFID is a generic term for technologies that use radio waves to automatically identify people or objects. There are several methods of identification, but the most common is to store a serial number that identifies a person or object, and perhaps other information, on a microchip that is attached to an antenna — the chip and the antenna together are called an RFID transponder or an RFID tag. The antenna enables the chip to transmit the identification information to a reader. The reader converts the radio waves reflected back from the RFID tag into digital information that can then be passed on to computers that can make use of it.") RFID will allow Wal-Mart to track any pallet or box at each stage in its supply chain and know exactly what product from which manufacturer is inside, with what expiration date. If a grocery item has to be stored at a certain temperature, the RFID tag will tell Wal-Mart when the temperature is too high or too low. Because each of these tags costs around 20¢, Wal-Mart is reserving them now for big boxes and pallets, not individual items. But this is clearly the wave of the future.

"When you have RFID," said Rollin Ford, the Wal-Mart logistics vice president, "you have more insights." You can tell even faster which stores sell more of which shampoo on Fridays and which ones on Sundays, and whether Hispanics prefer to shop more on Saturday nights rather than Mondays in the stores in their neighborhoods. "When all this information is fed into our demand models, we can become more efficient on when we produce [a product] and when we ship it and then put it on the trucks in exactly the right place inside the trucks so it can flow more efficiently," added Ford. "We used to have to count each piece, and scanning it at [the receiving end] was a bottleneck. Now [with RFID], we just scan the whole pallet under a bubble, and it says you have all thirty items you ordered and each box tells you, 'This is what I am and this is how I am feeling, this is what color I am, and am I in good shape' — so it makes receiving hugely easier." Procter & Gamble spokesperson Jeannie Tharrington talked to Salon.com (September 20, 2004) about Wal-Mart's move to RFID: "We see this as beneficial to the entire supply chain. Right now our out-of-stock levels are higher than we'd like and certainly higher than the consumer would like, and we think this technology can help us to keep the products on the shelf more often." RFID will also allow for quicker remixing of the supply chain in response to events.

During hurricanes, Wal-Mart officials told

me, Wal-Mart knows that people eat more things like Pop-Tarts — easy-to-store, non-perishable items — and that their stores also sell a lot of kids' games that don't require electricity and can substitute for TV. It also knows that when hurricanes are coming, people tend to drink more beer. So the minute Wal-Mart's meteorologists tell head-quarters a hurricane is bearing down on Florida, its supply chain automatically adjusts to a hurricane mix in the Florida stores — more beer early, more Pop-Tarts later.

Wal-Mart is constantly looking for new ways to collaborate with its customers. Lately, it has gone into banking. It found that in areas with large Hispanic populations, many people had no affiliation with a bank and were getting ripped off by check-cashing outlets. So Wal-Mart offered them payroll check cashing, money orders, money transfers, and even bill payment services for standard items like electricity bills — all for very small fees. Wal-Mart had an internal capability to do that for its own employees and simply turned it into an external business.

TOO MUCH OF A GOOD THING

Unfortunately for Wal-Mart, the same factors that drove its instinct for constant innovation — its isolation from the world, its need to dig inside itself, and its need to connect remote locations to a global supply chain — also got it in trouble. It is hard to exaggerate how isolated Bentonville, Arkansas, is from the currents of global debate on labor and human rights, and it is easy to see how this insular company, obsessed with lowering prices, could have gone over the edge in some of its practices.

Sam Walton bred not only a kind of ruthless quest for efficiency in improving Wal-Mart's supply chain but also a degree of ruthlessness period. I am talking about everything from Wal-Mart's recently exposed practice of locking overnight workers into its stores, to its allowing Wal-Mart's maintenance contractors to use illegal immigrants as janitors, to its role as defendant in the largest civil-rights class-action lawsuit in history, to its refusal to stock certain magazines — like *Playboy* — on its shelves, even in small towns where Wal-Mart is the only major store. This is all aside from the fact that some of Wal-Mart's biggest competitors complain that they have had to cut health-care benefits and create a lower wage tier to compete with Wal-Mart, which pays less and covers less than most big companies (more on this later). One can only hope that all the bad publicity Wal-Mart has received in the last few years will force it to understand that there is a fine line between a hyperefficient global supply chain that is helping people save money and improve their lives and one that has pursued cost cutting and profit margins to such a degree that whatever social benefits it is offering with one hand, it is taking away with the other.

Wal-Mart is the China of companies. It has so much leverage that it can grind down any supplier to the last halfpenny. And it is not at all hesitant about using its ability to play its foreign and domestic suppliers off against each other.

Some suppliers have found ways to flourish under the pressure and become better at what they do. If all of Wal-Mart's suppliers were being squeezed dry by Wal-Mart, Wal-Mart would have no suppliers. So obviously many of them are thriving as Wal-Mart's partners. But some no doubt have translated Wal-Mart's incessant price pressure into lower wages and benefits for their employees or watched as their business moved to China, whence Wal-Mart's supply chain pulled in $18 billion worth of goods in 2004 from five thousand Chinese suppliers. "If Wal-Mart were an individual economy, it would rank as China's eighth-biggest trading partner, ahead of Russia, Australia and Canada," Xu Jun, the spokesman for Wal-Mart China, told the

China Business Weekly (November 29, 2004).

The successor generation to Sam Walton's leadership seems to recognize that it has both an image and a reality to fix. How far Wal-Mart will adjust remains to be seen. But when I asked Wal-Mart's CEO, H. Lee Scott Jr., directly about all these issues, he did not duck. In fact, he wanted to talk about it. "What I think I have to do is institutionalize this sense of obligation to society to the same extent that we have institutionalized the commitment to the customer," said Scott. "The world has changed and we have missed that. We believed that good intentions and good stores and good prices would cause people to forgive what we are not as good at, and we were wrong." In certain areas, he added, "we are not as good as we should be. We just have to get better."

One trend that Wal-Mart insists it is not responsible for is the offshoring of manufacturing. "We are much better off if we can buy merchandise made in the United States," said Glass. "I spent two years going around this country trying to talk people into manufacturing here. We would pay more to buy it here because the manufacturing facilities in those towns [would create jobs for] all those people who shopped in our stores. Sanyo had a plant here [in Arkansas] making television sets for Sears, and Sears cut them off, so they decided they were closing the plant and going to move part to Mexico and part to Asia. Our governor asked if we would help. We decided we would buy television sets from Sanyo [if they would keep the plant in Arkansas], and they didn't want to do it. They wanted to move it, and [the governor] even talked to the [Japanese owning] family to try to persuade them to stay. Between his efforts and ours, we persuaded them to do it. They are now the world's largest producer of televisions. We just bought our fifty millionth set from them. But for the most part people in this country have just abandoned the manufacturing process. They say, 'I want to sell to you, but I don't want the responsibility for the buildings and employees [and health care]. I want to source it somewhere else.' So we were forced to source merchandise in other places in the world." He added, "One of my concerns is that, with the manufacturing out of this country, one day we'll all be selling hamburgers to each other."

The best way to get a taste of Wal-Mart's power as a global flattener is to visit Japan.

Commodore Matthew Calbraith Perry opened a largely closed Japanese society to the Western world on July 8, 1853, when he arrived in Edo (Tokyo) Bay with four big black steamships bristling with guns. According to the Naval Historical Center Web site, the Japanese, not knowing that steamships even existed, were shocked by the sight of them and thought they were "giant dragons puffing smoke." Commodore Perry returned a year later, and on March 31, 1854, concluded the Treaty of Kanagawa with the Japanese authorities, gaining U.S. vessels access to the ports of Shimoda and Hakodate and opening a U.S. consulate in Shimoda. This treaty led to an explosion of trade between Japan and the United States, helped open Japan to the Western world generally, and is widely credited with triggering the modernization of the Japanese state, as the Japanese realized how far behind they were and rushed to catch up. And catch up they did. In so many areas, from automobiles to consumer electronics to machine tools, from the Sony Walkman to the Lexus, the Japanese learned every lesson they could from Western nations and then proceeded to beat us at our own game — except one: retailing, especially discount retailing. Japan could make those Sonys like nobody else, but when it came to selling them at a discount, well, that was another matter.

So almost exactly 150 years after Commodore Perry signed that treaty, another lesser-known treaty was signed, actually a business partnership. Call it the Seiyu–Wal-Mart Treaty of 2003. Unlike Commodore Perry, Wal-Mart did not have to muscle its way into Japan with warships. Its reputation preceded it, which is why it was invited in by Seiyu, a struggling Japanese retail chain desperate to adapt the Wal-Mart formula in Japan, a country notorious for resisting big-box discount stores. As I traveled on the bullet train from Tokyo to Numazu, Japan, site of the first Seiyu store that was using the Wal-Mart methods, the *New York Times* translator pointed out that this store was located about one hundred miles from Shimoda and that first U.S. consulate. Commodore Perry probably would have loved shopping in the new Seiyu store, where all the music piped in consists of Western tunes designed to lull shoppers into filling their carts, and where you can buy a man's suit — made in China — for $65 and a white shirt to go with it for $5. That's what they call around Wal-Mart EDLP — Every Day Low Prices — and it was one of the first phrases Wal-Mart folks learned to say in Japanese.

Wal-Mart's flattening effects are fully on display in the Seiyu store in Numazu — not just the everyday low prices, but the wide aisles, the big pallets of household goods, the huge signs displaying the lowest prices in each category, and the Wal-Mart supply-chain computer system so that store managers can quickly adjust stock.

I asked Seiyu's CEO, Masao Kiuchi, why he had turned to Wal-Mart. "The first time I knew about Wal-Mart was about fifteen years ago," explained Kiuchi. "I went to Dallas to see the Wal-Mart stores, and I thought this was a very rational method. It was two things: One was the signage showing the prices. It was very easy for us to understand." The second, he said, was that the Japanese thought a discount store meant that you sold cheap products at cheap prices. What he realized from shopping at Wal-Mart, and seeing everything from plasma TVs to top-brand pet products, was that Wal-Mart sold quality products at low prices.

"At the store in Dallas, I took pictures, and I brought those pictures to my colleagues in Seiyu and said, 'Look, we have to see what Wal-Mart is doing on the other side of the planet.' But showing pictures was not good enough, because how can you understand by just looking at pictures?" recalled Kiuchi. Eventually, Kiuchi approached Wal-Mart, and they signed a partnership on December 31, 2003. Wal-Mart bought a piece of Seiyu; in return, Wal-Mart agreed to teach Seiyu its unique form of collaboration: global supply-chaining to bring consumers the best goods at the lowest prices.

There was one big thing, though, that Seiyu had to teach Wal-Mart, Kiuchi told me: how to sell raw fish. Japanese discounters and department stores all have grocery sections, and they all carry fish for very discriminating Japanese consumers. Seiyu will discount fish several times during each day, as the freshness declines.

"Wal-Mart doesn't understand raw fish," said Kiuchi. "We are expecting their help with general merchandising."

Give Wal-Mart time. I expect that in the not-too-distant future we will see Wal-Mart sushi.

Somebody had better warn the tuna.

Flattener #8
Insourcing
What the Guys in Funny Brown Shorts Are Really Doing

One of the most enjoyable things about researching this book has been discovering all sorts of things happening in the world around me of which I had no clue. Nothing was more surprisingly interesting than pulling the curtain back on UPS, United Parcel Service. Yes, those folks, the ones who wear the homely brown shorts and drive those ugly brown trucks. Turns out that while I was sleeping, stodgy old UPS became a huge force flattening the world.

Once again, it was one of my Indian tutors, Nandan Nilekani, the Infosys CEO, who tipped me off to this. "FedEx and UPS should be one of your flatteners. They're not just delivering packages, they are doing logistics," he told me on the phone from Bangalore one day. Naturally, I filed the thought away, making a note to check it out, without having any clue what he was getting at. A few months later I went to China, and while there I was afflicted with jet lag one night and was watching CNN International to pass the wee hours of the morning. At one point, a commercial came on for UPS, and its tag line was UPS's new slogan: "Your World Synchronized."

The thought occurred to me: That must be what Nandan was talking about! UPS, I learned, was not just delivering packages anymore; it was synchronizing global supply chains for companies large and small. The next day I made an appointment to visit UPS headquarters in Atlanta. I later toured the UPS Worldport distribution hub adjacent to the Louisville International Airport, which at night is basically taken over by the UPS fleet of cargo jets, as packages are flown in from all over the world, sorted, and flown back out again a few hours later. (The UPS fleet of 270 aircraft is the eleventh largest airline in the world.) What I discovered on these visits was that this is not your father's UPS. Yes, UPS still pulls in most of its $36 billion in sales by shipping more than 13.5 million packages a day from point A to point B. But behind that innocuous façade, the company founded in Seattle in 1907 as a messenger service has reinvented itself as a dynamic supply-chain manager.

Consider this: If you own a Toshiba laptop computer that is under warranty and it breaks and you call Toshiba to have it repaired, Toshiba will tell you to drop it off at a UPS store and have it shipped to Toshiba, and it will get repaired and then be shipped back to you. But here's what they don't tell you: UPS doesn't just pick up and deliver your Toshiba laptop. UPS actually repairs the computer in its own UPS-run workshop dedicated to computer and printer repairs at its Louisville hub. I went to tour that hub expecting to see only packages moving around, and instead I found myself dressed in a blue smock, in a special clean room, watching UPS employees replacing motherboards in broken Toshiba laptops. Toshiba had developed an image problem several years ago, with some customers concluding that its repair process for broken machines took too long. So Toshiba came to UPS and asked it to design a better system. UPS said, "Look, instead of us picking up the machine from your customers, bringing it to our hub, then flying it from our hub to your repair facility and then flying it back to our hub and then from our hub to your customer's house, let's cut out all the middle steps. We, UPS, will pick it up, repair it ourselves, and send it right back to your customer." It is now possible to send your Toshiba laptop in one day, get it repaired the next, and have it back the third day. The UPS repairmen and -women were all certified by Toshiba, and its customer complaints went down dramatically.

But this is just a sliver of what UPS does today. Eaten a Papa John's pizza lately? If you see the branded Papa John's supply truck go by, ask who's dispatching the drivers and scheduling the pickups of supplies, like tomatoes, pizza sauce, and onions. Answer: UPS. UPS comes inside a lot of companies now and takes over their branded vehicles to assure on-time delivery, which in the case of Papa John's includes getting the pizza dough from bakeries to outlets at exactly the right times each day. Tired of shopping for tennis shoes at the mall? Go online and order a pair of Nikes from its Web site, Nike.com.

The order, though, is actually routed to UPS, and a UPS employee picks, inspects, packs, and delivers your shoes for Nike on-line from a warehouse in Kentucky managed by UPS. Ditto if you order some underwear from Jockey.com. UPS employees, who manage Jockey products at a UPS warehouse, will actually fill the order, bag it, label it, and deliver it to you. Your HP printer breaks in Europe or Latin America? The field service repairman who comes to your door to fix it works for UPS, which manages the replacement parts and repairs divisions for HP in those markets. Order some tropical fish from Segrest Farms in Florida to be delivered to your door in Canada by UPS? UPS worked with the company to develop a special packaging for the fish so they would not be injured as they traveled through UPS's sorting systems. The fish are even mildly sedated for safe travel (like kids on Dramamine). "We wanted them to have a pleasant ride," said UPS spokesman Steve Holmes.

What is going on here? It's a process that has come to be called "insourcing" — a whole new form of collaboration and creating value horizontally, made possible by the flat world and flattening it even more. In the previous section I discussed why supply-chaining is so important in the flat world. But not every company, indeed very few companies, can afford to develop and support a complex global supply chain of the scale and scope that Wal-Mart has developed. That is what gave birth to insourcing. Insourcing came about because once the world went flat, the small could act big — small companies could suddenly see around the world. Once they did, they saw a lot of places where they could sell their goods, manufacture their goods, or buy their raw materials in a more efficient manner. But many of them either didn't know how to pull all this off or couldn't afford to manage a complex global supply chain on their own. Many big companies didn't want to manage this complexity, which they felt was not part of their core competency. Nike would rather spend its cash and energy designing better tennis shoes, not supply chains.

This created a whole new global business opportunity for traditional package delivery firms like UPS. In 1996, UPS went into the business of "synchronized commerce solutions." It has spent $1 billion since then to buy twenty-five different global logistics and freight-forwarding firms so that it could service virtually any supply chain from one corner of the flat earth to the other. The business took off right around 2000. I like the term "insourcing" because UPS engineers come right inside your company; analyze its manufacturing, packaging, and delivery processes; and then design, redesign, and manage your whole global supply chain. And, if necessary, they'll even finance parts of it, such as receivables and COD payments. There are companies today (many of them don't want their names mentioned) that never touch their own products anymore. UPS oversees the whole journey from factory to warehouse to customer to repair. It even collects the money from customers if need be. This form of deep collaboration, which involves a huge amount of trust and intimacy among UPS, its client, and its client's customers, is a uniquely new flattener.

"You know who the majority of our customers and partners are? Small businesses," said UPS chairman and CEO Mike Eskew. "That's right . . . They are asking us to take them global. We help these companies achieve parity with the bigger guys."

Indeed, when you are a small business or individual working at home, and you can plug into UPS and have it become your global supply-chain manager, you can pretend you are a lot bigger than you are. When the small can act big, it levels the competitive playing field even more. UPS bought Mail Boxes, Etc. (now "The UPS Store" in the United States) so that it could offer individuals and small businesses the power of its global supply-chain services. But UPS also helps the big to act small. When you are a huge conglomerate, like HP, and you can get packages delivered or goods repaired quickly anywhere in the world, you can act really small.

In addition, by making the delivery of goods and services around the world superefficient and superfast — and in huge volumes — UPS is helping to level customs barriers and harmonize trade by getting more and more people to adopt the same rules and labels and tracking systems for transporting goods. UPS has a smart label on all its packages so that package can be tracked and traced anywhere in its network.

Working with the U.S. Customs Service, UPS designed a software program that allows customs to say to UPS, "I want to see any package moving through your Worldport hub that was sent from Cali, Colombia, to Miami by someone named Carlos." Or, "I want to see any package sent from Germany to the United States by someone named Osama." When the package arrives for sorting, the UPS computers will then automatically route that package to a customs officer in the UPS hub. A computerized arm will literally slide it off the conveyor belt and dump it into a bin for a closer look. It makes the inspection process more efficient and does not interrupt the general flow of packages. These efficiencies of time and scale save UPS's clients money, enabling them to recycle their capital and fund more innovation. But the level of collaboration it requires between UPS and its clients is unusual.

Plow & Hearth is a large national catalog and Internet retailer specializing in "Products for Country Living." P&H came to UPS one day and said that too many of its furniture deliveries were coming to customers with a piece broken. Did UPS have any ideas? UPS sent its "package engineers" over and conducted a packaging seminar for the P&H procurement group. UPS also provided guidelines for them to use in the selection of their suppliers. The objective was to help P&H understand that its purchase decisions from its suppliers should be influenced not only by the quality of the products being offered but also by how those products were being packaged and delivered. UPS couldn't help its customer P&H without looking deep inside its business and then into its suppliers' businesses — what boxes and packing materials they were using. That is insourcing.

Consider the collaboration today among eBay sellers, UPS, PayPal, and eBay buyers. Say I offer to sell a golf club on eBay and you decide to buy it. I e-mail you a PayPal invoice, which has your name and mailing address on it. At the same time, eBay offers me an icon on its Web site to print out a UPS mailing label to you. When I print that mailing label on my own printer, it comes out with a UPS tracking bar code on it. At the same time, UPS, through its computer system, creates a tracking number that corresponds to that label, which automatically gets e-mailed to you — the person who bought my golf club — so you can track the package by yourself, online, on a regular basis and know exactly when it will reach you.

If UPS had not gone into this business, someone would have had to invent it. With so many more people working through horizontal global supply chains far from home, somebody had to fill in the inevitable holes and tighten the weak links. Said Kurt Kuehn, UPS's senior vice president for sales and marketing, "The Texas machine parts guy is worried that the customer in Malaysia is a credit risk. We step in as a trusted broker. If we have control of that package, we can collect funds subject to acceptance and eliminate letters of credit. Trust can be created through personal relations or through systems and controls. If you don't have trust, you can rely on a shipper who does not turn [your package] over until he is paid. We have more ability than a bank to manage this, because we have the package and the ongoing relationship with the customer as collateral, so we have two points of leverage."

More than sixty companies have moved operations closer to the UPS hub in Louisville since 1997, so they can make things and ship them straight from the hub, without having to warehouse them. But it is not just the little guys who benefit from the better logistics and more efficient supply chains that insourcing can provide. In 2001, Ford Motor Co. turned over its snarled and slow distribution network to UPS, allowing UPS to come deep inside Ford to figure out what its problems were and smooth out its supply chain.

"For years, the bane of most Ford dealers was the auto maker's Rube Goldberg–like system for getting cars from factory to showroom," *BusinessWeek* reported in its July 19, 2004, issue. "Cars could take as long as a month to arrive — that is, when they weren't lost along the way. And Ford Motor Co. was not always able to tell its dealers exactly what was coming, or even what was in inventory at the nearest rail yards. 'We'd lose track of whole trainloads of cars,' recalls Jerry Reynolds, owner of Prestige Ford in Garland, Tex. 'It was crazy.' " But after UPS got under Ford's hood, "UPS engineers . . . redesigned Ford's entire North American delivery network, streamlining every-thing from the route cars take from the factory to how they're processed at regional sorting hubs" — including pasting bar codes on the windshields of the 4 million cars coming out of Ford's U.S. plants so they could be tracked just like packages. As a result, UPS cut the time it takes autos to arrive at dealer lots by 40 percent, to ten days on average. *Business Week* reported: "That saves Ford millions in working capital each year and makes it easy for its 6,500 dealers to track down the models most in demand . . . 'It was the most amazing transformation I had ever seen,' marvels Reynolds. 'My last comment to UPS was: 'Can you get us spare parts like this?' "

UPS maintains a think tank, the Operations Research Division, in Timonium, Maryland, which works on supply-chain algorithms. This "school" of mathematics is called "package flow technology," and it is designed to constantly match the deployment of UPS trucks, ships, airplanes, and sorting capabilities with that day's flow of packages around the world. "Now we can make changes in our network in hours to adjust to changes in volume," says UPS CEO Eskew. "How I optimize the total supply chain is the key to the math." The sixty-person UPS team in Timonium is made up largely of people with engineering and math degrees, including several Ph.D.'s.

UPS also employs its own meteorologists and strategic threat analysts to track which atmospheric or geopolitical thunderstorms it will have to work around on any given day. To further grease its supply chains, UPS is the largest private user of wireless technology in the world, as its drivers alone make over 1 million phone calls a day in the process of picking up and delivering packages through its eighty-eight thousand package cars, vans, tractors, and motorcycles. On any given day, according to UPS, 2 percent of the world's GDP can be found in UPS delivery trucks or package cars. Oh, and did I mention that UPS also has a financing arm — UPS Capital — that will put up the money for the transformation of your supply chain, particularly if you are a small business and don't have the capital.

For example, notes Eskew, UPS was doing business with a small biotech company in Canada that sold blood adhesives, a highly perishable alternative to stitches. The company had a growing market among the major hospital chains, but it had a problem keeping up with demand and could not get financing. It had distribution centers on the East and West coasts. UPS redesigned the company's system based around a refrigerator hub in Dallas and extended it financing through UPS Capital. The result, said Eskew, was less inventory, better cash flow, better customer service — and an embedded customer for UPS. A maker of bridal headpieces and veils in Montreal wanted to improve its flow of business with the U.S. Eskew recalled, "We designed a system for consolidated [customs] clearances, so their veils and headpieces would not have to come over [the border] one by one. And then we put [the merchandise] in a warehouse in [upstate] New York. We took the orders by Internet, we put the labels on, we delivered the packages and collected the money, and we put that money through UPS Capital into their banks electronically so they had the cash back. That allows them to enter new markets and minimize their inventory."

Eskew explained, "When our grandfathers owned shops, inventory was what was in the back room. Now it is a box two hours away on a package car, or it might be hundreds more crossing the country by rail or jet, and you have thousands more crossing the ocean. And because we all have visibility into that supply chain, we can coordinate all those modes of transportation."

Indeed, as consumers have become more empowered to pull their own products via the Internet and customize them for themselves, UPS has found itself in the interesting position of being not only the company actually taking the orders but also, as the delivery service, the one handing the goods to the buyer at the front door. As a result, companies said, "Let's try to push as many differentiating things to the end of the supply chain, rather than the beginning." And because UPS was the last link in the supply chain before these goods were loaded onto planes, trains, and trucks, it took over many of these functions, creating a whole new business called End of Runway Services. The day I visited Louisville, two young UPS women were putting together Nikon cameras, with special memory cards and leather cases, which some store had offered as a weekend special. They were even putting them in special boxes just for that store. By taking over this function, UPS gives companies more options to customize products at the last minute.

UPS has also taken full advantage of the Netscape and work flow flatteners. Before 1995, all tracking and tracing of UPS packages for customers was done through a call center. You called a UPS 800 number and asked an operator where your package was. During the week before Christmas, UPS operators were fielding six hundred thousand calls on the peak days. Each one of those calls cost UPS $2.10 to handle. Then, through the 1990s, as more and more UPS customers became empowered and comfortable with the Internet, and as its own tracking and tracing system improved with advances in wireless technology, UPS invited its customers to track packages themselves over the Internet, at a cost to UPS of between 5¢ and 10¢ a query.

"So we dramatically reduced our service costs and increased service," said UPS vice president Ken Sternad, especially since UPS now pulls in 7 million tracking requests on an average day and a staggering 12 million on peak days. At the same time, its drivers also became more empowered with their DIADs — driver delivery information acquisition devices. These are the brown electronic clipboards that you always see the UPS drivers carrying around. The latest generation of them tells each driver where in his truck to load each package — exactly what position on the shelf. It also tells him where his next stop is, and if he goes to the wrong address, the GPS system built into the DIAD won't allow him to deliver the package. It also allows Mom to go online and find out when the driver will be in her neighborhood dropping off her package.

Insourcing is distinct from supply-chaining because it goes well beyond supply-chain management. Because it is third-party-managed logistics, it requires a much more intimate and extensive kind of collaboration among UPS and its clients and its clients' clients. In many cases today, UPS and its employees are so deep inside their clients' infrastructure that it is almost impossible to determine where one stops and the other starts. The UPS people are not just synchronizing your packages — they are synchronizing your whole company and its interaction with both customers and suppliers.

"This is no longer a vendor-customer relationship," said Eskew. "We answer your phones, we talk to your customers, we house your inventory, and we tell you what sells and doesn't sell. We have access to your information and you have to trust us. We manage competitors, and the only way for this to work, as our founders told Gimbel's and Macy's, is 'trust us.' I won't violate that. Because we are asking people to let go of part of their business, and that really requires trust."

UPS is creating enabling platforms for anyone to take his or her business global or to vastly improve the efficiency of his or her global supply chain. It is a totally new business, but UPS is convinced it has an almost limitless upside. Time will tell. Though margins are still thin in this kind of work, in 2003 alone insourcing pulled in $2.4 billion in revenues for UPS. My gut tells me the folks in the funny brown shorts and funny brown trucks are on to something big — something made possible only by the flattening of the world and something that is going to flatten it a lot more.

Flattener #9
In-forming
Google, Yahoo!, MSN Web Search

My friend and I met a guy at a restaurant. My friend was very taken with him, but I was suspiciously curious about this guy. After a few minutes of Googling, I found out that he was arrested for felony assault. Although I was once again disappointed with the quality of the dating pool, I was at least able to warn my friend about this guy's violent past. — *Testimonial from Google user*

I am completely delighted with the translation service. My partner arranged for two laborers to come and help with some demolition. There was a miscommunication: she asked for the workers to come at 11 am, and the labor service sent them at 8:30. They speak only Spanish, and I speak English

and some French. Our Hispanic neighbors were out. With the help of the
translation service, I was able to communicate with the workers, to apologize
for the miscommunication, establish the
expectation, and ask them to come back
at 11. Thank you for providing this
connection . . . Thank you Google.

— Testimonial from Google user

I just want to thank Google for teaching
me how to find love. While looking for
my estranged brother, I stumbled across
a Mexican Web site for male strippers
— and I was shocked. My brother was
working as a male prostitute! The first
chance I got, I flew to the city he was
working in to liberate him from this de-
grading profession. I went to the club
he was working at and found my
brother. But more than that, I met one
of his co-workers . . . We got married
last weekend [in Mexico], and I am
positive without Google's services, I
never would have found my brother, my
husband, or the surprisingly lucrative
nature of the male stripping industry in
Mexico!! Thank you, Google!

— Testimonial from Google user

Google headquarters in Mountain View,
California, has a certain Epcot Center feel

to it — so many fun space age toys to play with, so little time. In one corner is a spinning globe that emits light beams based on the volume of people searching on Google. As you would expect, most of the shafts of light are shooting up from North America, Europe, Korea, Japan, and coastal China. The Middle East and Africa remain pretty dark. In another corner is a screen that shows a sample of what things people are searching for at that moment, all over the world. When I was there in 2001, I asked my hosts what had been the most frequent searches lately. One, of course, was "sex," a perennial favorite of Googlers. Another was "God." Lots of people searching for Him or Her. A third was "jobs" — you can't find enough of those. And the fourth most searched item around the time of my visit? I didn't know whether to laugh or cry: "professional wrestling." The weirdest one, though, is the Google recipe book, where people just open their refrigerators, see what ingredients are inside, type three of them into Google, and see what recipes come up!

Fortunately, no single word or subject accounts for more than 1 or 2 percent of all Google searches at any given time, so no one should get too worried about the fate of humanity on the basis of Google's top search items on any particular day. Indeed, it is the remarkable diversity of searches going on via Google, in so many different tongues, that makes the Google search engine (and search engines in general) such huge flatteners. Never before in the history of the planet have so many people — *on their own* — had the ability to find so much information about so many things and about so many other people.

Said Google cofounder Russian-born Sergey Brin, "If someone has broadband, dial-up, or access to an Internet café, whether a kid in Cambodia, the university professor, or me who runs this search engine, all have the same basic access to overall research information that anyone has. It is a total equalizer. This is very different than how I grew up. My best access was some library, and it did not have all that much stuff, and you either had to hope for a miracle or search for something very simple or something very recent." When Google came along, he added, suddenly that kid had "universal access" to the information in libraries all over the world.

That is certainly Google's goal — to make easily available all the world's knowledge in every language. And Google hopes that in time, with a PalmPilot or a cell phone, everyone everywhere will be able to carry around access to all the world's knowledge in their pockets. "Everything" and "everyone" are key words that you hear around Google all the time. Indeed, the official Google history carried on its home page notes that the name "Google" is a play on the word " 'googol,' which is the number represented by the numeral 1 followed by 100 zeros. Google's use of the term reflects the company's mission to organize the immense, seemingly infinite amount of information available on the Web," just for you. What Google's success reflects is how much people are interested in having just that — all the world's knowledge at their fingertips. There is no bigger flattener than the idea of making all the world's knowledge, or even just a big chunk of it, available to anyone and everyone, anytime, anywhere.

"We do discriminate only to the degree that if you can't use a computer or don't have access to one, you can't use Google, but other than that, if you can type, you can use Google," said Google CEO Eric Schmidt. And surely if the flattening of the world means anything, he added, it means that "there is no discrimination in accessing knowledge. Google is now searchable in one hundred languages, and every time we find another we increase it. Let's imagine a group with a Google iPod one day and you can tell it to search by voice — that would take care of people who can't use a computer — and then [Google access] just becomes about the rate at which we can get cheap devices into people's hands."

How does searching fit into the concept of collaboration? I call it "in-forming." In-forming is the individual's personal analog to open-sourcing, outsourcing, insourcing, supply-chaining, and offshoring. In-forming is the ability to build and deploy your own personal supply chain — a supply chain of information, knowledge, and entertainment. In-forming is about self-collaboration — becoming your own self-directed and self-empowered researcher, editor, and selector of entertainment, without having to go to the library or the movie theater or through network television. In-forming is searching for knowledge. It is about seeking like-minded people and communities. Google's phenomenal global popularity, which has spurred Yahoo! and Microsoft (through its new MSN Search) also to make power searching and in-forming prominent features of their Web sites, shows how hungry people are for this form of collaboration. Google is now processing roughly one billion searches per day, up from 150 million just three years ago.

The easier and more accurate searching becomes, added Larry Page, Google's other cofounder, the more global Google's user base becomes, and the more powerful a flattener it becomes. Every day more and more people are able to in-form themselves in their own language. Today, said Page, "only a third of our searches are U.S.-based, and less than half are in English." Moreover, he added, "as people are searching for more obscure things, people are publishing more obscure things," which drives the flattening effect of in-forming even more. All the major search engines have also recently added the capability for users to search not only the Web for information but also their own computer's hard drive for words or data or e-mail they know is in there somewhere but have forgotten where. When you can search your own memory more efficiently, that is really in-forming. In late 2004, Google announced plans to scan the entire contents of both the University of Michigan and Stanford University Libraries, making tens of thousands of books available and searchable online.

In the earliest days of search engines, people were amazed and delighted to stumble across the information they sought; eureka moments were unexpected surprises, said Yahoo!'s cofounder Jerry Yang. "Today their attitudes are much more presumptive. They presume that the information they're looking for is certainly available and that it's just a matter of technologists making it easier to get to, and in fewer keystrokes," he said. "The democratization of information is having a profound impact on society. Today's consumers are much more efficient — they can find information, products, services, faster [through search engines] than through traditional means. They are better informed about issues related to work, health, leisure, etc. Small towns are no longer disadvantaged relative to those with better access to information. And people have the ability to be better connected to things that interest them, to quickly and easily become experts in given subjects and to connect with others who share their interests."

Google's founders understood that by the late 1990s hundreds of thousands of Web pages were being added to the Internet each day, and that existing search engines, which tended to search for keywords, could not keep pace. Brin and Page, who met as Stanford University graduate students in computer science in 1995, developed a mathematical formula that ranked a Web page by how many other Web pages were linked to it, on the assumption that the more people linked to a certain page, the more important the page. The key breakthrough that enabled Google to become first among search engines was its ability to combine its PageRank technology with an analysis of page content, which determines which pages are most relevant to the specific search being conducted. Even though Google entered the market after other major search players, its answers were seen by people as more accurate and relevant to what they were looking for. The fact that one search engine was just a little better than the others led a tidal wave of people to switch to it. (Google now employs scores of mathematicians working on its search algorithms, in an effort to always keep them one step more relevant than the competition.)

For some reason, said Brin, "people underestimated the importance of finding information, as opposed to other things you would do online. If you are searching for something like a health issue, you really want to know; in some cases it is a life-and-death matter. We have people who search Google for heart-attack symptoms and then call nine-one-one." But sometimes you really want to in-form yourself about something much simpler.

When I was in Beijing in June 2004, I was riding the elevator down one morning with my wife, Ann, and sixteen-year-old daughter, Natalie, who was carrying a fistful of postcards written to her friends.

Ann said to her, "Did you bring their addresses along?" Natalie looked at her as if she were positively nineteenth-century. "No," she said, with that you-are-so-out-of-it-Mom tone of voice. "I just Googled their phone numbers, and their home addresses came up."

Address book? You dummy, Mom.

All that Natalie was doing was informing, using Google in a way that I had no idea was even possible. Meanwhile, though, she also had her iPod with her, which empowered her to in-form herself in another way — with entertainment instead of knowledge. She had become her own music editor and downloaded all her favorite songs into her iPod and was carrying them all over China. Think about it: For decades the broadcast industry was built around the idea that you shoot out ads on network television or radio and hope that someone is watching or listening. But thanks to the flattening technologies in entertainment, that world is quickly fading away. Now with TiVo you can become your own TV editor. TiVo allows viewers to digitally record their favorite programs and skip the ads, except those they want to see. You watch what you want when you want. You don't have to make an appointment with a TV channel at the time and place someone else sets and watch the commercials foisted on you. With TiVo you can watch only your own shows and the commercials you want for only those products in which you might be interested.

But just as Google can track what you are searching for, so too can TiVo, which knows which shows and which ads you are freezing, storing, and rewinding on your own TV. So here's a news quiz: Guess what was the most rewound moment in TV history? Answer: Janet Jackson's breast exposure, or, as it was euphemistically called, her "wardrobe malfunction," at the 2004 Super Bowl. Just ask TiVo. In a press release it issued on February 2, 2004, TiVo said, "Justin Timberlake and Janet Jackson stole the show during Sunday's Super Bowl, attracting almost twice as many viewers as the most thrilling moments on the field, according to an annual measurement of second-by-second viewership in TiVo households. The Jackson-Timberlake moment drew the biggest spike in audience reaction TiVo has ever measured. TiVo said viewership spiked up to 180 percent as hundreds of thousands of households used TiVo's unique capabilities to pause and replay live television to view the incident again and again."

So if everyone can increasingly watch what he wants however many times he wants when he wants, the whole notion of broadcast TV — which is that we throw shows out there one time, along with their commercials, and then try to survey who is watching — will increasingly make less and less sense. The companies you want to bet on are those that, like Google or Yahoo! or TiVo, learn to collaborate with their users and offer them shows and advertisements tailored just for them. I can imagine a day soon when advertisers won't pay for anything other than that.

Companies like Google, Yahoo!, Amazon.com, and TiVo have learned to thrive not by pushing products and services on their customers as much as by building collaborative systems that enable customers to pull on their own, and then responding with lightning quickness to what they pull. It is so much more efficient.

"Search is so highly personal that searching is empowering for humans like nothing else," said Google CEO Eric Schmidt. "It is the antithesis of being told or taught. It is about self-empowerment; it is empowering individuals to do what they think best with the information they want. It is very different from anything else that preceded it. Radio was one-to-many. TV was one-to-many. The telephone was one-to-one. Search is the ultimate expression of the power of the individual, using a computer, looking at the world, and finding exactly what they want — and everyone is different when it comes to that."

Of course what made Google not just a search engine but a hugely profitable business was its founders' realization that they could build a targeted advertising model that would show you ads that are relevant to you when you searched for a specific topic and then could charge advertisers for the number of times Google users clicked on their ads. Whereas CBS broadcasts a movie and has a less exact idea who is watching it or the advertisements, Google knows exactly what you are interested in — after all, you are searching for it — and can link you up with advertisers directly or indirectly connected to your searches. In late 2004, Google began a service whereby if you are walking around Bethesda, Maryland, and are in the mood for sushi, you just send Google an SMS message on your cell phone that says "Sushi 20817" — the Bethesda zip code — and it will send you back a text message of choices. Lord only knows where this will go.

In-forming, though, also involves searching for friends, allies, and collaborators. It is empowering the formation of global communities, across all international and cultural boundaries, which is another critically important flattening function. People can now search out fellow collaborators on any subject, project, or theme — particularly through portals like Yahoo! Groups. Yahoo! has about 300 million users and 4 million active groups. Those groups have 13 million unique individuals accessing them each month from all over the world.

"The Internet is growing in the self-services area, and Yahoo! Groups exemplifies this trend," said Jerry Yang. "It provides a forum, a platform, a set of tools for people to have private, semiprivate, or public gatherings on the Internet regardless of geography or time. It enables consumers to gather around topics that are meaningful to them in ways that are either impractical or impossible offline. Groups can serve as support groups for complete strangers who are galvanized by a common issue (coping with rare diseases, first-time parents, spouses of active-duty personnel) or who seek others who share similar interests (hobbies as esoteric as dogsledding, blackjack, and indoor tanning have large memberships). Existing communities can migrate online and flourish in an interactive environment (local kids' soccer league, church youth group, alumni organizations), providing a virtual home for groups interested in sharing, organizing, and communicating information valuable to cultivating vibrant communities. Some groups exist only online and could never be as successful offline, while others mirror strong real-world communities. Groups can be created instantaneously and dissolved; topics can change or stay constant. This trend will only grow as consumers increasingly become publishers, and they can seek the affinity and community *they* choose — when, where, and how they choose it."

There is another side to in-forming that people are going to have to get used to, and that is other people's ability to in-form themselves about you from a very early age. Search engines flatten the world by eliminating all the valleys and peaks, all the walls and rocks, that people used to hide inside of, atop, behind, or under in order to mask their reputations or parts of their past. In a flat world, you can't run, you can't hide, and smaller and smaller rocks are turned over. Live your life honestly, because whatever you do, whatever mistakes you make, will be searchable one day. The flatter the world becomes, the more ordinary people become transparent — and available. Before my daughter Orly went off to college in the fall of 2003, she was telling me about some of her roommates. When I asked her how she knew some of the things she knew — had she spoken to them or received an e-mail from them? — she told me she had done neither. She just

Googled them. She came up with stuff from high school newspapers, local papers, etc., and fortunately no police records. These are high school kids!

"In this world you better do it right — you don't get to pick up and move to the next town so easily," said Dov Seidman, who runs a legal compliance and business ethics consulting firm, LRN. "In the world of Google, your reputation will follow you and precede you on your next stop. It gets there before you do . . . Reputation starts early now. You don't get to spend four years getting drunk. Your reputation is getting set much earlier in life. 'Always tell the truth,' said Mark Twain, 'that way you won't have to remember what you said.' " So many more people can be private investigators into your life, and they can also share their findings with so many more people.

In the age of the superpower search, everyone is a celebrity. Google levels information — it has no class boundaries or education boundaries. "If I can operate Google, I can find anything," said Alan Cohen, vice president of Airespace, which sells wireless technology. "Google is like God. God is wireless, God is everywhere, and God sees everything. Any questions in the world, you ask Google."

Some months after Cohen made that observation to me, I came across the following brief business story on CNET News.com: "Search giant Google said on Wednesday that it has acquired Keyhole, a company specializing in Web-based software that allows people to view satellite images from around the globe . . . The software gives users the ability to zoom in from space level; in some cases, it can zoom in all the way to a street-level view. The company does not have high-resolution imagery for the entire globe, but its Website offers a list of cities that are available for more detailed viewing. The company has focused most on covering large metropolitan areas in the United States and is working to expand its coverage."

Flattener #10
The Steroids
Digital, Mobile, Personal, and Virtual

But this iPaq's real distinction is its wirelessness. It's the first palmtop that can connect to the Internet and other gadgets in four wireless ways. For distances up to 30 inches, the iPaq can beam information, like your electronic business card, to another palmtop using an infrared transmitter. For distances up to 30 feet, it has built-in Bluetooth cir-

cuitry . . . For distances up to 150 feet, it has a Wi-Fi antenna. And for transmissions around the entire planet, the iPaq has one other trick up its sleeve: it's also a cell phone. If your office can't reach you on this, then you must be on the International Space Station.
— *From a* New York Times *article about HP's new PocketPC, July 29, 2004*

I am on the bullet train speeding southwest from Tokyo to Mishima. The view is spectacular: fishing villages on my left and a snow-dusted Mt. Fuji on my right. My colleague Jim Brooke, the Tokyo bureau chief for *The New York Times,* is sitting across the aisle and paying no attention to the view. He is engrossed in his computer. So am I, actually, but he's online through a wireless connection, and I'm just typing away on a column on my unconnected laptop. Ever since we took a cab together the other day in downtown Tokyo and Jim whipped out his wireless-enabled laptop in the backseat and e-mailed me something through Yahoo!, I have been exclaiming at the amazing degree of wireless penetration and connectivity in Japan. Save for a few remote islands and mountain villages, if you have a wireless card in your computer, or any Japanese cell phone, you can get online anywhere — from deep inside the subway stations to the bullet trains speeding through the countryside. Jim knows I am slightly obsessed with the fact that Japan, not to mention most of the rest of the world, has so much better wireless connectivity than America. Anyway, Jim likes to rub it in.

"See, Tom, I am online right now," he says, as the Japanese countryside whizzes by. "A friend of mine who's the *Times*'s stringer in Alma Ata just had a baby and I am congratulating him. He had a baby girl last night." Jim keeps giving me updates. "Now I'm reading the frontings!" — a summary of the day's *New York Times* headlines. Finally, I ask Jim, who is fluent in Japanese, to ask the train conductor to come over. He ambles by. I ask Jim to ask the conductor how fast we are going. They rattle back and forth in Japanese for a few seconds before Jim translates: "240 kilometers per hour." I shake my head. We are on a bullet train going 240 km per hour — that's 150 mph — and my colleague is answering e-mail from Kazakhstan, and I can't drive from my home in suburban Washington to downtown DC without my cell phone service being interrupted at least twice. The day before, I was in Tokyo waiting for an appointment with Jim's colleague Todd Zaun, and he was preoccupied with his Japanese cell phone, which easily connects to the Internet from anywhere. "I am a surfer," Todd explained, as he used his thumb to manipulate the keypad. "For $3 a month I subscribe to this [Japanese] site that tells me each morning how high the waves are at the beaches near my house. I check it out, and I decide where the best place to surf is that day."

(The more I thought about this, the more I wanted to run for president on a one-issue ticket: "I promise, if elected, that within four years America will have as good a cell phone coverage as Ghana, and in eight years as good as Japan — provided that the Japanese sign a standstill agreement and won't innovate for eight years so we can catch up." My campaign bumper sticker will be very simple: "Can You Hear Me Now?")

I know that America will catch up sooner or later with the rest of the world in wireless technology. It's already happening. But this section about the tenth flattener is not just about wireless. It is about what I call "the steroids." I call certain new technologies the steroids because they are amplifying and turbocharging all the other flatteners. They are taking all the forms of collaboration highlighted in this section — outsourcing, offshoring, open-sourcing, supply-chaining, insourcing, and informing — and making it possible to do each and every one of them in a way that is "digital, mobile, virtual, and personal," as former HP CEO Carly Fiorina put it in her speeches, thereby enhancing each one and making the world flatter by the day.

By "digital," Fiorina means that thanks to the PC–Windows–Netscape–work flow revolutions, all analog content and processes — everything from photography to entertainment to communication to word processing to architectural design to the management of my home lawn sprinkler system — are being digitized and therefore can be shaped, manipulated, and transmitted over computers, the Internet, satellites, or fiber-optic cable. By "virtual," she means that the process of shaping, manipulating, and transmitting this digitized content can be done at very high speeds, with total ease, so that you never have to think about it — thanks to all the underlying digital pipes, protocols, and standards that have now been installed. By "mobile," she means that thanks to wireless technology, all this can be done from anywhere, with anyone, through any device, and can be taken anywhere. And by "personal," she means that it can be done by you, just for you, on your own device.

What does the flat world look like when you take all these new forms of collaboration and turbocharge them in this way? Let me give just one example. Bill Brody, the president of Johns Hopkins, told me this story in the summer of 2004: "I am sitting in a medical meeting in Vail and the [doctor] giving a lecture quotes a study from Johns Hopkins University. And the guy speaking is touting a new approach to treating prostate cancer that went against the grain of the current surgical method. It was a minimally invasive approach to prostate cancer. So he quotes a study by Dr. Patrick Walsh, who had developed the state-of-the-art standard of care for prostate surgery. This guy who is speaking proposes an alternate method — which was controversial — but he quotes from Walsh's Hopkins study in a way that supported his approach. When he said that, I said to myself, 'That doesn't sound like Dr. Walsh's study.' So I had a PDA [personal digital assistant], and I immediately went online [wirelessly] and got into the Johns Hopkins portal and into Medline and did a search right while I was sitting there. Up come all the Walsh abstracts. I toggled on one and read it, and it was not at all what the guy was saying it was. So I raised my hand during the Q and A and read two lines from the abstract, and the guy just turned beet red."

The digitization and storage of all the Johns Hopkins faculty research in recent years made it possible for Brody to search it instantly and virtually without giving it a second thought. The advances in wireless technology made it possible for him to do that search from anywhere with any device. And his handheld personal computer enabled him to do that search personally — by himself, just for himself.

What are the steroids that made all this possible?

One simple way to think about computing, at any scale, is that it is comprised of three things: computational capability, storage capability, and input/output capability — the speed by which information is drawn in and out of the computer/storage complexes. And all of these have been steadily increasing since the days of the first bulky mainframes. This mutually reinforcing progress constitutes a significant steroid. As a result of it, year after year we have been able to digitize, shape, crunch, and transmit more words, music, data, and entertainment than ever before.

For instance, MIPS stands for "millions of instructions per second," and it is one measure of the computational capability of a computer's microchips. In 1971, the Intel 4004 microprocessor produced .06 MIPS, or 60,000 instructions per second. Today's Intel Pentium 4 Extreme Edition has a theoretical maximum of 10.8 billion instructions per second. In 1971, the Intel 4004 microprocessor contained 2,300 transistors. Today's Itanium 2 packs 410 million transistors. Meanwhile, inputting and outputting data have leaped ahead at a staggering rate. At the speeds that disk drives operated back in the early days of 286 and 386 chips, it would have taken about a minute to download a single photo from my latest digital camera. Today I can do that in less than a second on a USB 2.0 disk drive and a Pentium processor. The amount of stuff you can now store to input and output "is off the charts, thanks to the steady advances in storage devices," said Craig Mundie, Microsoft's chief technology officer. "Storage is growing exponentially, and this is really as much a factor in the revolution as anything else." It's what is allowing all forms of content to become digital and to some extent portable. It is also becoming cheap enough that you can put massive amounts on even the personal devices people carry around with them. Five years ago, no one would have believed that you would be able to sell iPods with 40 gigabytes of storage, capable of holding thousands of songs, for prices that teenagers could afford. Now it's seen as ho-hum. And when it comes to moving all these bits around, the computing world has been turbocharged. Advances in fiber optics will soon allow a single fiber to carry 1 terabit per second. With 48 fibers in a cable, that's 48 terabits per second. Henry Schacht, the former CEO of Lucent, which specialized in this technology, pointed out that with that much capacity, you could "transmit all the printed material in the world in minutes in a single cable. This means unlimited transmitting capacity at zero incremental cost." Even though the speeds that Schacht was talking about apply only to the backbone of the fiber network, and not that last mile into your house and into your computer, we are still talking about a quantum leap forward.

In *The Lexus and the Olive Tree*, I wrote about a 1999 Qwest commercial showing a businessman, tired and dusty, checking in to a roadside motel in the middle of nowhere. He asks the bored-looking desk clerk whether they have room service and other amenities. She says yes. Then he asks her whether entertainment is available on his room television, and the clerk answers in a what-do-you-think-you-idiot monotone, "All rooms have every movie ever made in every language, anytime, day or night." I wrote about that back then as an example of what happens when you get connected to the Internet. Today it is an example of how much you can now get *disconnected* from the Internet, because in the next few years, as storage continues to advance and become more and more miniaturized, you will be able to buy enough storage to carry many of those movies around in your pocket.

Then add another hardware steroid to the mix: file sharing. It started with Napster paving the way for two of us to share songs stored on each other's computers. "At its peak," according to Howstuffworks.com, "Napster was perhaps the most popular Website ever created. In less than a year, it went from zero to 60 million visitors per month. Then it was shut down by a court order because of copyright violations, and wouldn't re-launch until 2003 as a legal music-download site. The original Napster became so popular so quickly because it offered a unique product — free music that you could obtain nearly effortlessly from a gigantic database." That database was actually a file-sharing architecture by which Napster facilitated a connection ·between my computer and yours so that we could swap music files. The original Napster is dead, but file-sharing technology is still around and is getting more sophisticated every day, greatly enhancing collaboration.

Finally, add one last hardware steroid that brings these technology breakthroughs together for consumers: the steady breakthrough in multipurpose devices — ever smaller and more powerful laptops, cell phones, and handheld personal organizers that can keep your appointments, make calls, send e-mail, take pictures, and even serve as video cameras.

Collaborating with all this digitized data is going to be made even easier and cheaper thanks to another burgeoning steroid — voice over Internet protocol service, known as VoIP. VoIP allows you to make phone calls over the Internet by turning voices into data packets that are sent down Internet networks and converted back into voices on the other end. VoIP allows anyone who subscribes to the service through his phone company or private operator to receive unlimited local and long-distance phone calls, via the Internet, over his personal computer, laptop, or PDA — with just a small microphone attachment. It is personal and it will be delivered virtually — the underlying pipes will make it happen without your having to think about it at all. It will make every business and personal phone call to anywhere in the world as cheap as a local call — i.e., almost free. If that won't amplify every form of collaboration, I don't know what will.

Consider this item from the November 1, 2004, *BusinessWeek*, about the pioneering VoIP company Skype: "Eriksen Translations Inc. is a small business with a big footprint. The Brooklyn (N.Y.) company relies on 5,000 freelancers scattered around the world to help translate business documents in 75 languages for U.S. clients. That means phone bills of about $1,000 a month. So when business development manager Claudia Waitman heard about a new company called Skype Technologies that offers free voice calls over the Internet to other Skype users anywhere in the world, she jumped. Six months after signing up, Eriksen's phone costs already have fallen 10 percent. Even better, its employees and freelancers confer more often, allowing them to work faster and more efficiently. 'It has changed the whole way we work,' Waitman says."

VoIP is going to revolutionize the telecommunications industry, which, since its inception, has been based on the simple notion that companies charge you for how long you talk and over what distance. As consumers get more VoIP choices, the competition will be such that telecom companies won't be able to charge for time and distance much longer. Voice will become free. What phone companies will compete over, and charge for, will be the add-ons. The old voice platform did not lend itself well to innovation. But when you put voice on an Internet platform, all sorts of innovative options for collaboration become possible. You will have a buddy list of people and all you will have to do is double-click on a name and the call will go through. You want caller ID? The caller's picture will come up on your screen. Companies will compete over SoIP (services over the Internet protocol): who can offer you the best videoconferencing while you are talking over your computer, PDA or laptop; who can enable you to talk to someone while easily inviting a third or fourth person into the conversation; who can enable you to talk and swap document files and send text messages at the same time, so you can actually speak and work on a document together while talking. You will be able to leave someone a voice message that can be converted to text, along with a document attachment that the two of you may be working on. Said Mike Volpi, Cisco's senior vice president for routing technology, "It won't be about distance and how long you talk, but how you create value around voice communication. The voice will be free; it's what you enable customers to do around it that will differentiate companies."

People who live in Bangalore or Beijing will be able to get themselves listed in the Yellow Pages in New York. Looking for an accountant? Just double-click Hang Zhou in Beijing or Vladimir Tolstoy in Moscow or Ernst & Young in New York. Take your choice for accounting: Tiananmen Square, Red Square, or Union Square. They'll be happy to collaborate with you in filling out your tax returns.

There is another steroid, related to VoIP, which will turbocharge this turbocharger: the breakthrough improvements in videoconferencing. HP and the film company DreamWorks SKG collaborated on the design of a videoconferencing suite — with DreamWorks bringing its movie and sound expertise and HP contributing its computing and compression technology — that is breathtaking. Each party to the videoconference sits at a long table facing a wall of flat-panel TV screens and cameras pointed at them. The flat-panel screens display the people at the other site, which could be anywhere in the world. It creates an effect of everyone sitting around a single conference table and is apparently a qualitatively different experience from anything that has been on the market before. I had a chance to participate in a demonstration of it, and it was so realistic that you could practically feel the breath of the other parties to the videoconference, when in fact half of us were in Santa Barbara and half were five hundred miles away. Because DreamWorks is doing film and animation work all over the world, it felt that it had to have a videoconferencing solution where its creative people could really communicate all their thoughts, facial expressions, feelings, ire, enthusiasm, and raised eyebrows. HP's chief strategy and technology officer, Shane Robison, told me that HP plans to have these videoconferencing suites for sale by 2005 at a cost of roughly $250,000 each. That is nothing compared to the airline tickets and wear and tear on executives having to travel regularly to London or Tokyo for face-to-face meetings. Companies could easily make one of these suites pay for itself in a year. This level of videoconferencing, once it proliferates, will make remote development, outsourcing, and offshoring that much easier and more efficient.

And now the icing on the cake, the übersteroid that makes it all mobile: wireless. Wireless is what will allow you take everything that has been digitized, made virtual and personal, and do it from anywhere.

"The natural state of communications is wireless," argued Alan Cohen, the senior vice president at Airespace. It started with voice, because people wanted to be able to make a phone call anytime, from anyplace, to anywhere. That is why for many people the cell phone is the most important phone they own. By the early twenty-first century, people began to develop that same expectation and with it the desire for data communication — the ability to access the Internet, e-mail, or any business files anytime, anywhere, using a cell phone, PalmPilot, or some other personal device. (And now a third element is entering the picture, creating more demand for wireless technology and enhancing the flattening of the earth: machines talking to machines wirelessly, such as Wal-Mart's RFID chips, little wireless devices that automatically transmit information to suppliers' computers, allowing them to track inventory.)

In the early days of computing (Globalization 2.0), you worked in the office. There was a big mainframe computer, and you literally had to walk over and get the people running the mainframe to extract or input information for you. It was like an oracle. Then, thanks to the PC and the Internet, e-mail, the laptop, the browser, and the client server, I could access from my own screen all sorts of data and information being stored on the network. In this era you were delinked from the office and could work at home, at the beach house, or in a hotel. Now we are in Globalization 3.0, where, thanks to digitization, miniaturization, virtualization, personalization, and wireless, I can be processing, collecting, or transmitting voice or data from anywhere to anywhere — as an individual or as a machine.

"Your desk goes with you everywhere you are now," said Cohen. And the more people have the ability to push and pull information from anywhere to anywhere faster, the more barriers to competition and communication disappear. All of a sudden, my business has phenomenal distribution. I don't care whether you are in Bangalore or Bangor, I can get to you and you can get to me. More and more, people now want and expect wireless mobility to be there, just like electricity. We are rapidly moving into the age of the "mobile me," said Padmasree Warrior, the chief technology officer of Motorola. If consumers are paying for any form of content, whether it is information, entertainment, data, games, or stock quotes, they increasingly want to be able to access it anytime, anywhere.

Right now consumers are caught in a maze of wireless technology offerings and standards that are still not totally interoperable. As we all know, some wireless technology works in one neighborhood, state, or country and not in another.

The "mobile me" revolution will be complete when you can move seamlessly around the town, the country, or the world with whatever device you want. The technology is getting there. When this is fully diffused, the "mobile me" will have its full flattening effect, by freeing people to truly be able to work and communicate from anywhere to anywhere with anything.

I got a taste of what is coming by spending a morning at the Tokyo headquarters of NTT DoCoMo, the Japanese cellular giant that is at the cutting edge of this process and far ahead of America in offering total interoperability inside Japan. DoCoMo is an abbreviation for Do Communications Over the Mobile Network; it also means "anywhere" in Japanese. My day at DoCoMo's headquarters started with a tour conducted by a robot, which bowed in perfect Japanese fashion and then gave me a spin around DoCoMo's showroom, which now features handheld video cell phones so you can see the person you are speaking with.

"Young people are using our mobile phones today as two-way videophones," explained Tamon Mitsuishi, senior VP of the Ubiquitous Business Department at DoCoMo. "Everyone takes out their phones, they start dialing each other and have visual conversations. Of course there are some people who prefer not to see each other's faces." Thanks to DoCoMo technology, if you don't want to show your face you can substitute a cartoon character for yourself and manipulate the keyboard so that it not only will speak for you but also will get angry for you and get happy for you. "So this is a mobile phone, and video camera, but it has also evolved to the extent that it has functions similar to a PC," he added. "You need to move your buttons quickly [with your thumb]. We call ourselves 'the thumb people.' Young girls in high school can now move their thumbs faster than they can type on a PC."

By the way, I asked, what does the "Ubiquitous Department" do?

"Now that we have seen the spread of the Internet around the world," answered Mitsuishi, "what we believe we have to offer is the next step. Internet communication until today has been mostly between individuals — e-mail and other information. But what we are already starting to see is communication between individuals and machines and between machines. We are moving into that kind of phenomenon, because people want to lead a richer lifestyle, and businesses want more efficient practices . . . So young people in their business life use PCs in the offices, but in their private time they base their lifestyles on a mobile phone. There is now a growing movement to allow payment by mobile phone. [With] a smart card you will be able to make payments in virtual shops and smart shops. So next to the cash register there will be a reader of the card, and you just scan your phone and it becomes your credit card too . . .

"We believe that the mobile phone will become the essential controller of a person's life," added Mitsuishi, oblivious of the double meaning of the English word "control." "For example, in the medical field it will be your authentication system and you can examine your medical records, and to make payments you will have to hold a mobile phone. You will not be able to lead a life without a mobile phone, and it will control things at home too. We believe that we need to expand the range of machines that can be controlled by mobile phone."

There is plenty to worry about in this future, from kids being lured by online sexual predators through their cell phones, to employees spending too much time playing mindless phone games, to people using their phone cameras for all sorts of illicit activities. Some Japanese were going into bookstores, pulling down cookbooks, and taking pictures of the recipes and then walking out. Fortunately, camera phones are now being enabled to make a noise when they shoot a picture, so that a store owner, or the person standing next to you in the locker room, will know if he is on *Candid Camera*. Because your Internet-enabled camera phone is not just a camera; it is also a copy machine, with worldwide distribution potential.

DoCoMo is now working with other Japanese companies on an arrangement by which you may be walking down the street and see a poster of a concert by Madonna in Tokyo. The poster will have a bar code and you can buy your tickets by just scanning the bar code. Another poster might be for a new Madonna CD. Just scan the bar code with your cell phone and it will give you a sample of the songs. If you like them, scan it again and you can buy the whole album and have it home-delivered. No wonder my *New York Times* colleague in Japan, Todd Zaun, who is married to a Japanese woman, remarked to me that there is so much information the Japanese can now access from their Internet-enabled wireless phones that "when I am with my Japanese relatives and someone has a question, the first thing they do is reach for the phone."

I'm exhausted just writing about all this. But it is hard to exaggerate how much this tenth flattener — the steroids — is going to amplify and further empower all the other forms of collaboration. These steroids should make open-source innovation that much more open, because they will enable more individuals to collaborate with one another in more ways and from more places than ever before. They will enhance outsourcing, because they will make it so much easier for a single department of any company to collaborate with another company. They will enhance supply-chaining, because headquarters will be able to be connected in real time with every individual employee stocking the shelves, every individual package, and every Chinese factory manufacturing the stuff inside them. They will enhance insourcing — having a company like UPS come deep inside a retailer and manage its whole supply chain, using drivers who can interact with its warehouses, and with every customer, carrying his own PDA. And most obviously, they will enhance in-forming — the ability to manage your own knowledge supply chain.

Sir John Rose, the chief executive of Rolls-Royce, gave me a wonderful example of how wireless and other steroids are enhancing Rolls-Royce's ability to do work flow and other new forms of collaboration with its customers. Let's say you are British Airways and you are flying a Boeing 777 across the Atlantic. Somewhere over Greenland, one of your Rolls-Royce engines gets hit with lightning. The passengers and pilots might be worried, but there is no need. Rolls-Royce is on the case. That Rolls-Royce engine is connected by transponder to a satellite and is beaming data about its condition and performance, at all times, down into a computer in Rolls-Royce's operations room. That is true of many Rolls-Royce airplane engines in operation. Thanks to the artificial intelligence in the Rolls-Royce computer, based on complex algorithms, it can track anomalies in its engines while in operation. The artificial intelligence in the Rolls-Royce computer knows that this engine was probably hit by lightning, and feeds out a report to a Rolls-Royce engineer.

"With the real-time data we receive via satellites, we can identify an 'event' and our engineers can make remote diagnoses," said Rose. "Under normal circumstances, after an engine gets hit by lightning you would have to land the plane, call in an engineer, do a visual inspection, and make a decision about how much damage might have been done and whether the plane has to be delayed in order to do a repair.

"But remember, these airlines do not have much turnaround time. If this plane is delayed, you throw off the crews, you drop out of your position to fly back home. It gets very costly. We can monitor and analyze engine performance automatically in

311

real time, with our engineers making decisions about exactly what is needed by the time the plane has landed. And if we can determine by all the information we have about the engine that no intervention or even inspection is needed, the airplane can return on schedule, and that saves our customers time and money."

Engines talking to computers, talking to people, talking back to the engines, followed by people talking to people — all done from anywhere to anywhere. That is what happens when all the flatteners start to get turbocharged by all the steroids.

Can you hear me now?

THREE

The Triple Convergence

What is the triple convergence? In order to explain what I mean, let me tell a personal story and share one of my favorite television commercials.

The story took place in March 2004. I had made plans to fly from Baltimore to Hartford on Southwest Airlines to visit my daughter Orly, who goes to school in New Haven, Connecticut. Being a tech-savvy guy, I didn't bother with a paper ticket but ordered an e-ticket through American Express. As anyone who flies regularly on Southwest knows, the cheapo airline has no reserved seats. When you check in, your ticket says simply A, B, or C, with the As boarding first, the Bs boarding second, and the Cs boarding last. As veterans of Southwest also know, you do not want to be a C. If you are, you will almost certainly end up in a middle seat with no space to put your carry-ons in the overhead bin. If you want to sit in a window or aisle seat and be able to store your stuff, you want to be an A. Since I was carrying some bags of clothing for my daughter, I definitely wanted to be an A. So I got up early to make sure I got to the Baltimore airport ninety-five minutes before my scheduled departure. I walked up to the Southwest Airlines e-ticket machine, stuck in my credit card, and used the touch screen to get my ticket — a thoroughly modern man, right? Well, out came the ticket and it said B.

I was fuming. "How in the world could I be a B?" I said to myself, looking at my watch. "There is no way that many people got here before me. This thing is rigged! This is fixed! This is nothing more than a slot machine!"

I stomped off, went through security, bought a Cinnabon, and glumly sat at the back of the B line, waiting to be herded on board so I could hunt for space in the overhead bins. Forty minutes later, the flight was called. From the B line, I enviously watched all the As file on board ahead of me, with a certain barely detectable air of superiority. And then I saw it.

Many of the people in the A line didn't have normal e-tickets like mine. They were just carrying what looked to me like crumpled pieces of white printer paper, but they weren't blank. They had boarding passes and bar codes printed on them, as if the As had downloaded their boarding passes off the Internet at home and printed them out on their home printers. Which, I quickly learned, *was exactly what they had done.* I didn't know it, but Southwest had recently announced that beginning at 12:01 a.m. the night before a flight, you could download your ticket at home, print it out, and then just have the bar code scanned by the gate agent before you boarded.

"Friedman," I said to myself, looking at this scene, "you are so twentieth-century . . . You are so Globalization 2.0." In Globalization 1.0 there was a ticket agent. In Globalization 2.0 the e-ticket machine replaced the ticket agent. In Globalization 3.0 *you* are your own ticket agent.

The television commercial is from Konica Minolta Business Technologies for a new multipurpose device it sells called bizhub, a piece of office machinery that allows you to do black-and-white or color printing, copy a document, fax it, scan it, scan it to e-mail, or Internet-fax it — all from the same machine. The commercial begins with a rapid cutting back and forth between two guys, one in his office and the other standing at the bizhub machine. They are close enough to talk by raising their voices. Dom is senior in authority but slow on the uptake — the kind of guy who hasn't kept up with changing technology (my kind of guy!). He can see Ted standing at the bizhub machine when he leans back in his chair and peers out his office doorway.

> Dom: (*At his desk*) Hey, I need that chart.
> Ted: (*At the bizhub*) I'm e-mailing it now.
> Dom: You're e-mailing from the copy machine?
> Ted: No, I'm e-mailing from bizhub.
> Dom: Bizhub? Wait, did you make my copies yet?
> Ted: Right after I scan this.
> Dom: You're scanning at an e-mail machine?
> Ted: E-mail machine? I'm at the bizhub machine.
> Dom: (*Bewildered*) Copying?
> Ted: (*Trying to be patient*) E-mailing, *then* scanning, *then* copying.
> Dom: (*Long pause*) Bizhub?
> VO: (*Over an animated graphic of bizhub illustrating its multiple functions*) Amazing versatility *and* affordable color. That's bizhub, from Konica Minolta.
> (*Cut to Dom alone at the bizhub machine, trying to see if it will also dispense coffee into his mug.*)

Southwest was able to offer its at-home ticketing, and Konica Minolta could offer bizhub, because of what I call the triple convergence. What are the components of this triple convergence? The short answer is this: First, right around the year 2000, all ten of the flatteners discussed in the previous chapter started to converge and work together in ways that created a new, flatter, global playing field. As this new playing field became established, both businesses and individuals began to adopt new habits, skills, and processes to get the most out of it. They moved from largely vertical means of creating value to more horizontal ones. The merger of this new playing field for doing business with the new ways of doing business was the second convergence, and it actually helped to flatten the world even further. Finally, just when all of this flattening was happening, a whole new group of people, several billion, in fact, walked out onto the playing field from China, India, and the former Soviet Empire. Thanks to the new flat world, and its new tools, some of them were quickly able to collaborate and compete directly with everyone else. This was the third convergence. Now let's look at each in detail.

Convergence I

All ten flatteners discussed in the previous chapter have been around, we know, since the 1990s, if not earlier. But they had to spread and take root and connect with one another to work their magic on the world. For instance, at some point around 2003, Southwest Airlines realized that there were enough PCs around, enough bandwidth, enough computer storage, enough Internet-comfortable customers, and enough software know-how for Southwest to create a work flow system that empowered its customers to download and print out their own boarding passes at home, as easily as downloading a piece of e-mail. Southwest could collaborate with its customers and they with Southwest in a new way. And somewhere around the same time, the work flow software and hardware converged in a way that enabled Konica Minolta to offer scanning, e-mailing, printing, faxing, and copying *all from the same machine*. This is the first convergence.

As Stanford University economist Paul Romer pointed out, economists have known for a long time that "there are goods that are complementary — whereby good A is a lot more valuable if you also have good B. It was good to have paper and then it was good to have pencils, and soon as you got more of one you got more of the other, and as you got a better quality of one and better quality of the other, your productivity improved. This is known as the simultaneous improvement of complementary goods."

It is my contention that the opening of the Berlin Wall, Netscape, work flow, outsourcing, offshoring, open-sourcing, insourcing, supply-chaining, in-forming, and the steroids amplifying them all reinforced one another, like complementary goods. They just needed time to converge and start to work together in a complementary, mutually enhancing fashion. That tipping point arrived sometime around the year 2000.

The net result of this convergence was the creation of a global, Web-enabled playing field that allows for multiple forms of collaboration — the sharing of knowledge and work — in real time, without regard to geography, distance, or, in the near future, even language. No, not everyone has access yet to this platform, this playing field, but it is open today to more people in more places on more days in more ways than anything like it ever before in the history of the world. **This is what I mean when I say the world has been flattened.** It is the complementary convergence of the ten flatteners, creating this new global playing field for multiple forms of collaboration.

Convergence II

Great, you say, but why is it only in the past few years that we started to see in the

United States the big surges in productivity that should be associated with such a technological leap? Answer: Because it always takes time for all the flanking technologies, and the business processes and habits needed to get the most out of them, to converge and create that next productivity breakthrough.

Introducing new technology alone is never enough. The big spurts in productivity come when a new technology is combined with new *ways* of doing business. Wal-Mart got big productivity boosts when it combined big box stores — where people could buy soap supplies for six months — with new, horizontal supply-chain management systems that allowed Wal-Mart instantly to connect what a consumer took off the shelf from a Wal-Mart in Kansas City with what a Wal-Mart supplier in coastal China would produce.

When computers were first introduced into offices, everyone expected a big boost in productivity. But that did not happen right away, and it sparked both disappointment and a little confusion. The noted economist Robert Solow quipped that computers are everywhere — except "in the productivity statistics."

In a pathbreaking 1989 essay, "Computer and Dynamo: The Modern Productivity Paradox in a Not-Too Distant

Mirror," the economic historian Paul A. David explained such a lag by pointing to a historical precedent. He noted that while the lightbulb was invented in 1879, it took several decades for electrification to kick in and have a big economic and productivity impact. Why? Because it was not enough just to install electric motors and scrap the old technology — steam engines. The whole way of doing manufacturing had to be reconfigured. In the case of electricity, David pointed out, the key breakthrough was in how buildings, and assembly lines, were redesigned and managed. Factories in the steam age tended to be heavy, costly multistory buildings designed to brace the weighty belts and other big transmission devices needed to drive steam-powered systems. Once small, powerful electric motors were introduced, everyone hoped for a quick productivity boost. It took time, though. To get all the savings, you needed to redesign enough buildings. You needed to have long, low, cheaper-to-build single-story factories, with small electric motors powering machines of all sizes. Only when there was a critical mass of experienced factory architects and electrical engineers and managers, who understood the complementarities among the electric motor, the redesign of the factory, and the redesign of the production line, did electrification really deliver the productivity breakthrough in manufacturing, David wrote.

The same thing is happening today with the flattening of the world. Many of the ten flatteners have been around for years. But for the full flattening effects to be felt, we needed not only the ten flatteners to converge but also something else. We needed the emergence of a large cadre of managers, innovators, business consultants, business schools, designers, IT specialists, CEOs, and workers to get comfortable with, and develop, the sorts of horizontal collaboration and value-creation processes and habits that could take advantage of this new, flatter playing field. In short, the convergence of the ten flatteners begat the convergence of a set of business practices and skills that would get the most out of the flat world. And then the two began to mutually reinforce each other.

"When people asked, 'Why didn't the IT revolution lead to more productivity right away?' it was because you needed more than just new computers," said Romer. "You needed new business processes and new types of skills to go with them. The new way of doing things makes the information technologies more valuable, and the new and better information technologies make the new ways of doing things more possible."

Globalization 2.0 was really the era of mainframe computing, which was very vertical — command-and-control oriented, with companies and their individual departments tending to be organized in vertical silos. Globalization 3.0, which is built around the convergence of the ten flatteners, and particularly the combination of the PC, the microprocessor, the Internet, and fiber optics, flipped the playing field from largely top-down to more side to side. And this naturally fostered and demanded new business practices, which were less about command and control and more about connecting and collaborating horizontally.

"We have gone from a vertical chain of command for value creation to a much more horizontal chain of command for value creation," explained Carly Fiorina. Innovations in companies like HP, she said, now come more and more often from horizontal collaboration among different departments and teams spread all across the globe. For instance, HP, Cisco, and Nokia recently collaborated on the development of a camera/cell phone that beams its digitized pictures to an HP printer, which quickly prints them out. Each company had developed a very sophisticated technological specialty, but it could add value only when its specialty was horizontally combined with the specialties of the other two companies.

"How you collaborate horizontally and manage horizontally requires a totally different set of skills" from traditional top-down approaches, Fiorina added.

Let me offer just a few examples. In the past five years, HP has gone from a company that had eighty-seven different supply chains — each managed vertically and independently, with its own hierarchy of managers and back-office support — to a company with just five supply chains that manage $50 billion in business, and where functions like accounting, billing, and human resources are handled through a companywide system.

Southwest Airlines took advantage of the convergence of the ten flatteners to create a system where its customers can download their boarding passes at home. But until I personally altered my ticket-buying habits and reengineered myself to collaborate horizontally with Southwest, this technological breakthrough didn't produce a productivity breakthrough for me or Southwest. What the bizhub commercial is about is the difference between the employee who understands the convergent technologies in the new bizhub machine (and how to get the most out of them) and the employee in the very same office who does not. Not until the latter changes his work habits will productivity in that fictional office go up, even though the office has this amazing new machine.

Finally, consider the example of WPP — the second-largest advertising-marketing-communications consortium in the world. WPP, which is based in England, did not exist as we now know it twenty years ago. It is a product of the consolidation of some of the biggest names in the business — from Young & Rubicam to Ogilvy & Mather to Hill & Knowlton. The alliance was put together to capture more and more of big clients' marketing needs, such as advertising, direct mail, media buying, and branding.

"For years the big challenge for WPP was how to get its own companies to collaborate," said Allen Adamson, managing director of WPP's branding firm, Landor Associates. "Now, though, it is often no longer enough just to get the companies in WPP to work together per se. Increasingly, we find ourselves pulling together individuals from within each of these companies to form a customized collaborative team just for one client. The solution that will create value for that client did not exist in any one company or even in the traditional integration of the companies. It had to be much more specifically tailored. So we had to go down inside the whole group and pluck the individual who is the right ad person, to work with the right branding person, to work with the right media person for this particular client."

When GE decided in 2003 to spin off its insurance businesses into a separate company, WPP assembled a customized team to handle everything from the naming of the new company — Genworth — all the way down to its first advertising campaign and direct-marketing program. "As a leader within this organization," said Adamson, "what you have to do is figure out the value proposition that is needed for each client and then identify and assemble the individual talents within WPP's workforce that will in effect form a virtual company just for that client. In the case of GE, we even gave a name to the virtual collaborative team we formed: Klamath Communications."

When the world went flat, WPP adapted itself to get the most out of itself. It changed its office architecture and practices, just like those companies that adjusted their steam-run factories to the electric motor. But WPP not only got rid of all its walls, it got rid of all its floors. It looked at all its employees from all its companies as a vast pool of individual specialists who could be assembled horizontally into collaborative teams, depending on the unique demands of any given project.

And that team would then become a de facto new company with its own name.

It will take time for this new playing field and the new business practices to be fully aligned. It's a work in progress. But here's a little warning. It is happening much faster than you think, and it is happening globally.

Remember, this was a triple convergence!

Convergence III

How so? Just as we finished creating this new, more horizontal playing field, and companies and individuals primarily in the West started quickly adapting to it, 3 billion people who had been frozen out of the field suddenly found themselves liberated to plug and play with everybody else.

Save for a tiny minority, these 3 billion people had never been allowed to compete and collaborate before, because they lived in largely closed economies with very vertical, hierarchical political and economic structures. I am talking about the people of China, India, Russia, Eastern Europe, Latin America, and Central Asia. Their economies and political systems all opened up during the course of the 1990s, so that their people were increasingly free to join the free-market game. And when did these 3 billion people converge with the new playing field and the new processes? Right when the field was being flattened, right when millions of them could compete and collaborate more equally, more horizontally, and with cheaper and more readily available tools than ever before. Indeed, thanks to the flattening of the world, many of these new entrants didn't even have to leave home to participate. Thanks to the ten flatteners, the playing field came to them!

It is this triple convergence — of new players, on a new playing field, developing new processes and habits for horizontal collaboration — that I believe is the most important force shaping global economics and politics in the early twenty-first century. Giving so many people access to all these tools of collaboration, along with the ability through search engines and the Web to access billions of pages of raw information, ensures that the next generation of innovations will come from all over Planet Flat. The scale of the global community that is soon going to be able to participate in all sorts of discovery and innovation is something the world has simply never seen before.

Throughout the Cold War there were just three major trading blocs — North America, Western Europe, and Japan plus East Asia — and the competition among the three was relatively controlled, since they were all Cold War allies on the same side of the great global divide. There were also still a lot of walls around for labor and industries to hide behind. The wage rates in these three trading blocs were roughly the same, the workforces roughly the same size, and the education levels roughly equivalent. "You had a gentlemanly competition," noted Intel's Chairman Craig Barrett.

Then along came the triple convergence. The Berlin Wall came down, the Berlin mall opened up, and suddenly some 3 billion people who had been behind walls walked onto the flattened global piazza.

Here's what happened in round numbers: According to a November 2004 study by Harvard University economist Richard B. Freeman, in 1985 "the global economic world" comprised North America, Western Europe, Japan, as well as chunks of Latin America, Africa, and the countries of East Asia. The total population of this global economic world, taking part in international trade and commerce, said Freeman, was about 2.5 billion people.

By 2000, as a result of the collapse of communism in the Soviet Empire, India's turn from autarky, China's shift to market capitalism, and population growth all over, the global economic world expanded to encompass 6 billion people.

As a result of this widening, another roughly 1.5 billion new workers entered the global economic labor force, Freeman said, which is almost exactly double the number we would have had in 2000 had China, India, and the Soviet Empire not joined.

True, maybe only 10 percent of this new 1.5 billion–strong workforce entering the global economy have the education and connectivity to collaborate and compete at a meaningful level. But that is still 150 million people, roughly the size of the entire U.S. workforce. Said Barrett, "You don't bring three billion people into the world economy overnight without huge consequences, especially from three societies [like India, China, and Russia] with rich educational heritages."

That is exactly right. And a lot of those new workers are not just walking onto the playing field. No, this is no slow-motion triple convergence. They are jogging and even sprinting there. Because once the world has been flattened and the new forms of collaboration made available to more and more people, the winners will be those who learn the habits, processes, and skills most quickly — and there is simply nothing that guarantees it will be Americans or Western Europeans permanently leading the way. And be advised, these new players are stepping onto the playing field legacy free, meaning that many of them were so far behind they can leap right into the new technologies without having to worry about all the sunken costs of old systems. It means that they can move very fast to adopt new, state-of-the-art technologies, which is why there are already more cell phones in use in China today than there are people in the United States. Many Chinese just skipped over the landline phase. South Koreans put Americans to shame in terms of Internet usage and broadband penetration.

We tend to think of global trade and economics as something driven by the IMF, the G-8, the World Bank, the WTO, and the trade treaties forged by trade ministers. I don't want to suggest that these governmental agencies are irrelevant. They are not. But they are going to become less important. In the future globalization is going to be increasingly driven by the *individuals* who understand the flat world, adapt themselves quickly to its processes and technologies, and start to march forward — without any treaties or advice from the IMF. They will be every color of the rainbow and from every corner of the world.

The global economy from here forward will be shaped less by the ponderous deliberations of finance ministers and more by the spontaneous explosion of energy from the zippies. Yes, Americans grew up with the hippies in the 1960s. Thanks to the high-tech revolution, many of us became yuppies in the 1980s. Well, now let me introduce the zippies.

"The Zippies Are Here," declared the Indian weekly magazine *Outlook*. Zippies are the huge cohort of Indian youth who are the first to come of age since India shifted away from socialism and dived headfirst into global trade and the information revolution by turning itself into the world's service center. *Outlook* called India's zippies "Liberalization's Children" and defined a zippie as a "young city or suburban resident, between 15 and 25 years of age, with a zip in the stride. Belongs to Generation Z. Can be male or female, studying or working. Oozes attitude, ambition and aspiration. Cool, confident and creative. Seeks challenges, loves risks and shuns fear." Indian zippies feel no guilt about making money or spending it. They are, says one Indian analyst quoted by *Outlook*, "destination driven, not destiny driven, outward looking, not inward, upwardly mobile, not stuck-in-my-station-in-life." With 54 percent of India under the age of twenty-five — that's 555 million people — six out of ten Indian households have at least one potential zippie. And the zippies don't just have a pent-up demand for good jobs; they want the good life.

It all happened so fast. P. V. Kannan, the CEO and cofounder of the Indian call-center company 24/7 Customer, told me that in the last decade, he went from sweating out whether he would ever get a chance to work in America to becoming one of the leading figures in the outsourcing of services from America to the rest of the world.

"I will never forget when I applied for a visa to come to the United States," Kannan recalled. "It was March 1991. I had gotten a B.A. in chartered accountancy from the [Indian] Institute of Chartered Accountants. I was twenty-three, and my girlfriend was twenty-five. She was also a chartered accountant. I had graduated at age twenty and had been working for the Tata Consultancy group. So was my girlfriend. And we both got job offers through a body shop [a recruiting firm specializing in importing Indian talent for companies in America] to work as programmers for IBM. So we went to the U.S. consulate in Bombay. The recruiting service was based in Bombay. In those days, there was always a very long line to get visas to the United States, and there were people who would actually sleep in the line and hold places and you could go buy their place for 20 rupees. But we went by ourselves and stood in line and we finally got in to see the man who did the interview. He was an American [consular official]. His job was to ask questions and try to figure out whether we were going to do the work and then come back to India or try to stay in America. They judge by some secret formula. We used to call it 'the lottery' — you went and stood in line and it was a life lottery, because everything was dependent on it."

There were actually books and seminars in India devoted entirely to the subject of how to prepare for a work visa interview at the U.S. embassy. It was the only way for skilled Indian engineers really to exploit their talent. "I remember one tip was to always go professionally dressed," said Kannan, "so [my girlfriend and I] were both in our best clothes. After the interview is over, the man doesn't tell you anything. You had to wait until the evening to know the results. But meanwhile, the whole day was hell. To distract our minds, we just walked the streets of Bombay and went shopping. We would go back and forth, 'What if I get in and you don't? What if you get in and I don't?' I can't tell you how anxious we were, because so much was riding on it. It was torture. So in the evening we go back and both of us got visas, but I got a five-year multiple entry and my girlfriend got a six-month visa. She was crying. She did not understand what it meant. 'I can only stay for six months?' I tried to explain to her that you just need to get in and then everything can be worked out."

While many Indians still want to come to America to work and study, thanks to the triple convergence many of them can now compete at the highest levels, and be decently paid, by staying at home. In a flat world, you can innovate without having to emigrate. Said Kannan, "My daughter will never have to sweat that out." In a flat world, he explained, "there is no one visa officer who can keep you out of the system . . . It's a plug-and-play world."

One of the most dynamic pluggers and players I met in India was Rajesh Rao, founder and CEO of Dhruva Interactive, a small Indian game company based in Bangalore. If I could offer you one person who embodies the triple convergence, it is Rajesh. He and his firm show us what happens when an Indian zippie plugs into the ten flatteners.

Dhruva is located in a converted house on a quiet street in a residential neighborhood of Bangalore. When I stopped in for a visit, I found two floors of Indian game designers and artists, trained in computer graphics, working on PCs, drawing various games and animated characters for American and European clients. The artists and designers were listening to music on headphones as they worked. Occasionally, they took a break by playing a group computer game, in which all the designers could try to chase and kill one another at once on their computer screens. Dhruva has already produced some very innovative games — from a computer tennis game you can play on the screen of your cell phone to a computer pool game you can play on your PC or laptop. In 2004, it bought the rights to use Charlie Chaplin's image for mobile computer games. That's right — a start-up Indian game company today owns the Chaplin image for use in mobile computer games.

In Bangalore and in later e-mail conversations, I asked Rajesh, who is in his early thirties, to walk me through how he became a player in the global game business from Bangalore.

"The first defining moment for me dates back to the early nineties," said Rajesh, a smallish, mustachioed figure with the ambition of a heavyweight boxer. "Having lived and worked in Europe, as a student, I was clear in my choice that I would not leave India. I wanted to do my thing from India, do something that would be globally respected and something that would make a difference in India. I started my company in Bangalore as a one-man operation on March 15, 1995. My father gave me the seed money for the bank loan that bought me a computer and a 14.4 kbp modem. I set out to do multimedia applications aimed at the education and industry sectors. By 1997, we were a five-man team. We had done some pathbreaking work in our chosen field, but we realized that this was not challenging us enough. End of Dhruva 1.0.

"In March 1997, we partnered with Intel and began the process of reinventing ourselves into a gaming company. By mid-1998, we were showing global players what we were capable of by way of both designing games and developing the outsourced portions of games designed by others. On November 26, 1998, we signed our first major game development project with Infogrames Entertainment, a French gaming company. In hindsight, I think the deal we landed was due to the pragmatism of one man in Infogrames more than anything else. We did a great job on the game, but it was never published. It was a big blow for us, but the quality of our work spoke for itself, so we survived. The most important lesson we learned: We could do it, but we had to get smart. Going for all or nothing — that is, signing up to make only a full game or nothing at all — was not sustainable. We had to look at positioning ourselves differently. End of Dhruva 2.0."

This led to the start of Dhruva's 3.0 era — positioning Dhruva as a provider of game development services. The computer game business is already enormous, every year grossing more revenue than Hollywood, and it already had some tradition of outsourcing game characters to countries like Canada and Australia. "In March 2001, we sent out our new game demo, Saloon, to the world," said Rajesh. "The theme was the American Wild Wild West, and the setting was a saloon in a small town after business hours, with the barman cleaning up . . . None of us had ever seen a real saloon before, but we researched the look and feel [of a saloon] using the Internet and Google. The choice of the theme was deliberate. We wanted potential clients in the U.S.A. and Europe to be convinced that Indians can 'get it.' The demo was a hit, it landed us a bunch of outsourced business, and we have been a successful company ever since."

Could he have done this a decade earlier, before the world got so flat?

"Never," said Rajesh. Several things had to come together. The first was to have enough installed bandwidth so he could e-mail game content and instructions back and forth between his own company and his American clients. The second factor, said Rajesh, was the spread of PCs for use in both business and at home, with people getting very comfortable using them in a variety of tasks. "PCs are everywhere," he said. "The penetration is relatively decent even in India today."

The third factor, though, was the emergence of the work flow software and Internet applications that made it possible for a Dhruva to go into business as a minimultinational from day one: Word, Outlook, NetMeeting, 3D Studio MAX. But Google is the key. "It's fantastic," said Rajesh. "One of the things that's always an issue for our clients from the West is, 'Will you Indians be able to understand the subtle nuances of Western content?' Now, to a large extent, it was a very valid question. But the Internet has helped us to be able to aggregate different kinds of content at the touch of a button, and today if someone asks you to make something that looks like Tom and Jerry, you just say 'Google Tom & Jerry' and you've got tons and tons of pictures and information and reviews and write-ups about Tom and Jerry, which you can read and simulate."

While people were focusing on the boom and bust of the dot-coms, Rajesh explained, the real revolution was taking place more quietly. It was the fact that all over the world, people, en masse, were starting to get comfortable with the new global infrastructure. "We are just at the beginning of being efficient in using it," he said. "There is a lot more we can do with this infrastructure, as more and more people shift to becoming paperless in their offices and realize that distances really [do] not matter . . . It will supercharge all of this. It's really going to be a different world."

Moreover, in the old days, these software programs would have been priced beyond the means of a little Indian game start-up, but not anymore, thanks in part to the open-source free software movement. Said Rajesh, "The cost of software tools would have remained where the interested parties wanted them to be if it was not for the deluge of rather efficient freeware and shareware products that sprung up in the early 2000s. Microsoft Windows, Office, 3D Studio MAX, Adobe Photoshop — each of these programs would have been priced higher than they are today if not for the many freeware/shareware programs that were comparable and compelling. The Internet brought to the table the element of choice and instant comparison that did not exist before for a little company like ours . . . Already we have in our gaming industry artists and designers working from home, something unimaginable a few years back, given the fact that developing games is a highly interactive process. They connect into the company's internal system over the Internet, using a secure feature called VPN [virtual private network], making their presence no different from the guy in the next cubicle."

The Internet now makes this whole world "like one marketplace," added Rajesh. "This infrastructure is not only going to facilitate sourcing of work to the best price, best quality, from the best place, it is also going to enable a great amount of sharing of practices and knowledge, and it's going to be 'I can learn from you and you can learn from me' like never before. It's very good for the world. The economy is going to drive integration and the integration is going to drive the economy."

There is no reason the United States should not benefit from this trend, Rajesh insisted. What Dhruva is doing is pioneering computer gaming within Indian society. When the Indian market starts to embrace gaming as a mainstream social activity, Dhruva will already be positioned to take advantage. But by then, he argued, the market "will be so huge that there will be a lot of opportunity for content to come from outside. And, hey, the Americans are way ahead in terms of the ability to know what games can work and what won't work and in terms of being at the cutting edge of design — so this is a bilateral thing . . . Every perceived dollar or opportunity that is lost today [from an American point of view because of outsourcing] is actually going to come back to you times ten, once the market here is unleashed . . . Just remember, we are a 300-million middle class — larger than the size of your country or Europe."

Yes, he noted, India right now has a great advantage in having a pool of educated, low-wage English speakers with a strong service etiquette in their DNA and an enterprising spirit. "So, sure, for the moment, we are leading the so-called wave of service outsourcing of various kinds of new things," said Rajesh. "But I believe that there should be no doubt that this is just the beginning. If [Indians] think that they've got something going and there is something they can keep that's not going to go anywhere, that will be a big mistake, because we have got Eastern Europe, which is waking up, and we have got China, which is waiting to get on the services bandwagon to do various things. I mean, you can source the best product or service or capacity or competency from anywhere in the world today, because of this whole infrastructure that is being put into place. The only thing that inhibits you from doing that is your readiness to make use of this infrastructure. So as different businesses, and as different people, get more comfortable using this infrastructure, you are going to see a huge explosion. It is a matter of five to seven years and we will have a huge batch of excellent English-speaking Chinese graduates coming out of their universities. Poles and Hungarians are already very well connected, very close to Europe, and their cultures are very similar [to Western Europe's]. So today India is ahead, but it has to work very hard if it wants to keep this position. It has to never stop inventing and reinventing itself."

The raw ambition that Rajesh and so many of his generation possess is worthy of note by Americans — a point I will elaborate on later.

"We can't relax," said Rajesh. "I think in the case of the United States that is what happened a bit. Please look at me: I am from India. We have been at a very different level before in terms of technology and business. But once we saw we had an infrastructure which made the world a small place, we promptly tried to make the best use of it. We saw there were so many things we could do. We went ahead, and today what we are seeing is a result of that . . . There is no time to rest. That is gone. There are dozens of people who are doing the same thing you are doing, and they are trying to do it better. It is like water in a tray, you shake it and it will find the path of least resistance. That is what is going to happen to so many jobs — they will go to that corner of the world where there is the least resistance and the most opportunity. If there is a skilled person in Timbuktu, he will get work if he knows how to access the rest of the world, which is quite easy today. You can make a Web site and have an e-mail address and you are up and running. And if you are able to demonstrate your work, using the same infrastructure, and if people are comfortable giving work to you, and if you are diligent and clean in your transactions, then you are in business."

Instead of complaining about outsourcing, said Rajesh, Americans and Western Europeans would "be better off thinking about how you can raise your bar and raise yourselves into doing something better. Americans have consistently led in innovation over the last century. Americans whining — we have never seen that before. People like me have learned a lot from Americans. We have learned to become a little more aggressive in the way we market ourselves, which is something we would not have done given our typical British background."

So what is your overall message? I asked Rajesh, before leaving with my head spinning.

"My message is that what's happening now is just the tip of the iceberg . . . What is really necessary is for everybody to wake up to the fact that there is a fundamental shift that is happening in the way people are going to do business. And everyone is going to have to improve themselves and be able to compete. It is just going to be one global market. Look, we just made [baseball] caps for Dhruva to give away. They came from Sri Lanka."

Not from a factory in South Bangalore? I asked.

"Not from South Bangalore," said Rajesh, "even though Bangalore is one of the export hubs for garments. Among the three or four caps we got quotations for, this [Sri Lankan one] was the best in terms of quality and the right price, and we thought the finish was great.

"This is the situation you are going to see moving forward," Rajesh concluded. "If you are seeing all this energy coming out of Indians, it's because we have been underdogs and we have that drive to kind of achieve and to get there . . . India is going to be a superpower and we are going to rule."

Rule whom? I asked.

Rajesh laughed at his own choice of words. "It's not about ruling anybody. That's the point. There is nobody to rule anymore. It's about how you can create a great opportunity for yourself and hold on to that or keep creating new opportunities where you can thrive. I think today that rule is about efficiency, it's about collaboration and it is about competitiveness and it is about being a player. It is about staying sharp and being in the game . . . The world is a football field now and you've got to be sharp to be on the team which plays on that field. If you're not good enough, you're going to be sitting and watching the game. That's all."

How Do You Say "Zippie" in Chinese?

As in Bangalore ten years ago, the best place to meet zippies in Beijing today is in the line at the consular section of the U.S. embassy. In Beijing in the summer of 2004, I discovered that the quest by Chinese students for visas to study or work in America was so intense that it had spawned dedicated Internet chat rooms, where Chinese students swapped stories about which arguments worked best with which U.S. embassy consular officials. They even gave the U.S.

346

diplomats names like "Amazon Goddess," "Too Tall Baldy," and "Handsome Guy." Just how intensely Chinese students strategize over the Internet was revealed, U.S. embassy officials told me, when one day a rookie U.S. consular official had student after student come before him with the same line that some chat room had suggested would work for getting a visa: "I want to go to America to become a famous professor."

After hearing this all day, the U.S. official was suddenly surprised to get one student who came before him and pronounced, "My mother has an artificial limb and I want to go to America to learn how to build a better artificial limb for her." The official was so relieved to hear a new line that he told the young man, "You know, this is the best story I've heard all day. I really salute you. I'm going to give you a visa."

You guessed it.

The next day, a bunch of students showed up at the embassy saying they wanted a visa to go to America to learn how to build better artificial limbs for their mothers.

Talking to these U.S. embassy officials in Beijing, who are the gatekeepers for these visas, it quickly became apparent to me that they had mixed feelings about the process. On the one hand, they were pleased that so many Chinese wanted to come study and work in America. On the other hand, they wanted to warn American kids: Do you realize what is coming your way? As one U.S. embassy official in Beijing said to me, "What I see happening [in China] is what has been going on for the last several decades in the rest of Asia — the tech booms, the tremendous energy of the people. I saw it elsewhere, but now it is happening here."

I was visiting Yale in the spring of 2004. As I was strolling through the central quad, near the statue of Elihu Yale, two Chinese-speaking tours came through, with Chinese tourists of all ages. Chinese have started to tour the world in large numbers, and as China continues to develop toward a more open society, it is quite likely that Chinese leisure tourists will alter the whole world-tourism industry.

But Chinese are not visiting Yale just to admire the ivy. Consider these statistics from Yale's admissions office. The fall 1985 class had 71 graduate and undergraduate students from China and 1 from the Soviet Union. The fall 2003 class had 297 Chinese graduate and undergraduate students and 23 Russians. Yale's total international student contingent went from 836 in the fall of 1985 to 1,775 in the fall of 2003. Applications from Chinese and Russian high school students to attend Yale as undergraduates have gone from a total of 40 Chinese for the class of 2001 to 276 for the class of 2008, and 18 Russians for the class of 2001 to 30 for the class of 2008. In 1999, Yiting Liu, a schoolgirl from Chengdu, China, got accepted to Harvard on a full scholarship. Her parents then wrote a build-your-own handbook about how they managed to prepare their daughter to get accepted to Harvard. The book, in Chinese, titled *Harvard Girl Yiting Liu*, offered "scientifically proven methods" to get your Chinese kid into Harvard. The book became a runaway best seller in China. By 2003 it had sold some 3 million copies and spawned more than a dozen copycat books about how to get your kid into Columbia, Oxford, or Cambridge.

While many Chinese aspire to go to Harvard and Yale, they aren't just waiting around to get into an American university. They are also trying to build their own at home. In 2004, I was a speaker for the 150th anniversary of Washington University in St. Louis, a school noted for its strength in science and engineering. Mark Wrighton, the university's thoughtful chancellor, and I were chatting before the ceremony. He mentioned in passing that in the spring of 2001 he had been invited (along with many other foreign and American academic leaders) to Tsinghua University in Beijing, one of the finest in China, to participate in the celebration of its ninetieth anniversary. He said the invitation left him scratching his head at first: Why would any university celebrate its ninetieth anniversary — not its hundredth?

"Perhaps a Chinese tradition?" Wrighton asked himself. When he arrived at Tsinghua, though, he learned the answer. The Chinese had brought academics from all over the world to Tsinghua — more than ten thousand people attended the ceremony — in order to make the declaration "that at the one hundredth anniversary Tsinghua University would be among the world's premier universities," Wrighton later explained to me in an e-mail. "The event involved all of the leaders of the Chinese government, from the Mayor of Beijing to the head of state. Each expressed the conviction that an investment in the university to support its development as one of the world's great universities within ten years would be a rewarding one. With Tsinghua University already regarded as one of the leading universities in China, focused on science and technology, it was evident that there is a seriousness of purpose in striving for a world leadership position in [all the areas involved] in spawning technological innovation."

And as a result of China's drive to succeed, Microsoft chairman Bill Gates argued to me, the "ovarian lottery" has changed — as has the whole relationship between geography and talent. Thirty years ago, he said, if you had a choice between being born a genius on the outskirts of Bombay or Shanghai or being born an average person in Poughkeepsie, you would take Poughkeepsie, because your chances of thriving and living a decent life there, even with average talent, were much greater. But as the world has gone flat, Gates said, and so many people can now plug and play from anywhere, natural talent has started to trump geography.

"Now," he said, "I would rather be a genius born in China than an average guy born in Poughkeepsie."

That's what happens when the Berlin Wall turns into the Berlin mall and 3 billion people converge with all these new tools for collaboration. "We're going to tap into the energy and talent of five times as many people as we did before," said Gates.

From Russia with Love

I didn't get a chance to visit Russia and interview Russian zippies for this book, but I did the next best thing. I asked my friend

Thomas R. Pickering, the former U.S. ambassador to Moscow and now a top international relations executive with Boeing, to explain a new development I had heard about: that Boeing was using Russian engineers and scientists, who once worked on MiGs, to help design its next generation of passenger planes.

Pickering unraveled the story for me. Beginning in 1991, Boeing started assigning out work to Russian scientists to take advantage of their expertise in aerodynamic problems and new aviation alloys. In 1998, Boeing decided to take this a step further and open an aeronautical engineering design office in Moscow. Boeing located the office in the twelve-story Moscow tower that McDonald's built with all the rubles it made from selling Big Macs in Moscow before the end of communism — money that McDonald's had pledged not to take out of the country.

Seven years later, said Pickering, "we now have eight hundred Russian engineers and scientists working for us and we're going up to at least one thousand and maybe, over time, to fifteen hundred." The way it works, he explained, is that Boeing contracts with different Russian aircraft companies — companies that were famous in the Cold War for making warplanes, companies with names like Ilyushin, Tupolev, and Sukhoi — and they provide the engineers-to-order for Boeing's different projects. Using French-made airplane design software, the Russian engineers collaborate with their colleagues at Boeing America — in both Seattle and Wichita, Kansas — in computer-aided airplane designs. Boeing has set up a twenty-four-hour workday. It consists of two shifts in Moscow and one shift in America. Using fiber-optic cables, advanced compression technologies, and aeronautical work flow software, "they just pass their designs back and forth from Moscow to America," Pickering said. There are videoconferencing facilities on every floor of Boeing's Moscow office, so the engineers don't have to rely on e-mail when they have a problem to solve with their American counterparts. They can have a face-to-face conversation.

Boeing started outsourcing airplane design work to Moscow as an experiment, a sideline; but today, with a shortage of aeronautical engineers in America, it is a necessity. Boeing's ability to blend these lower-cost Russian engineers with higher-cost, more advanced American design teams is enabling Boeing to compete head-to-head with its archrival, Airbus Industries, which is subsidized by a consortium of European governments and is using Russian talent as well. A U.S. aeronautical engineer costs $120 per design hour; a

Russian costs about one-third of that.

But the outsourcees are also outsourcers. The Russian engineers have outsourced elements of their work for Boeing to Hindustan Aeronautics in Bangalore, which specializes in digitizing airplane designs so as to make them easier to manufacture. But this isn't the half of it. In the old days, explained Pickering, Boeing would say to its Japanese subcontractors, "We will send you the plans for the wings of the 777. We will let you make some of them and then we will count on you buying the whole airplanes from us. It's a win-win."

Today Boeing says to the giant Japanese industrial company Mitsubishi, "Here are the general parameters for the wings of the new 7E7. You design the finished product and build it." But Japanese engineers are very expensive. So what happens? Mitsubishi outsources elements of the outsourced 7E7 wing to the same Russian engineers Boeing is using for other parts of the plane. Meanwhile, some of these Russian engineers and scientists are leaving the big Russian airplane companies, setting up their own firms, and Boeing is considering buying shares in some of these start-ups to have reserve engineering capacity.

All of this global sourcing is for the purpose of designing and building planes faster and cheaper, so that Boeing can use its cash to keep innovating for the next generation and survive the withering competition from Airbus. Thanks to the triple convergence, it now takes Boeing eleven days to build a 737, down from twenty-eight days just a few years ago. Boeing will build its next generation of planes in three days, because all the parts are being computer-designed for assembly, and Boeing's global supply chain will enable it to move parts from one facility to another just in time.

To make sure that it is getting the best deals on its parts and other supplies, Boeing now runs regular "reverse auctions," in which companies bid down against each other rather than bid up against each other. They bid for contracts on everything from toilet paper for the Boeing factories to nuts and bolts — the off-the-shelf commodity parts — for Boeing's supply chain. Boeing will announce an auction for a stated time on a specially designed Internet site. It will begin the auction for each supply item at what it considers a fair price. Then it will just sit back and watch how far each supplier wants to undercut the others to win Boeing's business. Bidders are prequalified by Boeing, and everyone can see everyone else's bids as they are submitted.

"You can really see the pressures of the marketplace and how they work," said

Pickering. "It's like watching a horse race."

The Other Triple Convergence

I once heard Bill Bradley tell a story about a high-society woman from Boston who goes to San Francisco for the first time. When she comes home and is asked by a friend how she liked it, she says, "Not very much — it's too far from the ocean."

The perspective and predispositions that you carry around in your head are very important in shaping what you see and what you don't see. That helps to explain why a lot of people missed the triple convergence. Their heads were completely somewhere else — even though it was happening right before their eyes. Three other things — another convergence — came together to create this smoke screen.

The first was the dot-com bust, which began in March 2001. As I said earlier, many people wrongly equated the dot-com boom with globalization. So when the dot-com boom went bust, and so many dot-coms (and the firms that supported them) imploded, these same people assumed that globalization was imploding as well. The sudden flameout of dogfood.com and ten other Web sites offering to deliver ten pounds of puppy chow to your door in thirty minutes was supposed to be proof that globalization and the IT revolution were all sizzle and no beef.

This was pure foolishness. Those who thought that globalization was the same thing as the dot-com boom and that the dot-com bust marked the end of globalization *could not have been more wrong*. To say it again, the dot-com bust actually drove globalization into hypermode by forcing companies to outsource and offshore more and more functions in order to save on scarce capital. This was a key factor in laying the groundwork for Globalization 3.0. Between the dot-com bust and today, Google went from processing roughly 150 million searches per day to roughly one billion searches per day, with only a third coming from inside the United States. As its auction model caught on worldwide, eBay went from twelve hundred employees in early 2000 to sixty-three hundred by 2004, all in the period when globalization was supposed to be "over." Between 2000 and 2004, total global Internet usage grew 125 percent, including 186 percent in Africa, 209 percent in Latin America, 124 percent in Europe, and 105 percent in North America, according to Nielsen/NetRatings. Yes, globalization sure ended, all right.

It was not just the dot-com bust and all the hot air surrounding it that obscured all this from view. There were two other big clouds that moved in. The biggest, of course, was 9/11, which was a profound shock to the American body politic. Given 9/11, and the Afghanistan and Iraq invasions that followed, it's not surprising that the triple convergence was lost in the fog of war and the chatter of cable television. Finally, there was the Enron corporate governance scandal, quickly followed by blowups at Tyco and WorldCom — which all sent CEOs and the Bush administration running for cover. CEOs, with some justification, became guilty until proven innocent of boardroom shenanigans, and even the slavishly probusiness, pro-CEO Bush administration was wary of appearing — in public — to be overly solicitous of the concerns of big business. In the spring of 2004, I met with the head of one of America's biggest technology companies, who had come to Washington to lobby for more federal funding for the National Science Foundation to help nurture a stronger industrial base for American industry. I asked him why the administration wasn't convening a summit of CEOs to highlight this issue, and he just shook his head and said one word: "Enron."

The result: At the precise moment when the world was being flattened, and the triple convergence was reshaping the whole global business environment — requiring some very important adjustments in our own society and that of many other Western developed nations — American politicians not only were not educating the American public, they were actively working to make it stupid. During the 2004 election campaign we saw the Democrats debating whether NAFTA was a good idea and the Bush White House putting duct tape over the mouth of N. Gregory Mankiw, the chairman of the White House Council of Economic Advisers, and stashing him away in Dick Cheney's basement, because Mankiw, author of a popular college economics textbook, had dared to speak approvingly of oursourcing as just the "latest manifestation of the gains from trade that economists have talked about at least since Adam Smith."

Mankiw's statement triggered a competition for who could say the most ridiculous thing in response. The winner was Speaker of the House Dennis Hastert, who said that Mankiw's "theory fails a basic test of real economics." And what test was that, Dennis? Poor Mankiw was barely heard from again.

For all these reasons, most people missed the triple convergence. Something really big was happening, and it was simply not part of public discourse in America or Europe. Until I visited India in early 2004, I too was largely ignorant of it, although I was picking up a few hints that something was brewing. One of the most thoughtful business leaders I have come to know over the years is Nobuyuki Idei, the chairman of Sony. Whenever he speaks, I pay close attention. We saw each other twice during 2004, and both times he said something through his heavy Japanese accent that stuck in my ear. Idei said that a change was under way in the business-technology world that would be remembered, in time, like "the meteor that hit the earth and killed all the dinosaurs." Fortunately, the cutting-edge global companies knew what was going on out there, and the best companies were quietly adapting to it so that they would not be one of those dinosaurs.

As I started researching this book, I felt at times like I was in a *Twilight Zone* segment. I would interview CEOs and technologists from major companies, both American-based and foreign, and they would describe in their own ways what I came to call the triple convergence. But, for all the reasons I explained above, most of them weren't telling the public or the politicians. They were either too distracted, too focused on their own businesses, or too afraid. It was like they were all "pod people," living in a parallel universe, who were in on a big secret. Yes, they all knew the secret — *but nobody wanted to tell the kids.*

Well, here's the truth that no one wanted to tell you: The world has been flattened.

As a result of the triple convergence, global collaboration and competition — between individuals and individuals, companies and individuals, companies and companies, and companies and customers — have been made cheaper, easier, more friction-free, and more productive for more people from more corners of the earth than at any time in the history of the world.

You know "the IT revolution" that the business press has been touting for the last twenty years? Sorry, but that was only the prologue. The last twenty years were just about forging, sharpening, and distributing all the new tools with which to collaborate and connect. *Now* the real IT revolution is about to begin, as all the complementarities between these tools start to really work together to level the playing field. One of those who pulled back the curtain and called this moment by its real name was HP's Carly Fiorina, who in 2004 began to declare in her public speeches that the dot-com boom and bust were just "the end of the beginning." The last twenty-five years in technology, said Fiorina, then the CEO of HP, have been just "the warm-up act." Now we are going into the main event, she said, "and by the main event, I mean an era in which technology will literally transform every aspect of business, every aspect of life and every aspect of society."

FOUR

The Great Sorting Out

The triple convergence is not only going to affect how individuals prepare themselves for work, how companies compete, and how countries organize their economies and geopolitics. Over time, it is going to reshape political identities, recast political parties, and redefine who is a political actor. In short, in the wake of this triple convergence that we have just gone through, we are going to witness what I call "the great sorting out." Because when the world starts to move from a primarily vertical (command and control) value-creation model to an increasingly horizontal (connect and collaborate) creation model, it doesn't affect just how business gets done. It affects everything — how communities and companies define themselves, where companies and communities stop and start, how individuals balance their different identities as consumers, employees, shareholders, and citizens, and what role government has to play. All of this is going to have to be sorted out anew. The most common disease of the flat world is going to be multiple identity disorder, which is why, if nothing else, political scientists are going to have a field day with the flat world. Political science may turn out to be the biggest growth industry of all in this new era. Because as we go through this great sorting out over the next decade, we are going to see some very strange bedfellows making some very new politics.

I first began thinking about the great sorting out after a conversation with Harvard University's noted political theorist Michael J. Sandel. Sandel startled me slightly by remarking that the sort of flattening process that I was describing was actually first identified by Karl Marx and Friedrich Engels in the *Communist Manifesto*, published in 1848. While the shrinking and flattening of the world that we are seeing today constitute a difference of degree from what Marx saw happening in his day, said Sandel, it is nevertheless part of the same historical trend Marx highlighted in his writings on capitalism — the inexorable march of technology and capital to remove all barriers, boundaries, frictions, and restraints to global commerce.

"Marx was one of the first to glimpse the possibility of the world as a global market, uncomplicated by national boundaries," Sandel explained. "Marx was capitalism's fiercest critic, and yet he stood in awe of its power to break down barriers and create a worldwide system of production and consumption. In the *Communist Manifesto*, he described capitalism as a force that would dissolve all feudal, national, and religious identities, giving rise to a universal civilization governed by market imperatives. Marx considered it inevitable that capital would have its way — inevitable and also desirable. Because once capitalism destroyed all national and religious allegiances, Marx thought, it would lay bare the stark struggle between capital and labor. Forced to compete in a global race to the bottom, the workers of the world would unite in a global revolution to end oppression. Deprived of consoling distractions such as patriotism and religion, they would see their exploitation clearly and rise up to end it."

Indeed, reading the *Communist Manifesto* today, I am in awe at how incisively Marx detailed the forces that were flattening the world during the rise of the Industrial Revolution, and how much he foreshadowed the way these same forces would keep flattening the world right up to the present. In what is probably the key paragraph of the *Communist Manifesto*, Marx and Engels wrote:

All fixed, fast, frozen relations, with their train of ancient and venerable prejudices and opinions, are swept away, all new-formed ones become antiquated before they can ossify. All that is solid melts into air, all that is holy is profaned, and man is at last compelled to face with sober senses his real conditions of life and his relations with his kind. The need of a constantly expanding market for its products chases the bourgeoisie over the whole surface of the globe. It must nestle everywhere, settle everywhere, establish connections everywhere. The bourgeoisie has through its exploitation of the world market given a cosmopolitan character to production and consumption in every country. To the great chagrin of reactionaries, it has drawn from under the feet of industry the national ground on which it stood. All old-established national industries have been destroyed or are daily being destroyed. They are dislodged by new industries, whose introduction becomes a life and death question for all civilised nations, by industries that no longer work up indigenous raw material, but raw material drawn from the remotest zones; industries whose products are consumed, not only at home, but in every quarter of the globe. In place of the old wants, satisfied by the production of the country, we find new wants, requiring for their satisfaction the products of distant lands and climes. In place of the old local and national seclusion and self-sufficiency, we have intercourse in every direction, universal inter-dependence of nations. And as in material, so also in intellectual production. The intellectual creations of individual nations become common property. National one-sidedness and narrow-mindedness become more and more impossible, and from the numerous national and local literatures there arises a world literature.

The bourgeoisie, by the rapid improvement of all instruments of production, by the immensely facilitated means of communication, draws all, even the most barbarian nations into civilisation. The cheap prices of commodities are the heavy artillery with which it batters down all Chinese walls, with which it forces the barbarians' intensely obstinate hatred of foreigners to capitulate. It compels all nations, on pain of extinction, to adopt the bourgeois mode of production; it compels them to introduce what it calls civilisation into their midst, i.e., to become bourgeois themselves. In one word, it creates a world after its own image.

It is hard to believe that Marx published that in 1848. Referring to the *Communist*

Manifesto, Sandel told me, "You are arguing something similar. What you are arguing is that developments in information technology are enabling companies to squeeze out all the inefficiencies and friction from their markets and business operations. That is what your notion of 'flattening' really means. But a flat, frictionless world is a mixed blessing. It may, as you suggest, be good for global business. Or it may, as Marx believed, augur well for a proletarian revolution. But it may also pose a threat to the distinctive places and communities that give us our bearings, that locate us in the world. From the first stirrings of capitalism, people have imagined the possibility of the world as a perfect market — unimpeded by protectionist pressures, disparate legal systems, cultural and linguistic differences, or ideological disagreement. But this vision has always bumped up against the world as it actually is — full of sources of friction and inefficiency. Some obstacles to a frictionless global market are truly sources of waste and lost opportunities. But some of these inefficiencies are institutions, habits, cultures, and traditions that people cherish precisely because they reflect nonmarket values like social cohesion, religious faith, and national pride. If global markets and new communications technologies flatten those differences, we may lose something important. That is why the debate about capitalism has been, from the very beginning, about which frictions, barriers, and boundaries are mere sources of waste and inefficiency, and which are sources of identity and belonging that we should try to protect. From the telegraph to the Internet, every new communications technology has promised to shrink the distance between people, to increase access to information, and to bring us ever closer to the dream of a perfectly efficient, frictionless global market. And each time, the question for society arises with renewed urgency: To what extent should we stand aside, 'get with the program,' and do all we can to squeeze out yet more inefficiencies, and to what extent should we lean against the current for the sake of values that global markets can't supply? Some sources of friction are worth protecting, even in the face of a global economy that threatens to flatten them."

The biggest source of friction, of course, has always been the nation-state, with its clearly defined boundaries and laws. Are national boundaries a source of friction we should want to preserve, or even can preserve, in a flat world? What about legal barriers to the free flow of information, intellectual property, and capital — such as copyrights, worker protections, and minimum wages? In the wake of the triple convergence, the more the flattening forces reduce friction and barriers, the sharper the challenge they will pose to the nation-state and to the particular cultures, values, national identities, democratic traditions, and bonds of restraint that have historically provided some protection and cushioning for workers and communities. Which do we keep and which do we let melt away into air so we can all collaborate more easily?

This will take some sorting out, which is why the point that Michael Sandel raises is critical and is sure to be at the forefront of political debate both within and between nation-states in the flat world. As Sandel argued, what I call collaboration could be seen by others as just a nice name for the ability to hire cheap labor in India. You cannot deny that when you look at it from an American perspective. But that is only if you look at it from one side. From the Indian worker's perspective, that same form of collaboration, outsourcing, could be seen as another name for empowering individuals in the developing world as never before, enabling them to nurture, exploit, and profit from their God-given intellectual talents — talents that before the flattening of the world often rotted on the docks of Bombay and Calcutta. Looking at it from the American corner of the flat world, you might conclude that the frictions, barriers, and values that restrain outsourcing should be maintained, maybe even strengthened. But from the point of view of Indians, fairness, justice, and their own aspirations demand that those same barriers and sources of friction be removed. In the flat world, one person's economic liberation could be another's unemployment.

India versus Indiana: Who Is Exploiting Whom?

Consider this case of multiple identity disorder. In 2003, the state of Indiana put out to bid a contract to upgrade the state's computer systems that process unemployment claims. Guess who won? Tata America International, which is the U.S.-based subsidiary of India's Tata Consultancy Services Ltd. Tata's bid of $15.2 million came in $8.1 million lower than that of its closest rivals, the New York–based companies Deloitte Consulting and Accenture Ltd. No Indiana firms bid on the contract, because it was too big for them to handle.

In other words, an Indian consulting firm won the contract to upgrade the unemployment department of the state of Indiana! You couldn't make this up. Indiana was outsourcing the very department that would cushion the people of Indiana from the effects of outsourcing. Tata was planning to send some sixty-five contract employees to work in the Indiana Government Center, alongside eighteen state workers. Tata also said it would hire local subcontractors and do some local recruiting, but most workers would come from India to do the computer overhauls, which, once completed, were "supposed to speed the processing of unemployment claims, as well as save postage and reduce hassles for businesses that pay unemployment taxes," the *Indianapolis Star* reported on June 25, 2004. You can probably guess how the story ended. "Top aides to then-Gov. Frank O'Bannon had signed off on the politically sensitive, four-year contract before his death [on] September 13, [2003]," the *Star* reported. But when word of the contract was made public, Republicans made it a campaign issue. It became such a political hot potato that Governor Joe Kernan, a Democrat who had succeeded O'Bannon, ordered the state agency, which helps out-of-work Indiana residents, to cancel the contract — and also to put up some legal barriers and friction to prevent such a thing from happening again. He also ordered that the contract be broken up into smaller bites that Indiana firms could bid for — good for Indiana firms but very costly and inefficient for the state. The *Indianapolis Star* reported that a check for

$993,587 was sent to pay off Tata for eight weeks of work, during which it had trained forty-five state programmers in the development and engineering of up-to-date software: " 'The company was great to work with,' said Alan Degner, Indiana's commissioner of workforce development."

So now I have just one simple question: Who is the exploiter and who is the exploited in this India-Indiana story? The American arm of an Indian consulting firm proposes to save the taxpayers of Indiana $8.1 million by revamping their computers — using both its Indian employees and local hires from Indiana. The deal would greatly benefit the American arm of the Indian consultancy; it would benefit some Indiana tech workers; and it would save Indiana state residents precious tax dollars that could be deployed to hire more state workers somewhere else, or build new schools that would permanently shrink its roles of unemployed. And yet the whole contract, which was signed by pro-labor Democrats, got torn up under pressure from free-trade Republicans.

Sort that out.

In the old world, where value was largely being created vertically, usually within a single company and from the top down, it was very easy to see who was on the top and who was on the bottom, who was exploiting and who was being exploited. But when the world starts to flatten out and value increasingly gets created horizontally (through multiple forms of collaboration, in which individuals and little guys have much more power), who is on the top and who is on the bottom, who is exploiter and who is exploited, gets very complicated. Some of our old political reflexes no longer apply. Were the Indian engineers not being "exploited" when their government educated them in some of the best technical institutes in the world inside India, but then that same Indian government pursued a socialist economic policy that could not provide those engineers with work in India, so that those who could not get out of India had to drive taxis to eat? Are those same engineers now being exploited when they join the biggest consulting company in India, are paid a very comfortable wage in Indian terms, and, thanks to the flat world, can now apply their skills globally? Or are those Indian engineers now exploiting the people of Indiana by offering to revamp their state unemployment system for much less money than an American consulting firm? Or were the people of Indiana exploiting those cheaper Indian engineers? Someone please tell me: *Who is exploiting whom in this story?* With whom does the traditional Left stand in this story? With the knowledge workers from the developing world, being paid a decent wage, who are trying to use their hard-won talents in the developed world? Or with the politicians of Indiana, who wanted to deprive these Indian engineers of work so that it could be done, more expensively, by their constituents? And with whom does the traditional Right stand in this story? With those who want to hold down taxes and shrink the state budget of Indiana by outsourcing some work, or with those who say, "Let's raise taxes more in order to reserve the work here and reserve it just for people from Indiana"? With those who want to keep some friction in the system, even though that goes against every Republican instinct on free trade, just to help people from Indiana? If you are against globalization because you think it harms people in developing countries, whose side are you on in this story: India's or Indiana's?

The India versus Indiana dispute highlights the difficulties in drawing lines between the interests of two communities that never before imagined they were connected, much less collaborators. But suddenly they each woke up and discovered that in a flat world, where work increasingly becomes a horizontal collaboration, they were not only connected and collaborating but badly in need of a social contract to govern their relations.

The larger point here is this: Whether we are talking about management science or political science, manufacturing or research and development, many, many players and processes are going to have to come to grips with "horizontalization." And it is going to take a lot of sorting out.

Where Do Companies Stop and Start?

Just as the relationship between different groups of workers will have to be sorted out in a flat world, so too will the relationship between companies and the communities in which they operate. Whose values will govern a particular company and whose interests will that company respect and promote? It used to be said that as General Motors goes, so goes America. But today it would be said, "As Dell goes, so goes Malaysia, Taiwan, China, Ireland, India . . ." HP today has 142,000 employees in 178 countries. It is not only the largest consumer technology company in the world; it is the largest IT company in Europe, the largest IT company in Russia, the largest IT company in the Middle East, and the largest IT company in South Africa. Is HP an American company if a majority of its employees and customers are outside of America, even though it is headquartered in Palo Alto?

Corporations cannot survive today as entities bounded by any single nation-state, not even one as big as the United States. So the current keep-you-awake-at-night issue for nation-states and their citizens is how to deal with corporations that are no longer bounded by a thing called the nation-state. To whom are they loyal?

"Corporate America has done very well, and there is nothing wrong with that, but it has done well by aligning itself with the flat world," said Dinakar Singh, the hedge fund manager. "It has done that by outsourcing as many components as possible to the cheapest, most efficient suppliers. If Dell can build every component of its computers in coastal China and sell them in coastal America, Dell benefits, and American consumers benefit, but it is hard to make the case that American labor benefits." So Dell wants as flat a world as possible, with as little friction and as few barriers as possible. So do most other corporations today, because this allows them to build things in the most low-cost, efficient markets and sell in the most lucrative markets. There is almost nothing about Globalization 3.0 that is not good for capital. Capitalists can sit back, buy up any innovation, and then hire the best, cheapest labor input from anywhere into the world to research it, develop it, produce it, and distribute it. Dell stock does well, Dell shareholders do well, Dell customers do well, and the Nasdaq does well. All the things related to capital do fine. But only some American workers will benefit, and only some communities. Others will feel the pain that the flattening of the world brings about.

Since multinationals first started scouring the earth for labor and markets, their interests have always gone beyond those of the nation-state in which they were headquartered. But what is going on today, on the flat earth, is such a difference of degree that it amounts to a difference in kind. Companies have never had more freedom, and less friction, in the way of assigning research, low-end manufacturing, and high-end manufacturing anywhere in the world. What this will mean for the long-term relationship between companies and the country in which they are headquartered is simply unclear.

Consider this vivid example: On December 7, 2004, IBM announced that it was selling its whole Personal Computing Division to the Chinese computer company Lenovo to create a new worldwide PC company — the globe's third largest — with approximately $12 billion in annual revenue. Simultaneously, though, IBM said that it would be taking an 18.9 percent equity stake in Lenovo, creating a strategic alliance between IBM and Lenovo in PC sales, financing, and service worldwide. The new combined company's worldwide headquarters, it was announced, would be in New York, but its principal manufacturing operations would be in Beijing and Raleigh, North Carolina; research centers would be in China, the United States, and Japan; and sales offices would be around the world. The new Lenovo will be the preferred supplier of PCs to IBM, and IBM will also be the new Lenovo's preferred supplier of services and financing.

Are you still with me? About ten thousand people will move from IBM to Lenovo, which was created in 1984 and was the first company to introduce the home computer concept in China. Since 1997, Lenovo has been the leading PC brand in China. My favorite part of the press release is the following, which identifies the new company's senior executives.

"Yang Yuanqing — Chairman of the Board. [He's currently CEO of Lenovo.] Steve Ward — Chief Executive Officer. [He's currently IBM's senior vice president and general manager of IBM's Personal Systems Group.] Fran O'Sullivan — Chief Operating Officer. [She's currently general manager of IBM's PC division.] Mary Ma — Chief Financial Officer. [She's currently CFO of Lenovo.]"

Talk about horizontal value creation: This

new Chinese-owned computer company headquartered in New York with factories in Raleigh and Beijing will have a Chinese chairman, an American CEO, an American CPO, and a Chinese CFO, and it will be listed on the Hong Kong stock exchange. Would you call this an American company? A Chinese company? To which country will Lenovo feel most attached? Or will it just see itself sort of floating above a flat earth?

This question was anticipated in the press release announcing the new company: "Where will Lenovo be headquartered?" it asked.

Answer: "As a global business, the new Lenovo will be geographically dispersed, with people and physical assets located worldwide."

Sort that out.

The cold, hard truth is that management, shareholders, and investors are largely indifferent to where their profits come from or even where the employment is created. But they do want sustainable companies. Politicians, though, are compelled to stimulate the creation of jobs in a certain place. And residents — whether they are Americans, Europeans, or Indians — want to know that the good jobs are going to stay close to home.

The CEO of a major European multinational remarked to me, "We are a global research company now." That's great news for his shareholders and investors. He is accessing the best brains on the planet, wherever they are, and almost certainly saving money by not doing all the research in his backyard. "But ultimately," he confided to me, "this is going to have implications down the road on jobs in my own country — maybe not this year but in five or fifteen years." As a CEO and European Union citizen, "you might have a dialogue with your government about how we can retain capabilities in [our own country] — but day by day you have to make decisions with the shareholders in mind."

Translation: If I can buy five brilliant researchers in China and/or India for the price of one in Europe or America, I will buy the five; and if, in the long run, that means my own society loses part of its skills base, so be it. The only way to converge the interests of the two — the company and its country of origin — is to have a really smart population that can not only claim its slice of the bigger global pie but invent its own new slices as well. "We have grown addicted to our high salaries, and now we are really going to have to earn them," the CEO said.

But even identifying a company's country of origin today is getting harder and harder. Sir John Rose, the chief executive of Rolls-

Royce, told me once, "We have a big business in Germany. We are the biggest high-tech employer in the state of Brandenburg. I was recently at a dinner with Chancellor [Gerhard] Schroeder. And he said to me, 'You are a German company, why don't you come along with me on my next visit to Russia' — to try to drum up business there for German companies." The German chancellor, said Rose, "was recognizing that although my headquarters were in London, my business was involved in creating value in Germany, and that could be constructive in his relationship with Russia."

Here you have the quintessential British company, Rolls-Royce, which, though still headquartered in England, now operates through a horizontal global supply chain, and its CEO, a British citizen knighted by the queen, is being courted by the chancellor of Germany to help him drum up business in Russia, because one link in the Rolls-Royce supply chain happens to run through Brandenburg.

Sort that out.

From Command and Control to Collaborate and Connect

Before Colin Powell stepped down as secretary of state, I went in for an interview, which was also attended by two of his press advisers, in his seventh-floor State Department suite. I could not resist asking him about where he was when he realized the world had gone flat. He answered with one word: "Google." Powell said that when he took over as secretary of state in 2001, and he needed some bit of information — say, the text of a UN resolution — he would call an aide and have to wait for minutes or even hours for someone to dig it up for him.

"Now I just type into Google 'UNSC Resolution 242' and up comes the text," he said. Powell explained that with each passing year, he found himself doing more and more of his own research, at which point one of his press advisers remarked, "Yes, now he no longer comes asking for information. He already has the information. He comes asking for action."

Powell, a former member of the AOL board, also regularly used e-mail to contact other foreign ministers and, according to one of his aides, kept up a constant instant-messaging relationship with Britain's foreign secretary, Jack Straw, at summit meetings, as if they were a couple of college students. Thanks to the cell phone and wireless technology, said Powell, no foreign minister can run and hide from him. He said he had been looking for Russia's foreign minister the previous week. First he tracked him down on his cell phone in Moscow, then on his cell phone in Iceland, and then on his cell phone in Vientiane, Laos. "We have everyone's cell phone number," said Powell of his fellow foreign ministers.

The point I take away from all this is that when the world goes flat, hierarchies are not being leveled just by little people being able to act big. They are also being leveled by big people being able to act really small — in the sense that they are enabled to do many more things on their own. It really hit me when Powell's junior media adviser, a young woman, walked me down from his office and remarked along the way that because of e-mail, Powell could get hold of her and her boss at any hour, via their BlackBerrys — and did.

"I can't get away from the guy," she said jokingly of his constant e-mail instructions. But in the next breath she added that on the previous weekend, she was shopping at the mall with some friends when she got an instant message from Powell asking her to do some public affairs task. "My friends were all impressed," she said. "Little me, and I'm talking to the secretary of state!"

This is what happens when you move from a vertical (command and control) world to a much more horizontal (connect and collaborate) flat world. Your boss can do his job *and your job*. He can be secretary of state and his own secretary. He can give you instructions day or night. So you are never out. You are always in. Therefore, you are always on. Bosses, if they are inclined, can collaborate more directly with more of their staff than ever before — no matter who they are or where they are in the hierarchy. But staffers will also have to work much harder to be better informed than their bosses. There are a lot more conversations between bosses and staffers today that start like this: "I know that already! I Googled it myself. Now what do I do about it?"

Sort that out.

Multiple Identity Disorder

It is not only communities and companies that have multiple identities that will need sorting out in a flat world. So too will individuals. In a flat world, the tensions among our identities as consumers, employees, citizens, taxpayers, and shareholders are going to come into sharper and sharper conflict.

"In the nineteenth century," said business consultant Michael Hammer, "the great conflict was between labor and capital. Now it is between customer and worker, and the company is the guy in the middle. The consumer turns to the company and says, 'Give me more for less.' And then companies turn to employees and say, 'If we don't give them more for less, we are in trouble. I can't guarantee you a job and a union steward can't guarantee you a job, only a customer can.' "

The New York Times reported (November 1, 2004) that Wal-Mart spent about $1.3 billion of its $256 billion in revenue in 2003 on employee health care, to insure about 537,000 people, or about 45 percent of its workforce. Wal-Mart's biggest competitor, though, Costco Wholesale, insured 96 percent of its eligible full-time or part-time employees. Costco employees become eligible for health insurance after three months working full-time or six months working part-time. At Wal-Mart, most full-time employees have to wait six months to become eligible, while part-timers are not eligible for at least two years. According to the *Times*, full-time employees at Wal-Mart make about $1,200 per month, or $8 per hour. Wal-Mart requires employees to cover 33 percent of the cost of their benefits, and it plans to reduce that employee contribution to 30 percent. Wal-Mart-sponsored health plans have monthly premiums for family coverage ranging as high as $264 and out-of-pocket expenses as high as $13,000 in some cases, and such medical costs make health coverage unaffordable even for many Wal-Mart employees who are covered, the *Times* said.

But the same article went on to say this: "If there is any place where Wal-Mart's labor costs find support, it is Wall Street, where Costco has taken a drubbing from analysts who say its labor costs are too high." Wal-Mart has taken more fat and friction out than Costco, which has kept more in, because it feels a different obligation to its workers. Costco's pretax profit margin is only 2.7 percent of revenue, less than half Wal-Mart's margin of 5.5 percent.

The Wal-Mart shopper in all of us wants the lowest price possible, with all the middlemen, fat, and friction removed. And the Wal-Mart shareholder in us wants Wal-Mart to be relentless about removing the fat and friction in its supply chain and in its employee benefits packages, in order to fatten the company's profits. But the Wal-Mart worker in us hates the benefits and pay packages that Wal-Mart offers its starting employees. And the Wal-Mart citizen in us knows that because Wal-Mart, the biggest company in America, doesn't cover all its employees with health care, some of them will just go to the emergency ward of the local hospital and the taxpayers will end up picking up the tab. The *Times* reported that a survey by Georgia officials found that "more than 10,000 children of

Wal-Mart employees were in the state's health program for children at an annual cost of nearly $10 million to taxpayers." Similarly, it said, a "North Carolina hospital found that 31 percent of 1,900 patients who described themselves as Wal-Mart employees were on Medicaid, while an additional 16 percent had no insurance at all."

In her 2004 book, *Selling Women Short: The Landmark Battle for Workers' Rights at Wal-Mart*, journalist Liza Featherstone followed the huge women's discrimination suit against Wal-Mart. In an interview about the book with Salon.com (November 22, 2004), she made the following important point: "American taxpayers chip in to pay for many full-time Wal-Mart employees because they usually require incremental health insurance, public housing, food stamps — there are so many ways in which Wal-Mart employees are not able to be self-sufficient. This is very ironic, because Sam Walton is embraced as the American symbol of self-sufficiency. It is really troubling and dishonest that Wal-Mart supports Republican candidates in the way that they do: 80 percent of their corporate campaign contributions go to Republicans. But Republicans tend not to support the types of public assistance programs that Wal-Mart depends on. If anything, Wal-Mart should be crusading for national health insurance. They should at least be acknowledging that because they are unable to provide these things for their employees, we should have a more general welfare state."

As you sort out and weigh your multiple identities — consumer, employee, citizen, taxpayer, shareholder — you have to decide: Do you prefer the Wal-Mart approach or the Costco approach? This is going to be an important political issue in a flat world: Just how flat do you want corporations to be when you factor in all your different identities? Because when you take the middleman out of business, when you totally flatten your supply chain, you also take a certain element of humanity out of life.

The same question applies to government. How flat do you want government to be? How much friction would you like to see government remove, through deregulation, to make it easier for companies to compete on Planet Flat?

Said Congressman Rahm Emanuel, an Illinois Democrat who was a senior adviser to President Clinton, "When I served in the White House, we streamlined the FDA's drug approval process in response to concerns about its cumbersome nature. We took those steps with one objective in mind: to move drugs to the marketplace more quickly. The result, however, has been an increasingly cozy relationship between the FDA and the pharmaceutical industry, which has put public health at risk. The Vioxx debacle [over an anti-inflammatory drug that was found to lead to an increased risk for heart attacks and strokes] shows the extent to which drug safety has taken a backseat to speedy approval. A recent Senate hearing on Vioxx's recall revealed major deficiencies in the FDA's ability to remove dangerous drugs from the market."

As consumers we want the cheapest drugs that the global supply chains can offer, but as citizens we want and need government to oversee and regulate that supply chain, even if it means preserving or adding friction.

Sort that out.

Who Owns What?

Something else is absolutely going to have to be sorted out in a flat world: Who owns what? How do we build legal barriers to protect an innovator's intellectual property so he or she can reap its financial benefits and plow those profits into a new invention? And from the other side, how do we keep walls low enough so that we encourage the sharing of intellectual property, which is required more and more to do cutting-edge innovation?

"The world is decidedly not flat when it comes to uniform treatment of intellectual property," said Craig Mundie, Microsoft's chief technology officer. It is wonderful, he noted, to have a world where a single innovator can summon so many resources by himself or herself, assemble a team of partners from around the flat world, and make a real breakthrough with some product or service. But what does that wonderful innovative engineer do, asked Mundie, "when someone else uses the same flat-world platform and tools to clone and distribute his wonderful new product?" This happens in the world of software, music, and pharmaceuticals every day. And the technology is reaching a point now where "you should assume that there isn't anything that can't be counterfeited quickly" — from Microsoft Word to airplane parts, he added. The flatter the world gets, the more we are going to need a system of global governance that keeps up with all the new legal and illegal forms of collaboration.

We can also see this in the case of patent law as it has evolved inside the United States. Companies can do one of three things with an innovation. They can patent the widget they invent and sell it themselves; they can patent it and license it to someone else to manufacture; and they can patent it and cross-license with several other companies so that they all have freedom of action to make a product — like a PC — that comes from melding many different patents. American patent law is technically neutral on this. But the way established case law has evolved, experts tell me, it is decidedly biased against cross-licensing and other arrangements that encourage collaboration or freedom of action for as many players as possible; it is more focused on protecting the rights of individual firms to manufacture their own patents. In a flat world, companies need a patent system that encourages both. The more your legal structure fosters cross-licensing and standards, the more collaborative innovation you will get. The PC is the product of a lot of cross-licensing between the company that had the patent on the cursor and the company that had the patent on the mouse and the screen.

The free-software person in all of us wants no patent laws. But the innovator in all of us wants a global regime that protects against intellectual property piracy. The innovator in us also wants patent laws that encourage cross-licensing with companies that are ready to play by the rules.

"Who owns what?" is sure to emerge as one of the most contentious political and geopolitical questions in a flat world — especially if more and more American companies start feeling ripped off by more and more Chinese companies. If you are in the business of selling words, music, or pharmaceuticals and you are not worried about protecting your intellectual property, you are not paying attention.

And while you are sorting that out, sort this out as well. On November 13, 2004, Lance Cpl. Justin M. Ellsworth, twenty, was killed by a roadside bomb during a foot patrol in Iraq. On December 21, 2004, the Associated Press reported that his family was demanding that Yahoo! give them the password for their deceased son's e-mail account so they could have access to all his e-mail, including notes to and from others. "I want to be able to remember him in his words. I know he thought he was doing what he needed to do. I want to have that for the future," John Ellsworth, Justin's father, told the AP. "It's the last thing I have of my son." We are moving into a world where more and more communication is in the form of bits traveling through cyberspace and stored on servers located all over the world. No government controls this cyber-realm. So the question is: Who owns your bits when you die? The

AP reported that Yahoo! denied the Ellsworth family their son's password, citing the fact that Yahoo! policy calls for erasing all accounts that are inactive for ninety days and the fact that all Yahoo! users agree at sign-up that rights to a member's ID or account contents terminate upon death. "While we sympathize with any grieving family, Yahoo! accounts and any contents therein are nontransferable" even after death, Karen Mahon, a Yahoo! spokeswoman told the AP. As we get rid of more and more paper and communicate through more and more digitized formats, you better sort out before you die, and include in your will, to whom, if anyone, you want to leave your bits. This is very real. I stored many chapters of this book in my AOL account, feeling it would be safest in cyberspace. If something had happened to me during my writing, my family and publisher would have had to sue AOL to try to get this text. Somebody, please, sort all this out.

Death of the Salesmen

In the fall of 2004, I went out to Minneapolis to visit my mother and had three world-is-flat encounters right in a row. First, before I left home in Washington, I dialed 411 — directory assistance — to try to get a friend's phone number in Minneapolis. A computer answered and a computerized voice asked me to pronounce the name of the person whose number I was requesting. For whatever reason, I could not get the computer to hear me correctly, and it kept saying back to me in a computerized voice, "Did you say . . . ?" I kept having to say the family name in a voice that masked my exasperation (otherwise the computer never would have understood me). "No, I didn't say that . . . I said . . ." Eventually, I was connected to an operator, but I did not enjoy this friction-free encounter with directory information. I craved the friction of another human being. It may be cheaper and more efficient to have a computer dispense phone numbers, but for me it brought only frustration.

When I arrived in Minneapolis, I had dinner with family friends, one of whom has spent his life working as a wholesaler in the Midwest, selling goods to the biggest retailers in the region. He is a natural salesman. When I asked him what was new, he sighed and said that business just wasn't what it used to be. Everything was now being sold at 1 percent margins, he explained. No problem. He was selling mostly commodity items so that, given his volumes, he could handle the slim profit margin. But what bothered him, he mentioned, was the fact that he no longer had human contact with some of his biggest accounts. Even commodities and low-cost goods have certain differentiating elements that need to be sold and highlighted. "Everything is by e-mail now," he said. "I am dealing with a young kid at [one of the biggest retailers in the nation], and he says, 'Just e-mail me your bid.' I've never met him. Half the time he doesn't get back to me. I am not sure how to deal with him . . . In the old days, I used to stop by the office, give the buyers a few Vikings tickets. We were friends . . . Tommy, all anyone cares about today is price."

Fortunately, my friend is a successful businessman and has a range of enterprises. But as I reflected later on what he was saying, I was drawn back to that scene in *Death of a Salesman* in which Willy Loman says that, unlike his colleague Charley, he intends to be "well liked." He tells his sons that in business and in life, character, personality, and human connections are more important than smarts. Says Willy, "The man who makes an appearance in the business world, the man who creates personal interest, is the man who gets ahead. Be liked and you will never want."

Not when the world goes flat. It's hard to create a human bond with e-mail and streaming Internet. The next day, I had dinner with my friend Ken Greer, who runs a media company that I discuss in greater detail later. Ken had a similar lament: So many contracts were going these days to the advertising firms that were selling just numbers, not creative instinct. Then Ken said something that really hit home with me: "It is like they have cut all the fat out of the business" and turned everything into a numbers game. "But fat is what gives meat its taste," Ken added. "The leanest cuts of meat don't taste very good. You want it marbled with at least a little fat."

The flattening process relentlessly trims the fat out of business and life, but, as Ken noted, fat is what gives life taste and texture. Fat is also what keeps us warm.

Yes, the consumer in us wants Wal-Mart prices, with all the fat gone. But the employee in us wants a little fat left on the bone, the way Costco does it, so that it can offer health care to almost all its employees, rather than just less than half of them, as Wal-Mart does. But the shareholder in us wants Wal-Mart's profit margins, not Costco's. Yet the citizen in us wants Costco's benefits, rather than Wal-Mart's, because the difference ultimately may have to be paid for by society. The consumer in me wants lower phone bills, but the human being in me also wants to speak to an operator when I call 411. Yes, the reader in me loves to surf the Net and read the bloggers, but the citizen in me also wishes that some of those bloggers had an editor, a middleman, to tell them to check some of their facts one more time before they pressed the Send button and told the whole world that something was wrong or unfair.

Given these conflicting emotions and pressures, there is potential here for American politics to get completely reshuffled — with workers and corporate interests realigning themselves into different parties. Think about it: Social conservatives from the right wing of the Republican party, who do not like globalization or closer integration with the world because it brings too many foreigners and foreign cultural mores into America, might align themselves with unions from the left wing of the Democratic Party, who don't like globalization for the way it facilitates the outsourcing and offshoring of jobs. They might be called the Wall Party and militate for more friction and fat everywhere. Let's face it: Republican cultural conservatives have much more in common with the steelworkers of Youngstown, Ohio, the farmers of rural China, and the mullahs of central Saudi Arabia, who would also like more walls, than they do with investment bankers on Wall Street or service workers linked to the global economy in Palo Alto, who have been enriched by the flattening of the world.

Meanwhile, the business wing of the Republican Party, which believes in free trade, deregulation, more integration, and lower taxes — everything that would flatten the world even more — may end up aligning itself with the social liberals of the Democratic Party, many of whom are East Coast or West Coast global service industry workers. They might also be joined by Hollywood and other entertainment workers. All of them are huge beneficiaries of the flat world. They might be called the Web Party, whose main platform would be to promote more global integration. Many residents of Manhattan and Palo Alto have more interests in common with the people of Shanghai and Bangalore than they do with the residents of Youngstown or Topeka. In short, in a flat world, we are likely to see many social liberals, white-collar global service industry workers, and Wall Street types driven together, and many social conservatives, white-collar local service industry workers, and labor unions driven together.

The *Passion of the Christ* audience will be in the same trench with the Teamsters and the AFL-CIO, while the Hollywood and Wall Street liberals and the *You've Got Mail* crowd will be in the same trench with the high-tech workers of Silicon Valley and the global service providers of Manhattan and San Francisco. It will be Mel Gibson and Jimmy Hoffa Jr. versus Bill Gates and Meg Ryan.

More and more, politics in the flat world will consist of asking which values, frictions, and fats are worth preserving — which should, in Marx's language, be kept solid — and which must be left to melt away into the air. Countries, companies, and individuals will be able to give intelligent answers to these questions only if they understand the real nature and texture of the global playing field and how different it is from the one that existed in the Cold War era and before. And countries, companies, and individuals will be able to make sound political choices only if they fully appreciate the flattened playing field and understand all the new tools now available to them for collaborating and competing on it. I hope this book will provide a nuanced framework for this hugely important political debate and the great sorting out that is just around the corner.

To that end, the next three sections look at how the flattening of the world and the triple convergence will affect Americans, developing countries, and companies.

Brace yourself: You are now about to enter the flat world.

AMERICA
AND THE FLAT WORLD

FIVE

America and Free Trade

Is Ricardo Still Right?

As an American who has always believed in the merits of free trade, I had an important question to answer after my India trip: Should I still believe in free trade in a flat world? Here was an issue that needed sorting out immediately — not only because it was becoming a hot issue in the presidential campaign of 2004 but also because my whole view of the flat world would depend on my view of free trade. I know that free trade won't necessarily benefit every American, and that our society will have to help those who are harmed by it. But for me the key question was: Will free trade benefit America *as a whole* when the world becomes so flat and so many more people can collaborate, and compete, with my kids? It seems that so many jobs are going to be up for grabs. Wouldn't individual Americans be better off if our government erected some walls and banned some outsourcing and offshoring?

I first wrestled with this issue while filming the Discovery Times documentary in Bangalore. One day we went to the Infosys campus around five p.m. — just when the Infosys call-center workers were flooding into the grounds for the overnight shift on foot, minibus, and motor scooter, while many of the more advanced engineers were leaving at the end of the day shift. The crew and I were standing at the gate observing this river of educated young people flowing in and out, many in animated conversation. They all looked as if they had scored 1,600 on their SATs, and I felt a real mind-eye split overtaking me.

My mind just kept telling me, "Ricardo is right, Ricardo is right, Ricardo is right." David Ricardo (1772–1823) was the English economist who developed the free-trade theory of comparative advantage, which stipulates that if each nation specializes in the production of goods in which it has a comparative cost advantage and then trades with other nations for the goods in which they specialize, there will be an overall gain in trade, and overall income levels should rise in each trading country. So if all these Indian techies were doing what was their comparative advantage and then turning around and using their income to buy all the products from America that are our comparative advantage —

from Corning Glass to Microsoft Windows — both our countries would benefit, even if some individual Indians or Americans might have to shift jobs in the transition. And one can see evidence of this mutual benefit in the sharp increase in exports and imports between the United States and India in recent years.

But my eye kept looking at all these Indian zippies and telling me something else: "Oh, my God, there are so many of them, and they all look so serious, so eager for work. And they just keep coming, wave after wave. How in the world can it possibly be good for my daughters and millions of other young Americans that these Indians can do the same jobs as they can for a fraction of the wages?"

When Ricardo was writing, goods were tradable, but for the most part knowledge work and services were not. There was no undersea fiber-optic cable to make knowledge jobs tradable between America and India back then. Just as I was getting worked up with worry, the Infosys spokeswoman accompanying me casually mentioned that last year Infosys India received "one million applications" from young Indians for nine thousand tech jobs.

Have a nice day.

I struggled over what to make of this

scene. I don't want to see any American lose his or her job to foreign competition or to technological innovation. I sure wouldn't want to lose mine. When you lose your job, the unemployment rate is not 5.2 percent; it's 100 percent. No book about the flat world would be honest if it did not acknowledge such concerns, or acknowledge that there is some debate among economists about whether Ricardo *is* still right.

Having listened to the arguments on both sides, though, I come down where the great majority of economists come down — that Ricardo is still right and that more American individuals will be better off if we don't erect barriers to outsourcing, supply-chaining, and offshoring than if we do. The simple message of this chapter is that even as the world gets flat, America as a whole will benefit more by sticking to the basic principles of free trade, as it always has, than by trying to erect walls.

The main argument of the anti-outsourcing school is that in a flat world, not only are goods tradable, but many services have become tradable as well. Because of this change, America and other developed countries could be headed for an absolute decline, not just a relative one, in their economic power and living standards unless they move to formally protect certain jobs from foreign competition. So many new players cannot enter the global economy — in service and knowledge fields now dominated by Americans, Europeans, and Japanese — without wages settling at a newer, lower equilibrium, this school argues.

The main counterargument from free-trade/outsourcing advocates is that while there may be a transition phase in certain fields, during which wages are dampened, there is no reason to believe that this dip will be permanent or across the board, as long as the global pie keeps growing. To suggest that it will be is to invoke the so-called lump of labor theory — the notion that there is a fixed lump of labor in the world and that once that lump is gobbled up, by either Americans or Indians or Japanese, there won't be any more jobs to go around. If we have the biggest lump of labor now, and then Indians offer to do this same work for less, they will get a bigger piece of the lump, and we will have less, or so this argument goes.

The main reason the lump of labor theory is wrong is that it is based on the assumption that everything that is going to be invented has been invented, and that therefore economic competition is a zero-sum game, a fight over a fixed lump. This assumption misses the fact that although jobs are often lost in bulk — to outsourcing or offshoring — by big individual companies, and this loss tends to make headlines, new jobs are also being created in fives, tens, and twenties by small companies that you can't see. It often takes a leap of faith to believe that it is happening. *But it is happening.* If it were not, America's unemployment rate would be much higher today than 5 percent. The reason it is happening is that as lower-end service and manufacturing jobs move out of Europe, America, and Japan to India, China, and the former Soviet Empire, the global pie not only grows larger — because more people have more income to spend — it also grows more complex, as more new jobs, and new specialties, are created.

Let me illustrate this with a simple example. Imagine that there are only two countries in the world — America and China. And imagine that the American economy has only 100 people. Of those 100 people, 80 are well-educated knowledge workers and 20 are less-educated low-skilled workers. Now imagine that the world goes flat and America enters into a free-trade agreement with China, which has 1,000 people but is a less developed country. So today China too has only 80 well-educated knowledge workers out of that 1,000, and it has 920 low-skilled workers. Before America entered into its free-trade agreement with China, there were only 80 knowledge workers in its world. Now there are 160 in our two-country world. The American knowledge workers feel like they have more competition, and they do. But if you look at the prize they are going after, it is now a much expanded and more complex market. It went from a market of 100 people to a market of 1,100 people, with many more needs and wants. So it should be win-win for both the American and Chinese knowledge workers.

Sure, some of the knowledge workers in America may have to move *horizontally* into new knowledge jobs, because of the competition from China. But with a market that big and complex, you can be sure that new knowledge jobs will open up at decent wages for anyone who keeps up his or her skills. So do not worry about our knowledge workers or the Chinese knowledge workers. They will both do fine with this bigger market.

"What do you mean, don't worry?" you ask. "How do we deal with the fact that those eighty knowledge workers from China will be willing to work for so much less than the eighty knowledge workers from America? How will this difference get resolved?"

It won't happen overnight, so some American knowledge workers may be affected in the transition, but the effects will not be permanent. Here, argues Stanford new economy specialist Paul Romer, is what you need to understand: The wages for the Chinese knowledge workers were so low because, although their skills were marketable globally like those of their American counterparts, they were trapped inside a stifled economy. Imagine how little a North Korean computer expert or brain surgeon is paid inside that huge prison of a nation! But as the Chinese economy opens up to the world and reforms, the wages of Chinese knowledge workers will rise up to American/world levels. Ours will not go down to the level of a stifled, walled-in economy. You can already see this happening in Bangalore, where competition for Indian software writers is rapidly pushing up their wages toward American/European levels — after decades of languishing while the Indian economy was closed. It is why Americans should be doing all they can to promote more and faster economic reform in India and China.

Do worry, though, about the 20 low-skilled Americans, who now have to compete more directly with the 920 low-skilled Chinese. One reason the 20 low-skilled Americans were paid a decent wage before was that, relative to the 80 skilled Americans, there were not that many of them.

Every economy needs some low-skilled manual labor. But now that China and America have signed their free-trade pact, there are a total of 940 low-skilled workers and 160 knowledge workers in our two-country world. Those American low-skilled workers doing fungible jobs — jobs that can easily be moved to China — will have a problem. There is no denying this. Their wages are certain to be depressed. In order to maintain or improve their living standards, they will have to move *vertically,* not horizontally. They will have to upgrade their education and upgrade their knowledge skills so that they can occupy one of the new jobs sure to be created in the much expanded United States–China market. (In Chapter 8 I will talk about our society's obligation to ensure that everyone gets a chance to acquire those skills.)

As Romer notes, we know from the history of our own country that an increase in knowledge workers does not necessarily lead to a decrease in their pay the way it does with low-skilled workers. From the 1960s to the 1980s, the supply of college-educated workers grew dramatically, and yet their wages grew even faster. Because as the pie grew in size and complexity, so too did people's wants, and this increased the demand for people able to do complex work and specialized tasks.

Romer explains this in part by the fact that "there is a difference between idea-based goods and physical goods." If you are a knowledge worker making and selling some kind of idea-based product — consulting or financial services or music or software or marketing or design or new drugs — the bigger the market is, the more people there are out there to whom you can sell your product. And the bigger the market, the more new specialties and niches it will create. If you come up with the next Windows or Viagra, you can potentially sell one to everyone in the world. So idea-based workers do well in globalization, and fortunately America as a whole has more idea-driven workers than any country in the world.

But if you are selling manual labor — or a piece of lumber or a slab of steel — the value of what you have to sell does not necessarily increase when the market expands, and it may decrease, argues Romer. There are only so many factories that will buy your manual labor, and there are many more people selling it. What the manual laborer has to sell can be bought by only one factory or one consumer at a time, explains Romer, while what the software writer or drug inventor has to sell — idea-based products — can be sold to everyone in the global market at once.

That is why America, as a whole, will do fine in a flat world with free trade — provided it continues to churn out knowledge workers who are able to produce idea-based goods that can be sold globally and who are able to fill the knowledge jobs that will be created as we not only expand the global economy but connect all the knowledge pools in the world. There may be a limit to the number of good factory jobs in the world, *but there is no limit to the number of idea-generated jobs in the world.*

If we go from a world in which there were fifteen drug companies and fifteen software companies in America (thirty in all) and two drug companies and two software companies in China (four in all) to a world in which there are thirty drug and software companies in America and thirty drug and software companies in China, it is going to mean more innovation, more cures, more new products, more niches to specialize in, and many more people with higher incomes to buy those products.

"The pie keeps growing because things that look like wants today are needs tomorrow," argued Marc Andreessen, the Netscape cofounder, who helped to ignite a whole new industry, e-commerce, that now employs millions of specialists around the world, specialists whose jobs weren't even imagined when Bill Clinton became president. I like going to coffee shops occasionally, but now that Starbucks is here, I *need* my coffee, and that new need has spawned a whole new industry. I always wanted to be able to search for things, but once Google was created, I *must* have my search engine. So a whole new industry has been built up around search, and Google is hiring math Ph.D.'s by the bushel — before Yahoo! or Microsoft hires them. People are always assuming that everything that is going to be invented must have been invented already. *But it hasn't.*

"If you believe human wants and needs are infinite," said Andreesen, "then there are infinite industries to be created, infinite businesses to be started, and infinite jobs to be done, and the only limiting factor is human imagination. The world is flattening and rising at the same time. And I think the evidence is overwhelmingly clear: If you look over the sweep of history, every time we had more trade, more communications, we had a big upswing in economic activity and standard of living."

America integrated a broken Europe and Japan into the global economy after World War II, with both Europe and Japan every year upgrading their manufacturing, knowledge, and service skills, often importing and sometimes stealing ideas and equipment from the United States, just as

America did from Britain in the late 1770s. Yet in the sixty years since World War II, our standard of living has increased every decade, and our unemployment rate — even with all the outcry about outsourcing — stands at only a little above 5 percent, roughly half that of the most developed countries in Western Europe.

"We just started a company that created 180 new jobs in the middle of a recession," said Andreessen, whose company, Opsware, uses automation and software to replace human beings in the operation of huge server farms in remote locations. By automating these jobs, Opsware enables companies to save money and free up talented brainpower from relatively mundane tasks to start new businesses in other areas. You should be afraid of free markets, argued Andreessen, only if you believe that you will never need new medicines, new work flow software, new industries, new forms of entertainment, new coffeehouses.

"Yes," he concluded, "it takes a leap of faith, based on economics, to say there will be new things to do." But there always have been new jobs to do, and there is no fundamental reason to believe the future will be different. Some 150 years ago, 90 percent of Americans worked in agriculture and related fields. Today, it's only 3 or 4 percent. What if the government had decided to protect and subsidize all those agricultural jobs and not embrace industrialization and then computerization? Would America as a whole really be better off today? Hardly.

As noted, it is true that as Indians or Chinese move up the value chain and start producing more knowledge-intensive goods — the sorts of things Americans have been specializing in — our comparative advantage in some of these areas will diminish, explains Jagdish Bhagwati, the Columbia University expert on free trade. There will be a downward pressure on wages in certain fields, and some of the jobs in those fields may permanently migrate abroad. That is why some knowledge workers will have to move horizontally. But the growing pie will surely create new specialties for them to fill that are impossible to predict right now.

For instance, there was a time when America's semiconductor industry dominated the world, but then companies from other countries came along and gobbled up the low end of the market. Some even moved into the higher end. American companies were then forced to find newer, deeper specialties in the expanded market. If that weren't happening, Intel would be out of business today. Instead, it is thriving. Paul Otellini, Intel's president, told *The Economist* (May 8, 2003) that as chips become good enough for certain applications, new applications pop up that demand more powerful and more complex chips, which are Intel's specialty.

Once Google starts offering video searches, for instance, there will be demand for new machines and the chips that power them, of which no one was even dreaming five years ago. This process takes time to unfold. But it will, argued Bhagwati, because what is happening in services today is the same thing that happened in manufacturing as trade barriers were lowered. In manufacturing, said Bhagwati, as the global market expanded and more and more players came onto the field, you saw greater and greater "intraindustry trade, with more and more specialization," and as we move into the knowledge economy, you are now seeing more and more intraservice trade, with more and more specialization.

Don't be surprised if your son or daughter graduates from college and calls you one day and says he or she is going to be a "search engine optimizer."

A what?

A slew of firms has started up around Google, Yahoo!, and Microsoft to help retailers strategize on how to improve their rankings, and increase the number of click-throughs to their Web sites, on these major search engines. It can mean millions of dollars in extra profits if, when someone searches for "video camera," your company's product comes up first, because the people who click through to your Web site are those most likely to buy from you. What these search engine optimizers (SEOs as they are called in the trade) do is constantly study the algorithms being used by the major search engines and then design marketing and Web strategies that will push you up the rankings. The business involves a combination of math and marketing — a whole new specialty created entirely by the flattening of the world.

And always remember: *The Indians and Chinese are not racing us to the bottom. They are racing us to the top — and that is a good thing!* They want higher standards of living, not sweatshops; they want brand names, not junk; they want to trade their motor scooters for cars and their pens and pencils for computers. And the more they do that, the higher they climb, the more room is created at the top — because the more they have, the more they spend, the more diverse product markets become, and the more niches for specialization are created as well.

Look at what is happening already: As American companies send knowledge work to India, Indian companies are turning around and using their earnings and insights to start inventing new products that poorer Indians can use to lift themselves out of poverty into the middle class, where they will surely become consumers of American products. *BusinessWeek* cited the Tata Motors factory, near Pune, south of Mumbai, "where a group of young designers, technicians, and marketers pore over drawings and examine samples of steel and composite plastics. By early next year, they plan to design a prototype for Tata Group's most ambitious project yet: a compact car that will sell for $2,200. The company hopes the car will beat out Suzuki's $5,000 Maruti compact to become India's cheapest car — and an export model for the rest of the developing world. 'This is the need of the day in India — a people's car,' says Ratan Tata, chairman of the $12.5 billion Tata Group. Indians are increasingly demanding better products and services at an affordable cost. Strong economic growth this year will only enlarge that demand. The phrase 'Made in India' may come to represent low-cost innovation in the new global economy" (October 11, 2004).

Raghuram Rajan, the director of research for the International Monetary Fund, sits on the board of a company that puts Indian students to work tutoring students in Singapore. The students, from the Indian Institute of Technology in Madras, go online to help students in Singapore, from grades six to twelve, on their math homework. They also help teachers in Singapore develop lesson plans and prepare PowerPoint presentations or other jazzy ways for them to teach math. The company, called Heymath.com, is paid for by the schools in Singapore. Cambridge University in England is also part of this equation, providing the overall quality controls and certifying the lesson plans and teaching methods.

"Everyone wins," says Rajan. "The company is run by two Indians who worked for Citibank and CSFB in London and came back to India to start this business . . . Cambridge University is making money from a company that has created a whole new niche. The Indian students are making pocket money. And the Singapore students are learning better." Meanwhile, the underlying software is probably being provided by Microsoft and the chips by Intel, and the enriched Indian students are probably buying cheap personal computers from Apple, Dell, or HP. *But you can't really see any of this.* "The pie grew, but no one saw it," said Rajan.

An essay in the *McKinsey Quarterly*, "Beyond Cheap Labor: Lessons for Developing Economies" (January 2005), offers a nice example of this: "In northern Italy's textile and apparel industry . . . the majority of garment production has moved to lower-cost locations, but employment remains stable because companies have put more resources into tasks such as designing clothes and coordinating global production networks."

It is so easy to demonize free markets — and the freedom to outsource and offshore — because it is so much easier to see people being laid off than being hired. But occasionally a newspaper tries to dig deep into the issue. My hometown paper, the Minneapolis *Star Tribune*, did just that. It looked at exactly how the Minnesota economy was being affected by the flattening of the world, actually daring to run an article on September 5, 2004, headlined, "Offshore Jobs Bring Gains at Home." The article, datelined Wuxi, China, began like this: "Outside the air is dank, dusty and hot as tropical fever. Inside, in an environment that's dry, spotless and cool, hundreds of former farm laborers covered head to toe in suits looking like something out of NASA are performing work for Bloomington-based Donaldson Co. Inc. . . . In Donaldson's case, the company has twice as many workers in China

— 2,500 — as the 1,100 it has in Bloomington. The Chinese operation not only has allowed Donaldson to keep making a product it no longer could make at a profit in the United States, it also has helped boost the company's Minnesota employment, up by 400 people since 1990. Donaldson's highly paid engineers, chemists and designers in Minnesota spend their days designing updated filters that the Chinese plant will make for use in computers, MP3 players and digital video recorders. The falling disk-drive prices made possible by Chinese production are feeding demand for the gadgets. 'If we didn't follow [the trend], we'd be out of business,' said David Timm, general manager of Donaldson's disk-drive and microelectronics unit. In Minnesota, Global Insight estimates that 1,854 jobs were created as a result of foreign outsourcing in 2003. By 2008, the firm expects nearly 6,700 new jobs in Minnesota as a consequence of the trend."

Economists often compare China's and India's entry into the global economy to the moment when the railroad lines crossing America finally connected New Mexico to California, with its much larger population. "When the railroad comes to town," noted Vivek Paul, the Wipro president, "the first thing you see is extra capacity, and all the people in New Mexico say those people — Californians — will wipe out all our factories along the line. That will happen in some areas, and some companies along the line will go out of business. But then capital will get reallocated. In the end, everyone along the line will benefit. Sure, there is fear, and that fear is good because that stimulates a willingness to change and explore and find more things to do better."

It happened when we connected New York, New Mexico, and California. It happened when we connected Western Europe, America, and Japan. And it will happen when we connect India and China with America, Europe, and Japan. The way to succeed is not by stopping the railroad line from connecting you, but by upgrading your skills and making the investment in those practices that will enable you and your society to claim your slice of the bigger but more complex pie.

SIX

The Untouchables

So if the flattening of the world is largely (but not entirely) unstoppable, and holds out the potential to be as beneficial to American society as a whole as past market evolutions have been, how does an individual get the best out of it? What do we tell our kids?

There is only one message: You have to constantly upgrade your skills. There will be plenty of good jobs out there in the flat world for people with the knowledge and ideas to seize them.

I am not suggesting this will be simple. It will not be. There will be a lot of other people out there also trying to get smarter. It was never good to be mediocre in your job, but in a world of walls, mediocrity could still earn you a decent wage. In a flatter world, you *really* do not want to be mediocre. You don't want to find yourself in the shoes of Willy Loman in *Death of a Salesman*, when his son Biff dispels his idea that the Loman family is special by declaring, "Pop! I'm a dime a dozen, and so are you!" An angry Willy retorts, "I am not a dime a dozen! I am Willy Loman, and you are Biff Loman!"

I don't care to have that conversation with my girls, so my advice to them in this flat world is very brief and very blunt: "Girls, when I was growing up, my parents used to say to me, 'Tom, finish your dinner — people in China and India are starving.' My advice to you is: Girls, finish your homework — people in China and India are starving for your jobs."

The way I like to think about this for our society as a whole is that every person should figure out how to make himself or herself into an untouchable. That's right. When the world goes flat, the caste system gets turned upside down. In India untouchables may be the lowest social class, but in a flat world everyone should want to be an untouchable. Untouchables, in my lexicon, *are people whose jobs cannot be outsourced.*

So who are the untouchables, and how do you or your kids get to be one? Untouchables come in four broad categories: workers who are "special," workers who are "specialized," workers who are "anchored," and workers who are "really adaptable."

Workers who are special are people like Michael Jordan, Bill Gates, and Barbra

Streisand. They have a global market for their goods and services and can command global-sized pay packages. Their jobs can never be outsourced.

If you can't be special — and only a few people can be — you want to be specialized, so that your work cannot be outsourced. This applies to all sorts of knowledge workers — from specialized lawyers, accountants, and brain surgeons, to cutting-edge computer architects and software engineers, to advanced machine tool and robot operators. These are skills that are always in high demand and are not fungible. ("Fungible" is an important word to remember. As Infosys CEO Nandan Nilekani likes to say, in a flat world there is "fungible and nonfungible work." Work that can be easily digitized and transferred to lower-wage locations is fungible. Work that cannot be digitized or easily substituted is nonfungible. Michael Jordan's jump shot is nonfungible. A bypass surgeon's technique is nonfungible. A television assembly-line worker's job is now fungible. Basic accounting and tax preparation are now fungible.)

If you cannot be special or specialized, you want to be anchored. That status applies to most Americans, everyone from my barber, to the waitress at lunch, to the chefs in the kitchen, to the plumber, to nurses, to many doctors, many lawyers, entertainers, electricians, and cleaning ladies. Their jobs are simply anchored and always will be, because they must be done in a specific location, involving face-to-face contact with a customer, client, patient, or audience. These jobs generally cannot be digitized and are not fungible, and the market wage is set according to the local market conditions. But be advised: There are fungible parts of even anchored jobs, and they can and will be outsourced — either to India or to the past — for greater efficiency. (Yes, as David Rothkopf notes, more jobs are actually "outsourced to the past," thanks to new innovations, than are outsourced to India.) For instance, you are not going to go to Bangalore to find an internist or a divorce lawyer, but your divorce lawyer may one day use a legal aide in Bangalore for basic research or to write up vanilla legal documents, and your internist may use a nighthawk radiologist in Bangalore to read your CAT scan.

This is why if you cannot be special or specialized, you don't want to count on being anchored so you won't be outsourced. You actually want to become really adaptable. You want constantly to acquire new skills, knowledge, and expertise that enable you constantly to be able to create value — something more than vanilla ice cream. You want to learn how to make the latest chocolate sauce, the whipped cream, or the cherries on top, or to deliver it as a belly dancer — in whatever your field of endeavor. As parts of your work become commoditized and fungible, or turned into vanilla, adaptable people will always learn how to make some other part of the sundae. Being adaptable in a flat world, knowing how to "learn how to learn," will be one of the most important assets any worker can have, because job churn will come faster, because innovation will happen faster.

Atul Vashistha, CEO of NeoIT, a California consulting firm that specializes in helping U.S. firms do outsourcing, has a good feel for this: "What you can do and how you can adapt and how you can leverage all the experience and knowledge you have when the world goes flat — that is the basic component [for survival]. When you are changing jobs a lot, and when your job environment is changing a lot, being adaptable is the number one thing. The people who are losing out are those with solid technical skills who have not grown those skills. You have to be skillfully adaptable and socially adaptable."

The more we push out the boundaries of knowledge and technology, the more complex tasks that machines can do, the more those with specialized education, or the ability to learn how to learn, will be in demand, and for better pay. And the more those without that ability will be less generously compensated. What you don't want to be is a not very special, not very specialized, not very anchored, or not very adaptable person in a fungible job. If you are in the low-margin, fungible end of the work food chain, where businesses have an incentive to outsource to lower-cost, equally efficient producers, there is a much greater chance that your job will be outsourced or your wages depressed.

"If you are a Web programmer and are still using only HTML and have not expanded your skill set to include newer and creative technologies, such as XML and multimedia, your value to the organization gets diminished every year," added Vashistha. New technologies get introduced that increase complexity but improve results, and as long as a programmer embraces these and keeps abreast of what clients are looking for, his or her job gets hard to outsource. "While technology advances make last year's work a commodity," said Vashistha, "reskilling, continual professional education and client intimacy to develop new relationships keeps him or her ahead of the commodity curve and away from a potential offshore."

My childhood friend Bill Greer is a good example of a person who faced this challenge and came up with a personal strategy to meet it. Greer is forty-eight years old and has made his living as a freelance artist and graphic designer for twenty-six years. From the late 1970s until right around 2000, the way Bill did his job and served his clients was pretty much the same.

"Clients, like *The New York Times*, would want a finished piece of artwork," Bill explained to me. So if he was doing an illustration for a newspaper or a magazine, or proposing a new logo for a product, he would actually create a piece of art — sketch it, color it, mount it on an illustration board, cover it with tissue, put it in a package that was opened with two flaps, and have it delivered by messenger or FedEx. He called it "flap art." In the industry it was known as "camera-ready art," because it needed to be shot, printed on four different layers of color film, or "separations," and prepared for publication. "It was a finished product, and it had a certain preciousness to it," said Bill. "It was a real piece of art, and sometimes people would hang them on their walls. In fact, *The New York Times* would have shows of works that were created by illustrators for its publications."

But in the last few years "that started to change," Bill told me, as publications and ad agencies moved to digital preparation, relying on the new software — namely, Quark, Photoshop, and Illustrator, which graphic artists refer to as "the trinity" — which made digital computer design so much easier. Everyone who went through art school got trained on these programs. Indeed, Bill explained, graphic design got so much easier that it became a commodity. It got turned into vanilla ice cream. "In terms of design," he said, "the technology gave everyone the same tools, so everyone could do straight lines and everyone could do work that was halfway decent. You used to need an eye to see if something was in balance and had the right typeface, but all of a sudden anyone could hammer out something that was acceptable."

So Greer pushed himself up the knowledge ladder. As publications demanded that all final products be presented as digital files that could be uploaded, and there was no longer any more demand for that precious flap art, he transformed himself into an ideas consultant. "Ideation" was what his clients, including McDonald's and Unilever, wanted. He stopped using pens and ink and would just do pencil sketches, scan them into his computer, color them by using the computer's mouse, and then e-mail them to the client, which would have some less skilled artists finish them.

"It was unconscious," said Greer. "I had to look for work that not everyone else could do, and that young artists couldn't do with technology for a fraction of what I was being paid. So I started getting offers where people would say to me, 'Can you do this and just give us the big idea?' They would give me a concept, and they would just want sketches, ideas, and not a finished piece of art. I still use the basic skill of drawing, but just to convey an idea — quick sketches, not finished artwork. And for these ideas they will still pay pretty good money. It has actually taken me to a different level. It is more like being a consultant rather than a JAFA (Just Another Fucking Artist). There are a lot of JAFAs out there. So now I am an idea man, and I have played off that. My clients just buy concepts." The JAFAs then do the art in-house or it gets outsourced. "They can take my raw sketches and finish them and illustrate them using computer programs, and it is not like I would do it, but it is good enough," Greer said.

But then another thing happened. While the evolving technology turned the lower end of Greer's business into a commodity, it opened up a whole new market at the upper end: Greer's magazine clients. One day, one of his regular clients approached him and asked if he could do morphs.

Morphs are cartoon strips in which one character evolves into another. So Martha Stewart is in the opening frame and morphs into Courtney Love by the closing frame. Drew Barrymore morphs into Drew Carey. Mariah Carey morphs into Jim Carrey. Cher morphs into Britney Spears. When he was first approached to do these, Greer had no idea where to begin. So he went onto Amazon.com and located some specialized software, bought it, tried it out for a few days, and produced his first morph. Since then he has developed a specialty in the process, and the market for them has expanded to include *Maxim* magazine, *More*, and *Nickelodeon* — one a men's magazine, one a middle-aged women's magazine, and one a kids' magazine.

In other words, someone invented a whole new kind of sauce to go on the vanilla, and Greer jumped on it. This is exactly what happens in the global economy as a whole. "I was experienced enough to pick these [morphs] up pretty quickly," said Greer. "Now I do them on my Mac laptop, anywhere I am, from Santa Barbara to Minneapolis to my apartment in New York. Sometimes clients give me a subject, and sometimes I just come up with them. Morphing used to be one of those really high-end things you saw on TV, and then they came out with this consumer [software] program and people could do it themselves, and I shaped them so magazines could use them. I just upload them as a series of JPEG files . . . Morphs have been a good business for different magazines. I even get fan mail from kids!"

Greer had never done morphs until the technology evolved and created a new, specialized niche, just when a changing market for his work made him eager to learn new skills. "I wish I could say it was all intentional," he confessed. "I was just available for work and just lucky they gave me a chance to do these things. I know so many artists who got washed out. One guy who was an illustrator has become a package designer, some have gotten out of the field altogether; one of the best designers I know became a landscape architect. She is still a designer but changed her medium altogether. Visual people can adapt, but I am still nervous about the future."

I told Greer his story fit well into some of the terms I was using in this book. He began as a chocolate sauce (a classic illustrator), was turned into a vanilla commodity (a classic illustrator in the computer age), upgraded his skills to become a special chocolate sauce again (a design consultant), then learned how to become a cherry on top (a morphs artist) by fulfilling a new demand created by an increasingly specialized market.

Greer contemplated my compliment for a moment and then said, "And here all I was trying to do was survive — and I still am." As he got up to leave, though, he told me that he was going out to meet a friend "to juggle together." They have been juggling partners for years, just a little side business they sometimes do on a street corner or for private parties. Greer has very good hand-eye coordination. "But even juggling is being commoditized," he complained. "It used to be if you could juggle five balls, you were really special. Now juggling five balls is like just anteing up. My partner and I used to perform together, and he was the seven-ball champ when I met him. Now fourteen-year-old kids can juggle seven balls, no problem. Now they have these books, like *Juggling for Dummies*, and kits that will teach you how to juggle. So they've just upped the standard."

As goes juggling, so goes the world.

These are our real choices: to try to put up walls of protection or to keep marching forward with the confidence that American society still has the right stuff, even in a flatter world. I say march forward. As long as we keep tending to the secrets of our sauce, we will do fine. There are so many things about the American system that are ideally suited for nurturing individuals who can compete and thrive in a flat world.

How so? It starts with America's research universities, which spin off a steady stream of competitive experiments, innovations, and scientific breakthroughs — from mathematics to biology to physics to chemistry. It is a truism, but the more educated you are, the more options you will have in a flat world. "Our university system is the best," said Bill Gates. "We fund our universities to do a lot of research and that is an amazing thing. High-IQ people come here, and we allow them to innovate and turn [their innovations] into products. We reward risk taking. Our university system is competitive and experimental. They can try out different approaches. There are one hundred universities making contributions to robotics. And each one is saying that the other is doing it all wrong, or my piece actually fits together with theirs. It is a chaotic system, but it is a great engine of innovation in the world, and with federal tax money, with some philanthropy on top of that, [it will continue to flourish] . . . We will really have to screw things up for our absolute wealth not to increase. If we are smart, we can increase it faster by embracing this stuff."

The Web browser, magnetic resonance imaging (MRI), superfast computers, global position technology, space exploration devices, and fiber optics are just a few of the many inventions that got started through basic university research projects. The BankBoston Economics Department did a study titled "MIT: The Impact of Innovation." Among its conclusions was that MIT graduates have founded 4,000 companies, creating at least 1.1 million jobs worldwide and generating sales of $232 billion.

What makes America unique is not that it built MIT, or that its grads are generating economic growth and innovation, but that every state in the country has universities trying to do the same. "America has 4,000 colleges and universities," said Allan E. Goodman, president of the Institute of International Education. "The rest of the world combined has 7,768 institutions of higher education. In the state of California alone, there are about 130 colleges and universities. There are only 14 countries in the world that have more than that number."

Take a state you normally wouldn't think of in this regard: Oklahoma. It has its own Oklahoma Center for the Advancement of Science and Technology (OCAST), which, on its Web site, describes its mission as follows: "In order to compete effectively in the new economy, Oklahoma must continue to develop a well-educated population; a collaborative, focused university research and technology base; and a nurturing environment for cutting-edge businesses, from the smallest start-up to the largest international headquarters . . . [OCAST promotes] University-Business technology centers, which may span several schools and businesses, resulting in new businesses being spawned, new products being manufactured, and new manufacturing technologies employed." No wonder that in 2003, American universities reaped $1.3 billion from patents, according to the Association of University Technology Managers.

Coupled with America's unique innovation-generating machines — universities, public and private research labs, and retailers — we have the best-regulated and most efficient capital markets in the world for taking new ideas and turning them into products and services. Dick Foster, director of McKinsey & Co. and the author of two books on innovation, remarked to me, "We have an 'industrial policy' in the U.S. — it is called the stock exchange, whether it is the NYSE or the Nasdaq." That is where risk capital is collected and assigned to emerging ideas or growing companies, Foster said, and no capital market in the world does that better and more efficiently than the American one.

What makes capital provision work so well here is the security and regulation of our capital markets, where minority share-holders are protected. Lord knows, there are scams, excesses, and corruption in our capital markets. That always happens when a lot of money is at stake. What distinguishes our capital markets is not that Enrons don't happen in America — they sure do. It is that when they happen, they usually get exposed, either by the Securities and Exchange Commission or by the business press, and get corrected. What makes America unique is not Enron but Eliot Spitzer, the attorney general of New York State, who has doggedly sought to clean up the securities industry and corporate boardrooms. This sort of capital market has proved very, very difficult to duplicate outside of New York, London, Frankfurt, and Tokyo. Said Foster, "China and India and other Asian countries will not be successful at innovation until they have successful capital markets, and they will not have successful capital markets until they have rule of law which protects minority interests under conditions of risk . . . We in the U.S. are the lucky beneficiaries of centuries of economic experimentation, and we are the experiment that has worked."

While these are the core secrets of America's sauce, there are others that need to be preserved and nurtured. Sometimes you have to talk to outsiders to appreciate them, such as Indian-born Vivek Paul of Wipro. "I would add three to your list," he said to me. "One is the sheer openness of American society." We Americans often forget what an incredibly open, say-anything-do-anything-start-anything-go-bankrupt-and-start-anything-again society the United States is. There is no place like it in the world, and our openness is a huge asset and attraction to foreigners, many of whom come from countries where the sky is not the limit.

Another, said Paul, is the "quality of American intellectual property protection," which further enhances and encourages people to come up with new ideas. In a flat world, there is a great incentive to develop a new product or process, because it can achieve global scale in a flash. But if you are the person who comes up with that new idea, you want your intellectual property protected. "No country respects and protects intellectual property better than America," said Paul, and as a result, a lot of innovators want to come here to work and lodge their intellectual property.

The United States also has among the most flexible labor laws in the world. The easier it is to fire someone in a dying industry, the easier it is to hire someone in a rising industry that no one knew would exist five years earlier. This is a great asset, especially when you compare the situation in the United States to inflexible, rigidly regulated labor markets like Germany's, full of government restrictions on hiring and firing. Flexibility to quickly deploy labor and capital where the greatest opportunity exists, and the ability to quickly redeploy it if the earlier deployment is no longer profitable, is essential in a flattening world.

Still another secret to America's sauce is the fact that it has the world's largest domestic consumer market, with the most first adopters, in the world, which means that if you are introducing a new product, technology, or service, you have to have a presence in America. All this means a steady flow of jobs for Americans.

There is also the little-discussed American attribute of political stability. Yes, China has had a good run for the past twenty-five years, and it may make the transition from communism to a more pluralistic system without the wheels coming off. But it may not. Who would want all his or her eggs in that basket?

Finally, the United States has become one of the great meeting points in the world, a place where lots of different people bond and learn to trust one another. An Indian student who is educated at the University of Oklahoma and then gets his first job with a software firm in Oklahoma City forges bonds of trust and understanding that are really important for future collaboration, even if he winds up returning to India. Nothing illustrates this point better than Yale University's outsourcing of research to China. Yale president Richard C. Levin explained to me that Yale has two big research operations running in China today, one at Peking University in Beijing and the other at Fudan University in Shanghai. "Most of these institutional collaborations arise not from top-down directives of university administrators, but rather from long-standing personal relationships among scholars and scientists," said Levin.

How did the Yale-Fudan collaboration arise? To begin with, said Levin, Yale professor Tian Xu, its director, had a deep affiliation with both institutions. He did his undergraduate work at Fudan and received his Ph.D. from Yale. "Five of Professor Xu's collaborators, who are now professors at Fudan, were also trained at Yale," explained Levin. One was Professor Xu's friend when both were Yale graduate students; another was a visiting scholar in the laboratory of a Yale colleague; one was an exchange student who came to Yale from Fudan and returned to earn his Ph.D. in

China; and the other two were postdoctoral fellows in Professor Xu's Yale lab. A similar story underlies the formation of the Peking-Yale Joint Center for Plant Molecular Genetics and Agrobiotechnology.

Professor Xu is a leading expert on genetics and has won grants from the National Institutes of Health and the Howard Hughes Foundation to study the connection between genetics and cancer and certain neurodegenerative diseases. This kind of research requires the study of large numbers of genetic mutations in lab animals. "When you want to test many genes and trace for a given gene that may be responsible for certain diseases, you need to run a lot of tests. Having a bigger staff is a huge advantage," explained Levin. So what Yale did was essentially outsource the lab work to Fudan by creating the Fudan-Yale Biomedical Research Center. Each university pays for its own staff and research, so no money changes hands, but the Chinese side does the basic technical work using large numbers of technicians and lab animals, which cost so much less in China, and Yale does the high-end analysis of the data. The Fudan staff, students, and technicians get great exposure to high-end research, and Yale gets a large-scale testing facility that would have been prohibitively expensive if Yale had tried to duplicate it in New

Haven. A support lab in America for a project like this one might have 30 technicians, but the one in Fudan has 150.

"The gains are very much two-way," said Levin. "Our investigators get substantially enhanced productivity, and the Chinese get their graduate students trained, and their young faculty become collaborators with our professors, who are the leaders in their fields. It builds human capital for China and innovation for Yale." Graduate students from both universities go back and forth, forging relationships that will no doubt produce more collaborations in the future. At the same time, he added, a lot of legal preparation went into this collaboration to make sure that Yale would be able to harvest the intellectual property that is created.

"There is one world of science out there," said Levin, "and this kind of international division of labor makes a lot of sense." Yale, he said, also insisted that the working conditions at the Chinese labs be world-class, and, as a result, it has also helped to lift the quality of the Chinese facilities. "The living conditions of the lab animals are right up to U.S. standards," remarked Levin. "These are not mouse sweatshops."

Every law of economics tells us that if we

connect all the knowledge pools in the world, and promote greater and greater trade and integration, the global pie will grow wider and more complex. And if America, or any other country, nurtures a labor force that is increasingly made up of men and women who are special, specialized, or constantly adapting to higher-value-added jobs, it will grab its slice of that growing pie. But we will have to work at it. Because if current trends prevail, countries like India and China and whole regions like Eastern Europe are certain to narrow the gap with America, just as Korea and Japan and Taiwan did during the Cold War. They will keep upping their standards.

So are we still working at it? Are we tending to the secrets of our sauce? America still looks great on paper, especially if you look backward, or compare it only to India and China of today and not tomorrow. But have we really been investing in our future and preparing our children the way we need to for the race ahead? See the next chapter. But here's a quick hint: The answer is no.

SEVEN

The Quiet Crisis

Close games for the Americans were rare in previous Olympics, but now it appears to be something the Americans should get used to.
— From an August 17, 2004, AP article from the Athens Olympics titled "U.S. Men's Basketball Team Narrowly Beats Greece"

You could find no better metaphor for the way the rest of the world can now compete head-to-head more effectively than ever with America than the struggles of the U.S. Olympic basketball team in 2004. The American team, made up of NBA stars, limped home to a bronze medal after losing to Puerto Rico, Lithuania, and Argentina. Previously, the United States Olympic basketball team had lost only one game in the history of the modern Olympics. Remember when America sent only NCAA stars to the Olympic basketball events? For a long time these teams totally dominated all comers. Then they started getting challenged. So we sent our pros. And they started getting challenged. Because the world keeps learning, the diffusion of knowledge happens faster; coaches in other countries now download American coaching methods off the Internet and watch NBA games in their own living rooms on satellite TV. Many of them can even get ESPN and watch the highlight reels. And thanks to the triple convergence, there is a lot of new raw talent walking onto the NBA courts from all over the world — including many new stars from China, Latin America, and Eastern Europe. They go back and play for their national teams in the Olympics, using the skills they honed in America. So the automatic American superiority of twenty years ago is now gone in Olympic basketball. The NBA standard is increasingly becoming a global commodity — pure vanilla. If the United States wants to continue to dominate in Olympic basketball, we must, in that great sports cliché, step it up a notch. The old standard won't do anymore. As Joel Cawley of IBM remarked to me, "Star for star, the basketball teams from places like Lithuania or Puerto Rico still don't rank well versus the Americans, but when they play as a team — when they *collaborate* better than we do — they are extremely competitive."

Sports writer John Feinstein could have been referring to either American engineering skills or American basketball skills when he wrote in an August 26, 2004, AOL essay on Olympic basketball that the performance of the U.S. basketball team is a result of "the rise of the international player" and "the decline and fall of the U.S. game." And the decline and fall of the U.S. game, argued Feinstein, is a result of two long-term trends. The first is a steady decline "in basketball skills," with American kids just wanting to shoot either three-point shots or dunk — the sort of stuff that gets you on ESPN's *SportsCenter* highlight reel — instead of learning how to make precise passes, or go into the lane and shoot a pull-up jumper, or snake through big men to get to the basket. Those skills take a lot of hard work and coaching to learn. Today, said Feinstein, you have an American generation that relies almost completely on athleticism and almost not at all on basketball skills. And there is also that ugly little problem of ambition. While the rest of the world was getting better in basketball, "more and more NBA players were yawning at the notion of playing in the Olympics," noted Feinstein. "We have come a long way from 1984, when Bob Knight told Charles Barkley to show up to the second Olympic training camp at 265 pounds or else. Barkley showed up weighing 280. Knight cut him that day. In today's world, the Olympic coach wouldn't even have checked Barkley's weight in the first place. He would have sent a limousine to the airport to get him and stopped at Dunkin' Donuts on the way to the hotel if the player requested it . . . The world changes. In the case of American basketball, it hasn't changed for the better."

There is something about post–World War II America that reminds me of the classic wealthy family that by the third generation starts to squander its wealth. The members of the first generation are nose-to-the-grindstone innovators; the second generation holds it all together; then their kids come along and get fat, dumb, and lazy and slowly squander it all. I know that is both overly harsh and a gross generalization, but there is, nevertheless, some truth in it. American society started to coast in the 1990s, when our third postwar generation came of age. The dot-com boom left too many people with the impression that they could get rich without investing in hard work. All it took was an MBA and a quick IPO, or one NBA contract, and you were set for life. But while we were admiring the flat world we had created, a lot of people in India, China, and Eastern Europe were busy figuring out how to take advantage of it. Lucky for us, we were the only economy standing after World War II, and we had no serious competition for forty years. That gave us a huge head of steam but also a huge sense of entitlement and complacency — not to mention a certain tendency in recent years to extol consumption over hard work, investment, and long-term thinking. When we got hit with 9/11, it was a once-in-a-generation opportunity to summon the nation to sacrifice, to address some of its pressing fiscal, energy, science, and education shortfalls — all the things that we had let slide. But our president did not summon us to sacrifice. He summoned us to go shopping.

In the previous chapters, I showed why both classic economic theory and the inherent strengths of the American economy have convinced me that American individuals have nothing to worry about from a flat world — provided we roll up our sleeves, be ready to compete, get every individual to think about how he or she upgrades his or her educational skills, and keep investing in the secrets of the American sauce. Those chapters were all about what we must do and can do.

This chapter is about how we Americans, individually and collectively, have not been doing all these things that we should be doing and what will happen down the road if we don't change course.

★ ★ ★

The truth is, we are in a crisis now, but it is a crisis that is unfolding very slowly and very quietly. It is "a quiet crisis," explained Shirley Ann Jackson, the 2004 president of the American Association for the Advancement of Science and president of Rensselaer Polytechnic Institute since 1999. (Rensselaer is America's oldest technological college, founded in 1824.) And this quiet crisis involves the steady erosion of America's scientific and engineering base, which has always been the source of American innovation and our rising standard of living.

"The sky is not falling, nothing horrible is going to happen today," said Jackson, a physicist by training who chooses her words carefully. "The U.S. is still the leading engine for innovation in the world. It has the best graduate programs, the best scientific infrastructure, and the capital markets to exploit it. But there is a quiet crisis in U.S. science and technology that we have to wake up to. The U.S. today is in a truly global environment, and those competitor countries are not only wide awake, they are running a marathon while we are running sprints. If left unchecked, this could challenge our preeminence and capacity to innovate."

And it is our ability to constantly inno-

451

vate new products, services, and companies that has been the source of America's horn of plenty and steadily widening middle class for the last two centuries. It was American innovators who started Google, Intel, HP, Dell, Microsoft, and Cisco, and it matters where innovation happens. The fact that all these companies are headquartered in America means that most of the high-paying jobs are here, even if these companies outsource or offshore some functions. The executives, the department heads, the sales force, and the senior researchers are all located in the cities where the innovation happened. And their jobs create more jobs. The shrinking of the pool of young people with the knowledge skills to innovate won't shrink our standard of living overnight. It will be felt only in fifteen or twenty years, when we discover we have a critical shortage of scientists and engineers capable of doing innovation or even just high-value-added technology work. Then this won't be a quiet crisis anymore, said Jackson, "it will be the real McCoy."

Shirley Ann Jackson knows of what she speaks, because her career exemplifies as well as anyone's both why America thrived so much in the past fifty years and why it won't automatically do the same in the next fifty. An African-American woman, Jackson was born in Washington, D.C., in

1946. She started kindergarten in a segregated public school but was one of the first public school students to benefit from desegregation, as a result of the Supreme Court ruling in *Brown v. Board of Education*. Just when she was getting a chance to go to a better school, the Russians launched Sputnik in 1957, and the U.S. government became obsessed with educating young people to become scientists and engineers, a trend that was intensified by John F. Kennedy's commitment to a manned space program. When Kennedy spoke about putting a man on the moon, Shirley Ann Jackson was one of the millions of American young people who were listening. His words, she recalled, "inspired, assisted, and launched many of my generation into science, engineering and mathematics," and the breakthroughs and inventions they spawned went well beyond the space program. "The space race was really a science race," she said.

Thanks in part to desegregation, both Jackson's inspiration and intellect were recognized early, and she ultimately became the first African-American woman to earn a Ph.D. in physics from MIT (her degree was in theoretical elementary particle physics). From there, she spent many years working for AT&T Bell Laboratories, and in 1995 was appointed by President

Clinton to chair the U.S. Nuclear Regulatory Commission.

As the years went by, though, Jackson began to notice that fewer and fewer young Americans were captivated by national challenges like the race to the moon, or felt the allure of math, science, and engineering. In universities, she noted, graduate enrollment in science and engineering programs, having grown for decades, peaked in 1993, and despite some recent progress, it remains today below the level of a decade ago. So the science and engineering generations that followed Jackson's got smaller and smaller relative to our needs. By the time Jackson took the job as Rensselaer Polytechnic's president to put her heart and soul into reinvigorating American science and engineering, she realized, she said, that a "perfect storm" was brewing — one that posed a real long-term danger to America's economic health — and she started speaking out about it whenever she could.

"The phrase 'the perfect storm' is associated with meteorological events in October 1991," said Jackson in a speech in May 2004, when "a powerful weather system gathered force, ravaging the Atlantic Ocean over the course of several days, [and] caused the deaths of several Massachusetts-based fishermen and billions of dollars of damage. The event became a book, and, later, a movie. Meteorologists observing the event emphasized . . . the unlikely confluence of conditions . . . in which multiple factors converged to bring about an event of devastating magnitude. [A] similar worst-case scenario could arrest the progress of our national scientific and technological capacity. The forces at work are multiple and complex. They are demographic, political, economic, cultural, even social." Individually, each of these forces would be problematic, added Jackson. In combination, they could be devastating. "For the first time in more than a century, the United States could well find itself falling behind other countries in the capacity for scientific discovery, innovation and economic development."

The way to avoid being caught in such a storm is to identify the confluence of factors and to change course — even though right now the sky is blue, the winds are gentle, and the water seems calm. But that is not what has been going on in America in recent years. We are blithely sailing along, heading straight for the storm, with both politicians and parents insisting that no dramatic changes or sacrifices are required now. After all, look how calm and sunny it is outside, they tell us. In the fiscal year 2005 budget passed by the Republican-led Congress in November 2004, the budget for the National Science Foundation, which is the federal body most responsible for promoting research and funding more and better science education, was actually cut by 1.9 percent, or $105 million. History will show that when America should have been doubling the NSF funding, its Congress passed a pork-laden budget that actually cut assistance for science and engineering.

Don't be fooled by the calm. That's always the time to change course — not when you're just about to get hit by the typhoon. We don't have any time to waste in addressing the "dirty little secrets" of our education system.

Dirty Little Secret #1:
The Numbers Gap

In the Cold War, one of the deepest causes of American worries was the so-called missile gap between us and the Soviet Union. The perfect storm Shirley Ann Jackson is warning about could best be described as the confluence of three new gaps that have been slowly emerging to sap America's prowess in science, math, and engineering. They are the numbers gap, the ambition gap, and the education gap. In the Age of

Flatism, these gaps are what most threaten our standard of living.

Dirty little secret number one is that the generation of scientists and engineers who were motivated to go into science by the threat of Sputnik in 1957 and the inspiration of JFK are reaching their retirement years and are not being replaced in the numbers that they must be if an advanced economy like that of the United States is to remain at the head of the pack. According to the National Science Foundation, half of America's scientists and engineers are forty years or older, and the average age is steadily rising.

Just take one example — NASA. An analysis of NASA records conducted by the newspaper *Florida Today* (March 7, 2004), which covers the Kennedy Space Center, showed the following: Nearly 40 percent of the 18,146 people at NASA are age fifty or older. Those with twenty years of government service are eligible for early retirement. Twenty-two percent of NASA workers are fifty-five or older. NASA employees over sixty outnumber those under thirty by a ratio of about three to one. Only 4 percent of NASA workers are under thirty. A 2003 Government Accounting Office study concluded that NASA was having difficulty hiring people with the sufficient science, engineering, and information-technology skills that are critical to its operations. Many of these jobs are reserved for American citizens, because of national security concerns. Then–NASA administrator Sean O'Keefe testified before Congress in 2002: "Our mission of understanding and protecting our home planet and exploring the universe and searching for life will not be carried out if we don't have the people to do it." The National Commission on Mathematics and Science Teaching for the Twenty-first Century, chaired by the former astronaut and senator John Glenn, found that two-thirds of the nation's mathematics and science teaching force will retire by 2010.

Traditionally we made up for any shortages of engineers and science faculty by educating more at home and importing more from abroad. But both of those remedies have been stalled of late.

Every two years the National Science Board supervises the collection of a very broad set of data trends in science and technology in the United States, which it publishes as *Science and Engineering Indicators*. In preparing *Indicators* 2004, the NSB said, "We have observed a troubling decline in the number of U.S. citizens who are training to become scientists and engineers, whereas the number of jobs requiring science and engineering (S&E) training continues to grow." These trends threaten the economic welfare and security of our country, it said, adding that if the trends identified in *Indicators* 2004 continue undeterred, three things will happen: "The number of jobs in the U.S. economy that require science and engineering training will grow; the number of U.S. citizens prepared for those jobs will, at best, be level; and the availability of people from other countries who have science and engineering training will decline, either because of limits to entry imposed by U.S. national security restrictions or because of intense global competition for people with these skills."

The NSB report found that the number of American eighteen-to-twenty-four-year-olds who receive science degrees has fallen to seventeenth in the world, whereas we ranked third three decades ago. It said that of the 2.8 million first university degrees (what we call bachelor's degrees) in science and engineering granted worldwide in 2003, 1.2 million were earned by Asian students in Asian universities, 830,000 were granted in Europe, and 400,000 in the United States. In engineering specifically, universities in Asian countries now produce eight times as many bachelor's degrees as the United States.

Moreover, "the proportional emphasis on science and engineering is greater in other nations," noted Shirley Ann Jackson. Science and engineering degrees now represent 60 percent of all bachelor's degrees earned in China, 33 percent in South Korea, and 41 percent in Taiwan. By contrast, the percentage of those taking a bachelor's degree in science and engineering in the United States remains at roughly 31 percent. Factoring out science degrees, the number of Americans who graduate with just engineering degrees is 5 percent, as compared to 25 percent in Russia and 46 percent in China, according to a 2004 report by Trilogy Publications, which represents the national U.S. engineering professional association.

The United States has always depended on the inventiveness of its people in order to compete in the world marketplace, said the NSB. "Preparation of the S&E workforce is a vital arena for national competitiveness. [But] even if action is taken today to change these trends, the reversal is 10 to 20 years away." The students entering the science and engineering workforce with advanced degrees in 2004 decided to take the necessary math courses to enable this career path when they were in middle school, up to fourteen years ago, the NSB noted. The students making that same decision in middle school today won't complete advanced training for science and engineering occupations until 2018 or 2020. "If action is not taken now to change these trends, we could reach 2020 and find that the ability of U.S. research and education institutions to regenerate has been damaged and that their preeminence has been lost to other areas of the world," the science board said.

These shortages could not be happening at a worse time — just when the world is going flat. "The number of jobs requiring science and engineering skills in the U.S. labor force," the NSB said, "is growing almost 5 percent per year. In comparison, the rest of the labor force is growing at just over 1 percent. Before September 11, 2001, the Bureau of Labor Statistics (BLS) projected that science and engineering occupations would increase at three times the rate of all occupations." Unfortunately, the NSB reported, the average age of the science and engineering workforce is rising.

"Many of those who entered the expanding S&E workforce in the 1960s and 1970s (the baby boom generation) are expected to retire in the next twenty years, and their children are not choosing science and engineering careers in the same numbers as their parents," the NSB report said. "The percentage of women, for example, choosing math and computer science careers fell 4 percentage points between 1993 and

1999." The 2002 NSB indicators showed that the number of science and engineering Ph.D.'s awarded in the United States dropped from 29,000 in 1998 to 27,000 in 1999. The total number of engineering undergraduates in America fell about 12 percent between the mid-1980s and 1998.

Nevertheless, America's science and engineering labor force grew at a rate well above that of America's production of science and engineering degrees, because a large number of foreign-born S&E graduates migrated to the United States. The proportion of foreign-born students in S&E fields and workers in S&E occupations continued to rise steadily in the 1990s. The NSB said that persons born outside the United States accounted for 14 percent of all S&E occupations in 1990. Between 1990 and 2000, the proportion of foreign-born people with bachelor's degrees in S&E occupations rose from 11 to 17 percent; the proportion of foreign-born with master's degrees rose from 19 to 29 percent; and the proportion of foreign-born with Ph.D.'s in the S&E labor force rose from 24 to 38 percent. By attracting scientists and engineers born and trained in other countries we have maintained the growth of the S&E labor force without a commensurate increase in support for the long-term costs of training and attracting native U.S citizens to these fields, the NSB said.

But now, the simultaneous flattening and wiring of the world have made it much easier for foreigners to innovate without having to emigrate. They can now do world-class work for world-class companies at very decent wages without ever having to leave home. As Allan E. Goodman, president of the Institute of International Education, put it, "When the world was round, they could not go back home, because there was no lab to go back to and no Internet to connect to. But now all those things are there, so they are going back. Now they are saying, 'I feel more comfortable back home. I can live more comfortably back home than in New York City and I can do good work, so why not go back?' " This trend started even before the visa hassles brought on by 9/11, said Goodman. "The brain gain started to go to brain drain around the year 2000."

As the NSB study noted, "Since the 1980s other countries have increased investment in S&E education and the S&E workforce at higher rates than the United States has. Between 1993 and 1997, the OECD countries [Organization for Economic Co-operation and Development, a group of 40 nations with highly developed market economies] increased their number of S&E research jobs 23 percent, more than twice the 11 percent increase in S&E research jobs in the United States."

In addition, it said, visas for students and S&E workers have been issued more slowly since the events of September 11, owing to both increased security restrictions and a drop in applications. The U.S. State Department issued 20 percent fewer visas for foreign students in 2001 than in 2000, and the rate fell farther in subsequent years. While university presidents told me in 2004 that the situation was getting better, and that the Department of Homeland Security was trying to both speed up and simplify its visa procedures for foreign students and scientists, a lot of damage has been done, and the situation for foreign students or scientists wanting to work in any areas deemed to have national security implications is becoming a real problem. No wonder *New York Times* education writer Sam Dillon reported on December 21, 2004, that "foreign applications to American graduate schools declined 28 percent this year. Actual foreign graduate student enrollments dropped 6 percent. Enrollments of all foreign students, in undergraduate, graduate and postdoctoral programs, fell for the first time in three decades in an annual census released this fall. Meanwhile, university enrollments have been surging in England, Germany and other countries . . . Chinese applications to American graduate schools fell 45 percent this year, while several European countries announced surges in Chinese enrollment."

Dirty Little Secret #2:
The Ambition Gap

The second dirty little secret, which several prominent American CEOs told me only in a whisper, goes like this: When they send jobs abroad, they not only save 75 percent on wages, they get a 100 percent increase in productivity. Part of that is understandable. When you take a low-wage, low-prestige job in America, like a call center operator, and bring it over to India, where it becomes a high-wage, high-prestige job, you end up with workers who are paid less but motivated more. "The dirty little secret is that not only is [outsourcing] cheaper and efficient," the American CEO of a London-headquartered multinational told me, "but the quality and productivity [boost] is huge." In addition to the wage compression, he said, one Bangalore Indian retrained will do the work of two or three Europeans, and the Bangalore employees don't take six weeks of holidays. "When you think it's only about wages," he added, "you can still hold your dignity, but the fact that they work better is awful."

A short time after returning from India, I was approached in an airport by a young man who wanted to talk about some columns I had written from there. We had a nice chat, I asked him for his card, and we struck up an e-mail friendship. His name is Mike Arguello, and he is an IT systems architect living in San Antonio. He does high-end IT systems design and does not feel threatened by foreign competition. He also teaches computer science. When I asked him what we needed to do in America to get our edge back, he sent me this e-mail:

> I taught at a local university. It was disheartening to see the poor work ethic of many of my students. Of the students I taught over six semesters, I'd only consider hiring two of them. The rest lacked the creativity, problem-solving abilities and passion for learning. As you well know, India's biggest advantage over the Chinese and Russians is that they speak English. But it would be wrong to assume the top Indian developers are better than their American counterparts. The advantage they have is the number of bodies they can throw at a problem. The Indians that I work

with are the cream of the crop. They are educated by the equivalents of MIT back in India and there are plenty of them. If you were to follow me in my daily meetings it would become very obvious that a great deal of my time is spent working with Indians. Most managers are probably still under the impression that all Indians are doing is lower-end software development — "software assembly." But technologies, such as Linux, are allowing them to start taking higher-paying system design jobs that had previously been the exclusive domain of American workers. It has provided them with the means to move up the technology food chain, putting them on par with domestic workers. It's brain power against brain power, and in this area they are formidable. From a technology perspective, the world is flat and getting flatter (if that is possible). The only two areas that I have not seen Indian labor in are networking architects and system architects, but it is only a matter of time. Indians are very bright and they are quickly learning from their interaction with system architects just how all of the pieces of the IT puzzle fit together . . . Were Congress to pass legislation to stop the flow of Indian labor, you would have major software systems that would have nobody who knew what was going on. It is unfortunate that many management positions in IT are filled with non-technical managers who may not be fully aware of their exposure . . . I'm an expert in information systems, not economics, but I know a high-paying job requires one be able to produce something of high value. The economy is producing the jobs both at the high end and low end, but increasingly the high-end jobs are out of reach of many. Low education means low-paying jobs, plain and simple, and this is where more and more Americans are finding themselves. Many Americans can't believe they aren't qualified for high-paying jobs. I call this the "*American Idol* problem." If you've ever seen the reaction of contestants when Simon Cowell tells them they have no talent, they look at him in total disbelief. I'm just hoping someday I'm not given such a rude awakening.

In the winter of 2004 I had tea in Tokyo with Richard C. Koo, chief economist for the Nomura Research Institute. I tested out on Richard my "coefficient of flatness": the notion that the flatter one's country is — that is, the fewer natural resources it has — the better off it will be in a flat world. The ideal country in a flat world is the one with *no natural resources,* because countries with no natural resources tend to dig inside themselves. They try to tap the energy, entrepreneurship, creativity, and intelligence of their own people — men and women — rather than drill an oil well. Taiwan is a barren rock in a typhoon-laden sea, with virtually no natural resources — nothing but the energy, ambition, and talent of its own people — and today it has the third-largest financial reserves in the world. The success of Hong Kong, Japan, South Korea, and coastal China can all be traced to a similar flatness.

"I am a Taiwanese-American with a father from Taiwan and with a Japanese mother," Koo told me. "I was born in Japan and went to Japanese elementary school and then moved to the States. There is a saying in China that whatever you put in your head and your stomach, no one can take away from you. In this whole region, that is in the DNA. You just have to study hard and move forward. I was told relatively early by my teachers, 'We can never live like Americans and Canadians. We have no resources. We have to study hard, work hard, and export hard.' "

A few weeks later I had breakfast in Washington with P. V. Kannan, CEO of 24/7 Customer. When it comes to the flat world, said P.V., he had just one question: "Is America prepared? It is not . . . You've gotten a little contented and slow, and the people who came into the field with [the triple convergence] are really hungry. Immigrants are always hungry — and they don't have a backup plan."

A short time later I read a column by Steven Pearlstein, *The Washington Post*'s business columnist/reporter, under the headline "Europe's Capitalism Curtain." From Wroclaw, Poland (July 23, 2004), Pearlstein wrote: "A curtain has descended across Europe. On one side are hope, optimism, freedom and prospects for a better life. On the other side, fear, pessimism, suffocating government regulations and a sense that the best times are in the past." This new curtain, Pearlstein argued, demarks Eastern Europe, which is embracing capitalism, and Western Europe, which is wishing desperately that it would go away.

"This time, however, it is the East that is likely to prevail," he continued. "The energy and sense of possibility are almost palpable here . . . Money and companies are pouring in — not just the prestige nameplates like Bombardier, Siemens, Whirlpool, Toyota and Volvo, but also the network of suppliers that inevitably follows them. At first, most of the new jobs were of the semi-skilled variety. Now they have been followed by design and engineering work that aims to tap into the largest concentration of university students in Eastern Europe . . . The secret isn't just lower wages. It's also the attitude of workers who take pride and are willing to do what is necessary to succeed, even if it means outsourcing parts production or working on weekends or altering vacation schedules — things that would almost certainly trigger months of acrimony and negotiation in Western Europe. 'The people back home, they haven't got any idea how much they need to change if they want to preserve what they have,' said Jose Ugarte [a Basque who heads the appliance manufacturing operations of Mondragon, the giant Spanish industrial cooperative]. 'The danger to them is enormous. They don't realize how fast this is happening . . .' It's not the dream of riches that animates the people of Wroclaw so much as the determination to work hard, sacrifice what needs to be sacrificed and change what needs to be changed to close the gap with the West. It is that pride and determination, says Wroclaw's mayor, Rafal Dutkiewicz, that explain why they are such a threat to the 'leisure-time society' on the other side of the curtain."

I heard a similar refrain in a discussion with consular officials who oversee the granting of visas at the U.S. embassy in Beijing. As one of them put it to me, "I do think Americans are oblivious to the huge changes. Every American who comes over to visit me [in China] is just blown away . . . Your average kid in the U.S. is growing up in a wealthy country with many opportunities, and many are the kids of advantaged educated people and have a sense of entitlement. Well, the hard reality for that kid is that fifteen years from now Wu is going to be his boss and Zhou is going to be the doctor in town. The competition is coming, and many of the kids are going to move into their twenties clueless about these rising forces."

When I asked Bill Gates about the supposed American education advantage — an education that stresses creativity, not rote learning — he was utterly dismissive. In his view, those who think that the more rote learning systems of China and Japan can't turn out innovators who can compete with Americans are sadly mistaken. Said Gates, "I have never met the guy who doesn't know how to multiply who created software . . . Who has the most creative video games in the world? Japan! I never met these 'rote people' . . . Some of my best software developers are Japanese. You need to understand things in order to invent beyond them."

One cannot stress enough: Young Chinese, Indians, and Poles are not racing us to the bottom. They are racing us to the top. They do not want to work for us; they don't even want to be us. They want to dominate us — in the sense that they want to be creating the companies of the future that people all over the world will admire and clamor to work for. They are in no way content with where they have come so far. I was talking to a Chinese-American who works for Microsoft and has accompanied Bill Gates on visits to China. He said Gates is recognized everywhere he goes in China. Young people there hang from the rafters and scalp tickets just to hear him speak. Same with Jerry Yang, the founder of Yahoo!

In China today, Bill Gates is Britney Spears. In America today, Britney Spears is Britney Spears — and that is our problem.

Dirty Little Secret #3:
The Education Gap

All of this helps to explain the third dirty little secret: A lot of the jobs that are starting to go abroad today are very high-end research jobs, because not only is the talent abroad cheaper, but a lot of it is as educated as American workers — or even more so. In China, where there are 1.3 billion people and the universities are just starting to crack the top ranks, the competition for top spots is ferocious. The math/science salmon that swims upstream in China and gets itself admitted to a top Chinese university or hired by a foreign company is one smart fish. The folks at Microsoft have a saying about their research center in Beijing, which, for scientists and engineers, is one of the most sought-after places to work in all of China. "Remember, in China when you are one in a million — there are 1,300 other people just like you."

The brainpower that rises to the Microsoft research center in Beijing is already one in a million.

Consider the annual worldwide Intel International Science and Engineering Fair. About forty countries participate by nominating talent through local affiliate affairs. In 2004, the Intel Fair attracted around sixty-five thousand American kids, according to Intel. How about in China? I asked Wee Theng Tan, the president of Intel China, during a visit to Beijing. In China, he told me, there is a national affiliate science fair, which acts as a feeder system to select kids for the global Intel fair. "Almost every single province has students going to one of these affiliate fairs," said Tan. "We have as many as six million kids competing, although not all are competing for the top levels . . . [But] you know how seriously they take it. Those selected to go to the international [Intel] fair are immediately exempted from college entrance exams" and basically get their choice of any top university in China. In the 2004 Intel Science Fair, China came home with thirty-five awards, more than any other country in Asia, including one of the top three global awards.

Microsoft has three research centers in the world: in Cambridge, England; in Redmond, Washington, its headquarters; and in Beijing. Bill Gates told me that within just a couple of years of its opening in 1998, Microsoft Research Asia, as the center in Beijing is known, had become the most productive research arm in the Microsoft system "in terms of the quality of the ideas that they are turning out. It is mind-blowing."

Kai-Fu Li is the Microsoft executive who was assigned by Gates to open the Microsoft research center in Beijing. My first question to him was, "How did you go about recruiting the staff?" Li said his team went to universities all over China and simply administered math, IQ, and programming tests to Ph.D.-level students or scientists.

"In the first year, we gave about 2,000

tests all around," he said. From the 2,000, they winnowed the group down to 400 with more tests, then 150, "and then we hired 20." They were given two-year contracts and told that at the end of two years, depending on the quality of their work, they would either be given a longer-term contract or granted a postdoctoral degree by Microsoft Research Asia. Yes, you read that right. The Chinese government gave Microsoft the right to grant postdocs. Of the original twenty who were hired, twelve survived the cut. The next year, nearly four thousand people were tested. After that, said Li, "we stopped doing the test. By that time we became known as the number one place to work, where all the smart computer and math people wanted to work . . . We got to know all the students and professors. The professors would send their best people there, knowing that if the people did not work out, it would be their credibility [on the line]. Now we have the top professors at the top schools recommending their top students. A lot of students want to go to Stanford or MIT, but they want to spend two years at Microsoft first, as interns, so they can get a nice recommendation letter that says these are MIT quality." Today Microsoft has more than two hundred researchers in its China lab and some four hundred students who come in and out on projects and become recruiting material for Microsoft.

"They view this as a once-in-a-lifetime income opportunity," said Li of the team at Microsoft Research Asia. "They saw their parents going through the Cultural Revolution. The best they could do was become a professor, do a little project on the side because a professor's pay is horrible, and maybe get one paper published. Now they have this place where all they do is research, with great computers and lots of resources. They have administrators — we hire people to do the dirty work. They just could not believe it. They voluntarily work fifteen to eighteen hours a day and come in on weekends. They work through holidays, because their dream is to get to Microsoft." Li, who had worked for other American high-tech firms before coming to Microsoft, said that until starting Microsoft Research Asia, he had never seen a research lab with the enthusiasm of a start-up company.

"If you go in at two a.m. it is full, and at eight a.m. it is full," he said.

Microsoft is a stronger American company for being able to attract all this talent, said Li. "Now we have two hundred more brilliant people building [intellectual property] and patents. These two hundred people are not replacing people in

Redmond. They are doing new research in areas applicable worldwide."

Microsoft Research Asia has already developed a worldwide reputation for producing cutting-edge papers for the most important scientific journals and conferences. "This is the culture that built the Great Wall," he added, "because it is a dedicated and direction-following culture." Chinese people, explained Li, have both a superiority and an inferiority complex at the same time, which helps explain why they are racing America to the top, not the bottom. There is a deep and widely shared view that China was once great, that it succeeded in the past but now is far behind and must catch up again. "So there is a patriotic desire," he said. "If our lab can do as well as the Redmond lab, that could be really exciting."

That sort of inspired leadership in science and engineering education is now totally missing in the United States.

Said Intel chairman Craig Barrett, "U.S. technological leadership, innovation, and jobs of tomorrow require a commitment to basic research funding today." According to a 2004 study by the Task Force on the Future of American Innovation, an industry-academic coalition, basic research performed at leading U.S. universities — research in chemistry, physics, nanotechnology, genomics, and semiconductor manufacturing — has created four thousand spin-off companies that hired 1.1 million employees and have annual world sales of $232 billion. But to keep moving ahead, the study said, there must be a 10 to 12 percent increase each year for the next five to seven years in the budgets of key research-funding agencies: the National Institute for Science and Technology, the National Science Foundation, the Department of Energy's Office of Science, and the Department of Defense research accounts.

Unfortunately, federal funding for research in physical and mathematical sciences and engineering, as a share of GDP, actually declined by 37 percent between 1970 and 2004, the task force found. At a time when we need to be doubling our investments in basic research to overcome the ambition and education gaps, we are actually cutting that funding.

In the wake of the Bush administration and the Republican Congress's decision to cut the National Science Foundation funding for 2005, Republican congressman Vern Ehlers of Michigan, a voice in the wilderness, made the following statement: "While I understand the need to make hard choices in the face of fiscal constraint, I do not see the wisdom in putting science funding behind other priorities. We have cut NSF despite the fact that this omnibus bill increases spending for the 2005 fiscal year, so clearly we could find room to grow basic research while maintaining fiscal constraint. But not only are we not keeping pace with inflationary growth, we are actually cutting the portion basic research receives in the overall budget. This decision shows dangerous disregard for our nation's future, and I am both concerned and astonished that we would make this decision at a time when other nations continue to surpass our students in math and science and consistently increase their funding of basic research. We cannot hope to fight jobs lost to international competition without a well-trained and educated workforce."

No, we cannot, and the effects are starting to show. According to the National Science Board, the percentage of scientific papers written by Americans has fallen 10 percent since 1992. The percentage of American papers published in the top physics journal, *Physical Review*, has fallen from 61 percent to 29 percent since 1983. And now we are starting to see a surge in patents awarded to Asian countries. From 1980 to 2003, Japan's share of world industrial patents rose from 12 percent to 21 percent, and Taiwan's from 0 percent to 3 percent. By contrast, the U.S. share of patents has fallen from 60 percent to 52 percent since 1980.

Any honest analysis of this problem should note that there are some skeptics who believe that the sky is not falling and that scientists and the technology industry might be hyping some of this data, just to get more funding. A May 10, 2004, article in the *San Francisco Chronicle* quoted Daniel S. Greenberg, former news editor of the journal *Science* and author of the book *Science, Money and Politics*, who argues that "inside-the-Beltway science (lobbying) has always been insatiable. If you double the NIH (National Institutes of Health) budget in five years (as recently happened), they're (still) screaming their heads off: 'We need more money.' " Greenberg also questioned the science lobbyists' interpretation of a number of statistics.

Quoting Greenberg, the *Chronicle* said, "To put scientific publishing trends in context . . . it's important to look not only at overall percentiles but also at the actual numbers of published papers. At first, it may sound startling to hear that China quadrupled its scientific publication rate between 1986 and 1999. But it sounds somewhat less startling if one realizes that the actual number of Chinese papers published rose from 2,911 to 11,675. By comparison, close to a third of all the world's scientific papers were published by Americans — 163,526 out of 528,643. In other words, China, a nation with almost four times the population of the United States, published (as of 1999) only one-fourteenth as many scientific papers as the United States."

While I think a dose of skepticism is always in order, I also think the skeptics would be wise to pay more heed to the flattening of the world and how quickly some of these trends could change. It is why I favor Shirley Ann Jackson's approach: The sky is not falling today, but it might be in fifteen or twenty years if we don't change our ways, and all signs are that we are not changing, especially in our public schools. Help is not on the way. The American education system from kindergarten through twelfth grade just is not stimulating enough young people to want to go into science, math, and engineering. My wife teaches first-grade reading in a local public school, so she gets *Education Week*, which is read by educators all over America. One day she pointed out an article (July 28, 2004) headlined, "Immigrants' Children Inhabit the Top Ranks of Math, Science Meets."

It went on to say, "Research conducted by the National Foundation for American Policy shows that 60 percent of the nation's top science students and 65 percent of the top mathematics students are children of recent immigrants, according to an analysis of award winners in three scholastic competitions . . . the Intel Science Talent Search, the U.S. team for the International Mathematical Olympiad, and the U.S. Physics Team." The study's author attributed the immigrant students' success "partly to their parents' insistence that they manage study time wisely," *Education Week* said. "Many immigrant parents also encouraged their children to pursue mathematics and science interests, believing those skills would lead to strong career opportunities and insulate them from bias and lack of connections in the workplace . . . A strong percentage of the students surveyed had parents who arrived in the United States on H-1B visas, reserved for professional workers. U.S. policymakers who back overly restrictive immigration policies do so at the risk of cutting off a steady infusion of technological and scientific skill," said the study's author, Stuart Anderson, the executive director of the foundation. The article quoted Andrei Munteanu, eighteen, a finalist for the 2004 Intel competition, whose parents had moved from Romania to the United States five years earlier. Munteanu started American school in the seventh grade, which he found a breeze compared to his Romanian school. "The math and science classes [covered the same subject matter] I was taking in Romania . . . when I was in fourth grade," he said.

For now, the United States still excels at teaching science and engineering at the graduate level, and also in university-based research. But as the Chinese get more feeder stock coming up through their improving high schools and universities, "they will get to the same level as us after a decade," said Intel chairman Barrett. "We are not graduating the volume, we do not have a lock on the infrastructure, we do not have a lock on the new ideas, and we are either flatlining, or in real dollars cutting back, our investments in physical science."

Every four years the United States takes part in the Trends in International Mathematics and Science Study, which assesses students after fourth grade and eighth grade. Altogether, the most recent study involved roughly a half million students from forty-one countries and the use of thirty languages, making it the largest and most comprehensive international study of education that has ever been undertaken.

The 2004 results (for tests taken in 2003) showed American students making only marginal improvements over the 2000 results, which showed the American labor force to be weaker in science than those of its peer countries. The Associated Press reported (December 4, 2004) that American eighth-graders had improved their scores in science and math since 1995, when the test first was given, but their math improvement came mainly between 1995 and 1999, and not in recent years. The rising scores of American eighth-graders in science was an improvement over 1999, and it lifted the United States to a higher ranking relative to other countries. The worrying news, though, was that the scores of American fourth-graders were stagnant, neither improving nor declining in science or math since 1995. As a result, they slipped in the international rankings as other countries made gains. "Asian countries are setting the pace in advanced science and math," Ina Mullis, codirector of the International Study Center at Boston College, which manages the study, told the AP. "As one example, 44 percent of eighth-graders in Singapore scored at the most advanced level in math, as did 38 percent in Taiwan. Only 7 percent in the United States did." Results from another international education test also came out in December 2004, from the Program for International Student Assessment. It showed that American fifteen-year-olds are below the international average when it comes to applying math skills to real-life tasks.

No wonder Johns Hopkins University president Bill Brody remarked to me, "Over 60 percent of our graduate students in the sciences are foreign students, and mostly from Asia. At one point four years ago all of our graduate students in mathematics were from the PRC [Communist China]. I only found out about it because we use them as [teaching assistants] and some of them don't speak English all that well." A Johns Hopkins parent wrote Brody to complain that his son could not understand his calculus professor because of his heavy Chinese accent and poor English.

No wonder there is not a major company that I interviewed for this book that is not investing significantly in research and development abroad. It is not "follow the money." It is "follow the brains."

"Science and math are the universal language of technology," said Tracy Koon, Intel's director of corporate affairs, who oversees the company's efforts to improve science education. "They drive technology and our standards of living. Unless our kids grow up knowing that universal language, they will not be able to compete. We are not in the business of manufacturing somewhere else. This is a company that was founded here, but we have two raw materials — sand, which we have a ready supply of, and talent, which we don't." (Silicon comes from sand.)

"We looked at two things," she continued. "We looked at the fact that in disciplines that were relevant to our industry, the number of U.S. students graduating at the master's and Ph.D. levels was declining in absolute numbers and relative to other countries. In our K to twelve we were doing okay at the fourth-grade level, we were doing middle-of-the-road in the eighth grade, and by the twelfth grade we were hovering near the bottom in international tests related to math. So the longer kids were in school, the dumber they were getting . . . You have teachers turning off kids because they were not trained. You know the old saw about the football coach teaching science — people who do not have the ability to make this accessible and gripping for kids."

One of the problems in remedying the situation, said Koon, is the fact that education in America is relatively decentralized and fragmented. If Intel goes to India or China or Jordan and introduces a teacher education program for making science more interesting, it can get into schools all over the country at once. In America, the public schools are overseen by fifty different state governments. While Intel does sponsor research at the university level that will benefit its own product development, it is growing increasingly concerned about the feeder system into those universities and the job market.

"Have we seen any change here? No, not really," said Koon. So Intel has been lobbying the INS for an increase in the number of advanced foreign engineers allowed into the United States on temporary work visas. "When we look at the kinds of people that we are trying to hire here — the master's and Ph.D. levels in photonics and optics engineering and very large-scale computer architecture — what we are finding is that as you go up the food chain from bachelor's to master's to Ph.D.'s, the number of people graduating from top-tier universities in those fields are increasingly foreign-born. So what do you do? For years [America] could count on the fact that we still have the best higher-education system in the world. And we made up for our deficiencies in K through twelve by being able to get all these good students from abroad. But now fewer are coming and fewer are staying . . . We have no God-given right to be able to hire all these people, and little by little we won't have the first-round draft choices. People who graduate in these very technical fields that are critical to our industries should get a green card stapled to their diploma."

It appears that young people wanting to be lawyers started to swamp those wanting to be engineers and scientists in the 1970s and early 1980s. Then, with the dot-com boom, those wanting to go to business school and earn MBAs swamped engineering students and lawyers in the 1990s. One can also hope that the marketplace will address the shortage of engineers and scientists by changing the incentives.

"Intel has to go where the IQ is," said Koon. Remember, she repeated, Intel's chips are made from just two things — sand and brains, "and right now the brains are the problem . . . We will need a stronger and more supportive immigration system if we want to hire the people who want to stay here. Otherwise, we will go where they are. What are the alternatives? I am not talking about data programmers or [people with] B.S. degrees in computer science. We are talking about high-end specialized engineering. We have just started a whole engineering function in Russia, where engineers have wonderful training — and talk about underemployed! We are beefing that up. Why wouldn't you?"

Wait a minute: Didn't *we* win the Cold War? If one of America's premier technology companies feels compelled to meet its engineering needs by going to the broken-down former Soviet Union, where the only thing that seems to work is old-school math and science education, then we've got a quiet little crisis on our hands. One cannot stress enough the fact that in the flat world the frontiers of knowledge get pushed out farther and farther, faster and faster. Therefore, companies need the brainpower that can not only reach the new frontiers but push them still farther. That is where the breakthrough drugs and software and hardware products are going to be found. And America either needs to be training that brainpower itself or importing it from somewhere else — or ideally both — if it wants to dominate the twenty-first century the way it dominated the twentieth — and that simply is not happening.

"There are two things that worry me right now," said Richard A. Rashid, the director of research for Microsoft. "One is the fact that we have really dramatically shut down the pipeline of very smart people coming to the United States. If you believe that we have the greatest research universities and opportunities, it all has to be driven by IQ. In trying to create processes that protect the country from undesirables, [the government] has done a much better job of keeping out desirables. A really significant fraction of the top people graduated from our universities [in science and engineering] were not born here, but stayed here and created the businesses, and became the professors, that were engines for our economic growth. We want these people. In a world where IQ is one of the most important commodities, you want to get as many smart people as you can."

Second, said Rashid, "We have done a very poor job of conveying to kids the value of science and technology as a career choice that will make the world a better place. Engineering and science is what led to so many improvements in our lives. But you talk to K through twelve kids about changing the world and they don't look at computer science as a career that is going to be a great thing. The amazing thing is that it is hard to get women into computer science now, and getting worse. Young women in junior high are told this is a really wretched lifestyle. As a result, we are not getting enough students through our systems who want to be computer scientists and engineers, and if we cut off the flow from abroad, the confluence of those two will potentially put us in a very difficult position ten or fifteen years from now. It is a pipeline process. It won't come to roost right away, but fifteen or twenty years from now, you'll find you don't have the people and the energy in these areas where you need them."

From Richard Rashid at Microsoft in the Northwest to Tracy Koon at Intel in Silicon Valley to Shirley Ann Jackson at Rensselaer on the East Coast, the people who understand these issues the best and are closest to them have the same message: Because it takes fifteen years to create a scientist or advanced engineer, starting from when that young man or woman first gets hooked on science and math in elementary school, we should be embarking on an all-hands-on-deck, no-holds-barred, no-budget-too-large crash program for science and engineering education immediately. The fact that we are not doing so is our quiet crisis. Scientists and engineers don't grow on trees. They have to be educated through a long process, because, ladies and gentlemen, this really *is* rocket science.

EIGHT

This Is Not a Test

We have the power to shape the civilization that we want. But we need your will, your labor, your hearts, if we are to build that kind of society. Those who came to this land sought to build more than just a new country. They sought a new world. So I have come here today to your campus to say that you can make their vision our reality. So let us from this moment begin our work so that in the future men will look back and say: It was then, after a long and weary way, that man turned the exploits of his genius to the full enrichment of his life.

— "Great Society" speech,
Lyndon B. Johnson, 1964

As a person who grew up during the Cold War, I'll always remember driving along down the highway and listening to the radio, when suddenly the music would stop and a grim-voiced announcer would come on the air and say, "This is a test of the emergency

493

broadcast system," and then there would be a thirty-second high-pitched siren sound. Fortunately, we never had to live through a moment in the Cold War where the announcer came on and said, "This is not a test." That, however, is exactly what I want to say here: *This is not a test.*

The long-term opportunities and challenges that the flattening of the world puts before the United States are profound. Therefore, our ability to get by doing things the way we've been doing them — which is to say, not always tending to our secret sauce and enriching it — will not suffice anymore. "For a country as wealthy as we are, it is amazing how little we are doing to enhance our natural competitiveness," said Dinakar Singh, the Indian-American hedge fund manager. "We are in a world that has a system that now allows convergence among many billions of people, and we had better step back and figure out what it means. It would be a nice coincidence if all the things that were true before are still true now — but there are quite a few things you actually need to do differently . . . You need to have a much more thoughtful national discussion." The flat world, Singh argued, is now the elephant in the room, and the question is, What is it going to do to us, and what are we going to do to it?

If this moment has any parallel in American history, it is the height of the Cold War, around 1957, when the Soviet Union leaped ahead of America in the space race by putting up the Sputnik satellite. Yes, there are many differences between that age and our own. The main challenge then came from those who wanted to put up walls; the main challenge to America today comes from the fact that all the walls are being taken down, and other countries can now compete with us much more directly. The main challenge in that world was from those practicing extreme communism, namely, Russia, China, and North Korea. The main challenge to America today is from those practicing extreme capitalism, namely, China, India, and South Korea. The main objective in that era was building a strong state; the main objective in this era is building strong individuals.

What this era has in common with the Cold War era, though, is that to meet the challenges of flatism requires as comprehensive, energetic, and focused a response as did meeting the challenge of communism. It requires our own version of the New Frontier and Great Society adapted to the age of flatness. It requires a president who can summon the nation to get smarter and study harder in science, math, and engineering in order to reach the new frontiers of knowledge that the flat world is rapidly opening up and pushing out. And it requires a Great Society that commits our government to building the infrastructure, safety nets, and institutions that will help every American become more employable in an age when no one can be guaranteed lifetime employment. I call my own version of this approach *compassionate flatism.*

Getting Americans to rally around compassionate flatism is much more difficult than getting them to rally around anticommunism. "National peril is a lot easier to convey than individual peril," noted Johns Hopkins University foreign policy expert Michael Mandelbaum. Economics, as noted, is not like war, because economics can always be a win-win game. But sometimes I wish economics were more like war. In the Cold War, we actually got to see the Soviets parade their missiles in Red Square. We all got to be scared together, from one end of the country to the other, and all our politicians had to be focused and serious about marshaling the resources and educational programs to make sure Americans could keep pace with the Soviet Union.

But today, alas, there is no missile threat coming from India. The "hot line," which used to connect the Kremlin with the White House, has been replaced by the "help line," which connects everyone in

America to call centers in Bangalore. While the other end of the hotline might have had Leonid Brezhnev threatening nuclear war, the other end of the help line just has a soft voice eager to help you sort out your AOL bill or collaborate with you on a new piece of software. No, that voice has none of the menace of Nikita Khrushchev pounding a shoe on the table at the UN, and it has none of the sinister snarl of the bad guys in *From Russia with Love.* There is no Boris or Natasha saying "We will bury you" in a thick Russian accent. No, that voice on the help line just has a friendly Indian lilt that masks any sense of threat or challenge. It simply says: "Hello, my name is Rajiv. Can I help you?"

No, Rajiv, actually, you can't.

When it comes to responding to the challenges of the flat world, there is no help line we can call. We have to dig into ourselves. We in America have all the tools to do that, as I argued in Chapter 6. But, as I argued in Chapter 7, we have not been tending to those tools as we should. Hence, our quiet crisis. The assumption that because America's economy has dominated the world for more than a century, it will and must always be that way is as dangerous an illusion today as the illusion that America would always dominate in science and technology was back in 1950. But this is not going to be easy. Getting our society up to speed for a flat world is going to be extremely painstaking. We are going to have to start doing a lot of things differently. It is going to take the sort of focus and national will that President John F. Kennedy called for in his famous May 25, 1961, speech to Congress on "urgent national needs." At that time, America was recovering from the twin shocks of Sputnik and the Soviet space launch of a cosmonaut, Yuri Gagarin, less than two months before Kennedy's speech. Kennedy knew that while America had enormous human and institutional assets — far more than the Soviet Union — they were not being fully utilized.

"I believe we possess all the resources and talents necessary," said President Kennedy. "But the facts of the matter are that we have never made the national decisions or marshaled the national resources required for such leadership. We have never specified long-range goals on an urgent time schedule, or managed our resources and our time so as to ensure their fulfillment." After then laying out his whole program for putting a man on the moon within ten years, President Kennedy added, "Let it be clear that I am asking the Congress and the country to accept a firm commitment to a new course of action, a course which will last for many years and carry very heavy costs . . . This decision demands a major national commitment of scientific and technical manpower, materiel and facilities, and the possibility of their diversion from other important activities where they are already thinly spread. It means a degree of dedication, organization and discipline which have not always characterized our research and development efforts."

In that speech, Kennedy made a vow that has amazing resonance today: "I am therefore transmitting to the Congress a new Manpower Development and Training program, to train or retrain several hundred thousand workers, particularly in those areas where we have seen chronic unemployment as a result of technological factors, in new occupational skills over a four-year period — in order to replace those skills made obsolete by automation and industrial change with the new skills which the new processes demand."

Amen. We too have to do things differently. We are going to have to sort out what to keep, what to discard, what to adapt, what to adopt, where to redouble our efforts, and where to intensify our focus. That is what this chapter is about. This is just an intuition, but the flattening of the world is going to be hugely disruptive to both traditional and developed societies. The weak will fall farther behind faster. The traditional will feel the force of modernization much more profoundly. The new will get turned into old quicker. The developed will be challenged by the underdeveloped much more profoundly. I worry, because so much political stability is built on economic stability, and economic stability is not going to be a feature of the flat world. Add it all up and you can see that the disruptions are going to come faster and harder. Think about Microsoft trying to figure out how to deal with a global army of people writing software for free! We are entering an era of creative destruction on steroids. Even if your country has a comprehensive strategy for dealing with flatism, it is going to be a challenge of a whole new dimension. But if you don't have a strategy at all . . . well, you've been warned.

This is not a test.

Being an American, I am most focused on my own country. How do we go about maximizing the benefits and opportunities of the flat world, and providing protection for those who have difficulty with the transition, without resorting to protectionism or runaway capitalism? Some will offer traditional conservative responses; some will offer traditional liberal ones. I offer compassionate flatism, which is a policy blend built around five broad categories of action for the age of flat: leadership, muscle building, cushioning, social activism, and parenting.

Leadership

The job of the politician in America, whether at the local, state, or national level, should be, in good part, to help educate and explain to people what world they are living in and what they need to do if they want to thrive within it. One problem we have today, though, is that so many American politicians don't seem to have a clue about the flat world. As venture capitalist John Doerr once remarked to me, "You talk to the leadership in China, and they are all the engineers, and they get what is going on immediately. The Americans don't, because they're all lawyers." Added Bill Gates, "The Chinese have risk taking down, hard work down, education, and when you meet with Chinese politicians, they are all scientists and engineers. You can have a numeric discussion with them — you are never discussing 'give me a one-liner to embarrass [my political rivals] with.' You are meeting with an intelligent bureaucracy."

I am not saying we should require all

politicians to hold engineering degrees, but it would be helpful if they had a basic understanding of the forces that are flattening the world, were able to educate constituents about them and galvanize a response. We have way too many politicians in America today who seem to do the opposite. They seem to go out of their way actually to make their constituents stupid — encouraging them to believe that certain jobs are "American jobs" and can be protected from foreign competition, or that because America has always dominated economically in our lifetimes it always will, or that compassion should be equated with protectionism. It is hard to have an American national strategy for dealing with flatism if people won't even acknowledge that there is an education gap emerging and that there is an ambition gap emerging and that we are in a quiet crisis. For instance, of all the policy choices that the Republican-led Congress could have made in forging the FY 2005 budget, how in the world could it have decided to cut the funding of the National Science Foundation by more than $100 million?

We need politicians who are able and willing to both explain and inspire. And what they most need to explain to Americans is pretty much what Lou Gerstner explained to the workforce of IBM when he took over as chairman in 1993, when the company was losing billions of dollars. At the time, IBM was facing a near-death experience owing to its failure to adapt to and capitalize on the business computing market that it invented. IBM got arrogant. It had built its whole franchise around helping customers solve problems. But after a while it stopped listening to its customers. It thought it didn't have to. And when IBM stopped listening to its customers, it stopped creating value that mattered for its customers, and that had been the whole strength of its business. A friend of mine who worked at IBM back then told me that when he was in his first year at the company and taking an internal course, his IBM instructor boasted to him that IBM was such a great company, it could do "extraordinary things with just average people." As the world started to flatten, though, IBM found that it could not continue thriving with an overabundance of average people working for a company that had stopped being a good listener.

But when a company is the pioneer, the vanguard, the top dog, the crown jewel, it is hard to look in the mirror and tell itself it is in a not-so-quiet crisis and better start to make a new history or become history. Gerstner decided that he would be that mirror. He told IBM it was ugly and that a strategy built largely around designing and selling computers — rather than the services and strategies to get the most out of those computers for each customer — didn't make sense. Needless to say, this was a shock for IBMers.

"Transformation of an enterprise begins with a sense of crisis or urgency," Gerstner told students at Harvard Business School, in a December 9, 2002, talk. "No institution will go through fundamental change unless it believes it is in deep trouble and needs to do something different to survive." It is impossible to ignore the parallel with America as a whole in the early twenty-first century.

When Lou Gerstner came in, one of the first things he did was replace the notion of lifetime employment with the notion of lifetime employability. A friend of mine, Alex Attal, a French-born software engineer who was working for IBM at the time, described the shift this way: "Instead of IBM giving you a guarantee that you will be employed, you had to guarantee that you could stay employable. The company would give you the framework, but you had to build it yourself. It's all about adapting. I was head of sales for IBM France at the time. It was the mid-nineties. I told my people that in the old days [the concept of] lifetime employment was only a company's responsibility, not a personal responsibility. But once we move to a model of employability, that becomes a shared responsibility. The company will give you access to knowledge, but you have to take advantage of it . . . You have to build the skills because it will be you against a lot of other people."

When Gerstner started to change the paradigm at IBM, he kept stressing the issue of individual empowerment. Said Attal, "He understood that an extraordinary company could only be built on a critical mass of extraordinary people."

As at IBM, so in America. Average Joe has to become special, specialized, or adaptable Joe. The job of government and business is not to guarantee anyone a lifetime job — those days are over. That social contract has been ripped up with the flattening of the world. What government can and must guarantee people is the chance to make themselves more employable. We don't want America to be to the world what IBM was becoming to the computer industry in the 1980s: the people who opened the field and then became too timid, arrogant, and ordinary to play on it. We want America to be the born-again IBM.

Politicians not only need to explain to people the flat world, they need to inspire them to rise to the challenge of it. There is more to political leadership than a competition for who can offer the most lavish safety nets. Yes, we must address people's fears, but we must also nurse their imaginations. Politicians can make us more fearful and thereby be disablers, or they can inspire us and thereby be enablers.

To be sure, it is not easy to get people passionate about the flat world. It takes some imagination. President Kennedy understood that the competition with the Soviet Union was not a space race but a science race, which was really an education race. Yet the way he chose to get Americans excited about sacrificing and buckling down to do what it took to win the Cold War — which required a large-scale push in science and engineering — was by laying out the vision of putting a man on the moon, not a missile into Moscow. If President Bush is looking for a similar legacy project, there is one just crying out — a national science initiative that would be our generation's moon shot: a crash program for alternative energy and conservation to make America energy-independent in ten years. If President Bush made energy independence his moon shot, in one fell swoop he would dry up revenue for terrorism, force Iran, Russia, Venezuela, and Saudi Arabia onto the path of reform —

which they will never do with $50-a-barrel oil — strengthen the dollar, and improve his own standing in Europe by doing something huge to reduce global warming. He would also create a real magnet to inspire young people to contribute to both the war on terrorism and America's future by again becoming scientists, engineers, and mathematicians. "This is not just a win-win," said Michael Mandelbaum. "This is a win-win-win-win-win."

I have consistently been struck that my newspaper columns that have gotten far and away the most positive feedback over the years, especially from young people, have been those that urged the president to call the nation to this task. Summoning all our energies and skills to produce a twenty-first-century fuel is George W. Bush's opportunity to be both Nixon to China and JFK to the moon in one move. Unfortunately for America, it appears as though I will go to the moon before President Bush will go down this road.

Muscles

Since lifetime employment is a form of fat that a flat world simply cannot sustain any longer, compassionate flatism seeks to focus its energy on how government and business can enhance every worker's *lifetime employability*. Lifetime employment depends on preserving a lot of fat. Lifetime employability requires replacing that fat with muscle. The social contract that progressives should try to enforce between government and workers, and companies and workers, is one in which government and companies say, "We cannot guarantee you any lifetime employment. But we can guarantee you that government and companies will focus on giving you the tools to make you more lifetime employable." The whole mind-set of a flat world is one in which the individual worker is going to become more and more responsible for managing his or her own career, risks, and economic security, and the job of government and business is to help workers build the necessary muscles to do that.

The "muscles" workers need most are portable benefits and opportunities for lifelong learning. Why those two? Because they are the most important assets in making a worker mobile and adaptable. As Harvard University economist Robert Lawrence notes, the greatest single asset that the American economy has always had is the flexibility and mobility of its labor force and labor laws. That asset will become even more of an advantage in the flat world, as job creation and destruction both get speeded up.

Given that reality, argues Lawrence, it becomes increasingly important for society, to the extent possible, to make benefits and education — the two key ingredients of employability — as flexible as possible. You don't want people to feel that they have to stay with a company forever simply to keep their pension and health benefits. The more the workforce feels mobile — in terms of health care, pension benefits, and lifelong learning possibilities — the more it will be willing and able to jump into the new industries and new job niches spawned by the flat world and to move from dying companies to thriving companies.

Creating legal and institutional frameworks for universal portability of pensions and health care — in addition to Social Security, Medicare, and Medicaid — will help people build up such muscles. Today roughly 50 percent of Americans don't have a job-based pension plan, other than Social Security. Those who are fortunate enough to have one cannot easily take it with them from job to job. What is needed is one simple universal portable pension scheme, along the lines proposed by the Progressive Policy Institute, that would get rid of the confusing welter of sixteen different tax-deferred options now offered by the government and consolidate them all into a single vehicle. This universal plan, which you would open with your first job, would encourage workers to establish 401(k) tax-deferred savings programs. Each worker and his or her employer could make contributions of cash, bonuses, profit sharing, or stock, depending on what sorts of benefits the specific employer offered. These assets would be allowed to build up tax-free in whatever savings or investment portfolio options the worker chose. But if and when it came time to change jobs, the worker could take the whole portfolio with him or her and not have to either cash it out or leave it under the umbrella of the previous employer. Rollover provisions do exist today, but they are complicated and many workers don't take advantage of them because of that.

The universal pension format would make rollover simple, easy, and expected, so pension lockup per se would never keep someone from moving from one job to another. Each employer could still offer his or her own specific 401(k) benefit plan, as an incentive to attract employees. But once a worker moved to another job, the investments in that particular 401(k) would just automatically dump into his or her universal pension account. With each new job, a new 401(k) could be started, and with each move, the benefits deposited in that same universal pension account.

In addition to this simple, portable, and universal pension program, Will Marshall, president of the Progressive Policy Institute, proposes legislation that would make it much easier and more likely for workers to obtain stock options in the companies for which they work. Such legislation would give tax incentives to companies to give more workers more options earlier and penalize companies that do not. Part of making workers more mobile is creating more ways to make more workers owners of financial assets, not just their own labor. "We want a public that sees itself as stakeholders, sharing in the capital-creating side of the flat world, not just competing in global labor markets," argued Marshall. "We all have to be owners as well as wage earners. That is where public policy has to be focused — to make sure that people have wealth-producing assets as they enter the twenty-first century, the way homeownership accomplished that in the twentieth century."

Why? Because there is an increasing body of literature that says people who are stakeholders, people who have a slice of the pie, "are more deeply invested in our system of democratic capitalism and the policies that keep it dynamic," said Marshall. It is another way, besides homeownership, to underpin the legitimacy of democratic capitalism. It is also another way to energize it, because workers who are also owners are more productive on the job. Moreover, in a flat world where every worker is going to face stiffer competition, the more opportunities everyone has to build wealth through the power of markets and compounding interest, the more he or she will be able to be self-reliant. We need to give workers every stabilizer we can and make it as easy for them to get stock options as it is for the plutocrats. Instead of just being focused on protecting those with existing capital, as conservatives so often seem to be, let's focus instead on widening the circle of capital owners.

On the health-care side, which I won't delve into in great detail, since that would be a book unto itself, it is essential that we develop a scheme for portable health insurance that reduces some of the burden on employers for providing and managing coverage. Virtually every entrepreneur I talked to for this book cited soaring and uncontrolled health-care costs in America as a reason to move factories abroad to countries where benefits were more limited, or nonexistent, or where there was national health insurance. Again, I favor the type of portable health-care program proposed by PPI. The idea is to set up state-by-state collective purchasing pools, the way Congress and federal employees now cover themselves. These pools would set the rules and create the marketplace in which insurance companies could offer a menu of options. Each employer would then be responsible for offering this menu of options to each new employee. Workers could choose high, medium, or low coverage. Everyone, though, would have to be covered. Depending on the employer, he or she would cover part or all of the premiums and the employee the rest. But employers would not be responsible for negotiating plans with insurance companies, where they have little individual clout.

The state or federal pools would do that. This way employees would be totally mobile and could take their health-care coverage wherever they went. This type of plan has worked like a charm for members of Congress, so why not offer it to the wider public? Needy and low-income workers who could not afford to join a plan would get some government subsidy to do so. But the main idea is to establish a government-supervised, -regulated, and -subsidized private insurance market in which government sets the broad rules so that there is no cherry-picking of healthy workers or arbitrary denial of treatment. The health care itself is administered privately, and the job of employers is to facilitate their workers' entry into one of these state pools and, ideally, help them pay for some or all of the premiums, but not be responsible for the health care themselves. In the transition, though, employers could continue to offer health-care plans as an incentive, and workers would have the option of going with either the plan offered by their employers or the menu of options available through the state purchasing pools. (For details, go to ppionline.org.)

One can quibble about the details of any of these proposals, but I think the basic inspiration behind them is exactly right: In a flattening world, where worker security can no longer be guaranteed by Fortune 500 corporations with top-down pension and health plans, we need more collaborative solutions — among government, labor, and business — that will promote self-reliant workers but not just leave them to fend for themselves.

When it comes to building muscles of employability, government has another critical role to play. Each century, as we push out the frontiers of human knowledge, work at every level becomes more complex, requiring more pattern recognition and problem solving. In the preindustrial age, human strength really mattered. Strength was a real service that lots of people could sell on the farm or in the workshop. With the invention of the electric motor and steam engine, though, physical strength became less important. Small women could drive big trucks. There is little premium for strength anymore. But there is an increasing premium for pattern recognition and complex problem solving, even down on the farm. Farming became a more knowledge-intensive activity, with GPS satellites guiding tractors to make sure all the rows being planted were straight. That modernization, plus fertilizer, put a lot of people out of work at the *previous wage* they were earning in agriculture.

Society as a whole looked at this transition from traditional agriculture to industrialization and said, "This is great! We will have more food and better food at lower costs, plus more people to work in factories." However, muscle-bound field hands and their families said, "This is a tragedy. How will I ever get a job in the industrial economy with only muscles and a sixth-grade education? I won't be able to eat any of that better, cheaper, plentiful food coming off the farms. We need to stop this move to industrialization."

Somehow we got through this transition from an agriculture-based society one hundred years ago to an industrial-based one — and still ended up with a higher standard of living for the vast majority of Americans. How did we do it?

"We said everyone is going to have to have a secondary education," said Stanford University economist Paul Romer. "That was what the high school movement in the early part of the twentieth century was all about." As economic historians have demonstrated in a variety of research (see particularly the work of Harvard economists Claudia Goldin and Larry Katz), both technology and trade are making the pie bigger, but they are also shifting the shares of that pie away from low-skilled labor to high-skilled labor. As American society produced more higher-skilled people by making high school mandatory, it empowered more people to get a bigger slice of the bigger, more complex economic pie. As that century progressed, we added, on top of the high school movement, the GI Bill and the modern university system.

"These were big ideas," noted Romer, "and what is missing at the moment is a political imagination of how do we do something just as big and just as important for the transition into the twenty-first century as we did for the nineteenth and twentieth." The obvious challenge, Romer added, is to make tertiary education, if not compulsory, then government-subsidized for at least two years, whether it is at a state university, a community college, or a technical school. Tertiary education is more critical the flatter the world gets, because technology will be churning old jobs, and spawning new, more complex ones, much faster than during the transition from the agricultural economy to the industrial one.

Educating more people at the tertiary level has two effects. One is that it produces more people with the skills to claim higher-value-added work in the new niches. And two, it shrinks the pool of people able to do lower-skilled work, from road maintenance to home repair to Starbucks. By shrinking the pool of lower-skilled workers, we help to stabilize their wages (provided we control immigration), because there are fewer people available to do those jobs. It is not an accident that plumbers can charge $75 an hour in major urban areas or that good housekeepers or cooks are hard to find.

America's ability from the mid-nineteenth century on into the mid-twentieth century to train people, limit immigration, and make low-skilled work scarce enough to win decent wages was how we created a middle class without too disparate an income gap. "Indeed," noted Romer, "from the end of the nineteenth century to the middle of the twentieth, we had a narrowing of the income gap. Now we have seen an increase of that gap over the last twenty or thirty years. That is telling us that you have to run faster in order to stay in the same place." With each advance in technology and increase in the complexity of services, you need an even higher level of skills to do the new jobs. Moving from being a farmhand to a phone operator who spoke proper English and could be polite was one thing. But moving from being a phone operator after the job got outsourced to India, to being able to install or repair phone-mail systems — or write their software — requires a whole new leap upward.

While expanding research universities on the high end of the spectrum is important, so is expanding the availability of technical schools and community colleges. Everyone should have a chance to be educated beyond high school. Otherwise upper-income kids will get those skills and their slice, and the lower-income kids will never get a chance. We have to increase the government subsidies that make it possible for more and more kids to attend community colleges and more and more low-skilled workers to get retrained.

JFK wanted to put a man on the moon. My vision is to put every American man or woman on a campus.

Employers have a critical contribution to make to lifetime learning and fostering employability, as opposed to guaranteed employment. Take, for instance, CapitalOne, the global credit card company, which began outsourcing elements of its backroom operations to Wipro and Infosys in India over the past few years. Competing in the global financial services market, the company felt it had to take advantage of all the cost-saving opportunities that its competitors were. CapitalOne began, though, by trying to educate its workers through workshops about the company's competitive predicament. It made clear that there is no safe haven where lifetime employment is possible anymore — inside CapitalOne or outside. Then it developed a whole program for cross-training of computer programmers, those most affected by outsourcing. The company would take a programmer who specialized in mainframes and teach him or her to be a distributed systems programmer as well. CapitalOne did similar cross-training on its business side, in everything from auto loans to risk management. As a result, the workers who were eventually let go in an outsourcing move were in a much better position to get new jobs, because they were cross-trained and therefore more employable. And those who were cross-trained but retained were more versatile and therefore more valuable to CapitalOne, because they could do multiple tasks.

What CapitalOne was doing, out of both its own self-interest and a feeling of obligation to workers it was letting go, was trying to make more and more of its workers into versatilists. The word "versatilist" was coined by Gartner Inc., the technology consultants, to describe the trend in the information technology world away from specialization and toward employees who are more adaptable and versatile. Building employee versatility and finding employees who already are or are willing to become versatilists "will be the new watchword for career planning," according to a Gartner study quoted by TechRepublic.com. "Enterprises that focus on technical aptitude alone will fail to align workforce performance with business value," the Gartner study said. "Instead, they need to build a team of versatilists who build a rich portfolio of knowledge and competencies to fuel [multiple] business objectives." The Gartner study noted that "specialists generally have deep skills and narrow scope, giving them expertise that is recognized by peers but seldom valued outside their immediate domain. Generalists have broad scope and shallow skills, enabling them to respond or act reasonably quickly but often without gaining or demonstrating the confidence of their partners or customers. Versatilists, in contrast, apply depth of skill to a progressively widening scope of situations and experiences, gaining new competencies, building relationships, and assuming new roles." TechRepublic quoted Joe Santana, director of training at Siemens Business Services: "With flat or even smaller budgets and fewer people, managers need to make the most of the people they have . . . They can no longer see people as specialty tools. And their people need to become less like specialty tools and more like Swiss Army knives. Those 'Swiss Army knives' are the versatilists."

In addition to their own self-interest in making more of their own employees into human Swiss Army knives, companies should be encouraged, with government subsidies or tax incentives, to offer as wide an array as possible of in-house learning opportunities. The menu of Internet-based worker-training programs today is enormous — from online degree programs to in-house guided training for different specializations. Not only is the menu enormous, but the cost to the company for offering these educational options is very low. The more lifetime learning opportunities that companies provide, the more they are both widening the skill base of their own workforce and fulfilling a moral obligation to workers whose jobs are outsourced to see to it that they leave more employable than they came. If there is a new social contract implicit between employers and employees today, it should be this: You give me your labor, and I will guarantee that as long as you work here, I will give you every opportunity — through either career advancement or training — to become more employable, more versatile.

While we need to redouble our efforts to build the muscles of each individual American, we have to continue to import muscles from abroad as well. Most of the Indian, Chinese, Russian, Japanese, Korean, Iranian, Arab, and Israeli engineers, physicists, and scientists who come to work or study in the United States make great citizens. They are family-oriented, educated, and hardworking, and most would jump at the chance to become an American. They are exactly the type of people this country needs, and we cannot let the FBI, CIA, and Homeland Security, in their zeal to keep out the next Mohammed Atta, also keep out the next Sergey Brin, one of the cofounders of Google, who was born in Russia. As a computer architect friend of mine says, "If a foreign-born person is one day going to take my job, I'd prefer they be American citizens helping pay for my retirement benefits."

I would favor an immigration policy that gives a five-year work visa to any foreign student who completes a Ph.D. at an accredited American university in any subject. I don't care if it is Greek mythology or mathematics. If we can cream off the first-round intellectual draft choices from around the world, it will always end up a net plus for America. If the flat world is about connecting all the knowledge pools together, we want our knowledge pool to be the biggest. Said Bill Brody, the president of Johns Hopkins, "We are in a global talent search, so anything we can do in America to get those top draft choices we should do, because one of them is going to be Babe Ruth, and why should we let him or her go somewhere else?"

Good Fat
Cushions Worth Keeping

While many of the old corporate and government safety nets will vanish under global competition in the flat world, some fat still needs to be maintained, and even added. As everyone who worries about his or her health knows, there is "good fat" and "bad fat" — but everybody needs some fat. That is also true of every country in the flat world. Social Security is good fat. We need to keep it. A welfare system that discourages people from working is bad fat. The sort of good fat that actually needs to be added for a flat world is wage insurance.

According to a study by Lori Kletzer, an economist at the University of California, Santa Cruz, in the 1980s and '90s, two-thirds of workers who lost jobs in manufacturing industries hit by overseas competition earned less on their next job. A quarter of workers who lost their jobs and were reemployed saw their income fall 30 percent or more. Losing a job for any reason is a trauma — for the worker and his or her family — but particularly for older workers who are less able to adapt to new production techniques or lack the education to move up into more skilled service jobs.

This idea of wage insurance was first proposed in 1986 by Harvard's Robert Lawrence and Robert E. Litan of the Brookings Institution, in a book called *Saving Free Trade*. The idea languished for a while until it started to catch fire again with an updated analysis by Kletzer and Litan in 2001. It got further political clout from the bipartisan U.S. Trade Deficit Commission in 2001. This commission couldn't agree on anything — including the causes of or what to do about the trade deficit — other than the wisdom of wage insurance.

"Trade creates winners and losers, and what we were thinking about were mechanisms by which the winners could compensate the losers, and particularly losers who were enjoying high wages in a particular job and suddenly found their new employment at much lower wages," said Lawrence. The way to think about this, he explained, is that every worker has "general skills and specific skills" for which they are paid, and when you switch jobs you quickly discover which is which. So you might have a college and CPA degree, or you might have a high school degree and the ability to operate a lathe. Both skills were reflected in your wages. But suppose one day your lathe job gets moved to China or your basic accounting work is outsourced to India and you have to go out and find a new job. Your new employer will not likely compensate you much for your specific skills, because your knowledge as a machine tool operator or a general accountant is probably of less use to him or her. You will be paid largely for your general skills, your high school education or college degree. Wage insurance would compensate you for your old specific skills, for a set period of time, while you take a new job and learn new specific skills.

The standard state-run unemployment insurance program eases some of this pain for workers, but it does not address their bigger concerns of declining wages in a new job and the inability to pay for health insurance while they are unemployed and searching. To qualify for wage insurance, workers seeking compensation for job loss would have to meet three criteria. First, they would have to have lost their job through some form of displacement — offshoring, outsourcing, downsizing, or factory closure. Second, they would have to have held the job for at least two years. And third, the wage insurance would not be paid until the workers found new jobs, which would provide a strong incentive to look for work quickly and increase the chances that they would get on-the-job retraining. On-the-job training is always the best way to learn new skills — instead of having to sign up for some general government training program, with no promise of a job at the other end, and go through that while remaining unemployed.

Workers who met those three conditions would then receive payments for two years, covering half the drop in their income from their previous job (capped at $10,000 a year). Kletzer and Litan also proposed that the government pay half the health insurance premiums for all "displaced" workers for up to six months. Wage insurance seems to me a much better idea than relying only on the traditional unemployment insurance offered by states, which usually covers only about 50 percent of most workers' previous wages, is limited to six months, and does not help workers who suffer a loss of earnings after they take a new job.

Moreover, as Kletzer and Litan noted, although all laid-off workers now have the right to purchase unsubsidized health insurance from their former employer if health coverage was offered when they were employed, many jobless workers do not have the money to take advantage of this guarantee. Also, while unemployed workers can earn an additional fifty-two weeks of unemployment insurance if they enroll in an approved retraining program, workers have no guarantee that when they finish such a program they will have a job.

For all these reasons, the Kletzer-Litan proposal makes a lot of sense to me as the right benefit for cushioning workers in a flat world. Moreover, such a program would be eminently affordable. Litan estimated that at an unemployment rate of 5 percent, the wage insurance and health-care subsidy today would cost around $8 billion a year, which is peanuts compared to the positive impact it could have on workers. This program would not replace classic state-run unemployment insurance for workers who opt for that, but if it worked as projected, it could actually reduce the cost of such programs by moving people back to work quicker.

Some might ask, Why be compassionate at all? Why keep any fat, friction, or barriers? Let me put it as bluntly as I can: If you are not a compassionate flatist — if you are just a let 'er rip free-market flatist — you are not only cruel, you are a fool. You are courting a political backlash by those who can and will get churned up by this flattening process, and that backlash could become ferocious if we hit any kind of prolonged recession.

The transition to a flat world is going to stress many people. As Joshua S. Levine, E★Trade's chief technology officer, put it to me, "You know how sometimes you go through a harrowing experience and you need a respite, but the respite never seems to come. Look at the airline workers. They go through this [terrible] event like 9/11, and management and the airline unions all negotiate for four months and management says, 'If the unions don't cut $2 billion in salary and benefits they will have to shut the airline down.' And after these wrenching negotiations the unions agree. I just have to laugh, because you know that in a few months management is going to come right back . . . There is no end. No one has to ask me to cut my budget each year. We all just know that each year we will be expected to do more with less. If you are a revenue producer, you are expected to come up with more revenue every year, and if you are an expense saver, you are expected to come up with more savings every year. You never get a break from it."

If societies are unable to manage the strains that are produced by this flattening, there will be a backlash, and political forces will attempt to reinsert some of the frictions and protectionist barriers that the flattening forces have eliminated, but they will do it in a crude way that will, in the name of protecting the weak, end up lowering everyone's standard of living. Former Mexican president Ernesto Zedillo is very sensitive to this problem, having had to manage Mexico's transition into NAFTA, with all of the strains that put on Mexican society. Speaking of the flattening process, he said to me, "It would be very hard to stop, but it can be stopped for a time. Maybe you can't stop it totally, but you can slow it down. And it makes a difference whether you get there in twenty-five years or fifty years. In between, two or three generations — who could have benefited a lot from more trade and globalization — will end up with crumbs."

Always remember, said Zedillo, that behind all this technology is a political infrastructure that enables it to play out. "There have been a series of concrete political decisions, taken over the last fifty years, that put the world where it is right now," he said. "Therefore, there are political decisions that could screw up the whole process too."

As the saying goes: If you want to live like a Republican, vote like a Democrat — take good care of the losers and left-behinds. The only way to be a flatist is to be a compassionate flatist.

Social Activism

One new area that is going to need sorting out is the relationship between global corporations and their own moral consciences. Some may laugh at the notion that a global corporation even has a moral conscience, or should ever be expected to develop one. But some do and others are going to have to develop one, for one simple reason: In the flat world, with lengthy global supply chains, the balance of power between global companies and the individual communities in which they operate is tilting more and more in favor of the companies, many of them American-based. As such, these companies are going to command more power, not only to create value but also to transmit values, than any transnational institutions on the planet. Social and environmental activists and progressive companies can now collaborate in ways that can make both the companies more profitable and the flat earth more livable. Compassionate flatism very much seeks to promote this type of collaboration.

Let me illustrate this notion with a couple of examples. If you think about the forces that are gobbling up biodiversity around the planet, none are more powerful than farmers. It is not that they are intending to be harmful, it is just in the nature of what they do. So how and where people farm and fish really matter to whether we preserve natural habitats and species. Conservation International, one of the biggest environmental NGOs in the world, has as its main mission preserving biodiversity. It is also a big believer in trying, when possible, to collaborate with big business, because when you bring a major global player around, it can have a huge impact on the environment. In 2002, McDonald's and Conservation International forged a partnership to use the McDonald's global supply chain — a behemoth that sucks beef, fish, chicken, pork, bread, lettuce, pickles, tomatoes, and potatoes from all four corners of the flat world — to produce not just value but also different values about the environment. "We and McDonald's looked at a set of environmental issues and said, 'Here are the things the food suppliers could do to reduce the environmental impact at little or no cost,'" explained Glenn Prickett, senior vice president of Conservation International.

McDonald's then met with its key suppliers and worked out, with them and with CI, a set of guidelines for what McDonald's calls "socially responsible food supply." "For conservationists the challenge is how do you get your arms around hundreds of millions of decisions and decision makers involved in agriculture and fisheries, who are not coordinated in any way except by the market," said Prickett. "So what we look for are partners who can put their purchasing power behind a set of environmentally friendly practices in a way that is good for them, works for the producers, and is good for biodiversity. In that way, you can start to capture so many more decision makers . . . There is no global government authority to protect biodiversity. You have to collaborate with the players who can make a difference, and one of them is McDonald's."

Conservation International is already seeing improvements in conservation of water, energy, and waste, as well as steps to encourage better management of fisheries, among McDonald's suppliers. But it is still early, and one will have to assess over a period of years, with comprehensive data collection, whether this is really having a positive impact on the environment. This form of collaboration cannot and should never be a substitute for government rules and oversight. But if it works, it can be a vehicle for actually getting government rules implemented. Environmentalists who prefer government regulation to these more collaborative efforts often ignore the fact that strong rules imposed against the will of farmers end up being weakly enforced — or not enforced at all.

What is in this for McDonald's? It is a huge opportunity to improve its global brand by acting as a good global citizen. Yes, this is, at root, a business opportunity for McDonald's. Sometimes the best way to change the world is by getting the big players to do the right things for the wrong reasons, because waiting for them to do the right things for the right reasons can mean waiting forever. Conservation International has struck similar supply-chain collaborations with Starbucks, setting rules for its supply chain of coffee farmers, and Office Depot, with its supply chain of paper-product providers.

What these collaborations do is start to "break down the walls between different interest groups," said Prickett. Normally you would have the environmentalists on one side and the farmers on the other and each side trying to get the government to write the regulations in the way that would serve it. Government would end up writing the rules largely to benefit business. "Now, instead, we have a private entity saying, 'We want to use our global supply chain to do some good,' but we understand that to be effective it has to be a collaboration with the farmers and the environmentalists if it is going to have any impact," Prickett said.

In this same vein, as a compassionate flatist, I would like to see a label on every electronics good state whether the supply chain that produced it is in compliance with the standards set down by the new HP-Dell-IBM alliance. In October 2004, these three giants joined forces in a collaborative effort with key members of their computer and printer supply chains to promote a unified code of socially responsible manufacturing practices across the world.

The new Electronics Industry Code of Conduct includes bans on bribes, child labor, embezzlement and extortion, and violations of intellectual property, rules governing usage of wastewater, hazardous materials, pollutants, and regulations on the reporting of occupational injuries. Several major electronics manufacturers who serve the IBM, Dell, and HP supply chains collaborated on writing the code, including Celestica, Flextronics, Jabil, Sanmina-SCI, and Solectron.

All HP suppliers, for instance, will be required to follow the code, though there is flexibility in the timing of how they reach compliance. "We are completely prepared and have terminated relationships with suppliers we find to be repeatedly nonresponsive," said HP spokeswoman Monica Sarkar. As of October 2004, HP had assessed more than 150 of its 350 suppliers, including factories in China, Mexico, Southeast Asia, and Eastern Europe. It has set up a steering committee with IBM and Dell in order to figure out exactly how they collectively can review compliance and punish consistent violators. Compliance is everything, and so, again, it remains to be seen just how vigilant the corporations will be with their suppliers. Nevertheless, this use of supply chains to create values — not just value — could be a wave of the future.

"As we have begun to look to other [off-shore] suppliers to do most of our manu-facturing, it has become clear to us that we have to assume some responsibility for how they do that work," explained Debra Dunn, HP's senior vice president of corporate affairs and global citizenship. First and foremost, that is what many of HP's customers want. "Customers care," said Dunn, "and European customers lead the way in caring. And human rights groups and NGOs, who are gaining increasing global influence as trust in corporations declines, are basically saying, 'You guys have the power here. You are global companies, you can set expectations that will influence environmental practices and human rights practices in emerging markets.' "

Those voices are right, and what is more, they can use the Internet to great effect, if they want, to embarrass global corporations into compliance.

"When you have the procurement dollars that HP and McDonald's have," said Dunn, "people really want to do business with you, so you have leverage and are in a position to set standards and [therefore] you have a responsibility to set standards." The role of global corporations in setting standards in emerging markets is doubly important, because oftentimes local governments actually want to improve their environmental standards. They know it is important in the long run, but the pressure to create jobs and live within budget constraints is overwhelming and therefore the pressure to look the other way is overwhelming. Countries like China, noted Dunn, often actually want an outside force, like a global business coalition, to exert pressure to drive new values and standards at home that they are too weak to impose on themselves and their own bureaucrats. In *The Lexus and the Olive Tree* I called this form of value creation "globalution," or revolution from beyond.

Said Dunn: "We used to say that as long as we complied with the local law, that was all we could be expected to do. But now the imbalance of power is so huge it is not practical to say that Wal-Mart or HP can do whatever they want as long as a state government or country does not stop them. The leverage HP would leave on the table would be immoral given its superior power . . . We have the power to transmit global governance to our universe of suppliers and employees and consumers, which is a pretty broad universe."

Dunn noted that in a country like China there is an intense competition by local companies to become part of the HP or Dell or Wal-Mart supply chain. Even though it is high pressure, it means a steady volume of considerable business — the kind that can make or break a company. As a result, HP has huge leverage over its Chinese suppliers, and they are actually very open to having their factory standards lifted, because they know that if they get up to the standards of HP they can leverage that to get business from Dell or Sony.

Advocates of compassionate flatism need to educate consumers to the fact that their buying decisions and buying power are political. Every time you as a consumer make a decision, you are supporting a whole set of values. You are voting about the barriers and friction you want to preserve or eliminate. Progressives need to make this information more easily available to consumers, so more of them can vote the right way and support the right kind of global corporate behavior.

Marc Gunther, a senior writer for *Fortune* magazine and the author of *Faith and Fortune: The Quiet Revolution to Reform American Business*, is one of the few business writers who have recognized how global corporations can be influenced by progressive politics. "To be sure," wrote Gunther in an essay in *The Washington Post* (November 14, 2004), "there are plenty of scoundrels out there, indifferent to the rights and wrongs of corporate behavior.

And some executives who talk of social issues may be only mouthing the words. But the bottom line is that a growing number of companies have come to believe that moral values, broadly and liberally defined, can help drive shareholder values. And that is a case study from which everyone could learn."

This progressive tilt of big business has not generated much press attention, Gunther noted. "Partly that's because scandal stories are juicier. Mostly it's because changes in corporate practices have been incremental — and because reporters tend to dismiss talk of corporate social responsibility as mere public relations. But chief executives of closely-watched firms like General Electric do not promise to become better global citizens unless they intend to follow through. 'If you want to be a great company today,' Jeff Immelt, GE's CEO, likes to say, 'you have to be a good company.' When I asked him why GE has begun to talk more openly about corporate citizenship, he said: 'The reason why people come to work for GE is that they want to be about something that is bigger than themselves.' As Immelt suggests, the biggest driver of corporate reform is the desire of companies to attract people who seek meaning as well as money from their work. Few of us go to our jobs every day to enhance shareholder value. Younger people, especially, want to work for companies with a mission that goes beyond the bottom line."

In sum, we are now in a huge transition as companies are coming to understand not only their power in a flat world but also their responsibilities. Compassionate flatists believe that this is no time to be sitting on one's hands, thinking exclusively in traditional left-right, consumer-versus-company terms. Instead we should be thinking about how collaboration between consumers and companies can provide an enormous amount of protection against the worst features of the flattening of the world, without opting for classic protectionism.

"Compassionate capitalism. Think it sounds like an oxymoron? Think again," said Gunther. "Even as America is supposedly turning conservative on social issues, big business is moving in the other direction."

Parenting

No discussion of compassionate flatism would be complete without also discussing the need for improved parenting. Helping individuals adapt to a flat world is not only the job of governments and companies. It is also the job of parents. They too need to know in what world their kids are growing up and what it will take for them to thrive. Put simply, we need a new generation of parents ready to administer tough love: There comes a time when you've got to put away the Game Boys, turn off the television set, put away the iPod, and get your kids down to work.

The sense of entitlement, the sense that because we once dominated global commerce and geopolitics — and Olympic basketball — we always will, the sense that delayed gratification is a punishment worse than a spanking, the sense that our kids have to be swaddled in cotton wool so that nothing bad or disappointing or stressful ever happens to them at school is, quite simply, a growing cancer on American society. And if we don't start to reverse it, our kids are going to be in for a huge and socially disruptive shock from the flat world. While a different approach by politicians is necessary, it is not sufficient.

David Baltimore, the Nobel Prize–winning president of Caltech, knows what it takes to get your child ready to compete against the cream of the global crop. He told me that he is struck by the fact that almost all the students who make it to Caltech, one of the best scientific universities in the world, come from public schools, not from private schools that sometimes nurture a sense that just because you are there, you are special and entitled. "I look at the kids who come to Caltech, and they grew up in families that encouraged them to work hard and to put off a little bit of gratification for the future and to understand that they need to hone their skills to play an important role in the world," Baltimore said. "I give parents enormous credit for this, because these kids are all coming from public schools that people are calling failures. Public education is producing these remarkable students — so it *can* be done. Their parents have nurtured them to make sure that they realize their potential. I think we need a revolution in this country when it comes to parenting around education."

Clearly, foreign-born parents seem to be doing this better. "About one-third of our students have an Asian background or are recent immigrants," he said. A significant majority of the students coming to Caltech in the engineering disciplines are foreign-born, and a large fraction of its current faculty is foreign-born. "In biology, at the postdoc level, the dominance of Chinese students is overwhelming," said Baltimore. No wonder that at the big scientific conferences today, a majority of the research papers dealing with cutting-edge bioscience have at least one Chinese name on them.

My friends Judy Estrin and Bill Carrico have started several networking companies in Silicon Valley. At one time, Judy was chief technology officer for Cisco. I sat with them one afternoon and talked about this problem. "When I was eleven years old," said Bill, "I knew I was going to be an engineer. I dare you to find an eleven-year-old in America who wants to be an engineer today. We've turned down the ambition level."

Added Judy, "More of the problem [can be solved by good] parenting than can be solved from a regulatory or funding move. Everyone wants to fund more of this and that, but where it starts is with the parents. Ambition comes from the parents. People have to get it. It will probably take a crisis [to get us refocused]."

In July 2004, comedian Bill Cosby used an appearance at Jesse Jackson's Rainbow/PUSH Coalition & Citizenship Education Fund's annual conference to upbraid African-Americans for not teaching their children proper grammar and for black kids not striving to learn more themselves. Cosby had already declared, "Everybody knows it's important to speak English except these knuckleheads. You can't be a doctor with that kind of crap coming out of your mouth." Referring to African-Americans who squandered their chances for a better life, Cosby told the Rainbow Coalition, "You've got to stop beating up your women because you can't find a job, because you didn't want to get an education and now you're [earning] minimum wage. You should have thought more of yourself when you were in high school, when you had an opportunity." When Cosby's remarks attracted a lot of criticism, Reverend Jackson defended him, arguing, "Bill is saying, let's fight the right fight. Let's level the playing field. Drunk people can't do that. Illiterate people can't do that."

That is right. Americans are the ones who increasingly need to level the playing field — not by pulling others down, not by feeling sorry for ourselves, but by lifting ourselves up. But when it comes to how to do that, Cosby was saying something that is important for black and white Americans, rich and poor. Education, whether it comes from parents or schools, has to be about more than just cognitive skills. It also has to include character building. The fact is, parents and schools and cultures can and do shape people. The most important influence in my life, outside of my family, was my high school journalism teacher, Hattie M. Steinberg. She pounded the fundamentals of journalism into her students — not simply how to write a lead or accurately transcribe a quote but, more important, how to comport yourself in a professional way. She was nearing sixty at the time I had her as my teacher and high school newspaper adviser in the late 1960s. She was the polar opposite of "cool," but we hung around her classroom like it was the malt shop and she was Wolfman Jack. None of us could have articulated it then, but it was because we enjoyed being harangued by her, disciplined by her, and taught by her. She was a woman of clarity and principles in an age of uncertainty. I sit up straight just thinking about her! Our children will increasingly be competing head-to-head with Chinese, Indian, and Asian kids, whose parents have a lot more of Hattie's character-building approach than their own American parents. I am not suggesting that we militarize education, but I am suggesting that we do more to push our young people to go beyond their comfort zones, to do things right, and to be ready to suffer some short-run pain for longer gain.

I fear, though, that things will have to get worse before they get better. As Judy Estrin said, it will probably take a crisis. I would simply add: The crisis is already here. It is just playing out in slow motion. The flattening of the world is moving ahead apace, and barring war or some catastrophic terrorist event, nothing is going to stop it. But what can happen is a decline in our standard of living, if more Americans are not empowered and educated to participate in a world where all the knowledge centers are being connected. We have within our society all the ingredients for American individuals to thrive in this world, but if we squander those ingredients, we will stagnate.

I repeat: *This is not a test*. This is a crisis, and as Paul Romer has so perceptively warned, "A crisis is a terrible thing to waste."

DEVELOPING COUNTRIES AND THE FLAT WORLD

NINE

The Virgin of Guadalupe

It's not that we are becoming more Anglo-Saxon. It's that we are having an encounter with reality.
— Frank Schirrmacher, publisher of the German newspaper *Frankfurter Allgemeine Zeitung*, commenting to *The New York Times* about the need for German workers to retool and work longer hours

Seek knowledge even unto China.
— saying of the Prophet Muhammad

The more I worked on this book, the more I found myself asking people I met around the world where they were when they first discovered that the world was flat.

In the space of two weeks, I got two revealing answers, one from Mexico, one from Egypt. I was in Mexico City in the spring of 2004, and I put the question on the table during lunch with a few Mexican journalist colleagues. One of them said he realized that he was living in a new world when he started seeing reports appearing in the Mexican media and on the Internet that some statuettes of Mexico's patron saint, the Virgin of Guadalupe, were being imported into Mexico from China, probably via ports in California. When you are Mexico and your claim to fame is that you are a low-wage manufacturing country, and some of your people are importing statuettes of your own patron saint from China, because China can make them and ship them all the way across the Pacific more cheaply than you can produce them, you are living in a flat world.

You've also got a problem. Over at the Central Bank of Mexico, I asked its governor, Guillermo Ortiz, whether he was aware of this issue. He rolled his eyes and told me that for some time now he could feel the competitive playing field being leveled — and that Mexico was losing some of its natural geographic advantages with the U.S. market — by just staring at the numbers on his computer screen. "We started looking at the numbers in 2001 — it was the first year in two decades that [Mexico's] exports to the U.S. declined," said Ortiz. "That was a real shock. We started reducing our gains in market share and then started losing them. We said that there is a real change here . . . And it was about China."

China is such a powerhouse of low-cost manufacturing that even though the

NAFTA accord has given Mexico a leg up with the United States, and even though Mexico is right next door to us, China in 2003 replaced Mexico as the number two exporter to the United States. (Canada remains number one.) Though Mexico still has a strong position in big-ticket exports that are costly to ship, such as cars, auto parts, and refrigerators, China is coming on strong and has already displaced Mexico in areas such as computer parts, electrical components, toys, textiles, sporting goods, and tennis shoes. But what's even worse for Mexico is that China is displacing some Mexican companies in Mexico, where Chinese-made clothing and toys are now showing up on store shelves everywhere. No wonder a Mexican journalist told me about the day he interviewed a Chinese central bank official, who told him something about China's relationship with America that really rattled him: "First we were afraid of the wolf, then we wanted to dance with the wolf, and now we want to be the wolf."

A few days after returning from Mexico, I had breakfast in Washington with a friend from Egypt, Lamees El-Hadidy, a longtime business reporter in Cairo. Naturally I asked her where she was when she discovered the world was flat. She answered that it was a just few weeks earlier, during the Muslim holy month of Ramadan. She had done a story for CNBC Arabiya Television about the colorful lanterns called *fawanis*, each with a burning candle inside, that Egyptian schoolchildren traditionally carried around during Ramadan, a tradition dating back centuries to the Fatimid period in Egypt. Kids swing the lanterns and sing songs, and people give them candy or gifts, as in America on Halloween. For centuries, small, low-wage workshops in Cairo's older neighborhoods have manufactured these lanterns — until the last few years.

That was when plastic Chinese-made Ramadan lanterns, each with a battery-powered light instead of a candle, began flooding the market, crippling the traditional Egyptian workshops. Said Lamees, "They are invading our tradition — in an innovative way — and we are doing nothing about it . . . These lanterns come out of our tradition, our soul, but [the Chinese versions] are more creative and advanced than the Egyptian ones." Lamees said that when she asked Egyptians, "Do you know where these are made?," they would all answer no. Then they would turn the lamps over and see that they came from China.

Many mothers, like Lamees, though, appreciated the fact that the Chinese versions are safer than the traditional Egyptian ones, which are made with sharp metal edges and glass, and usually still use candles. The Chinese versions are made of plastic and feature flashing lights and have an embedded microchip that plays traditional Egyptian Ramadan tunes and even the theme song to the popular Ramadan TV cartoon series *Bakkar*. As *Business Monthly*, published by the American Chamber of Commerce in Egypt, reported in its December 2001 issue, Chinese importers "are pitted not only against each other, but also against the several-hundred-year-old Egyptian industry. But the Chinese models are destined to prevail, according to [a] famous importer, Taha Zayat. 'Imports have definitely cut down on sales of traditional fawanis,' he said. 'Of all fawanis on the market, I don't think that more than 5 percent are now made in Egypt.' People with ties to the Egyptian [fawanis] industry believe China has a clear advantage over Egypt. With its superior technology, they said, China can make mass quantities, which helps to keep prices relatively low. Egypt's traditional [fawanis] industry, by contrast, is characterized by a series of workshops specialized in different stages of the production process. Glassmakers, painters, welders and metal craftsmen all have their role to play. 'There will always be fawanis in Ramadan, but in the future I think Egyptian-made ones could become extinct,' Zayat said. 'There is no way they can ever compete with things made in China.' "

Think how crazy that statement is: Egypt has masses of low-wage workers, like China. It sits right next to Europe, on the Suez Canal. It could be and should be the Taiwan of the eastern Mediterranean, but instead it is throwing in the towel to atheistic China on the manufacture of one of Muslim Egypt's most cherished cultural artifacts. Ibrahim El Esway, one of the main importers from China of fawanis, gave *The Business Monthly* a tour of his warehouse in the Egyptian town of Muski: He had imported sixteen different models of Ramadan lanterns from China in 2004. "Amid the crowds at Muski, [El Esway] gestured to one of his employees, who promptly opened a dust-covered box and pulled out a plastic fawanis shaped like the head of Simba, from *The Lion King*. 'This is the first model we imported back in 1994,' he said. He switched it on. As the blue-colored lion's head lit up, the song 'It's a Small World' rang out."

Introspection

The previous section of this book looked at how individuals, particularly Americans, should think about meeting the challenge posed by the flattening of the world. This chapter focuses on what sort of policies

554

developing countries need to undertake in order to create the right environment for their companies and entrepreneurs to thrive in a flat world, although many of the things I am about to say apply to many developed countries as well.

When developing countries start thinking about the challenge of flatism, the first thing they need to do is engage in some brutally honest introspection. A country, its people and leaders alike, has to be honest with itself and look clearly at exactly where it stands in relation to other countries and in relation to the ten flatteners. It has to ask itself, "To what extent is my country advancing or being left behind by the flattening of the world, and to what extent is it adapting to and taking advantage of all the new platforms for collaboration and competition?" As that Chinese banking official boasted to my Mexican colleague, China is the wolf. Of all the ten flatteners, the entry of China into the world market is the most important for developing countries, and for many developed countries. China can do high-quality low-cost manufacturing better than any other country, and increasingly, it also can do high-quality higher-cost manufacturing. With China and the other nine flatteners coming on so strong, no country today can afford to be anything less than brutally honest with itself.

To that end, I believe that what the world needs today is a club that would be modeled after Alcoholics Anonymous (A.A.). It would be called Developing Countries Anonymous (D.C.A.). And just as at the first A.A. meeting you attend you have to stand up and say, "My name is Thomas Friedman and I'm an alcoholic," so at Developing Countries Anonymous, countries would have to stand up at their first meeting and say, "My name is Syria and I'm underdeveloped." Or "My name is Argentina and I'm underachieving. I have not lived up to my potential."

Every country needs "the ability to make your own introspection," since "no country develops without going through an X-ray of where you are and where your limits are," said Luis de la Calle, one of Mexico's chief NAFTA negotiators. Countries that fall off the development wagon are a bit like drunks; to get back on they have to learn to see themselves as they really are. Development is a voluntary process. You need a positive decision to make the right steps, but it starts with introspection.

I Can Get It for You Wholesale

During the late 1970s, but particularly after the fall of the Berlin Wall, a lot of countries started to pursue development in a new way through a process that I call reform whole-sale. The era of Globalization 2.0, when the world shrank from a size medium to a size small, was the era of reform wholesale, an era of broad macroeconomic reform. These wholesale reforms were initiated by a small handful of leaders in countries like China, Russia, Mexico, Brazil, and India. These small groups of reformers often relied on the leverage of authoritarian political systems to unleash the state-smothered market forces in their societies. They pushed their countries into more export-oriented, free-market strat-egies — based on privatization of state com-panies, deregulation of financial markets, currency adjustments, foreign direct invest-ment, shrinking subsidies, lowering of pro-tectionist tariff barriers, and introduction of more flexible labor laws — from the top down without ever really asking the people. Ernesto Zedillo, who served as president of Mexico from 1994 to 2000 and was finance minister before that, once remarked to me that all the decisions to open the Mexican economy were taken by three people. How many people do you suppose Deng Xiaoping consulted before he declared, "To get rich is glorious," and opened the Chi-nese economy, or when he dismissed those who questioned China's move from commu-nism to free markets by saying that what mattered was jobs and incomes, not ideology? Deng tossed over decades of Communist ideology with one sentence: "Black cat, white cat, all that matters is that it catches mice." In 1991, when India's finance minister, Manmohan Singh, took the first tentative steps to open India's economy to more foreign trade, investment, and competition, it was a result not of some considered national debate and dialogue, but of the fact that India's economy at that moment was so sclerotic, so unappealing to foreign investors, that it had almost run out of foreign currency. When Mikhail Gorbachev started dabbling with perestroika, it was with his back up against the Kremlin wall and with few allies in the Soviet leadership. The same was true of Margaret Thatcher when she took on the striking coal miners' union in 1984 and forced reform wholesale onto the sagging British economy.

What all these leaders confronted was the irrefutable fact that more open and competitive markets are the only sustainable vehicle for growing a nation out of poverty, because they are the only guarantee that new ideas, technologies, and best practices are easily flowing into your country and that private enterprises, and even government, have the competitive incentive and flexibility to adopt those new ideas and turn them into jobs and products. This is why the nonglobalizing countries, those that refused to do any reform wholesale — North Korea, for instance — actually saw their per capita GDP growth shrink in the 1990s, while countries that moved from a more socialist model to a globalizing model saw their per capita GDP grow in the 1990s. As David Dollar and Art Kray conclude in their book *Trade, Growth, and Poverty,* economic growth and trade remain the best antipoverty program in the world.

The World Bank reported that in 1990 there were roughly 375 million people in China living in extreme poverty, on less than $1 per day. By 2001, there were 212 million Chinese living in extreme poverty, and by 2015, if current trends hold, there will be only 16 million living on less than $1 a day. In South Asia — primarily India, Pakistan, and Bangladesh — the numbers go from 462 million in 1990 living on less than $1 a day down to 431 million by 2001 and down to 216 million in 2015. In sub-Saharan Africa, by contrast, where globalization has been slow to take hold, there were 227 million people living on less than $1 a day in 1990, 313 million in 2001, and an expected 340 million by 2015.

The problem for any globalizing country lies in thinking you can stop with reform wholesale. In the 1990s, some countries thought that if you got your ten commandments of reform wholesale right — thou shall privatize state-owned industries, thou shall deregulate utilities, thou shall lower tariffs and encourage export industries, etc. — you had a successful development strategy. But as the world started to get smaller and flatter — enabling China to compete everywhere with everyone on a broad range of manufactured products, enabling India to export its brainpower everywhere, enabling corporations to outsource any task anywhere, and enabling individuals to compete globally as never before — reform wholesale was no longer sufficient to keep countries on a sustainable growth path.

A deeper process of reform was required — a process I would call reform retail.

I Can Only Get It for You Retail

What if regions of the world were like the neighborhoods of a city? What would the world look like? I'd describe it like this: Western Europe would be an assisted-living facility, with an aging population lavishly attended to by Turkish nurses. The United States would be a gated community, with a metal detector at the front gate and a lot of people sitting in their front yards complaining about how lazy everyone else was, even though out back there was a small opening in the fence for Mexican labor and other energetic immigrants who helped to make the gated community function. Latin America would be the fun part of town, the club district, where the workday doesn't begin until ten p.m. and everyone sleeps until midmorning. It's definitely the place to hang out, but in between the clubs, you don't see a lot of new businesses opening up, except on the street where the Chileans live. The landlords in this neighborhood almost never reinvest their profits here, but keep them in a bank across town. The Arab street would be a dark alley where outsiders fear to tread, except for a few side streets called Dubai, Jordan, Bahrain, Qatar, and Morocco. The only new businesses are gas stations, whose owners, like the elites in the Latin neighborhood, rarely reinvest their funds in the neighborhood. Many people on the Arab street have their curtains closed, their shutters drawn, and signs on their front lawn that say, "No Trespassing. Beware of Dog." India, China, and East Asia would be "the other side of the tracks." Their neighborhood is a big teeming market, made up of small shops and one-room factories, interspersed with Stanley Kaplan SAT prep schools and engineering colleges. Nobody ever sleeps in this neighborhood, everyone lives in extended families, and everyone is working and saving to get to "the right side of the tracks." On the Chinese streets, there's no rule of law, but the roads are all well paved; there are no potholes, and the streetlights all work. On the Indian streets, by contrast, no one ever repairs the streetlights, the roads are full of ruts, but the police are sticklers for the rules. You need a license to open a lemonade stand on the Indian streets. Luckily, the local cops can be bribed, and the successful entrepreneurs all have their own generators to run their factories and the latest cell phones to get around the fact that the local telephone poles are all down. Africa, sadly, is that part of town where the businesses are boarded up, life expectancy is declining, and the only new buildings are health-care clinics.

The point here is that every region of the world has its strengths and weaknesses, and all are in need of reform retail to some degree. What is reform retail? In the simplest terms, it is more than just opening your country to foreign trade and investment and making a few macroeconomic policy changes from the top. That is reform wholesale. Reform retail presumes you have already done reform wholesale. It involves looking at four key aspects of your society — infrastructure, regulatory institutions, education, and culture (the general way your country and leaders relate to the world) — and upgrading each one to remove as many friction points as possible. The idea of reform retail is to enable the greatest number of your people to have the best legal and institutional framework within which to innovate, start companies, and become attractive partners for those who want to collaborate with them from elsewhere in the world.

Many of the key elements of reform retail were best defined by the research done by the World Bank's International Finance Corporation (IFC) and its economic analysis team led by its chief economist, Michael Klein. What do we learn from their work? To begin with, you don't grow your country out of poverty by guaranteeing everyone a job. Egypt guarantees all college graduates a job each year, and it has been mired in poverty with a slow-growing economy for fifty years.

"If it were just a matter of the number of jobs, solutions would be easy," note Klein and Bita Hadjimichael in their World Bank Study, *The Private Sector in Development*. "For example, state-owned enterprises could absorb all those in need of employment. The real issue is not just employment, but increasingly productive employment that allows living standards to rise." State-owned enterprises and state-subsidized private firms usually have not delivered sustainable productivity growth, and neither have a lot of other approaches that people assume are elixirs of growth, they add. Just attracting more foreign investment into a country also doesn't automatically do it. And even massive investments in education won't guarantee it.

"Productivity growth and, hence, the way out of poverty, is not simply a matter of throwing resources at the problem," say Klein and Hadjimichael. "More important, it is a matter of using resources well." In other words, countries grow out of poverty not only when they manage their fiscal and monetary policies responsibly from above, i.e., reform wholesale. They grow out of poverty when they also create an environment below that makes it very easy for their people to start businesses, raise capital, and become entrepreneurs, and when they subject their people to at least some competition from beyond — because companies and countries with competitors always innovate more and faster.

The IFC drove home this point with a comprehensive study of more than 130 countries, called *Doing Business in 2004*. The IFC asked five basic questions about doing business in each of these countries, questions about how easy or difficult it is to 1) start a business in terms of local rules, regulations, and license fees, 2) hire and fire workers, 3) enforce a contract, 4) get credit, and 5) close a business that goes bankrupt or is failing. To translate it into my own lexicon, those countries that make all these things relatively simple and friction-free have undertaken reform retail, and those that have not are stalled in reform wholesale and are not likely to thrive in a flat world. The IFC's criteria were inspired by the brilliant and innovative work of Hernando de Soto, who has demonstrated in Peru and other developing nations that if you change the regulatory and business environment for the poor, and give them the tools to collaborate, they will do the rest.

Doing Business in 2004 tries to explain each of its points with a few colorful examples: "Teuku, an entreprenuer in Jakarta, wants to open a textile factory. He has customers lined up, imported machinery, and a promising business plan. Teuku's first encounter with the government is when registering his business. He gets the standard forms from the Ministry of Justice, and completes and notarizes them. Teuku proves that he is a local resident and does not have a criminal record. He obtains a tax number, applies for a business license, and deposits the minimum capital (three times national income per capita) in the bank. He then publishes the articles of association in the official gazette, pays a stamp fee, registers at the Ministry of Justice, and waits 90 days before filing for social security. One hundred sixty-eight days after he commences the process, Teuku can legally start operations. In the meantime, his customers have contracted with another business.

"In Panama, another entrepreneur, Ina, registers her construction company in only 19 days. Business is booming and Ina wants to hire someone for a two-year appointment. But the employment law only allows fixed-term appointments for specific tasks, and even then requires a maximum term of one year. At the same time, one of her current workers often leaves early, with no excuse, and makes costly mistakes. To replace him, Ina needs to notify and get approval from the union, and pay five months' severance pay. Ina rejects the more qualified applicant she would like to hire and keeps the underperforming worker on staff.

"Ali, a trader in the United Arab Emirates, can hire and fire with ease. But one of his customers refuses to pay for equipment delivered three months earlier.

It takes 27 procedures and more than 550 days to resolve the payment dispute in court. Almost all procedures must be made in writing, and require extensive legal justification and the use of lawyers. After this experience, Ali decides to deal only with customers he knows well.

"Timnit, a young entrepreneur in Ethiopia, wants to expand her successful consulting business by taking a loan. But she has no proof of good credit history because there are no credit information registries. Although her business has substantial assets in accounts receivable, laws restrict her bank from using these as collateral. The bank knows it cannot recover the debt if Timnit defaults, because courts are inefficient and laws give creditors few powers. Credit is denied. The business stays small.

"Having registered, hired workers, enforced contracts, and obtained credit, Avik, a businessman in India, cannot make a profit and goes out of business. Faced with a 10-year-long process of going through bankruptcy, Avik absconds, leaving his workers, the bank, and the tax agency with nothing."

If you want to know why two decades of macroeconomic reform wholesale at the top have not slowed the spread of poverty and produced enough new jobs in key countries of Latin America, Africa, the

Arab world, and the former Soviet Empire, it is because there has been too little reform retail. According to the IFC report, if you want to create productive jobs (the kind that lead to rising standards of living), and if you want to stimulate the growth of new businesses (the kind that innovate, compete, and create wealth), you need a regulatory environment that makes it easy to start a business, easy to adjust a business to changing market circumstances and opportunities, and easy to close a business that goes bankrupt, so that the capital can be freed up for more productive uses.

"It takes two days to start a business in Australia, but 203 days in Haiti and 215 days in the Democratic Republic of Congo," the IFC study found. "There are no monetary costs to start a new business in Denmark, but it costs more than five times income per capita in Cambodia and over thirteen times in Sierra Leone. Hong Kong, Singapore, Thailand and more than three dozen other economies require no minimum capital from start-ups. In contrast, in Syria the capital requirement is equivalent to fifty-six times income per capita . . . Businesses in the Czech Republic and Denmark can hire workers on part-time or fixed-term contracts for any job, without specifying maximum duration of the contract. In contrast, employment laws in El Salvador allow fixed-term contracts only for specific jobs, and set their duration to be at most one year . . . A simple commercial contract is enforced in seven days in Tunisia and thirty-nine days in the Netherlands, but takes almost 1,500 days in Guatemala. The cost of enforcement is less than 1 percent of the disputed amount in Austria, Canada and the United Kingdom, but more than 100 percent in Burkina Faso, the Dominican Republic, Indonesia . . . and the Philippines. Credit bureaus contain credit histories on almost every adult in New Zealand, Norway and the United States. But the credit registries in Cameroon, Ghana, Pakistan, Nigeria and Serbia and Montenegro have credit histories for less than 1 percent of adults. In the United Kingdom, laws on collateral and bankruptcy give creditors strong powers to recover their money if a debtor defaults. In Colombia, the Republic of Congo, Mexico, Oman and Tunisia, a creditor has no such rights. It takes less than six months to go through bankruptcy proceedings in Ireland and Japan, but more than ten years in Brazil and India. It costs less than 1 percent of the value of the estate to resolve insolvency in Finland, the Netherlands, Norway and Singapore — and nearly half the estate value in Chad, Panama, Macedonia, Venezuela, Serbia and Montenegro, and Sierra Leone."

As the IFC report notes, excessive regulation also tends to hurt most the very people it is supposed to protect. The rich and the well connected just buy or hustle their way around onerous regulations. In countries that have very regulated labor markets where it is difficult to hire and fire people, women, especially, have a hard time finding employment.

"Good regulation does not mean zero regulation," concludes the IFC study. "The optimal level of regulation is not none, but may be less than what is currently found in most countries, and especially poor ones." It offers what I call a five-step checklist for reform retail. One, simplify and deregulate wherever possible in competitive markets, because competition for consumers and workers can be the best source of pressure for best practices, and overregulation just opens the door for corrupt bureaucrats to demand bribes. "There is no reason for Angola to have one of the most rigid employment laws if Portugal, whose laws Angola adapted, has already revised them twice to make the labor market more flexible," says the IFC study. Two, focus on enhancing property rights. Under de Soto's initiative, the Peruvian government in the last decade has issued property titles to 1.2 million urban squatter households. "Secure property rights have enabled parents to leave their homes and find jobs instead of staying in to protect the property," says the IFC study. "The main beneficiaries are their children, who can now go to school." Three, expand the use of the Internet for regulation fulfillment. It makes it faster, more transparent, and far less open to bribery. Four, reduce court involvement in business matters. And last but certainly not least, advises the IFC study, "Make reform a continuous process . . . Countries that consistently perform well across the *Doing Business* indicators do so because of continuous reform."

In addition to the IFC's criteria, reform retail obviously has to include expanding the opportunities for your population to get an education at all levels and investing in the logistical infrastructure — roads, ports, telecommunications, and airports — without which no reform retail can take off and collaboration with others is impossible. Many countries today still have telecommunications systems dominated by state monopolies that make it either too expensive or too slow to get high-speed Internet access and wireless access, and to make cheap long-distance and overseas phone calls. Without reform retail in your telecom sector, reform retail in the other five areas, while necessary, will not be sufficient.

What is striking about the IFC's criteria is that a lot of people think they are relevant only for Peru and Argentina, but in fact some of the countries that score worst are places like Germany and Italy. (Indeed, the German government protested some of the findings.)

"When you and I were born," said Luis de la Calle, "our competition [was] our next-door neighbors. Today our competition is a Japanese or a Frenchman or a Chinese. You know where you rank very quickly in a flat world . . . You are now competing with everyone else." The best talent in a flat world will earn more, he added, "and if you don't measure up, someone will replace you — and it will not be the guy across the street."

If you don't agree, just ask some of the major players. Craig Barrett, the chairman of Intel, said to me, "With very few exceptions, when you would think about where to site a manufacturing plant, you would think about the cost of labor, transportation, and availability of utilities — that sort of stuff. The discussion has been expanded today, and so it is no longer where you put your plant but now where do you put your engineering resources, your research and development — where are the most efficient intellectual and other resources relative to cost? You now have the freedom to make that choice . . . Today we can be anywhere. Anywhere could be part of my supply chain now — Brazil, Vietnam, the Czech Republic, Ukraine. Many of us are limiting our scope today to a couple of countries for a very simple reason: Some can combine the availability of talent and a market — that is, India, Russia, and China." But for every country Intel considers going into, added Barrett, he asks himself the same question: "What inherent strength does [the] country bring to the party? India, Russia — crummy infrastructure, good educational level, you have a bunch of smart folks. China has a little bit of everything. China has good infrastructure, better than Russia or India. So if you go to Egypt, what unique capability [does that country have to offer]? Exceedingly low labor rates, but what is [the] infrastructure and education base? The Philippines or Malaysia have good literacy rates — you get to employ college grads in your manufacturing line. They did not have infrastructure, but they had a pool of educated people. You have got to have something to build on. When we go to India and are asked about opening plants, we say, 'You don't have infrastructure. Your electricity goes off four times a day.' "

Added John Chambers, the CEO of Cisco Systems, which uses a global supply chain to build the routers that run the Internet and is constantly being wooed to invest in one country or another, "The jobs are going to go where the best-educated workforce is with the most competitive infrastructure and environment for creativity and supportive government. It is inevitable. And by definition those people will have the best standard of living. This may or may not be the countries who led the Industrial Revolution."

But while the stakes in reform retail today are higher than ever, and countries know it, one need only look around the world to notice that not every country can pull it off. Unlike reform wholesale, which could be done by a handful of people using administrative orders or just authoritarian dictates, reform retail requires a much wider base of public and parliamentary buy-in if it is going to overcome vested economic and political interests.

In Mexico, "we did the first stages of structural reform from the top down," said Guillermo Ortiz. "The next stage is much more difficult. You have to work from the bottom up. You have to create the wider consensus to push the reforms in a democratic context." And once that happens, noted Moisés Naím, a former Economy Minister of Venezuela and now editor of *Foreign Policy* magazine, you have a much larger number of actors participating, making the internal logic and technical consistency of the reform policies much more vulnerable to the impact of political compromises, contradictions, and institutional failures. "Bypassing or ignoring the entrenched and defensive public bureaucracy — a luxury frequently enjoyed by the government teams that launch initial reform measures — is more difficult in this stage," Naim said.

So why does one country get over this reform retail hump, with leaders able to mobilize the bureaucracy and the public behind these more painful, more exacting micro-reforms, and another country get tripped up?

Culture Matters: Glocalization

One answer is culture.

To reduce a country's economic performance to culture alone is ridiculous, but to analyze a country's economic performance without reference to culture is equally ridiculous, although that is what many economists and political scientists want to do. This subject is highly controversial and is viewed as politically incorrect to introduce. So it is often the elephant in the room that no one wants to speak about. But I am going to speak about it here, for a very simple reason: As the world goes flat, and more and more of the tools of collaboration get distributed and commoditized, the gap between cultures that have the will, the way, and the focus to quickly adopt these new tools and apply them and those that do not will matter more. The differences between the two will become amplified.

One of the most important books on this subject is *The Wealth and Poverty of Nations* by the economist David Landes. He argues that although climate, natural resources, and geography all play roles in explaining why some countries are able to make the leap to industrialization and others are not, the key factor is actually a country's cultural endowments, particularly the degree to which it has internalized the values of hard work, thrift, honesty, patience, and tenacity, as well as the degree to which it is open to change, new technology, and equality for women. One can agree or disagree with the balance Landes strikes between these cultural mores and other factors shaping economic performance. But I find refreshing his insistence on elevating the culture question, and his refusal to buy into arguments that the continued stagnation of some countries is simply about Western colonialism, geography, or historical legacy.

In my own travels, two aspects of culture have struck me as particularly relevant in the flat world. One is how outward your culture is: To what degree is it open to foreign influences and ideas? How well does it "glocalize"? The other, more intangible, is how inward your culture is. By that I mean, to what degree is there a sense of national solidarity and a focus on development, to what degree is there trust within the society for strangers to collaborate together, and to what degree are the elites in the country concerned with the masses and ready to invest at home, or are they indifferent to their own poor and more interested in investing abroad?

The more you have a culture that naturally glocalizes — that is, the more your culture easily absorbs foreign ideas and best practices and melds those with its own traditions — the greater advantage you will have in a flat world. The natural ability to glocalize has been one of the strengths of Indian culture, American culture, Japanese culture, and, lately, Chinese culture. The Indians, for instance, take the view that the Moguls come, the Moguls go, the British come, the British go, we take the best and leave the rest — but we still eat curry, our women still wear saris, and we still live in tightly bound extended family units. That's glocalizing at its best.

"Cultures that are open and willing to change have a huge advantage in this world," said Jerry Rao, the MphasiS CEO who heads the Indian high-tech trade association. "My great-grandmother was illiterate. My grandmother went to grade two. My mother did not go to college. My sister has a master's degree in economics, and my daughter is at the University of Chicago. We have done all this in living memory, but we have been willing to change . . . You have to have a strong culture, but also the openness to adapt and adopt from others. The cultural exclusivists have a real disadvantage. Think about it, think about the time when the emperor in China threw out the British ambassador. Who did it hurt? It hurt the Chinese. Exclusivity is a dangerous thing."

Openness is critical, added Rao, "because you start tending to respect people for their talent and abilities. When you are chatting with another developer in another part of the world, you don't know what his or her color is. You are dealing with people on the basis of talent — not race or ethnicity — and that changes, subtly, over time your whole view of human beings, if you are in this talent-based and performance-based world rather than the background-based world."

This helps explain why so many Muslim

countries have been struggling as the world goes flat. For complicated cultural and historical reasons, many of them do not glocalize well, although there are plenty of exceptions — namely, Turkey, Lebanon, Bahrain, Dubai, Indonesia, and Malaysia. All of these latter countries, though, tend to be the more secular Muslim nations. In a world where the single greatest advantage a culture can have is the ability to foster adaptability and adoptability, the Muslim world today is dominated by a religious clergy that literally bans *ijtihad,* reinterpretation of the principles of Islam in light of current circumstances.

Think about the whole mind-set of bin Ladenism. It is to "purge" Saudi Arabia of all foreigners and foreign influences. That is exactly the opposite of glocalizing and collaborating. Tribal culture and thinking still dominate in many Arab countries, and the tribal mind-set is also anathema to collaboration. What is the motto of the tribalist? "Me and my brother against my cousin; me, my brother, and my cousin against the outsider." And what is the motto of the globalists, those who build collaborative supply chains? "Me and my brother and my cousin, three friends from childhood, four people in Australia, two in Beijing, six in Bangalore, three from Germany, and four people we've met only over the Internet all make up a single global supply chain." In the flat world, the division of labor is steadily becoming more and more complex, with a lot more people interacting with a lot of other people they don't know and may never meet. If you want to have a modern complex division of labor, you have to be able to put more trust in strangers.

In the Arab-Muslim world, argues David Landes, certain cultural attitudes have in many ways become a barrier to development, particularly the tendency to still treat women as a source of danger or pollution to be cut off from the public space and denied entry into economic activities. When a culture believes that, it loses a large portion of potential productivity of the society. A system that privileges the men from birth on, Landes also argues, simply because they are male, and gives them power over their sisters and other female members of society, is bad for the men. It builds in them a sense of entitlement that discourages what it takes to improve, to advance, and to achieve. This sort of discrimination, he notes, is not something limited to the Arab Middle East, of course. Indeed, strains of it are found in different degrees all around the world, even in so-called advanced industrial societies.

The Arab-Muslim world's resistance to

glocalization is something that some liberal Arab commentators are now focusing on. Consider a May 5, 2004, article in the Saudi English-language daily *Arab News* by liberal Saudi journalist Raid Qusti, titled "How Long Before the First Step?"

"Terrorist incidents in Saudi Arabia are more or less becoming everyday news. Every time I hope and pray that it ends, it only seems to get worse," Qusti wrote. "One explanation to why all of this is happening was brought up by the editor in chief of *Al-Riyadh* newspaper, Turki Al-Sudairi, on a program about determining the roots of the terrorist acts. He said that the people carrying out these attacks shared the ideology of the Juhaiman movement that seized the Grand Mosque in the seventies. They had an ideology of accusing others of being infidels and giving themselves a free hand to kill them, be it Westerners — who, according to them, ought to be kicked out of the Arabian Peninsula — or the Muslim believer who does not follow their path. They disappeared in the eighties and nineties from the public eye and have again emerged with their destructive ideology. The question Al-Sudairi forgot to bring up was: What are we Saudis going to do about it? If we as a nation decline to look at the root causes, as we have for the past two decades, it will only be a matter of time before another group of people with the same ideology spring up. Have we helped create these monsters? Our education system, which does not stress tolerance of other faiths — let alone tolerance of followers of other Islamic schools of thought — is one thing that needs to be re-evaluated from top to bottom. Saudi culture itself and the fact that the majority of us do not accept other lifestyles and impose our own on other people is another. And the fact that from fourth to 12th grade we do not teach our children that there are other civilizations in the world and that we are part of the global community and only stress the Islamic empires over and over is also worth re-evaluating."

It is simply too easily forgotten that when it comes to economic activities, one of the greatest virtues a country or community can have is a culture of tolerance. When tolerance is the norm, everyone flourishes — because tolerance breeds trust, and trust is the foundation of innovation and entrepreneurship. Increase the level of trust in any group, company, or society, and only good things happen. "China began its astounding commercial and industrial takeoff only when Mao Zedong's odiously intolerant form of communism was scrapped in favor of what might be called totalitarian laissez-faire," wrote British historian Paul Johnson in a June 21, 2004, essay in *Forbes*. "India is another example. It is the nature of the Hindu religion to be tolerant and, in its own curious way, permissive . . . When left to themselves, Indians (like the Chinese) always prosper as a community. Take the case of Uganda's Indian population, which was expelled by the horrific dictator Idi Amin and received into the tolerant society of Britain. There are now more millionaires in this group than in any other recent immigrant community in Britain. They are a striking example of how far hard work, strong family bonds and devotion to education can carry a people who have been stripped of all their worldly assets." Islam, down through the years, has thrived when it fostered a culture of tolerance, as in Moorish Spain. But in its modern form, in too many cases Islam has been captured and interpreted by spiritual leaders who do not embrace a culture of tolerance, change, or innovation, and that, Johnson noted, surely has contributed to lagging economic growth in many Muslim lands.

Here we come again to the coefficient of flatness. Countries without natural resources are much more likely, through human evolution, to develop the habits of openness to new ideas, because it is the only way they can survive and advance.

The good news, though, is that not only does culture matter, but culture can change. Cultures are not wired into our human DNA. They are a product of the context — geography, education level, leadership, and historical experience — of any society. As those change, so too can culture. Japan and Germany went from highly militarized societies to highly pacifist and staunchly democratic societies in the last fifty years. Bahrain was one of the first Arab countries to discover oil. It was the first Arab country to run out of oil. And it was the first Arab country in the Arab Gulf to hold an election for parliament where women could run and vote. China during the Cultural Revolution seemed like a nation in the grip of a culture of ideological madness. China today is a synonym for pragmatism. Muslim Spain was one of the most tolerant societies in the history of the world. Muslim Saudi Arabia today is one of the most intolerant. Muslim Spain was a trading and merchant culture where people had to live by their wits and therefore learned to live well with others; Saudi Arabia today can get by just selling oil. Yet right next to Saudi Arabia sits Dubai, an Arab city-state that has used its petrodollars to build *the* trading, tourist, service, and computing center of the Arab Gulf.

Dubai is one of the most tolerant, cosmopolitan places in the world, with, it often seems, more sushi bars and golf courses than mosques — and tourists don't even need a visa. So yes, culture matters, but culture is nested in contexts, not genes, and as those contexts, and local leaders, change and adapt, so too can culture.

The Intangible Things

You can tell a lot by just comparing skylines. Like many Indian Americans, Dinakar Singh, the hedge fund manager, regularly goes back to India to visit family. In the winter of 2004, he went back to New Delhi for a visit. When I saw him a few months later, he told me about the moment when he realized why India's economy, as a whole, still had not taken off as much as it should have — outside of the high-tech sector.

"I was on the sixth floor of a hotel in New Delhi," he recalled, "and when I looked out the window I could see for miles. How come? Because you do not have assured power in Delhi for elevators, so there are not many tall buildings." No sensible investor would want to build a tall building in a city where the power could go out at any moment and you might have to walk up twenty flights of stairs. The result is more urban sprawl and an inefficient use of space. I told Singh that his story reminded me of a trip I had just taken to Dalian, China. I had been to Dalian in 1998, and when I went back in 2004, I did not recognize the city. There were so many new buildings, including modern glass-and-steel towers, that I began to question whether I had actually visited there in 1998. Then I added another recollection. I went to school in Cairo in the summer of 1974. The three most prominent buildings in the city then were the Nile Hilton, the Cairo Tower, and the Egyptian TV building. Thirty years later, in 2004, they are still the most prominent buildings there; the Cairo skyline has barely changed. Whenever I go back to Cairo, I know exactly where I am. I visited Mexico City shortly before Dalian, where I had not visited in five years. I found it much cleaner than I had remembered, thanks to a citywide campaign by the mayor. There were also a few new buildings up, but not as many as I expected after a decade of NAFTA. Inside the buildings, though, I found my Mexican friends a little depressed. They told me that Mexico had lost its groove — it just wasn't growing like it had been, and people's self-confidence was waning.

So in Delhi, you can see forever. In

Cairo, the skyline seems forever the same. In China, if you miss visiting a city for a year, it's like you haven't been there in forever. And in Mexico City, just when Mexicans thought they had turned the corner forever, they ran smack into China, coming the other way and running much faster.

What explains these differences? We know the basic formula for economic success — reform wholesale, followed by reform retail, plus good governance, education, infrastructure, and the ability to glocalize. What we don't know, though, and what I would bottle and sell if I did, is the answer to the question of why one country gets its act together to do all these things in a sustained manner and why another one doesn't. Why does one country's skyline change overnight and another's doesn't change over half a century? The only answer I have been able to find is something that cannot be defined: I call it *the intangible things*. These are primarily two qualities: a society's ability and willingness to pull together and sacrifice for the sake of economic development and the presence in a society of leaders with the vision to see what needs to be done in terms of development and the willingness to use power to push for change rather than to enrich themselves and preserve the status quo. Some countries (such as Korea and

Taiwan) seem to be able to focus their energies on the priority of economic development, and others (such as Egypt and Syria) get distracted by ideology or local feuds. Some countries have leaders who use their time in office to try to drive modernization rather than personally enrich themselves. And some countries simply have venal elites, who use their time in office to line their pockets and then invest those riches in Swiss real estate. Why India had leaders who built institutes of technology and Pakistan had leaders who did not is a product of history, geography, and culture that I can only summarize as one of those intangible things. But even though these intangibles are not easily measured, they really do matter.

The best way I know to illustrate this is by comparing Mexico and China. Mexico, on paper, seemed perfectly positioned to thrive in a flat world. It was right next door to the biggest, most powerful economy in the world. It signed a free-trade agreement with the United States and Canada in the 1990s and was poised to be a springboard to Latin America for both these huge economies. And it had a valuable natural resource in oil, which accounted for more than a third of government income. China, by contrast, was thousands of miles away, burdened by overpopulation, with few natural resources, with its best labor crowded onto a coastal plain, and with a burdensome debt legacy from fifty years of Communist rule. Ten years ago, if you took the names off these two countries and just gave someone their profiles, he surely would have bet on Mexico. And yet China has replaced Mexico as the second-largest exporter of goods into the United States. And there is a general sense, even among Mexicans, that even though China is thousands of miles away from America, it is growing closer to America economically, while Mexico, right on America's border, is becoming thousands of miles away.

I am by no means writing Mexico off. Mexico, in the fullness of time, may turn out to be the slow-but-sure tortoise to China's hare. China still has a huge political transition to get through, which could derail it at any moment. Moreover, Mexico has many entrepreneurs who are as Chinese as the most entrepreneurial Chinese. Mexico would not have exported $138 billion worth of goods to the United States in 2003 if that were not the case. And you have many rural Chinese who are no more advanced or productive than rural Mexicans. But on balance, when you add it all up, the fact is that China has become the hare and Mexico has not, even though

Mexico seemed to start with so many more natural advantages when the world went flat. Why?

This is a question Mexicans themselves are asking. When you go to Mexico City these days, Mexicans will tell you that they are hearing that "giant sucking sound" in stereo. "We are caught between India and China," Jorge Castaneda, Mexico's former foreign minister, told me in 2004. "It is very difficult for us to compete with the Chinese, except with high-value-added industries. Where we should be competing, the services area, we are hit by the Indians with their back offices and call centers."

No doubt China is benefiting to some degree from the fact that it still has an authoritarian system that can steamroll vested interests and archaic practices. Beijing's leadership can order many reforms from the top down, whether it is a new road or accession to the World Trade Organization. But China today also has better intangibles — an ability to summon and focus local energies on reform retail. China may be an authoritarian state, but it nevertheless has strong state institutions and a bureaucracy that manages to promote a lot of people on merit to key decision-making positions, and it has a certain public-spiritedness. The Mandarin tradition of promoting bureaucrats who see their role as promoting and protecting the interests of the state is still alive and well in China. "China has a tradition of meritocracy — a tradition that is also carried on in Korea and Japan," said Francis Fukuyama, author of the classic *The End of History and the Last Man.* "All of them also have a basic sense of 'stateness' where [public servants] are expected to look to the long-term interests of the state" and are rewarded by the system for doing so.

Mexico, by contrast, moved during the 1990s from a basically one-party authoritarian state to a multiparty democracy. So just when Mexico needs to summon all its will and energy for reform retail on the micro level, it has to go through the much slower, albeit more legitimate, democratic process of constituency building. In other words, any Mexican president who wants to make changes has to aggregate so many more interest groups — like herding cats — to implement a reform than his autocratic predecessors, who could have done it by fiat. A lot of these interest groups, whether unions or oligarchs, have powerful vested interests in the status quo and the power to strangle reforms. And Mexico's state system, like that of so many of its Latin American neighbors, has a long history of simply being an instrument of patronage for the ruling party or local interests, not the national interest.

Another of these intangible things is how much your culture prizes education. India and China both have a long tradition of parents telling their children that the greatest thing they can be in life is an engineer or a doctor. But building the schools to make that happen in Mexico simply has not been done. India and China each have more than fifty thousand students studying in the United States today. They come from about twelve time zones away. Mexico, which is smaller but right next door, has only about ten thousand. Mexico is also right next door to the world's biggest economy, which speaks English. But Mexico has not launched any crash program in English education or invested in scholarships to send large numbers of Mexican students to the United States to study. There is a "disconnect," said President Zedillo, among Mexico's political establishment, the challenges of globalization, and the degree to which anyone is educating and harnessing the Mexican public to this task. You would have to look a long time for a graduate science or math program at an American university that is dominated by Mexican students the way most are dominated by Chinese and Indian students.

The government of President Vicente Fox had set out five areas for reform retail to make the Mexican economy more productive and flexible: labor market reform to make it easier to hire and fire workers, judicial reform to make Mexico's courts less corrupt and capricious, electoral and constitutional reform to rationalize politics, tax collection reform to increase the country's dismal tax harvest, and energy reform to open the energy and electricity markets to foreign investors so that Mexico, a major oil producer, gets out of the crazy bind of importing some natural gas and gasoline from America. But almost all of these initiatives got stalled in the Mexican parliament.

It would be easy to conclude from just looking at Mexico and China that democracy may be a hindrance to reform retail. I think it is premature to conclude that. I think the real issue is leadership. There are democracies that are blessed with leaders who are able to make the sale and get their people focused on reform retail — Margaret Thatcher in England comes to mind — and there are democracies that drift for a long time without biting the bullet — modern Germany, for example. There are autocracies that really get focused — modern China — and there are others that just drift aimlessly, unwilling really to summon their people because the leaders are so illegitimate they are afraid of inflicting any pain — Zimbabwe.

Mexico and Latin America generally have "fantastic potential," says President Zedillo. "Latin America was ahead of everyone thirty years ago, but for twenty-five years we have been basically stagnant and the others are moving closer and well ahead. Our political systems are not capable of processing and adopting and executing those [reform retail] ideas. We are still discussing prehistory. Things that are taken for granted everywhere we are still discussing as if we are living in the 1960s. To this day you cannot speak openly about a market economy in Latin America." China is moving every month, added Zedillo, "and we are taking years and years to decide on elementary reforms whose needs should be strikingly urgent for any human being. We are not competitive because we don't have infrastructure; you need people to pay taxes. How many new highways have been built connecting Mexico with the U.S. since NAFTA? [Virtually none.] Many people who would benefit from government expenditure don't pay taxes. The only way for government to serve is get people to pay higher taxes, [but] then the populism comes up and kills it."

A Mexican newspaper recently ran a story about how the Converse shoe company was making tennis shoes in China using Mexican glue. "The whole article was about why are we giving them our glue," said Zedillo, "when the right attitude would be how much more glue can we sell them? We still need to break some mental barriers."

It is not that Mexico has failed to modernize its export industries. It is losing ground to China primarily because China has changed even faster and more broadly, particularly in educating knowledge workers. As business consultant Daniel H. Rosen pointed out in an essay in *The International Economy* journal (Spring 2003), Mexico and China both saw their share of global exports grow in many of the same areas during the booming 1990s — from auto parts to electronics to toys and sporting goods — but China's share was growing faster. This was not just because of what China was doing right but because of what Mexico was doing wrong, which was not steadily honing its competitiveness with microreforms. What Mexico succeeded in doing was creating islands of competitiveness, like Monterrey, where it got things right and could take advantage of proximity to the United States, but the Mexican government never had a strategy for melting those islands into the rest of the country. This helps explain why from 1996 to 2002, Mexico's ranking in the Global Competitiveness Report actually fell while China's rose. And this was not just about cheap wages, said Rosen. It was about China's advantages in education, privatization, infrastructure, quality control, midlevel management, and the introduction of new technology.

"So China is eating Mexico's lunch," concluded Rosen, "but more due to the Mexican inability to capitalize on successes and induce broader reform than to China's lower wage workers per se." In other words, it's reform retail, stupid. According to the *Doing Business in 2005* report, it takes an average of fifty-eight days to start a business in Mexico, compared with eight in Singapore and nine in Turkey. It takes seventy-four days to register a property in Mexico, but only twelve in the United States. Mexico's corporate income tax rate of 34 percent is twice as high as China's.

The *McKinsey Quarterly* report "Beyond Cheap Labor" noted that since 2000, as China joined the WTO and started to take advantage of the flattening of the world, Mexico lost 270,000 assembly jobs, and hundreds of factories closed. But the main advice the report had for Mexico and other middle-income countries feeling squeezed by China was this: "Rather than fixating on jobs lost to China, these countries should remember a fact of economic life: no place can remain the world's low-cost producer forever — even China will lose that title one day. Instead of trying to defend low-wage assembly jobs, Mexico and other middle-income countries should focus on creating jobs that add higher value. Only if more productive companies with higher-value-added activities replace less productive ones can middle income economies continue down the development path."

In short, the only way for Mexico to thrive is with a strategy of reform retail that will enable it to beat China to the top, not the bottom, because China is not focused on beating Mexico as much as it is on beating America. But winning that kind of race to the top takes intangible focus and will.

You cannot maintain rising standards of living in a flattening world when you are up against competitors who are getting not only their fundamentals right but also their intangibles. China does not just want to get rich. It wants to get powerful. China doesn't just want to learn how to make GM cars. It wants to be GM and put GM out of business. Anyone who doubts that should spend time with young Chinese.

Said Luis Rubio, president of Mexico's Center of Research for Development, "The more self-confidence you have, the more it diminishes your mythologies and complexes. One of the great things about

Mexico in the early 1990s was that Mexicans saw that they could do it, they could make it." A lot of that self-confidence, though, has been lost in Mexico in recent years, because the government stopped reforming. "A lack of self-confidence leads a country to keep chewing on the past," added Rubio. "A lack of self-confidence [in Mexico] means that everyone in the country thinks the U.S. is going to take Mexico to the cleaners." That is why NAFTA was so important for Mexico's self-confidence. "What NAFTA accomplished was to get Mexicans to think forward and outward instead of inward and backward. [But] NAFTA was seen [by its architects] as an end more than a beginning. It was seen as the conclusion of a process of political and economic reforms." Unfortunately, he added, "Mexico did not have a strategy for going forward."

Will Rogers said it a long time ago: "Even if you're on the right track, you'll get run over if you just sit there." The flatter the world gets, the faster that will happen. Mexico got itself on the right track with reform wholesale, but then, for a lot of tangible and intangible reasons, it just sat there and reform retail stalled. The more Mexico just sits there, the more it is going to get run over. And it won't be alone.

COMPANIES AND THE FLAT WORLD

TEN

How Companies Cope

Out of clutter, find simplicity.
From discord, find harmony.
In the middle of difficulty, lies
    opportunity.
                    — Albert Einstein

As I conducted interviews for this book, I kept hearing the same phrase from different business executives. It was strange; they all used it, as if they had all been talking to each other. The phrase was, "Just in the last couple of years . . ." Time and again, entrepreneurs and innovators from all different types of businesses, large and small, told me that "just in the last couple of years" they had been able to do things they had never dreamed possible before, or that they were being forced to do things they had never dreamed necessary before.

I am convinced that these entrepreneurs and CEOs were responding to the triple convergence. Each was figuring out a strategy for his or her company to thrive or at least survive in this new environment. Just as individuals need a strategy for coping with the flattening of the world, so too do companies. My economics tutor Paul Romer is fond of saying, "Everyone wants economic growth, but nobody wants change." Unfortunately, you cannot have one without the other, especially when the playing field shifts as dramatically as it has since the year 2000. If you want to grow and flourish in a flat world, you better learn how to change and align yourself with it.

I am not a business writer and this is not a how-to-succeed-in-business book. What I have learned in researching this book, though, is that the companies that have managed to flourish today are the ones that best understand the triple convergence and have developed their own strategies for coping with it — as opposed to trying to resist it.

This chapter is an effort to highlight a few of their rules and strategies:

Rule #1: When the world goes flat — and you are feeling flattened — reach for a shovel and dig inside yourself. Don't try to build walls.

I learned this valuable lesson from my best friends from Minnesota, Jill and Ken Greer.

Going to India gave me an inkling that the world was flat, but only when I went back to my roots and spoke to my friends from Minnesota did I realize just how flat. Some twenty-five years ago Jill and Ken (whose brother Bill I profiled earlier) started their own multimedia company, Greer & Associates, which specialized in developing commercials for TV and doing commercial photography for retail catalogs. They have built up a nice business in Minneapolis, with more than forty employees, including graphic artists and Web designers, their own studio, and a small stable of local and national clients. As a midsize firm, Greer always had to hustle for work, but over the years Ken always found a way to make a good living.

In early April 2004, Ken and Jill came to Washington to spend a weekend for my wife's fiftieth birthday. I could tell that Ken had a lot on his mind regarding his business. We took a long walk one morning in rural Virginia. I told him about the book I was writing, and he told me about how his business was doing. After a while, we realized that we were both talking about the same thing: The world had grown flat, and it had happened so fast, and had affected his business so profoundly, that he was still wrestling with how to adjust. It was clear to him that he was facing competition and pricing pressure of a type and degree that he had never faced before.

"Freelancers," said Greer, speaking about these independent contractors as if they were a plague of locusts that suddenly had descended on his business, eating everything in sight. "We are now competing against freelancers! We never really competed against freelancers before. Our competition used to be firms of similar size and capability. We used to do similar things in somewhat different ways, and each firm was able to find a niche and make a living." Today the dynamic is totally different, he said. "Our competition is not only those firms we always used to compete against. Now we have to deal with giant firms, who have the capability to handle small, medium, and large jobs, and also with the solo practitioners working out of their home offices, who [by making use of today's technology and software] can theoretically do the same thing that a person sitting in our office can do. What's the difference in output, from our clients' point of view, between the giant company who hires a kid designer and puts him in front of a computer, and our company that hires a kid designer and puts him in front of a computer, and the kid designer with a computer in his own basement? . . . The technology and software are so empowering that it makes us all look the same. In the last month we have lost three jobs to freelance solo practitioners who used to work for good companies and have experience and then just went out on their own. Our clients all said the same thing to us: 'Your firm was really qualified. John was very qualified. John was cheaper.' We used to feel bad losing to another firm, but now we are losing to another *person!*"

How did this change happen so fast? I asked.

A big part of their business is photography — shooting both products and models for catalogs, Greer explained. For twenty-five years, the way the business worked was that Greer & Associates would get an assignment. The client would tell Greer exactly what sort of shot he was looking for and would "trust" the Greer team to come up with the right image. Like all commercial photographers, Greer would use a Polaroid camera to take a picture of the model or product he was shooting, to see if his creative instinct was right, and then shoot with real film. Once the pictures were taken, Greer would send the film out to a photo lab to be developed and color-separated. If a picture needed to be touched up, it would be sent to another lab that specialized in retouching.

"Twenty years ago, we decided we would

not process the film we shot," Greer explained. "We would leave that technical aspect to other professionals who had the exact technology, training, and expertise — and a desire to make money that way. We wanted to make money by taking the pictures. It was a good plan then, and may be a good plan today, but it is no longer possible."

Why? The world went flat, and every analog process went digital, virtual, mobile, and personal. In the last three years, digital cameras for professional photographers achieved a whole new technical level that made them equal to, if not superior to, traditional film cameras.

"So we experimented with several different cameras and chose the current state-of-the-art camera that was most like our [analog] film cameras," Greer said. "It's called a Canon D1, and it's the same exact camera as our film camera, except there's a computer inside with a little TV-screen display on the back that shows us what picture we're taking. But it uses all the same lenses, you set things the same way, shutter speed and aperture, it has the same ergonomics. It was the first professional digital camera that worked exactly like a film camera. This was a defining moment.

"After we got this digital camera, it was incredibly liberating at first," said Greer. "All of the thrill and excitement of photography were there — except that the film was free. Because it was digital, we didn't have to buy film and we didn't have to go to the lab to have it processed and wait to get it back. If we were on location and shooting something, we could see if we got the shot right away. There was instant gratification. We referred to it as an 'electronic Polaroid.' We used to have an art director who would oversee everything to make sure that we were capturing the image we were trying to create, but we would never really know until we got it developed. Everyone had to go on faith, on trust. Our clients paid us a professional fee because they felt they needed an expert who could not only click a button, but knew exactly how to shape and frame the image. And they *trusted* us to do that."

For a year or so there was this new sense of empowerment, freedom, creativity, and control. But then Ken and his team discovered that this new liberating technology could also be enslaving. "We discovered that not only did we now have the responsibility of shooting the picture and defining the desired artistic expression, we had to get involved in the technology of the photograph. We had to become the lab. We woke up one morning and said, 'We are the lab.' "

How so? Because digital cameras gave

Greer the ability to download those digital images into a PC or laptop and, with a little magic software and hardware, perform all sorts of new functions. "So in addition to being the photographer, we had to become the processing lab and the color separator," said Greer. Once the technology made that possible, Greer's customers demanded it. Because Greer *could* control the image farther down the supply chain, they said he *should* control it, he *must* control it. And then they also said because it was all digital now, and all under his control, it should be included among the services his team provided as the photographic creators of the image. "The clients said, 'We will not pay you extra for it,' " said Greer. "We used to go to an outside service to touch up the pictures — to remove red-eye or blemishes — but now we have to be the retouchers ourselves also. They expect [red-eye] to be removed by us, digitally, even before they see it. For twenty years we only practiced the art of photography — color and composition and texture and how to make people comfortable in front of a camera. This is what we were good at. Now we had to learn to be good at all these other things. It is not what we signed up for, but the competitive marketplace and the technology forced us into it."

Greer said every aspect of his company went through a similar flattening. Film production went digital, so the marketplace and the technology forced them to become their own film editors, graphics studio, sound production facility, and everything else, including producers of their own DVDs. Each of those functions used to be farmed out to a separate company. The whole supply chain got flattened and shrunk into one box that sat on someone's desktop. The same thing happened in the graphics part of their business: Greer & Associates became their own typesetters, illustrators, and sometimes even printers, because they owned digital color printers. "Things were supposed to get easier," he said. "Now I feel like I'm going to McDonald's, but instead of getting fast food, I'm being asked to bus my own table and wash the dishes too."

He continued: "It is as if the manufacturers of technology got together with our clients and outsourced all of these different tasks to us. If we put our foot down and say you have to pay for each of these services, there is someone right behind us saying, 'I will do it all.' So the services required go up significantly and the fees you can charge stay the same or go down."

It's called commoditization, and in the wake of the triple convergence, it is happening faster and faster across a whole range of industries. As more and more analog processes become digital, virtual, mobile, and personal, more and more jobs and functions are being standardized, digitized, and made both easy to manipulate and available to more players.

When everything is the same and supply is plentiful, said Greer, clients have too many choices and no basis on which to make the right choice. And when that happens, you're a commodity. You are vanilla.

Fortunately, Greer responded to commoditization by opting for the only survival strategy that works: a shovel, not a wall. He and his associates dug inside themselves to locate the company's real core competency, and this has become the primary energy source propelling their business forward in the flat world. "What we sell now," said Greer, "is strategic insight, creative instinct, and artistic flair. We sell inspired, creative solutions, we sell personality. Our core competence and focus is now on all those things that cannot be digitized. I know our clients today and our clients in the future will only come to us and stick with us for those things . . . So we hired more thinkers and outsourced more technology pieces."

In the old days, said Greer, many companies "hid behind technology. You could be very good, but you didn't have to be the world's best, because you never thought you were competing with the world. There was a horizon out there and no one could see beyond that horizon. But just in the space of a few years we went from competing with firms down the street to competing with firms across the globe. Three years ago it was inconceivable that Greer & Associates would lose a contract to a company in England, and now we have. Everyone can see what everyone else is doing now, and everyone has the same tools, so you have to be the very best, the most creative thinker."

Vanilla just won't put food on the table anymore. "You have to offer something totally unique," said Greer. "You need be able to make Chocolate Chip Cookie Dough, or Cherry (Jerry) Garcia, or Chunky Monkey" — three of the more exotic brands of Ben & Jerry's ice cream that are very nonvanilla. "It used to be about what you were able to do," said Greer. "Clients would say, 'Can you do this? Can you do that?' Now it's much more about the creative flair and personality you can bring to [the assignment] . . . It's all about imagination."

Rule #2: And the small shall act big . . . One way small companies flourish in

the flat world is by learning to act really big. And the key to being small and acting big is being quick to take advantage of all the new tools for collaboration to reach farther, faster, wider, and deeper.

I can think of no better way to illustrate this rule than to tell the story of another friend, Fadi Ghandour, the cofounder and CEO of Aramex, the first home-grown package delivery service in the Arab world and the first and only Arab company to be listed on the Nasdaq. Originally from Lebanon, Ghandour's family moved to Jordan in the 1960s, where his father, Ali, founded Royal Jordanian Airlines. So Ghandour always had the airline business in his genes. Shortly after graduating from George Washington University in Washington, D.C., Ghandour returned home and saw a niche business he thought he could develop: He and a friend raised some money and in 1982 started a mini–Federal Express for the Middle East to do parcel delivery. At the time, there was only one global parcel delivery service operating in the Arab world: DHL, today owned by the German postal service. Ghandour's idea was to approach American companies, like Federal Express and Airborne Express, that did not have a Middle East presence and offer to become their local delivery service, playing on the fact that an Arab company would know the region and how to get around unpleasantries like the Israeli invasion of Lebanon, the Iran-Iraq war, and the American invasion of Iraq.

"We said to them, 'Look, we don't compete with you locally in your home market, but we understand the Middle East market, so why not give your packages to us to deliver out here?" said Ghandour. "We will be your Middle East delivery arm. Why give them to your global competitor, like DHL?" Airborne responded positively, and Ghandour used that to build his own business and then buy up or partner with small delivery firms from Egypt to Turkey to Saudi Arabia and later all the way over to India, Pakistan, and Iran — creating his own regional network. Airborne did not have the money that Federal Express was investing in setting up its own operations in every region of the globe, so it created an alliance, bringing together some forty regional delivery companies, like Aramex, into a virtual global network. What Airborne's partners got was something none of them could individually afford to build at the time — a global geographic presence and a computerized package tracking and tracing system to compete with that of a FedEx or DHL.

Airborne "made their online computerized tracking and tracing system available to all its partners, so there was a unified language and set of quality standards for how everyone in the Airborne alliance would deliver and track and trace packages," explained Ghandour. With his company headquartered in Amman, Jordan, Ghandour tapped into the Airborne system by leasing a data line that was connected from Amman all the way to Airborne's big mainframe computer in its headquarters in Seattle. Through dumb terminals back in the Middle East, Aramex tracked and traced its packages using Airborne's back room. Aramex, in fact, was the earliest adopter of the Airborne system. Once Ghandour's Jordanian employees got up to speed on it, Airborne hired them to go around the world to install systems and train the other alliance partners. So these Jordanians, all of whom spoke English, went off to places like Sweden and the Far East and taught the Airborne methods of tracking and tracing. Eventually, Airborne bought 9 percent of Aramex to cement the relationship.

The arrangement worked well for everyone, and Aramex came to dominate the parcel delivery market in the Arab world, so well that in 1997, Ghandour decided to take the company public on Broadway, also known as the Nasdaq. Aramex continued to grow into a nearly $200-million-a-year company, with thirty-two hundred employees — and without any big government contracts. Its business was built for and with the private sector, highly unusual in the Arab world. Because of the dot-com boom, which deflected interest from brick-and-mortar companies like Aramex, and then the dot-com bust, which knocked out the Nasdaq, Aramex's stock price never really took off. Thinking that the market simply did not appreciate its value, Ghandour, along with a private equity firm from Dubai, bought the company back from its shareholders in early 2002.

Unbeknownst to Ghandour, this move coincided with the flattening of the world. He suddenly discovered that he not only could do new things, but he had to do new things he had never imagined doing before. He first felt the world going flat in 2003, when Airborne got bought out by DHL. Airborne announced that as of January 1, 2004, its tracking and tracing system would no longer be available to its former alliance partners. See you later. Good luck on your own.

While the flattening of the world enabled Airborne, the big guy, to get flatter, it allowed Ghandour, the little guy, to step up and replace it. "The minute Airborne announced that it was being bought and dissolving the alliance," said Ghandour, "I called a meeting in London of all the major partners in the group, and the first thing we did was found a new alliance." But Ghandour also came with a proposal: "I told them that Aramex was developing the software in Jordan to replace the Airborne tracking and tracing system, and I promised everyone there that our system would be up and running before Airborne switched theirs off."

Ghandour in effect told them that the mouse would replace the elephant. Not only would his relatively small company provide the same backroom support out of Amman that Airborne had provided out of Seattle with its big mainframe, but he would also find more global partners to fill in the holes in the alliance left by Airborne's departure. To do this, he told the prospective partners that he would hire Jordanian professionals to manage all the alliance's back-office needs at a fraction of the cost they were paying to have it all done from Europe or America. "I am not the largest company in the group," said Ghandour, who is now in his mid-forties and still full of energy, "but I took leadership. My German partners were a $1.2 billion company, but they could not react as fast."

How could he move so quickly? The triple convergence.

First of all, a young generation of Jordanian software and industrial engineers had just come of age and walked out onto the level playing field. They found that all the collaborative tools they needed to act big were as available to them as to Airborne's employees in Seattle. It was just a question of having the energy and imagination to adopt these tools and put them to good use.

"The key for us," said Ghandour, "was to come up with the technology and immediately replace the Airborne technology, because without online, real-time tracking and tracing, you can't compete with the big boys. With our own software engineers, we produced a Web-based tracking and tracing and shipment management system."

Managing the back room for all the alliance partners through the Internet was actually much more efficient than plugging everyone into Airborne's mainframe back in Seattle, which was very centralized and had already been struggling to adapt to the new Web architecture. With the Web, said Ghandour, every employee in every alliance company could access the Aramex tracking and tracing system through smart PC terminals or handheld devices, using the Internet and wireless. A couple of months after making his proposal in London,

Ghandour brought all the would-be partners together in Amman to show them the proprietary system that Aramex was developing and to meet some of his Jordanian software professionals and industrial engineers. (Some of the programming was being done in-house at Aramex and some was outsourced. Outsourcing meant Aramex too could tap the best brains.) The partners liked it, and thus the Global Distribution Alliance was born — with Aramex providing the back room from the backwater of Amman, where Lawrence of Arabia once prowled, replacing Airborne, which was located just down the highway from Microsoft and Bill Gates.

Another reason Ghandour could replace Airborne so quickly, he explained, was that he was not stuck with any "legacy" system that he had to adapt. "I could go right to the Internet and use the latest technologies," he said. "The Web enabled me to act big and replicate a massive technology that the big guys had invested millions in, at a fraction of the cost . . . From a cost perspective, for me as a small guy, it was ideal . . . I knew the world was flat. All my preaching to our employees as the CEO was that we can compete, we can have a niche, the rules of the game are changing, you don't need to be a giant, you can find a niche, and technology will enable us to

618

compete with the big boys."

When January 2004 rolled around and Airborne began switching off its system, Aramex was up and running for a seamless handoff. And because Aramex was able to run its new system off an Internet platform, with software designed primarily by lower-cost Jordanian programmers, installation of the new system took place virtually, without Aramex having to send its engineers to train any of the alliance partners. Each partner company could build its own client base over the Internet through the Aramex system, do its own tracking and tracing, and be part of the new virtual global air freight network.

"So now we are managing this global network, with forty alliance partners, and we cover every geographic area in the world," said Ghandour. "We saved so much money . . . With our Web-based system all you needed was a browser and a password to get into the Aramex network, and suddenly you're inside a global shipment management system." Aramex trained many of the employees of the other alliance companies how to use its system by using various online channels, including voice over the Internet, online chatting, and other virtual training tools available on Aramex's intranet — making the training incredibly cheap.

Like UPS, Aramex has quickly moved into insourcing. Arab and foreign banks in the Middle East have outsourced the delivery of their credit cards to Aramex; mobile phone companies are using Aramex delivery men to collect bills on their behalf, with the delivery men just scanning the customer's credit card and then issuing a receipt. (Aramex may be high-tech, but it has not shrunk from using donkeys to cross military roadblocks to deliver packages in the West Bank when Israeli-Palestinian clashes have closed roads.)

"We are a very flat organization," Ghandour explained. "This is not traditional, because Arab institutions in the private sector tend to look like the governments — very hierarchal and patriarchal. That is not how Aramex works. There are no more than two to three layers between me and anyone in the company. Every single knowledge worker in this organization has a computer with e-mail and Internet access. Right here from your computer I can access my intranet and see exactly what is happening in the organization without my senior people having to report to me."

In sum, Fadi Ghandour took advantage of several new forms of collaboration — supply-chaining, outsourcing, insourcing, and all the steroids — to make his little

$200-million-a-year company very big. Or, as he put it with a smile, "I was big locally and small internationally — and I reversed that."

Rule #3: And the big shall act small . . . One way that big companies learn to flourish in the flat world is by learning how to act really small by enabling their customers to act really big.

Howard Schultz, the founder and chairman of Starbucks, says that Starbucks estimates that it is possible to make nineteen thousand variations of coffee on the basis of the menus posted at any Starbucks outlet. What Starbucks did, in other words, was make its customers its drink designers and allow them to customize their drinks to their exact specifications. Starbucks never thought of offering soy milk, Schultz told me, until store managers started to get bombarded with demands for it from customers, to the point where they were going to the grocery store across the street in the middle of the day to buy cartons of soy milk. Starbucks learned from its customers, and today some 8 percent of all the drinks that Starbucks sells include soy milk. "We didn't dream up the different concoctions with soy milk," said Schultz, "the customers did." Starbucks just collaborated with them. The smartest big companies clearly understand that the triple convergence allows them to collaborate with their customers in a totally new fashion — and, by doing so, to act really small. The way that big companies act small is not by targeting each individual consumer and trying to serve that customer individually. That would be impossible and impossibly expensive. They do it by making their business, as much as possible, into a buffet. These companies create a platform that allows individual customers *to serve themselves* in their own way, at their own pace, in their own time, according to their own tastes. They are actually making their customers their employees and having them pay the company for that pleasure at the same time!

One of those big companies that have learned to act small in this way is E★Trade, the online bank and brokerage house. It did so, explained Mitchell H. Caplan, the CEO of E★Trade as well as a friend and neighbor, by recognizing that behind all the hoopla around the dot-com boom and bust, something very important was happening. "Some people thought the Internet was going to revolutionize everything in the world with no limits — it was going to cure the common cold," said Caplan. Sure, it was hype, and it led to crazy valuations and expectations, which eventually came crashing down. But meanwhile, with much less fanfare, the Internet was creating "a whole new distribution platform for companies to reach consumers in a whole new way and for consumers to reach your company in a whole new way," Caplan said. "While we were sleeping, my mom figured out how to use e-mail and connect with the kids. My kids were instant-messaging all their friends. My mom figured out how to go online and check her E★Trade balances."

Companies that were paying attention understood they were witnessing the birth of the "self-directed consumer," because the Internet and all the other tools of the flat world had created a means for every consumer to customize exactly the price, experience, and service he or she wanted. Big companies that could adapt their technology and business processes to empower this self-directed consumer could act very small *by enabling their customers to act very big*. They could make the consumer feel that every product or service was being tailored for his or her specific needs and desires, when in fact all that the company was doing was creating a digital buffet for them to serve themselves.

In the financial services industry, this constituted a profound change in approach. Historically, financial services was dominated by large banks, large brokerage houses, and large insurance companies that told you what you were getting, how you were getting it, when and where you were getting it, and the price you had to pay for it. Customers reacted to these big companies with emotions ranging from apathy to distaste. But if I didn't like the way my bank was treating me, I didn't have any real choice. Then the world was flattened and the Internet came along. Consumers started to feel that they could have more control, and the more they adapted their buying habits to the Internet, the more companies — from booksellers to financial services — had to adapt and offer them the tools to be in control.

"Sure, the Internet stocks blew up when the bubble burst," said Caplan, whose own company's stock price took a big dip in that market storm, "but underneath, consumers were getting a taste of power, and once they tasted it, things went from companies being in control of consumers' behavior to consumers being in control of companies' behavior. The rules of engagement changed, and if you did not respond and offer customers what they wanted, someone else would, and you would be dead." Where once the financial services companies acted big, now they strove to act small and to enable the consumer to act big. "Companies who prosper today," argued Caplan, "are the ones who understand the self-directed consumer." For E★Trade, that meant thinking of the company not as a collection of individual financial services — a bank, a brokerage, and a lending business — but as an integrated financial experience that could serve the most self-directed financial consumers. "The self-directed consumer wanted one-stop financial shopping," said Caplan. "When they came to our site they wanted everything integrated, with them in control. Only recently, though, did we have the technology to really integrate all our three businesses — banking, lending, and brokerage — and pull them together in a way that didn't just deliver the price, not just the service, but the total experience they wanted."

If you came to the E★Trade site just three or four years ago, you would see your brokerage account on one screen page and your lending on another. Today, said Caplan, "On one page you can now see exactly where you stand in terms of your brokerage in real time, including your buying power, and you see your bank account and the scheduled payments for your loans — what is pending, what is the balance on your home mortgage, and [what is your] line of credit — and you have the ability to move seamlessly between all three to maximize the benefit of your cash."

While Fadi Ghandour coped with the triple convergence by taking a small company and devising a strategy to make it act very big, Mitchell Caplan survived by taking a big company and making it act very small so that his customers could act very big.

Rule #4: The best companies are the best collaborators. In the flat world, more and more business will be done through collaborations within and between companies, for a very simple reason: The next layers of value creation — whether in technology, marketing, biomedicine, or manufacturing — are becoming so complex that no single firm or department is going to be able to master them alone.

"What we are seeing in so many different fields," said Joel Cawley, the head of IBM's strategic planning unit, "is that the next layers of innovation involve the intersection of very advanced specialties. The cutting edge of technical innovation in every field is increasingly specialized." In most cases, your own company's or your own department's specialization is going to be applicable to only a very small piece of any meaningful business or social challenge. "Therefore, to come up with any valuable new breakthrough, you have to be able to combine more and more of these increasingly granular specialties. That is why collaboration is so important," Cawley said. So you might find that a pharmaceutical company has invented a new stent that allows it to dispense a whole new class of drugs that a biomedical company has been working on, and the real breakthrough — where the real profit is created for both — is in their collaboration in getting the breakthrough drugs from one firm together with the breakthrough delivery system from another.

Or take a more colorful example: video games. Game makers have long been commissioning special music to go with games. They eventually discovered that when they combined the right music with the right game they not only sold many, many more copies of that game, but they could spin off the music for sale on CD or download as well. So some big game companies have recently started their own music divisions, and some artists have decided that they have a better chance of getting their music heard by launching it with a new digital game than on the radio. The more the flattening of the world connects all the knowledge pools together, the more specializations and specialists there will be out there, the more innovation will come from putting them together in different combinations, and the more management will be about the ability to do just that.

Perhaps the best way to illustrate this paradigm shift and how some companies have adapted to it is by looking at a very traditional manufacturer: Rolls-Royce. When you hear the word "Rolls-Royce," what immediately comes to mind is a shiny handmade car, with a uniformed chauffeur sitting in the driver's seat and a perfectly tailored couple in the back on their way to Ascot or Wimbledon. Rolls-Royce, the quintessential stodgy British company, right? What if I told you, though, that Rolls-Royce doesn't even make cars anymore (that business was sold in 1972 and the brand was licensed to BMW in 1998), that 50 percent of its income comes from services, and that in 1990 all of its employees were in Great Britain and today 40 percent are based outside of the United Kingdom, integrated into a global operation that stretches from China to Singapore to India to Italy to Spain to Germany to Japan and up to Scandinavia?

No, this is not your father's Rolls-Royce.

"Quite a long time ago we said, 'We cannot be just a U.K. company,' " Sir John Rose, chief executive of Rolls-Royce PLC, told me in an interview while we were both visiting China. "The U.K. is a tiny market. In the late 1980s, 60 percent of our business was defense [particularly jet engines] and our primary customer was Her Majesty's government. But we needed to become a world player, and if we were going to do that we had to recognize that the biggest customer in everything we could do was the U.S., and we had to be successful in nondefense markets. So we became a technology company [specializing in] power systems." Today Rolls-Royce's core competency is making gas turbines for civilian and military airplanes, for helicopters, for ships, and for the oil and gas and power-generation industries. Rolls-Royce has customers now in 120 countries and employs around thirty-five thousand people, but only twenty-one thousand are located in the United Kingdom, with the rest part of a global network of research, service, and manufacturing workers. Half of Rolls-Royce's revenue is now generated by businesses outside the United Kingdom. "In the U.K. we are thought of as a British company," said Rose, "but in Germany we are a German company. In America we are an American company, in Singapore we are a Singaporean company — you have to be in order to be close to the customer but also to the suppliers, employees, and communities in which we operate." Today Rolls-Royce employs people of about fifty nationalities in fifty countries speaking about fifty languages. It outsources and offshores about 75 percent of its components to its global supply chain. "The 25 percent that we make are the differentiating elements," said Rose. "These are the hot end of the engine, the turbines, the compressors and fans and the alloys, and the aerodynamics of how they are made. A turbine blade is grown from a single crystal in a vacuum furnace from a proprietary alloy, with a very complex cooling system. This very high-value-added manufacturing is one of our core competencies." In short, said Rose, "We still own the key technologies, we own the ability to identify and define what product is required by our customers, we own the ability to integrate the latest science into making these products, we own the route to the market for these products, and we own the ability to collect and understand the data generated by those customers using our products, enabling us to support that product while in service and constantly add value."

But outside of these core areas, Rolls-Royce has adopted a much more horizontal approach to outsourcing noncore components to suppliers anywhere in the world, and to seeking out IQ far beyond the British Isles. The sun may have set on the British Empire, and it used to set on the old Rolls-Royce. But it never sets on the new

Rolls-Royce. To produce breakthroughs in the power-generation business today, the company has to meld together the insights of many more specialists from around the world, explained Rose. And to be able to commercialize the next energy frontier — fuel cell technology — will require that even more.

"One of the core competencies of the business today is partnering," said Rose. "We partner on products and on service provisions, we partner with universities and with other participants in our industry. You have to be disciplined about what they can provide and what we can sensibly undertake . . . There is a market in R & D and a market in suppliers and a market in products, and you need to have a structure that responds to all of them."

A decade ago, he added, "We did 98 percent of our research and technology in the U.K. and now we do less than 40 percent in the U.K. Now we do it as well in the U.S., Germany, India, Scandinavia, Japan, Singapore, Spain, and Italy. We now recruit from a much more international group of universities to anticipate the mix of skills and nationalities we will want in ten or fifteen years."

When Rolls-Royce was a U.K.-centric company, he added, it was very vertically organized. "But we had to flatten ourselves," said Rose, as more and more markets opened worldwide that Rolls-Royce could sell into and from which it could extract knowledge.

And what does the future hold?

This approach to change that Rolls-Royce has perfected in response to the flattening of the world is going to become the standard for more and more new start-up companies. If you were to approach venture capital firms in Silicon Valley today and tell them that you wanted to start a new company but refused to outsource or offshore anything, they would show you the door immediately. Venture capitalists today want to know from day one that your start-up is going to take advantage of the triple convergence to collaborate with the smartest, most efficient people you can find anywhere in the world. Which is why in the flat world, more and more companies are now being born global.

"In the old days," said Vivek Paul, the Wipro president, "when you started a company, you might say to yourself, 'Boy, in twenty years, I hope we will be a multinational company.' Today, you say to yourself that on day two I will be a multinational. Today, there are thirty-person companies starting out with twenty employees in Silicon Valley and ten in India . . . And if you are a multiproduct company, you are probably going to have some manufacturing relationships in Malaysia and China, some design in Taiwan, some customer support in India and the Philippines, and possibly some engineering in Russia and the U.S." These are the so-called micromultinationals, and they are the wave of the future.

Today, your first management job out of business school could be melding the specialties of a knowledge team that is one-third in India, one-third in China, and a sixth each in Palo Alto and Boston. That takes a very special kind of skill, and it is going to be much in demand in the flat world.

Rule #5: In a flat world, the best companies stay healthy by getting regular chest X-rays and then selling the results to their clients.

Because niche businesses can get turned into vanilla commodity businesses faster than ever in a flat world, the best companies today really do get chest X-rays regularly — to constantly identify and strengthen their niches and outsource the stuff that is not very differentiating. What do I mean by chest X-rays? Let me introduce Laurie Tropiano, IBM's vice president for business consulting services, who is what I would call a corporate radiologist. What Tropiano and her team at IBM do is basically X-ray your company and break down every component of your business and then put it up on a wall-size screen so you can study your corporate skeleton. Every department, every function, is broken out and put in a box and identified as to whether it is a cost for the company or a source of income, or a little of both, and whether it is a unique core competency of the company or some vanilla function that anyone else could do — possibly cheaper and better.

"A typical company has forty to fifty components," Tropiano explained to me one day at IBM, as she displayed a corporate skeleton up on her screen, "so what we do is identify and isolate these forty to fifty components and then sit down and ask [the company], 'How much money are you spending in each component? Where are you best in class? Where are you differentiated? What are the totally nondifferentiated components of your business? Where do you think you have capabilities but are not sure you are ever going to be great there because you'd have to put more money in than you want?' "

When you are done, said Tropiano, you basically have an X-ray of the company, identifying four or five "hot spots." One or two might be core competencies; others might be skills that the company wasn't fully aware that it even had and that should be built up. Other hot spots on the X-ray, though, might be components where five different departments are duplicating the same functions or services that others outside the company could do better and more cheaply and so should be outsourced — provided there is still a savings to be made once all the costs and disruptions of outsourcing are taken into account.

"So you go look at this [X-ray] and say, 'I have these areas here that are going to be really hot and core,'" says Tropiano, "and then let go of the things that you can outsource, and free up those funds and focus on the projects that could one day be part of your core competency. For the average company, you are doing well if 25 percent is core competency and strategic and really differentiating, and the rest you may continue to do and try to improve or you may outsource."

I first got interested in this phenomenon when an Internet business news headline caught my eye: "HP bags $150 million India bank contract." The story on Computerworld.com (February 25, 2004) quoted a statement by HP saying that it had inked a ten-year outsourcing contract with the Bank of India in Mumbai. The $150 million contract was the largest ever won by HP Services in the Asia-Pacific region, according to Natarajan Sundaram, head of marketing for HP Services India. The deal called for HP to implement and manage a core banking system across 750 Bank of India branches. "This is the first time we at HP are looking at the outsourcing of the core banking function in the Asia-Pacific region," said Sundaram. Several multinational companies competed for the contract, including IBM. Under the contract, HP would take charge of data warehousing and document-imaging technology, telebanking, Internet banking, and automated teller machines for the whole bank chain.

Other stories explained that the Bank of India had been facing increasing competition from both public- and private-sector banks and multinational corporations. It realized that it needed to adopt Web-based banking, standardize and upgrade its computer systems, lower its transaction costs, and generally become more customer-friendly. So it did what any other multinational would do — it gave itself a chest X-ray and decided to outsource all the functions it did not believe were part of its core competency or that it simply did not have the internal skills to do at the highest level.

Still, when the Bank of India decides to outsource its back room to an American-owned computer company, well, that just seemed too weird for words. "Run that by me again," I said, rubbing my eyes. "HP, the folks I call when my printer breaks, won the outsourcing contract for managing the back room of India's 750-branch state-owned bank? What in the world does Hewlett-Packard know about running the backroom systems of an Indian bank?"

Out of curiosity, I decided to visit the HP headquarters in Palo Alto to find out. There, I met Maureen Conway, HP's vice president for emerging market solutions, and put the above question directly to her.

"How did we think we could take our internal capabilities and make them good for other people?" she answered rhetorically. In brief, she explained, HP is constantly hosting customer visits, where its corporate clients come to its headquarters and see the innovations that HP has brought to managing its own information systems. Many of those customers go away intrigued at how this big company has adapted itself to the flat world. How, they ask, did HP, which once had eighty-seven different supply chains — each managed vertically and independently, with its own hierarchy of managers and back-office support — compress them into just five supply chains that manage $50 billion in business, and in which functions like accounting, billing, and human resources are handled through a companywide system? What computers and business processes did HP install to consolidate all this efficiently? HP, which does business in 178 countries, used to handle all its accounts payable and receivable for each individual country in that country. It was totally chopped up. Just in the last couple of years, HP created three transaction-processing hubs — in Bangalore, Barcelona, and Guadalajara — with uniform standards and special work flow software that allowed HP offices in all 178 countries to process all billing functions through these three hubs.

Seeing the reaction of its customers to its own internal operations, HP said one day, "Hey, why don't we commercialize this?" Said Conway, "That became the nucleus of our business process outsourcing service . . . We were doing our own chest X-rays and discovered we had assets that other people cared about, and that is a business."

In other words, the flattening of the world was both the disease and the cure for the Bank of India. It clearly could not keep up with its competitors in the flattening banking environment of India, and, at the same time, it was able to get a chest X-ray and then outsource to HP all those things that it no longer made sense to do itself. And HP, having done its own chest X-ray, discovered that it was carrying a whole new consulting business inside its breast. Sure, most of the work for the Bank of India will be done by HP employees in India or Bank of India employees who will actually join HP. But some of the profits will find their way back to the mother ship in Palo Alto, which will be supporting the whole operation through its global knowledge supply chain.

Most of HP's revenues today come from outside the United States. But the core HP knowledge and infrastructure teams who can put together the processes that win those contracts — like running the back room of the Bank of India — are still in the United States.

"The ability to dream is here, more than in other parts of the world," said Conway. "The nucleus of creativity is here, not because people are smarter — it is the environment, the freedom of thought. The dream machine is still here."

Rule #6: The best companies outsource to win, not to shrink. They outsource to innovate faster and more cheaply in order to grow larger, gain market share, and hire more and different specialists — not to save money by firing more people.

Dov Seidman runs LRN, a business that

provides online legal, compliance, and ethics education to employees of global companies and helps executives and board members manage corporate governance responsibilities. We were having lunch in the fall of 2004 when Seidman casually mentioned that he had recently signed an outsourcing contract with the Indian consulting firm MindTree.

"Why are you cutting costs?" I asked him.

"I am outsourcing to win, not to save money," Seidman answered. "Go to our Web site. I currently have over thirty job openings, and these are knowledge jobs. We're expanding. We're hiring. I am adding people and creating new processes."

Seidman's experience is what most outsourcing is actually about — companies outsourcing to acquire knowledge talent to grow their business faster, not simply to cut costs and cut back. Seidman's company is a leader in one of those completely new industries that just appeared in the flat world — helping multinationals foster an ethical corporate culture around an employee base spread all over the world. Although LRN is a BE company — founded ten years before Enron exploded — demand for its services surged in the PE era — post-Enron. In the wake of the collapse of Enron and other corporate governance scandals, a lot more companies became interested in what LRN was offering — on-line programs for companies to forge common expectations and understandings of their legal and ethical responsibilities, from the boardroom to the factory floor. When companies sign up with LRN, their employees are given an online education, including tests that cover everything from your company's code of conduct to when you are allowed to accept a gift to what you need to think about before hitting Send on an e-mail to what constitutes a bribe of a foreign official.

As the whole issue of corporate governance began to mushroom in the early 2000s, Seidman realized that his customers, much like E★Trade, would need a more integrated platform. While it was great that he was educating their employees with one online curriculum and advising boards on ethics issues with another, he knew that company executives would want a one-stop Web-based interface where they could get a handle on all the governance and ethics issues facing their organizations — whether it was employee education, the reporting of any anomalous behavior, stewardship of a hard-earned corporate reputation, or government compliance — and where they could get immediate visibility into where their company stood.

So Seidman faced a double challenge. He

needed to do two things at once: keep growing his market share in the online compliance education industry, and design a whole new integrated platform for the companies he was already working with, one that would require a real technological leap. It was when faced with this challenge that he decided to enlist MindTree, the Indian consulting firm, in an outsourced relationship that offered him about five well-qualified software engineers for the price of one in America.

"Look," said Seidman, "when things are on sale, you tend to buy more. MindTree offered a sale not on last season's closeout, but on top-notch software engineering talent that I would have been hard-pressed to find elsewhere. I needed to spend a lot of money defending and extending my core business and continue to take care of my customers, who were working off my current programs. And at the same time, I had to make a giant leap to offer my customers what they were asking for next, which was a much more robust and total online solution to all their ethics, governance, and compliance questions. If I don't meet their needs, someone else will. Partnering with MindTree allows me to basically have two teams — one team [mostly Americans] that is focused on defending and extending our core business, and the other team, including our Indian consultants, focused on making our next strategic leap to grow our business."

Since ethics is at the core of Seidman's Los Angeles–headquartered business, *how* he went about outsourcing was as important as the ultimate results of the relationship. Rather than announcing the MindTree partnership as a done deal, Seidman conducted an all-hands town hall meeting of his 170 or so employees to discuss the outsourcing he had in mind. He laid out all the economic arguments, let his staff weigh in, and gave everyone a picture of which jobs would be needed in the future and how people could prepare themselves to fit in. "I needed to show my company that this is what it would take to win," he said.

Have no doubt, there are firms that do and will outsource good jobs just to save money and disperse it to shareholders or management. To think that is not happening or will not happen is beyond naïve. But firms that are using outsourcing primarily as a tool to cut costs, not enhance innovation and speed growth, are the minority, not the majority — and I would not want to own stock in any of them. The best companies are finding ways to leverage the best of what is in India with the best of what is in North Dakota with the best of what is in Los Angeles. In that sense, the word "outsourcing" should really be retired. The applicable word is really "sourcing." That is what the flat world both enables and demands, and the companies that do sourcing right end up with bigger market shares and more employees everywhere — not smaller and fewer.

"This is about trying to get bigger faster, about how we make our next leap in less time with greater assurance of success," said Seidman of his decision to source critical areas of development of his new platform to MindTree. "It is not about cutting corners. We have over two hundred clients all over the world now. If I can grow this company the way that I want to, I will be able to hire even more people in all our current offices, promote even more people, and give our current employees even more opportunities and more rewarding career paths — because LRN's agenda is going to be broader, more complex and more global . . . We are in a very competitive space. This [decision to use outsourcing] is all about playing offense, not defense. I am trying to run up the score before it's run up on me."

Rule #7: Outsourcing isn't just for Benedict Arnolds. It's also for idealists.

One of the newest figures to emerge on the world stage in recent years is the social entrepreneur. This is usually someone who burns with desire to make a positive social impact on the world, but believes that the best way of doing it is, as the saying goes, not by giving poor people a fish and feeding them for a day, but by teaching them to fish, in hopes of feeding them for a lifetime. I have come to know several social entrepreneurs in recent years, and most combine a business school brain with a social worker's heart. The triple convergence and the flattening of the world have been a godsend for them. Those who get it and are adapting to it have begun launching some very innovative projects.

One of my favorites is Jeremy Hockenstein, a young man who first followed a time-honored path of studying at Harvard and going to work for the McKinsey consulting firm, but then, with a colleague from McKinsey, veered totally off course and decided to start a not-for-profit data-entry firm that does outsourced data entry for American companies in one of the least hospitable business environments in the world, post–Pol Pot Cambodia.

Only in a flat world!

In February 2001, Hockenstein and some colleagues from McKinsey decided to go to Phnom Penh, half on vacation and half on a scouting mission for some social entrepreneurship. They were surprised to find a city salted with Internet cafés and schools for learning English — but with no jobs, or at best limited jobs, for those who graduated.

"We decided we would leverage our connections in North America to try to bridge the gap and create some income-generating opportunities for people," Hockenstein said. That summer, after another trip funded by themselves, Hockenstein and his colleagues opened Digital Divide Data, with a plan to start a small operation in Phnom Penh that would do data entry — hiring locals to type into computers printed materials that companies in the United States wanted in digitized form, so that it could be stored on databases and retrieved and searched on computers. The material would be scanned in the United States and the files transmitted over the Internet. Their first move was to hire two local Cambodian managers. Hockenstein's partner from McKinsey, Jaeson Rosenfeld, went to New Delhi and knocked on the doors of Indian data-entry companies to see if he could find one — just one — that would take on his two Cambodian managers as trainees. Nine of the Indian companies slammed their doors. The last thing they wanted was even lower-cost competition emerging in Cambodia. But a generous Hindu soul agreed, and Hockenstein got his managers trained. They then hired their first twenty data-entry operators, many of whom were Cambodian war refugees, and bought twenty computers and an Internet line that cost them $100 a month. The project was financed with $25,000 of their own money and a $25,000 grant from a Silicon Valley foundation. They opened for business in July 2001, and their first work assignment was for the *Harvard Crimson*, Harvard's undergraduate daily newspaper.

"The *Crimson* was digitizing their archives to make them available online, and because we were Harvard grads they threw some business our way," said Hockenstein. "So our first project was having Cambodians typing news articles from the *Harvard Crimson* from 1873 to 1899, which reported on Harvard-Yale crew races. Later, actually, when we got to the years 1969 to 1971, when the turmoil in Cambodia was all happening, they were typing [*Crimson* stories] about their own story . . . We would convert the old *Crimson*s, which were on microfilm, to digital images in the United States through a company in Oklahoma that specialized in that sort of thing, and then we would just transfer the digital images to Cambodia by FTP [file transfer protocol]. Now you can go to thecrimson.com and download these stories." The Cambodian typists did not have to know English, only how to type English characters; they worked in pairs, each typing the same article, and then the computer program compared their work to make sure that there were no errors.

Hockenstein said that each of the typists works six hours a day, six days a week, and is paid $75 a month, twice the minimum wage in Cambodia, where the average annual income is less than $400. In addition, each typist receives a matching scholarship for the rest of the workday to go to school, which for most means completing high school but for some has meant going to college. "Our goal was to break the vicious cycle there of [young people] having to drop out of school to support families," said Hockenstein. "We have tried to pioneer socially responsible outsourcing. The U.S. companies working with us are not just saving money they can invest somewhere else. They are actually creating better lives for some of the poor citizens of the world."

Four years after starting up, Digital Divide Data now has 170 employees in three offices: Phnom Penh; Battambang, the second-largest city in Cambodia; and a new office in Vientiane, Laos. "We recruited our first two managers in Phnom Penh and sent them to India to get trained in data entry, and then, when we opened the Laos office, we recruited two managers who were trained by our staff in the Phnom Penh office," Hockenstein said.

This tree has scattered all kinds of seeds. Besides the *Harvard Crimson*, one of the biggest sources of data-entry work was NGOs, which wanted the results of their surveys about health or families or labor conditions digitized. So some of the first wave of Digital Divide Data's Cambodian workers left the company and spun off their own firm to design databases for NGOs that want to do surveys! Why? Because while they were working for Digital Divide Data, said Hockenstein, they kept getting survey work from NGOs that needed to be digitized, but because the NGOs had not done enough work in advance to standardize all the data they were collecting, it was very hard to digitize in any efficient manner. So these Cambodian workers realized that there was value earlier in the supply chain and that they could get paid more for it — not for typing but for designing standardized formats for NGOs to collect survey data, which would make the surveys easier and cheaper to digitize, collate, and manipulate. So they started their own company to do just that — out of Cambodia.

Hockenstein argued that none of the jobs being done in Cambodia came from the

United States. This sort of basic data-entry work got outsourced to India and the Caribbean a long time ago, and, if anywhere, that is where the jobs were taken from. But none of this would have been possible to set up in Cambodia a decade ago. It all came together in just the last few years.

"My partner is a Cambodian," said Hockenstein. "His name is Sophary, and until 1992 he was living in a refugee camp on the Cambodia-Thai border while I was living in Harvard Square as an undergrad. We were worlds apart. After the UN peace treaty [in Cambodia], he walked home ten days to his village, and now today he lives in Phnom Penh running Digital Divide Data's office." They now instant-message each other each night to collaborate in the delivery of services to people and companies around the world. The type of collaboration that is possible today "allows us to be partners and equals," said Hockenstein. "It is not one of us dominating the other; it is real collaboration that is creating better futures for the people at the bottom and the top. It is making my life more meaningful and creating concrete opportunities for people living on a dollar or two a day . . . We see the self-respect and confidence that blossoms in people who never before would have had an on-ramp into the global economy."

So Hockenstein and his partners are getting calls now from Mongolia, Pakistan, Iran, and Jordan from people who want to provide IT services to the world and are wondering how they can get started. In mid-2004, a client approached Digital Divide Data to digitize an English-Arabic dictionary. Around the same time, Hockenstein's office received an unsolicited e-mail from a company in Iran that was running a data-entry firm there. "They found us through a Google search in trying to find ways of expanding their local data-entry business beyond the borders of Iran," said Hockenstein. So Hockenstein asked the Iranians whether they could do an English-Arabic dictionary, even though the language of Iran is Farsi, which uses some but not all of the same letters as Arabic. "He said they could," said Hockenstein, "so we partnered on a joint project for this client to digitize an Arabic dictionary." What I like most about the story, and why it is so telling of the flat world, is Hockenstein's kicker: "I still have never met the guy [in Iran]. We did the whole deal over Yahoo! instant messenger and e-mail. We wired him the money through Cambodia . . . I invited him to my wedding, but he wasn't able to come."

GEOPOLITICS
AND THE FLAT WORLD

ELEVEN

The Unflat World

No Guns or Cell Phones Allowed

To build may have to be the slow and laborious task of years. To destroy can be the thoughtless act of a single day.
— Sir Winston Churchill

On a trip back home to Minnesota in the winter of 2004, I was having lunch with my friends Ken and Jill Greer at Perkins pancake house when Jill mentioned that the state had recently passed a new gun law. The conceal and carry law, passed on May 28, 2003, established that local sheriffs had to issue permits for anyone — other than those with felony records or declared mentally ill — who requested to carry concealed firearms to work (unless the person's employer explicitly restricted that right). This law is supposed to deter criminals, because if they try to hold you up, they can't be sure that you too are not packing a weapon. The law, though, contained a provision to allow business owners to prevent nonemployees from bringing concealed weapons into a place of business, like a restaurant or health club. It said that any business could ban concealed handguns on its premises if it posted a sign at each entrance indicating that guns were not allowed there. (This reportedly led to some very creative signage, with one church suing the state for the right to use a biblical quote as its gun-banning sign and a restaurant using a picture of a woman in a cooking apron toting a machine gun.) The reason this all came up at our lunch was that Jill mentioned that at health clubs around the city, where she played tennis, she noticed two signs now popping up regularly, one right after the other. At their tennis club in Bloomington, for example, there is a sign right by the front door that says, "No Guns Allowed." And then nearby, outside the locker rooms, is another sign: "No Cell Phones Allowed."

Hmmm. No guns or cell phones allowed? Guns I understand, I said, but why cell phones?

Silly me. It was because some people were bringing cell phones with cameras into locker rooms, covertly taking pictures of naked men and women and then e-mailing them around the world. What will they think of next? Whatever the innovation, people will find a way to use it and abuse it.

While interviewing Promod Haque at

Norwest Venture Partners in Palo Alto, I was helped by the firm's public relations director, Katie Belding, who later sent me this e-mail: "I was chatting with my husband about your meeting with Promod the other day . . . He is a history teacher at a high school in San Mateo. I asked him, 'Where were you when the world went flat?' He said it just happened the other day at school when he was in a faculty meeting. A student was suspended for helping another student cheat on a test — we're not talking the traditional writing answers on the bottom of your shoe or passing a note, though . . ." Intrigued, I called her husband, Brian, and he picked up the story: "At the end of the period, when all of the tests were being passed up to the front of the classroom, this student very quickly and slyly pulled out his cell phone and somehow snapped a picture of some test questions, and instantly e-mailed it to his friend who was taking the same test the next period. His friend also had a cell phone with a digital camera and e-mail capabilities and was apparently able to view the questions before the next period. The student was caught by another teacher when he pulled out the cell phone between periods. It is against the rules to have a cell phone on campus — even though we know that all the kids do — so the teacher confiscated it and saw that the kid had a test on it. So the dean of discipline, at our regular faculty meeting, opened by saying, 'We have something new to worry about.' Essentially he said, 'Beware, keep your eyes open, because the kids are so far ahead of us in terms of the technology.'"

But things aren't all bad with this new technology, noted Brian: "I went to a Jimmy Buffett concert earlier this year. Cameras were not allowed, but cell phones were. So then the concert starts and everyone suddenly starts holding up their cell phones and taking pictures of Jimmy Buffett. I've got one right on my wall. We were sitting in the second row and the guy next to us held up his cell phone, and I said, 'Hey, would you mind e-mailing me some of those? No one will believe we sat this close.' He said 'Sure,' and we gave him a card with our e-mail [address]. We didn't really expect to see any, but the next day he e-mailed us a bunch."

My trip to Beijing described earlier fell right after the fifteenth anniversary of the Tiananmen Square massacre, which happened on June 4, 1989, that is, 6/4/89. My colleagues at the *Times* bureau informed me that on that day the Chinese government censors were blocking SMS messages on cell phones that contained any reference to Tiananmen Square or even the numbers

6 and 4. So if you happened to be dialing the phone number 664-6464, or sending a message in which you told someone you would meet at 6 p.m. on the 4th floor, the Chinese censors blocked it using their jamming technology.

Mark Steyn, writing in the *National Review* (October 25, 2004), related a story from the London Arabic newspaper *Al-Quds al-Arabi* about a panic that broke out in Khartoum, Sudan, after a crazy rumor swept the city, claiming that if an infidel shook a man's hand, that man could lose his manhood. "What struck me about the story," wrote Steyn, "was a detail: The hysteria was spread by cell phones and text messaging. Think about that: You can own a cell phone yet still believe a foreigner's handshake can melt away your penis. What happens when that kind of technologically advanced primitivism advances beyond text messaging?"

This is not a chapter about cell phones, so why do I raise these stories? Because ever since I began writing about globalization, I've been challenged by critics along one particular line: "Isn't there a certain technological determinism to your argument? To listen to you, Friedman, there are these ten flatteners, they are converging and flattening the earth, and there is nothing that people can do but bow to them and join the parade. And after a transition, everyone will get richer and smarter and it will all be fine. But you're wrong, because the history of the world suggests that ideological alternatives, and power alternatives, have always arisen to any system, and globalization will be no different."

This is a legitimate question, so let me try to answer it directly: *I am a technological determinist! Guilty as charged.*

I believe that capabilities create intentions. If we create an Internet where people can open an online store and have global suppliers, global customers, and global competitors, they will open that online store or bank or bookshop. If we create work flow platforms that allow companies to disaggregate any job and source it to the knowledge center anywhere in the world that can perform that task most efficiently at the lowest cost, companies will do that sort of outsourcing. If we create cell phones with cameras in them, people will use them for all sorts of tasks, from cheating on tests to calling Grandma in her nursing home on her ninetieth birthday from the top of a mountain in New Zealand. The history of economic development teaches this over and over: If you can do it, you must do it, otherwise your competitors will — and as this book has tried to demonstrate, there is a whole new universe of things that companies, countries, and individuals can and must do to thrive in a flat world.

But while I am a technological determinist, *I am not a historical determinist.* There is absolutely no guarantee that everyone will use these new technologies, or the triple convergence, for the benefit of themselves, their countries, or humanity. These are just technologies. Using them does not make you modern, smart, moral, wise, fair, or decent. It just makes you able to communicate, compete, and collaborate farther and faster. In the absence of a world-destabilizing war, every one of these technologies will become cheaper, lighter, smaller and more personal, mobile, digital, and virtual. Therefore, more and more people will find more and more ways to use them. We can only hope that more people in more places will use them to create, collaborate, and grow their living standards, not the opposite. But it doesn't have to happen. To put it another way, I don't know how the flattening of the world will come out.

Indeed, this is the point in the book where I have to make a confession: I know that the world is not flat.

Yes, you read me right: *I know that the world is not flat.* Don't worry. I know.

I am certain, though, that the world has been shrinking and flattening for some time now, and that process has quickened dramatically in recent years. Half the world today is directly or indirectly participating in the flattening process or feeling its effects. I have engaged in literary license in titling this book *The World Is Flat* to draw attention to this flattening and its quickening pace because I think it is the single most important trend in the world today.

But I am equally certain that it is not historically inevitable that the rest of the world will become flat or that the already flat parts of the world won't get unflattened by war, economic disruption, or politics. There are hundreds of millions of people on this planet who have been left behind by the flattening process or feel overwhelmed by it, and some of them have enough access to the flattening tools to use them against the system, not on its behalf. How the flattening could go wrong is the subject of this chapter, and I approach it by trying to answer the following questions: What are the biggest constituencies, forces, or problems impeding this flattening process, and how might we collaborate better to overcome them?

Too Sick

I once heard Jerry Yang, the cofounder of Yahoo!, quote a senior Chinese government official as saying, "Where people have hope, you have a middle class." I think this is a very useful insight. The existence of large, stable middle classes around the world is crucial to geopolitical stability, but middle class is a state of mind, not a state of income. That's why a majority of Americans always describe themselves as "middle class," even though by income statistics some of them wouldn't be considered as such. "Middle class" is another way of describing people who believe that they have a pathway out of poverty or lower-income status toward a higher standard of living and a better future for their kids. You can be in the middle class in your head whether you make $2 a day or $200, if you believe in social mobility — that your kids have a chance to live better than you do — and that hard work and playing by the rules of your society will get you where you want to go.

In many ways, the line between those who are in the flat world and those who are not is this line of hope. The good news in India and China and the countries of the former Soviet Empire today is that, with all their flaws and internal contradictions, these countries are now home to hundreds of millions of people who are hopeful enough to be middle class. The bad news in Africa today, as well as rural India, China, Latin America, and plenty of dark corners of the developed world, is that there are hundreds of millions of people who have no hope and therefore no chance of making it into the middle class. They have no hope for two reasons: Either they are too sick, or their local governments are too broken for them to believe they have a pathway forward.

The first group, those who are too sick, are those whose lives are stalked every day by HIV-AIDS, malaria, TB, and polio, and who do not even enjoy steady electricity or potable water. Many of these people live in shockingly close proximity with the flat world. While in Bangalore I visited an experimental school, Shanti Bhavan, or "Haven of Peace." It is located near the village of Baliganapalli, in Tamil Nadu Province, about an hour's drive from downtown Bangalore's glass-and-steel high-tech centers — one of which is aptly called "The Golden Enclave." On the drive there, the school's principal, Lalita Law, an intense, razor-sharp Indian Christian, explained to me, with barely controlled rage in her voice, that the school has 160 children, whose parents are all untouchables from the nearby village.

"These kids, their parents are ragpickers, coolies, and quarry laborers," she said as we bounced along in a jeep on the potholed roads to the school. "They come from homes below the poverty line, and from the lowest caste, the untouchables, who are supposed to be fulfilling their destiny and left where they are. We get these children at ages four and five. They don't know what it is to have a drink of clean water. They are used to drinking filthy gutter water, if they are lucky enough to have a gutter near where they live. They have never seen a toilet, they don't have baths . . . They don't even have proper scraps of clothing. We have to start by socializing them. When we first get them they run out and urinate and defecate wherever they want. [At first] we don't make them sleep on beds, because it is a culture shock."

I was typing frantically in the back of the jeep on my laptop to keep up with her scalding monologue about village life.

"This 'India Shining' thing [the slogan of the ruling Bharatiya Janata Party, BJP, in the 2004 election] irritates people like us," she added. "You have to come to the rural villages and see whether India is shining, and you look into a child's face and see whether India is shining. India is shining okay for the glossy magazines, but if you just go outside Bangalore you will see that everything about India shining is refuted . . . [In the villages] alcoholism is rife and female infanticide and crime are rising.

You have to bribe to get electricity, water; you have to bribe the tax assessor to assess your home correctly. Yes, the middle and upper classes are taking off, but the 700 million who are left behind, all they see is gloom and darkness and despair. They are born to fulfill their destiny and have to live this way and die this way. The only thing that shines for them is the sun, and it is hot and unbearable and too many of them die of heatstroke." The only "mouse" these kids have ever encountered, she added, is not one that rests next to a computer but the real thing.

There are thousands of such villages in rural India, China, Africa, and Latin America. And that is why it is no wonder that children in the developing world — the unflat world — are ten times more likely to die of vaccine-preventable diseases than are children in the developed flat world. In the worst-affected regions of rural southern Africa, a full one-third of pregnant women are reportedly HIV-positive. The AIDS epidemic alone is enough to put a whole society into a tailspin: Many teachers in these African countries are now afflicted with AIDS, so they cannot teach, and young children, especially girls, have to drop out either because they must tend to sick and dying parents or because they have been orphaned by AIDS and cannot afford the school fees. And without education, young people cannot learn how to protect themselves from HIV-AIDS or other diseases, let alone acquire the life-advancing skills that enable women to gain greater control over their own bodies and sexual partners. The prospect of a full-blown AIDS epidemic in India and China, of the sort that has already debilitated southern Africa, remains very real, largely because only one-fifth of the people at risk for HIV worldwide have access to prevention services. Tens of millions of women who want and would benefit from family-planning resources don't have them for lack of local funding. You cannot drive economic growth in a place where 50 percent of the people are infected with malaria or half of the kids are malnourished or a third of the mothers are dying of AIDS.

There is no question that China and India are better off for having at least part of their population in the flat world. When societies begin to prosper, you get a virtuous cycle going: They begin to produce enough food for people to leave the land, the excess labor gets trained and educated, it begins working in services and industry; that leads to innovation and better education and universities, freer markets, economic growth and development, better infrastructure, fewer diseases, and slower population growth. It is that dynamic that is going on in parts of urban India and urban China today, enabling people to compete on a level playing field and attracting investment dollars by the billions.

But there are many, many others living outside this cycle. They live in villages or rural areas that only criminals would want to invest in, regions where violence, civil war, and disease compete with one another to see which can ravage the civilian population most. The world will be entirely flat only when all these people are brought into it. One of the few people with enough dollars to make a difference who has stepped up to this challenge is Microsoft chairman Bill Gates, whose $27 billion Bill and Melinda Gates Foundation has focused on this huge, disease-ravaged, opportunity-deprived population. I have been a critic of some of Microsoft's business practices over the years, and I do not regret one word I have written about some of its anticompetitive tactics. But I have been impressed by Gates's personal commitment of money and energy to address the unflat world. Both times I spoke to Gates, this is the subject he wanted to talk about most and addressed with the most passion.

"No one funds things for that other 3 billion," said Gates. "Someone estimated that the cost of saving a life in the U.S. is

$5 or $6 million — that is how much our society is willing to spend. You can save a life outside of the U.S. for less than $100. But how many people want to make *that* investment?

"If it was just a matter of time," Gates continued, "you know, give it twenty or thirty years and the others will be there, then it would be great to declare that the whole world is flat. But the fact is, there is a trap that these 3 billion are caught in, and they may never get into the virtuous cycle of more education, more health, more capitalism, more rule of law, more wealth . . . I am worried that it could just be half the world that is flat and it stays that way."

Take malaria, a disease caused by a parasite carried by mosquitoes. It is the greatest killer of mothers on the planet right now. While virtually no one dies of malaria today in the flat world, more than 1 million people die from this disease each year in the unflat world, about seven hundred thousand of them children, most of them in Africa. Deaths from malaria have actually doubled in the last twenty years because mosquitoes have become resistant to many antimalarial drugs, and commercial drug companies have not invested much in new antimalarial vaccines because they believe there is no profitable market for them.

If this crisis were happening in a flat country, noted Gates, the system would work: Government would do what it needed to do to contain the disease, pharmaceutical companies would do what they needed to do to get the drugs to market, schools would educate young people about preventive measures, and the problem would be licked. "But this nice response works only when the people who have the problem also have some money," said Gates. When the Gates Foundation issued a $50 million grant to combat malaria, he added, "people said we just doubled the amount of money [worldwide] going to fight malaria . . . When the people who have the need don't have the money, it takes outside groups and charities to get them to the point where the system can kick in for them."

Up to now, though, argued Gates, "we have not given these people a chance [to be in the flat world]. The kid who is connected to the Internet today, if he has the curiosity and an Internet connection, is as [empowered] as me. But if he does not get the right nutrition, he will never play that game. Yes, the world is smaller, but do we really see the conditions that people live in? Isn't the world still really big enough that we don't see the real conditions that people live in, the kid whose life can be saved for $80?"

Let's stop here for a moment and imagine how beneficial it would be for the world, and for America, if rural China, India, and Africa were to grow into little Americas or European Unions in economic and opportunity terms. But the chances of their getting into such a virtuous cycle is tiny without a real humanitarian push by flat-world businesses, philanthropies, and governments to devote more resources to their problems. The only way out is through new ways of collaboration between the flat and unflat parts of the world.

In 2003, the Gates Foundation launched a project called Grand Challenges in Global Health. What I like about it is the way the Gates Foundation approached solving this problem. They didn't say, "We, the rich Western foundation, will now deliver you the solution," and then issue instructions and write some checks. They said, "Let's collaborate horizontally on defining both the problem and the solutions — let's create value that way — and then [the foundation] will invest our money in the solutions we both define." So the Gates Foundation placed ads on the Web and in more conventional channels across both the developed and the developing worlds, asking scientists to respond to one big question: What are the biggest problems that, if science attended to them and solved them, could most dramatically change the fate of the several billion people trapped in the vicious cycle of infant mortality, low life expectancy, and disease? The foundation got about eight thousand pages of ideas from hundreds of scientists from around the world, including Nobel laureates. It then culled through them and distilled them down to a list of fourteen Grand Challenges — challenges where a technological innovation could remove a critical barrier to the solving of an important health problem in the developing world. In the fall of 2003, it announced these fourteen Grand Challenges worldwide. They include the following: How to create effective single-dose vaccines that can be used soon after birth, how to prepare vaccines that do not require refrigeration, how to develop needle-free delivery systems for vaccines, how to better understand which immunological responses provide protective immunity, how to better control insects that transmit agents of disease, how to develop a genetic or chemical strategy to incapacitate a disease-transmitting insect population, how to create a full range of optimal bioavailable nutrients in a single staple plant species, and how to create immunological methods that can cure chronic infections. Within a year, the foundation received sixteen hundred proposals for ways to meet these challenges from scientists in seventy-five countries, and the foundation is now in the process of funding the best proposals with $250 million in cash.

"We're trying to accomplish two things with this program," explained Rick Klausner, a former head of the National Cancer Institute who now runs the global health programs for the Gates Foundation. "The first is [to make] a moral appeal to the scientific imagination, [pointing out] that there are great problems to be solved that we, the scientific community, have ignored, even though we pride ourselves in how international we are. We have not taken our responsibilities as global problem solvers as seriously as our self-identity as an international community. We wanted the Grand Challenges to say these are the most exciting, sexy, scientific things that anyone in the world could work on right now . . . The idea was to fire the imagination. The second thing is to actually direct some of the foundation's resources to see if we could do it."

Given the phenomenal advances in technology in the last twenty years, it is easy to assume that we already have all the tools to address some of these challenges and that the only thing lacking is money. I wish that were the case. But it is not. In the instance of malaria, for example, it isn't just the drugs that are missing. As anyone who has visited Africa or rural India knows, the health-care systems in these areas are often broken or functioning at a very low level. So the Gates Foundation is trying to stimulate the development of drugs and delivery systems that presume a broken health-care system and therefore can be safely self-administered by ordinary people in the field. That may be the grandest challenge of all: to use the tools of the flat world to design tools that work in an unflat world. "The most important health-care system in the world is a mother," said Klausner. "How do you get things in her hands that she understands and can afford and can use?"

The tragedy of all these people is really a dual tragedy, added Klausner. There is the individual tragedy of facing a death sentence from disease or a life sentence of broken families and limited expectations. And there is the tragedy for the world because of the incredible lost contribution that all these people still outside the flat world could be making. In a flat world, where we are connecting all the knowledge pools together, imagine what knowledge those people could bring to science or education. In a flat world, where innovation can come from anywhere, we are letting a huge pool of potential contributors and collaborators slip under the waves. There is no question that poverty causes ill health, but ill health also traps people in poverty, which in turn weakens them and keeps them from grasping the first rung of the ladder to middle-class hope. Until and unless we can meet some of these grand challenges, much of that 50 percent of the world that is still not flat will stay that way — no matter how flat the other 50 percent gets.

Too Disempowered

There's not just the flat world and the unflat world. Many people live in the twilight zone between the two. Among these are the people I call the too disempowered. They are a large group of people who have not been fully encompassed by the flattening of the world. Unlike the too sick, who have yet even to get a chance to step onto the flat world, the too disempowered are people who you might say are half flat. They are healthy people who live in countries with significant areas that have been flattened but who don't have the tools or the skills or the infrastructure to participate in any meaningful or sustained way. They have just enough information to know that the world is flattening around them and that they aren't really getting any of the benefits. Being flat is good but full of pressure, being unflat is awful and full of pain, but being half flat has its own special anxiety. As exciting and as visible as the flat Indian high-tech sector is, have no illusions: It accounts for 0.2 percent of employment in India. Add those Indians involved in manufacturing for export, and you get a total of 2 percent of employment in India.

The half flat are all those other hundreds of millions of people, particularly in rural India, rural China, and rural Eastern Europe, who are close enough to see, touch, and occasionally benefit from the flat world but who are not really living inside it themselves. We saw how big and how angry this group can be in the spring of 2004 Indian national elections, in which the ruling BJP was surprisingly tossed out of office — despite having overseen a surge in India's growth rate — largely because of the discontent of rural Indian voters with the slow pace of globalization outside the giant cities. These voters were not saying, "Stop the globalization train, we want to get off." They were saying, "Stop the globalization train, we want to get on, but someone needs to help us by building a better stepstool."

These rural voters — peasants and

farmers, who form the bulk of India's population — just had to spend a day in any nearby big city to see the benefits of the flat world: the cars, the houses, the educational opportunities. "Every time a villager watches the community TV and sees an ad for soap or shampoo, what they notice are not the soap and shampoo but the lifestyle of the people using them — the kind of motorbikes they ride, their dress, and their homes," explained Indian-born Nayan Chanda, editor of YaleGlobal Online. "They see a world they want access to. This election was about envy and anger. It was a classic case of revolutions happening when things are getting better but not fast enough for many people."

At the same time, these rural Indians understood, at gut level, exactly why it was not happening for them: because local governments in India have become so eaten away by corruption and mismanagement that they cannot deliver to the poor the schools and infrastructure they need to get a fair share of the pie. As some of these millions of Indians on the outside of the gated communities looking in lose hope, "they become more religious, more tied to their caste/subcaste, more radical in their thinking, more willing to snatch than create, [and] view dirty politics as being the only way to get mobility, since economic mobility is stalled," said Vivek Paul of Wipro. India can have the smartest high-tech vanguard in the world, but if it does not find a way to bring along more of those who are unable, disabled, undereducated, and underserved, it will be like a rocket that takes off but quickly falls back to earth for lack of sustained thrust.

The Congress Party got the message, which was why as soon as it took office it chose as its prime minister not some antiglobalizer but Manmohan Singh, the former Indian finance minister, who in 1991 first opened the Indian economy to globalization, placing an emphasis on exports and trade and reform wholesale. And Singh, in turn, pledged himself to vastly increase government investments in rural infrastructure and to bring more reform retail to rural government.

How can outsiders collaborate in this process? I think, first and foremost, they can redefine the meaning of global populism. If populists really want to help the rural poor, the way to do it is not by burning down McDonald's and shutting down the IMF and trying to put up protectionist barriers that will unflatten the world. That will help the rural poor not one iota. It has to be by refocusing the energies of the global populist movement on how to improve local government, infrastructure, and education in places like rural India and China, so the populations there can acquire the tools to collaborate and participate in the flat world. The global populist movement, better known as the antiglobalization movement, has a great deal of energy, but up to now it has been too divided and confused to effectively help the poor in any meaningful or sustained manner. It needs a policy lobotomy. The world's poor do not resent the rich any-where nearly as much as the left-wing par-ties in the developed world imagine. What they resent is not having any pathway to get rich and to join the flat world and cross that line into the middle class that Jerry Yang spoke about.

Let's pause for a minute here and trace how the antiglobalization movement lost touch with the true aspirations of the world's poor. The antiglobalization move-ment emerged at the World Trade Organi-zation conference in Seattle in 1999 and then spread around the world in subse-quent years, usually gathering to attack meetings of the World Bank, the IMF, and the G-8 industrialized nations. From its or-igins, the movement that emerged in Se-attle was a primarily Western-driven phenomenon, which was why you saw so few people of color in the crowds. It was driven by five disparate forces. One was upper-middle-class American liberal guilt at the incredible wealth and power that America had amassed in the wake of the fall of the Berlin Wall and the dot-com boom. At the peak of the stock market boom, lots of pampered American college kids, wearing their branded clothing, began to get interested in sweatshops as a way of expiating their guilt. The second force driving it was a rear-guard push by the Old Left — socialists, anarchists, and Trotsky-ites — in alliance with protectionist trade unions. Their strategy was to piggyback on rising concerns about globalization to bring back some form of socialism, even though these ideas had been rejected as bankrupt by the very people in the former Soviet Empire and China who had lived under them longest. (Now you know why there was no antiglobalization movement to speak of in Russia, China, or Eastern Europe.) These Old Left forces wanted to spark a debate about *whether we globalize.* They claimed to speak in the name of the Third World poor, but the bankrupt economic policies they advocated made them, in my view, the Coalition to Keep Poor People Poor. The third force was a more amorphous group. It was made up of many people who gave passive support to the antiglobalization movement from many countries, because they saw in it some kind of protest against the speed at which the old world was disappearing and becoming flat.

The fourth force driving the movement, which was particularly strong in Europe and in the Islamic world, was anti-Americanism. The disparity between American economic and political power and everybody else's had grown so wide after the fall of the Soviet Empire that America began to — or was perceived to — touch people's lives around the planet, directly or indirectly, more than their own governments did. As people around the world began to intuit this, a movement emerged, which Seattle both reflected and helped to catalyze, whereby people said, in effect, "If America is now touching my life directly or indirectly more than my own government, then I want to have a vote in America's power." At the time of Seattle, the "touching" that people were most concerned with was from American economic and cultural power, and therefore the demand for a vote tended to focus around economic rule-making institutions like the World Trade Organization. America in the 1990s, under President Clinton, was perceived as a big dumb dragon, pushing people around in the economic and cultural spheres, knowingly and unknowingly. We were Puff the Magic Dragon, and people wanted a vote in what we were puffing.

Then came 9/11. And America transformed itself from Puff the Magic Dragon, touching people around the world economically and culturally, into Godzilla with an arrow in his shoulder, spitting fire and tossing around his tail wildly, touching people's lives in military and security terms, not just economic and cultural ones. As that happened, people in the world began to say, "Now we *really* want a vote in how America wields its power" — and in many ways the whole Iraq war debate was a surrogate debate about that.

Finally, the fifth force in this movement was a coalition of very serious, well-meaning, and constructive groups — from environmentalists to trade activists to NGOs concerned with governance — who became part of the populist antiglobalization movement in the 1990s in the hopes that they could catalyze a global discussion about *how we globalize*. I had a lot of respect and sympathy for this latter group. But in the end they got drowned out by the whether-we-globalize crowd, which began to turn the movement more violent at the July 2001 Genoa G-8 summit, when an antiglobalization protester was killed while attacking an Italian police jeep with a fire extinguisher.

The combination of the triple convergence, the violence at Genoa, 9/11, and tighter security measures fractured the antiglobalization movement. The more serious how-we-globalize groups did not want to be in the same trench with anarchists out to provoke a public clash with police, and after 9/11, many American labor groups did not want to be associated with a movement that appeared to be taken over by anti-American elements. This became even more pronounced when in late September 2001, three weeks after 9/11, antiglobalization leaders attempted a rerun of Genoa in the streets of Washington, to protest the IMF and World Bank meetings there. After 9/11, though, the IMF and World Bank canceled their meetings, and many American protesters shied away. Those who did turn up in the streets of Washington turned the event into a march against the imminent American invasion of Afghanistan to remove Osama bin Laden and al-Qaeda. At the same time, with the triple convergence making the Chinese, Indians, and Eastern Europeans some of the biggest beneficiaries of globalization, it was no longer possible to claim that this phenomenon was devastating the world's poor. Just the opposite: Millions of Chinese and Indians were entering the world's middle class thanks to the flattening of the world and globalization.

So as the how-we-globalize forces drifted away, and as the number of Third World people benefiting from globalization began to grow, and as America under the Bush administration began to exercise more unilateral military power, the anti-American element in the antiglobalization movement began to assume a much louder voice and role. As a result, the movement itself became both more anti-American and more unable and unwilling to play any constructive role in shaping the global debate on how we globalize, precisely when such a role has become even more important as the world has gotten flatter. As Hebrew University political theorist Yaron Ezrahi so aptly noted, "The important task of enlisting the people's power to influence globalism — making it more compassionate, fair, and compatible with human dignity — is way too important to be wasted on crass anti-Americanism or left in the hands of only anti-Americans."

There is a huge political vacuum now waiting to be filled. There is a real role today for a movement that could advance the agenda of how we globalize — not whether we globalize. The best place such a movement could start is rural India.

"Both the Congress [Party] and its left allies would be risking India's future if they draw the wrong conclusion from this

[2004] election," Pratap Bhanu Mehta, who heads the Center for Policy Research in Delhi, wrote in *The Hindu* newspaper. "This is not a revolt against the market, it is a protest against the state; this is not resentment against the gains of liberalization, but a call for the state to put its house in order through even more reform . . . The revolt against holders of power is not a revolt of the poor against the rich: ordinary people are far less prone to resent other people's success than intellectuals suppose. It is rather an expression of the fact that the reform of the state has not gone far enough."

This is why the most important forces fighting poverty in India today, in my view, are those NGOs fighting for better local governance, using the Internet and other modern tools of the flat world to put a spotlight on corruption, mismanagement, and tax avoidance. The most important, effective, and meaningful populists in the world today are not those handing out money. They are those with an agenda to drive reform retail at the local level in their countries — to make it easier for the little man or woman to register his or her land, even if they are squatters; to start a business, no matter how small; and to get minimal justice from the legal system. Modern populism, to be effective and meaningful, should be about reform retail — making globalization workable, sustainable, and fair for more people by improving their local governance, so that the money that has already been earmarked for the poor actually gets to them and so that their natural entrepreneurship can get unlocked. It is through local government that people plug into the system and get to enjoy the benefits of the flattening world rather than just observe them. The average Indian villagers cannot be like the Indian high-tech companies and just circumvent the government by supplying their own electricity, their own water resources, their own security, their own bus system, and their own satellite dishes. *They need the state for that.* The market cannot be counted on to make up for the failure of the state to deliver decent governance. The state has to get better. Precisely because the Indian state opted for a globalization strategy in 1991 and abandoned fifty years of socialism — which had brought its foreign reserves to near zero — New Delhi had reserves in 2004 of $100 billion, giving it the resources to help more of its people into the flat arena.

Ramesh Ramanathan, an Indian-born former Citibank executive who returned to India to lead an NGO called Janaagraha, dedicated to improving local governance, is precisely the kind of new populist I have in mind. "In India," he said, "clients of public education are sending a signal about the quality of service delivery: Whoever can afford to opt out does so. The same goes for health care. Given the escalating costs of health care, if we had a solid public health-care system, most citizens would opt to use it, not just the poor. Ditto for roads, highways, water supply, sanitation, registration of births and deaths, crematoria, driver's licenses, and so on. Wherever the government provides these services, it [should be] for the benefit of all citizens. [But] in fact, in some of these, like water supply and sanitation, the poor are actually not even getting the same basic services as the middle class and the rich. The challenge here is therefore universal access." Getting NGOs that can collaborate on the local level to ensure that the poor get the infrastructure and budgets to which they are entitled could have a major impact on poverty alleviation.

So although this may sound odd coming from me, it is totally consistent with this whole book: What the world doesn't need now is for the antiglobalization movement to go away. We just need it to grow up. This movement had a lot of energy and a lot of mobilizing capacity. What it lacked was a coherent agenda for assisting the poor by collaborating with them in a way that could actually help them. The activist groups that are helping alleviate poverty the most are those working at the local village level in places like rural India, Africa, and China to spotlight and fight corruption and to promote accountability, transparency, education, and property rights. You don't help the world's poor by dressing up in a turtle outfit and throwing a stone through McDonald's window. You help them by getting them the tools and institutions to help themselves. It may not be as sexy as protesting against world leaders in the streets of Washington and Genoa, and getting lots of attention on CNN, but it is a lot more important. Just ask any Indian villager.

Collaboration in poverty alleviation is not just for NGOs. It is also for multinational corporations. The rural poor in India, Africa, and China represent a huge market, and it is possible to make money there and serve them — if companies are ready to collaborate horizontally with the poor. One of the most interesting examples I have come across of this form of collaboration is a program run by Hewlett-Packard. HP is not an NGO. HP began with a simple question: What do poor people need most that we could sell to them? You cannot design this stuff in Palo

Alto; you have to cocreate with the user-customer beneficiary. In order to answer that question, HP created a public-private partnership with the national government in India and the local government in Andhra Pradesh. Then a group of HP technologists convened a series of dialogues in the farming village of Kuppam. It asked residents two things: What are your hopes for the next three to five years? and What changes would really make your lives better? To help the villagers (many of them illiterate) express themselves, HP used a concept called graphic facilitation, whereby when people voiced their dreams and aspirations, a visual artist whom HP brought over from the United States drew images of those aspirations on craft paper put up on the walls around the room.

"When people, particularly people who are illiterate, say something and it gets immediately represented on the wall, they feel really validated, and therefore they get more animated and more engaged," said Maureen Conway, HP's vice president for emerging market solutions, who headed the project. "It raises self-esteem." Once these poor farmers living in a remote village got loose, they really started aspiring. "One of them said, 'What we really need here is an airport,' " said Conway.

After the visioning sessions were complete, HP employees spent more time in the village just observing how people lived. One technological thing missing in their lives was photography. Conway explained: "We noticed that there was a big demand for having pictures taken for identification purposes, for licenses, for applications and government permits, and we said to ourselves, 'Maybe there is an entrepreneurial opportunity here if we can turn people into village photographers.' There was one photo studio in downtown Kuppam. Everyone around [is] farmers. We noticed that people would come back in from villages on a bus, spend two hours, get their pictures taken, come back a week later for the pictures, and find out that they were not done or done wrong. Time is as important for them as for us. So we said, 'Wait a minute, we make digital cameras and portable printers. So what is the problem?' Why doesn't HP sell them a bunch of digital cameras and printers? The villagers came back with a very short answer: 'Electricity.' They had no assured supply of electricity and little money to pay for it.

"So we said, 'We are technologists. Let's get a solar panel and put it on a backpack on wheels and see if there is a business for people here, and for HP, if we make a mobile photo studio.' That is the approach we took. The solar panel can charge both the camera and the printer. Then we went to a self-help women's group. We picked five women and said, 'We will train you how to use this equipment.' We gave them two weeks of training. And we said, 'We will provide you with the camera and supplies, and we will share revenue with you on every picture.' " This was not charity. Even after buying all their supplies from HP and sharing some of the revenue with HP, the women in the photography group doubled their family incomes. "And to be honest, what we found out was that less than 50 percent of the pictures they took were for identification pictures and the rest were people just wanting pictures of their kids, weddings, and themselves," said Conway. The poor like family photo albums as much as the rich and are ready to pay for them. The local government also made this women's group its official photographers for public works projects, which added to their income.

End of story? Not quite. As I said, HP is not an NGO. "After four months we said, 'Okay, the experiment is over, we're taking the camera back,' " said Conway. "And they said, 'You're crazy.' " So HP told the women that if they wanted to keep the camera, printer, and solar panel, they had to come up with a plan to pay for them. They eventually proposed renting them for

$9 a month, and HP agreed. And now they are branching out into other villages. HP, meanwhile, has started working with an NGO to train multiple women's groups with the same mobile photography studio, and there is a potential here for HP to sell the studios to NGOs all over India, with all of them using HP ink and other supplies. And from India, who knows where?

"They are giving us feedback on the cameras and ease of use," said Conway. "What it has done to change the confidence of the women is absolutely amazing."

Too Frustrated

One of the unintended consequences of the flat world is that it puts different societies and cultures in much greater direct contact with one another. It connects people to people much faster than people and cultures can often prepare themselves. Some cultures thrive on the sudden opportunities for collaboration that this global intimacy makes possible. Others are threatened, frustrated, and even humiliated by this close contact, which, among other things, makes it very easy for people to see where they stand in the world vis-à-vis everyone else. All of this helps to explain the emergence of one of the most dangerous unflattening forces today —

the suicide bombers of al-Qaeda and the other Islamist terror organizations, who are coming out of the Muslim world and Muslim communities in Europe.

The Arab-Muslim world is a vast, diverse civilization, encompassing over one billion people and stretching from Morocco to Indonesia and from Nigeria all the way to the suburbs of London. It is very dangerous to generalize about such a complex religious community, made up of so many different ethnicities and nationalities. But one need only look at the headlines in any day's newspaper to appreciate that a lot of anger and frustration seems to be bubbling over from the Muslim world in general and from the Arab-Muslim world in particular, where many young people seem to be agitated by a combination of issues. One of the most obvious is the festering Arab-Israeli conflict, and the Israeli occupation of Palestinian land and East Jerusalem — a grievance which has a powerful emotional hold on the Arab-Muslim imagination and has long soured relations with America and the West.

But this is not the only reason for the brewing anger in these communities. This anger also has to do with the frustration of Arabs and Muslims at having to live, in many, many cases, under authoritarian governments, which not only deprive their people of a voice in their own future, but have deprived tens of millions of young people in particular of opportunities to achieve their full potential through good jobs and modern schools. The fact that the flat world enables people to so easily compare their circumstances with others only sharpens their frustrations.

Some of these Arab-Muslim young men and women have chosen to emigrate in order to find opportunities in the West; others have chosen to suffer in silence at home, hoping for some kind of change. The most powerful journalistic experiences I have had since 9/11 have been my encounters in the Arab world with some of these young people. Because my column with my picture runs in Arabic in the leading pan-Arab newspaper, the London-based *Al-Sharq Al-Awsat*, and because I often appear on Arab satellite-television news programs, many people in that part of the world know what I look like. I have been amazed by the number of young Arabs and Muslims — men and women — who have come up to me on the streets of Cairo or in the Arabian Gulf since 9/11, and said to me what one young man in Al-Azhar mosque did one Friday, after noon prayer: "You're Friedman, aren't you?"

I nodded yes.

"Keep writing what you're writing," he

said. And what he meant was writing about the importance of bringing more freedom of thought, expression, and opportunity to the Arab-Muslim world, so its young people can realize their potential.

Unfortunately, though, these progressive young people are not the ones defining the relationship between the Arab-Muslim community and the world at large today. Increasingly, that relationship is being dominated by, and defined by, religious militants and extremists, who give vent to the frustrations in that part of the world by simply lashing out. The question that I want to explore in this section is: What produced this violent Islamist fringe, and why has it found so much passive support in the Arab-Muslim world today — even though, I am convinced, the vast majority there do not share the violent agenda of these groups or their apocalyptic visions?

The question is relevant to a book about the flat world for a very simple reason: Should there be another attack on the United States of the magnitude of 9/11, or worse, walls would go up everywhere and the flattening of the world would be set back for a long, long time.

That, of course, is precisely what the Islamists want.

When Muslim radicals and fundamentalists look at the West, they see only the openness that makes us, in their eyes, decadent and promiscuous. They see only the openness that has produced Britney Spears and Janet Jackson. They do not see, and do not want to see, the openness — the freedom of thought and inquiry — that has made us powerful, the openness that has produced Bill Gates and Sally Ride. They deliberately define it all as decadence. Because if openness, women's empowerment, and freedom of thought and inquiry are the real sources of the West's economic strength, then the Arab-Muslim world would have to change. And the fundamentalists and extremists do not want to change.

To beat back the threat of openness, the Muslim extremists have, quite deliberately, chosen to attack the very thing that keeps open societies open, innovating, and flattening, and that is *trust*. When terrorists take instruments from our daily lives — the car, the airplane, the tennis shoe, the cell phone — and turn them into weapons of indiscriminate violence, they reduce trust. We trust when we park our car downtown in the morning that the car next to it is not going to blow up; we trust when we go to Disney World that the man in the Mickey Mouse outfit is not wearing a bomb-laden vest underneath; we trust when we get on the shuttle flight from Boston to New York that the foreign student seated next to us isn't going to blow up his tennis shoes. Without trust, there is no open society, because there are not enough police to patrol every opening in an open society. Without trust, there can also be no flat world, because it is trust that allows us to take down walls, remove barriers, and eliminate friction at borders. Trust is essential for a flat world, where you have supply chains involving ten, a hundred, or a thousand people, most of whom have never met face-to-face. The more open societies are exposed to indiscriminate terrorism, the more trust is removed, and the more open societies will erect walls and dig moats instead.

The founders of al-Qaeda are not religious fundamentalists per se. That is, they are not focused simply on the relationship between themselves and God, and on the values and cultural norms of the religious community. They are a political phenomenon more than a religious one. I like to call them Islamo-Leninists. I use the term "Leninists" to convey the utopian-totalitarian vision of al-Qaeda as well its self-image. As al-Qaeda's chief ideologist, Ayman al-Zawahiri, has put it, al-Qaeda is the ideological vanguard, whose attacks on the United States and other Western targets are designed to mobilize and energize the Muslim masses to rise up against their own corrupt rulers, who are propped up by America. Like all good Leninists, the Islamo-Leninists are certain that the Muslim masses are deeply dissatisfied with their lot and that one or two spectacular acts of jihad against the "pillars of tyranny" in the West will spark them to overthrow the secularizing, immoral, and unjust Arab-Muslim regimes that have defiled Islam. In their place, the Islamo-Leninists, however, do not want to establish a workers' paradise but rather a religious paradise. They vow to establish an Islamic state across the same territory that Islam ruled over at its height, led by a caliph, a supreme religious-political leader, who would unite all the Muslim peoples into a single community.

Islamo-Leninism, in many ways, emerged from the same historical context as the radical European ideologies of the nineteenth and twentieth centuries. Fascism and Marxist-Leninism grew out of the rapid industrialization and modernization of Germany and Central Europe, where communities living in tightly bonded villages and extended families suddenly got shattered and the sons and fathers went off to the urban areas to work for big industrial companies. In this age of transitions, young men in particular lost a sense of identity, rootedness, and personal dignity that had been provided by traditional social structures. In that vacuum, along came Hitler, Lenin, and Mussolini, who told these young men that they had an answer for their feelings of dislocation and humiliation: You may not be in the village or small town anymore, but you are still proud, dignified members of a larger community — the working class, or the Aryan nation.

Bin Laden offered the same sort of ideological response for young Arabs and Muslims. The first person to recognize the Islamo-Leninist character of these 9/11 hijackers — that they were not fundamentalists but adherents of an extreme, violent political cult — was Adrian Karatnycky, the president of Freedom House. In a November 5, 2001, article in the *National Review*, titled "Under Our Very Noses," Karatnycky makes the following argument: "The key hijackers . . . were well-educated children of privilege. None of them suffered first-hand economic privation or political oppression." And none of them seem to have been raised in a particularly fundamentalist household. Indeed, the top 9/11 operatives and pilots, like Mohammed Atta and Marwan al-Shehhi, who shared an apartment in Hamburg, where they both attended the Technical University of Hamburg-Harburg, all seem to have been recruited to al-Qaeda through cells and prayer groups — after they moved to Europe.

None of these plotters was recruited in the Middle East and then planted in Europe years in advance by bin Laden, notes Karatnycky. To the contrary, virtually all of them seem to have lived in Europe on their own, grown alienated from the European society around them, gravitated to a local prayer group or mosque to find warmth and solidarity, undergone a "born-again" conversion, gotten radicalized by Islamist elements, gone off for training in Afghanistan, and presto, a terrorist was born. Their discovery of religion was not just part of a personal search for meaning. It went far beyond fundamentalism. They converted Islam into a political ideology, a religious totalitarianism. Had the 9/11 hijackers been students at Berkeley in the early 1970's, they would have been Trotskyite radicals. "To understand the September 11 terrorists, we should have in mind the profile of the classic revolutionary: deracinated, middle class, shaped in part by exile. In other words, the image of Lenin in Zurich; or of Pol Pot or Ho Chi Minh in Paris . . . For them Islamism is the new universal revolutionary creed, and bin Laden is Sheikh Guevara," writes Karatnycky. "Like the leaders of America's Weather Underground, Germany's Baader-Meinhof Gang, Italy's Red Brigades, and

Japan's Red Army Faction, the Islamic terrorists were university-educated converts to an all-encompassing neo-totalitarian ideology."

My friend Abdallah Schleifer, a journalism professor in Cairo, actually knew Ayman al-Zawahiri, bin Laden's number two and chief ideologue, when al-Zawahiri was a young doctor on his way to becoming a young neo-Leninist Muslim revolutionary. "Ayman was attracted from the time he was a teenager into a utopian vision of an Islamic state," Schleifer told me on a visit to Cairo. But instead of being drawn to the traditional concern of religion — the relationship between oneself and God — al-Zawahiri became drawn to religion as a political ideology. Like a good Marxist or Leninist, al-Zawahiri was interested in "building the Kingdom of God on earth," said Schleifer, and Islamism became his Marxism — his "utopian ideology." And where Mohammed Atta meets al-Zawahiri is the intersection where rage and humiliation meet the ideology that is going to make it all right. "Ayman is saying to someone like Mohammed Atta, 'You see injustice? We have a system — *a system, mind you, a system* — that will give you [justice], not a religion, because religion gives you inner peace.' It doesn't necessarily solve any social problem. But [al-Zawahiri] is saying we have a system that will give you justice. You feel frustration? We have a system that will enable you to flower. The system is what we call Islamism — an ideological, highly politicized Islam, in which the spiritual content — the personal relationship [with God] — is taken out of Islam and instead it is transformed into a religious ideology like fascism or communism." But unlike the Leninists, who wanted to install the reign of the perfect class, the working class, and unlike Nazis, who wanted to install the reign of the perfect race, the Aryan race, bin Laden and al-Zawahiri wanted to install the reign of the perfect religion.

Unfortunately, bin Laden and his colleagues have found it all too easy to enlist recruits in the Arab-Muslim world. I think this has to do, in part, with the state of half-flatness that many Arab-Muslim young people are living in, particularly those in Europe. They have been raised to believe that Islam is the most perfect and complete expression of God's monotheistic message and that the Prophet Muhammed is God's last and most perfect messenger. This is not a criticism. This is Islam's self-identity. Yet, in a flat world, these youth, particularly those living in Europe, can and do look around and see that the Arab-Muslim world, in too many cases, has fallen behind the rest of the planet. It is not living as prosperously or democratically as other civilizations. How can that be? these young Arabs and Muslims must ask themselves. If we have the superior faith, and if our faith is all encompassing of religion, politics, and economics, why are others living so much better?

This is a source of real cognitive dissonance for many Arab-Muslim youth — the sort of dissonance, and loss of self-esteem, that sparks rage, and leads some of them to join violent groups and lash out at the world. It is also the sort of dissonance that leads many others, average folks, to give radical groups like al-Qaeda passive support. Again, the flattening of the world only sharpens that dissonance by making the backwardness of the Arab-Muslim region, compared to others, impossible to ignore. It has become so impossible to ignore that some Arab-Muslim intellectuals have started to point out this backwardness with brutal honesty and to demand solutions. They do this in defiance of their authoritarian governments, who prefer to use their media not to encourage honest debate, but rather to blame all their problems on others — on America, on Israel, or on a legacy of Western colonialism — on anything and anyone but the dead hand of these authoritarian regimes.

According to the second Arab Human

Development Report, which was written in 2003 for the United Nations Development Program by a group of courageous Arab social scientists, between 1980 and 1999, Arab countries produced 171 international patents. South Korea alone during that same period registered 16,328 patents. Hewlett-Packard registers, on average, 11 new patents a day. The average number of scientists and engineers working in research and development in the Arab countries is 371 per million people, while the world average, including countries in Africa, Asia, and Latin America, is 979, the report said. This helps to explain why although massive amounts of foreign technology are imported to the Arab regions, very little of it is internalized or supplanted by Arab innovations. Between 1995 and 1996, as many as 25 percent of the university graduates produced in the Arab world immigrated to some Western country. There are just 18 computers per 1,000 people in the Arab region today, compared with the global average of 78.3 per 1,000, and only 1.6 percent of the Arab population has Internet access. While Arabs represent almost 5 percent of the world population, the report said, they produce only 1 percent of the books published, and an unusually high percentage of those are religious books — over triple the world average. Of the 88 million unemployed males between fifteen and twenty-four worldwide, almost 26 percent are in the Middle East and North Africa, according to an International Labor Organization study (Associated Press, December 26, 2004).

The same study said the total population of Arab countries quadrupled in the past fifty years, to almost 300 million, with 37.5 percent under fifteen, and 3 million coming onto the job market every year. But the good jobs are not being produced at home, because the environment of openness required to attract international investment and stimulate local innovation is all too rare in the Arab-Muslim world today. That virtuous cycle of universities spinning off people and ideas, and then those people and ideas getting funded and creating new jobs, simply does not exist there. Theodore Dalrymple is a physician and psychiatrist who practices in England and writes a column for the *London Spectator*. He wrote an essay in *City Journal*, the urban policy magazine (Spring 2004), about what he learned from his contacts with Muslim youth in British prisons. Dalrymple noted that most schools of Islam today treat the Qu'ran as a divinely inspired text that is not open to any literary criticism or creative reinterpretation. It is a sacred book to be memorized, not adapted to the demands and opportunities of modern life. But without a culture that encourages, and creates space for, such creative reinterpretation, critical thought and original thinking tend to whither. This may explain why so few world-class scientific papers cited by other scholars come out of the Arab-Muslim universities.

If the West had made Shakespeare "the sole object of our study and the sole guide of our lives," said Dalrymple, "we would soon enough fall into backwardness and stagnation. And the problem is that so many Muslims want both stagnation and power: they want a return to the perfection of the seventh century and to dominate the twenty-first, as they believe is the birthright of their doctrine, the last testament of God to man. If they were content to exist in a seventh-century backwater, secure in a quietist philosophy, there would be no problem for them or us; their problem, and ours, is that they want the power that free inquiry confers, without either the free inquiry or the philosophy and institutions that guarantee that free inquiry. They are faced with a dilemma: either they abandon their cherished religion, or they remain forever in the rear of human technical advance. Neither alternative is very appealing, and the tension between their desire for power and success in the modern world on the one hand, and their desire not to abandon their religion on the other, is resolvable for some only by exploding themselves as bombs. People grow angry when faced with an intractable dilemma; they lash out."

Indeed, talk to young Arabs and Muslims anywhere, and this cognitive dissonance and the word "humiliation" always come up very quickly in conversation. It was revealing that when Mahathir Mohammed made his October 16, 2003, farewell speech as prime minister of Malaysia at an Islamic summit he was hosting in his own country, he built his remarks to his fellow Muslim leaders around the question of why their civilization had become so humiliated — a term he used five times. "I will not enumerate the instances of our humiliation," said Mahathir. "Our only reaction is to become more and more angry. Angry people cannot think properly. There is a feeling of hopelessness among the Muslim countries and their people. They feel they can do nothing right . . ."

This humiliation is the key. It has always been my view that terrorism is not spawned by the poverty of money. It is spawned by *the poverty of dignity*. Humiliation is the most underestimated force in international relations and in human relations. It is when people or nations are humiliated that they really lash out and engage in extreme violence. When you take the economic and political backwardness of much of the Arab-Muslim world today, add its past grandeur and self-image of religious superiority, and combine it with the discrimination and alienation these Arab-Muslim males face when they leave home and move to Europe, or when they grow up in Europe, you have one powerful cocktail of rage. As my friend the Egyptian playwright Ali Salem said of the 9/11 hijackers, they "are walking the streets of life, searching for tall buildings — for towers to bring down, because they are not able to be tall like them."

I fear that this sense of frustration that feeds recruits to bin Laden may get worse before it gets better. In the old days, leaders could count on walls and mountains and valleys to obstruct their people's view and keep them ignorant and passive about where they stood in comparison to others. You could see only to the next village. But as the world gets flatter, people can see for miles and miles.

In the flat world you get your humiliation dished up to you fiber-optically. I stumbled across a fascinating example of this involving bin Laden himself. On January 4, 2004, bin Laden issued one of his taped messages through al-Jazeera, the satellite television network based in Qatar. On March 7, the Web site of the Islamic Studies and Research Center published the entire text. One paragraph jumped out at me. It is in the middle of a section in which bin Laden is discussing the various evils of Arab rulers, particularly the Saudi ruling family.

"Thus, the situation of all Arab countries suffers from great deterioration in all walks of life, in religious and worldly matters," says bin Laden. "It is enough to know that the economy of all Arab countries is weaker than the economy of one country that had once been part of our [Islamic] world when we used to truly adhere to Islam. That country is the lost Andalusia. Spain is an infidel country, but its economy is stronger than our economy because the ruler there is accountable. In our countries, there is no accountability or punishment, but there is only obedience to the rulers and prayers of long life for them."

The hair on my arms stood up when I read that. Why? Because what bin Laden was referring to was the first Arab Human Development Report, which came out in July 2002, well after he had been evicted from Afghanistan and was probably hiding out in a cave somewhere. The Arab authors of the report wanted to grab the attention of the Arab world as to how far behind it had fallen. So they looked for a country that had a GDP slightly more than that of all twenty-two Arab states combined. When they ran down the tables, the country that fit that bill perfectly was Spain. It could have been Norway or Italy, but Spain happened to have a GDP just slightly larger than all the Arab states together. Somehow, bin Laden heard or read about this first Arab Human Development Report from his cave. For all I know, he may have read my own column about it, which was the first to highlight the report and stressed the comparison with Spain. Or maybe he got it off the Internet. The report was downloaded from the Internet some 1 million times. So even though he was off in a cave somewhere, he could still get this report, and its humiliating conclusion, shoved right in his face — negatively comparing the Arab states to Spain, no less! And when he heard that comparison, wherever he was hiding, bin Laden took it as an insult, as a humiliation — the notion that Christian Spain, a country that was once controlled by Muslims, had a greater GDP today than all the Arab states combined. The authors of this report were themselves Arabs and Muslims; they were not trying to humiliate anyone — but that was how bin Laden interpreted it. And I am certain he got this dose of humiliation over a modem at 56K. They may even have broadband now in Tora Bora.

And having gotten his dose of humiliation this way, bin Laden and his emulators have learned to give it right back in the same coin. Want to understand why the Islamo-Leninists behead Americans in Iraq and Saudi Arabia and then distribute pictures on the Internet with the bloody head of the body resting on the headless corpse? It is because there is no more humiliating form of execution than chopping off someone's head. It is a way of showing utter contempt for that person and his or her physical being. It is no accident that the groups in Iraq who beheaded Americans dressed them first in the same orange jumpsuits that al-Qaeda prisoners in Guantánamo Bay are forced to wear. They had to learn about those jumpsuits either over the Internet or satellite TV. But it amazes me that in the middle of the Iraq war they were able to have the exact same jumpsuits made in Iraq to dress their prisoners in. You humiliate me, I humiliate you. And what do you suppose terrorist leader Abu Musab al-Zarqawi said in his audiotape released on September 11, 2004, the third anniversary of 9/11? He said, "The holy warriors made the international coalition taste humiliation . . . lessons from which they are still burning." The tape was titled "Where Is the Honor?"

As I said, however, this frustration and humiliation is not confined to the Islamist fringes. The reason why the Islamo-Leninists have become the most energized and pronounced opponents of globalization/Americanization and the biggest threat to the flattening of the world today is not simply their extraordinary violence, but also because they enjoy some passive support around the Arab-Muslim world.

In part, this is because most governments in the Arab-Muslim world have refused to take on these radicals in a war of ideas. While Arab regimes have been very active in jailing their Islamo-Leninists when they can find and arrest them, they have been very passive in countering them with a modern, progressive interpretation of Islam. This is because almost all of these Arab-Muslim leaders are illegitimate themselves. Having come to power by force, they have no credibility as carriers of a moderate, progressive Islam, and they always feel vulnerable to hard-line Muslim preachers, who denounce them for not being good Muslims. So instead of taking on the Muslim radicals, the Arab regimes either throw them in jail or try to buy them off. This leaves a terrible spiritual and political void.

But the other reason for the passive support that the Islamo-Leninists enjoy — and the fact that they are able to raise so much money through charities and mosques in the Arab-Muslim world — is that too many good decent people there feel the same frustration and tinge of humiliation that many of their most enraged youth do. And there is a certain respect for the way these violent youth have been ready to stand up to the world and to their own leaders and defend the honor of their civilization. When I visited Qatar a few months after 9/11, a friend of mine there — a sweet, thoughtful, liberal person who works for the Qatari government — confided to me something in a whisper that was deeply troubling to him: "My eleven-year-old son thinks bin Laden is a good man."

Most middle-class Arabs and Muslims, I am convinced, were not celebrating the death of three thousand innocent Americans on 9/11. I know my Arab and Muslim friends were not. But many Arabs and Muslims were celebrating the idea of putting a fist in America's face — and they were quietly applauding the men who did it. They were happy to see someone humiliating the people and the country that they felt was humiliating them and supporting what they saw as injustice in their world — whether it is America's backing of Arab kings and dictators who export oil to it or America's backing of Israel whether it does the right things or the wrong things.

Most American blacks, I am sure, had little doubt that O. J. Simpson murdered his ex-wife, but they applauded his acquittal as a stick in the eye of the Los Angeles Police Department and a justice system that they saw as consistently humiliating and unfair to them. Humiliation does that to people. Bin Laden is to the Arab masses what O.J. was to many American blacks — the stick they poke in the eye of an "unfair" America and their own leaders. I once interviewed Dyab Abou Jahjah, often called the Malcolm X of Belgium's alienated Moroccan youth. I asked him what he and his friends thought when they saw the World Trade Center being smashed. He said, "I think if we are honest with ourselves, most of the Muslims all over the world felt that . . . America got hit in the face and that cannot be bad. I don't want to make an intellectual answer for that. I'll give it very simply. America was kicking our butts for fifty years. And really badly. Supporting the bullies in the region, whether it is Israel or our own regimes, [America] is giving us not only a bleeding nose, but breaking a lot of our necks."

Just as America's economic depression in the 1920s and 1930s made many normal, intelligent, thinking Americans passive or active supporters of communism, so the humiliating economic, military, and emotional depression of the Arab-Muslim world has made too many normal, intelligent, and thinking Arabs and Muslims passive supporters of bin Ladenism.

Former Kuwaiti minister of information Dr. Sa'd Bin Tefla, a journalist, wrote an essay in the London Arabic daily *Al-Sharq Al-Awsat* on the third anniversary of September 11 titled "We Are All Bin Laden," which went right to this point. He asked why it is that Muslim scholars and clerics eagerly supported fatwas condemning Salman Rushdie to death for writing an allegedly blasphemous novel, *The Satanic Verses*, that wove in themes about the Prophet Muhammad, but to this day no Muslim cleric has issued a fatwa condemning Osama bin Laden for murdering three thousand innocent civilians. After the fatwa was declared against Salman Rushdie, Muslims staged protests against the book at British embassies all over the Islamic world and burned Salman Rushdie dolls along with copies of his book. Nine people were killed in an anti-Rushdie protest in Pakistan.

"Religious legal rulings were disseminated one after another banning Salman Rushdie's book and calling for him to be killed," Bin

Tefla wrote. "Iran earmarked a reward of $1 million for whoever would implement Imam Khomeini's fatwa and kill Salman Rushdie." And bin Laden? Nothing — no condemnation. "Despite the fact that bin Laden murdered thousands of innocents in the name of our religion and despite the damage that he has caused to Muslims everywhere, and especially to innocent Muslims in the West, whose life is much better than the life of Muslims in Islamic lands, to this date not a single fatwa has been issued calling for the killing of bin Laden, on the pretext that bin Laden still proclaims 'there is no God other than Allah,' " Tefla wrote. Worse, he added, Arab and Muslim satellite television channels have "competed amongst themselves in broadcasting [bin Laden's] sermons and fatwas, instead of preventing their dissemination as they did in the case of Rushdie's book . . . With our equivocal stance on bin Laden, we from the very start left the world with the impression that we are all bin Laden."

Germany was humiliated after World War I, but it had the modern economic foundations to produce a state response to that humiliation — in the form of the Third Reich. The Arab world, by contrast, could not produce a state response to its humiliation. Instead, it has rattled the world stage in the last fifty years with two larger-than-life figures, rather than states, noted political theorist Yaron Ezrahi: One was the Saudi oil minister Ahmed Zaki Yamani, and the other was Osama bin Laden. Each achieved global notoriety, each briefly held the world in his palm — one by using oil as a weapon and the other by using the most unconventional suicide violence imaginable. Each gave a temporary "high" to the Arab-Muslim world, a feeling that it was exercising power on the world stage. But bin Laden and Yamani were only the illusions of power, noted Ezrahi: The Saudi oil weapon is economic power without productivity, and bin Laden's terrorism weapon is military force without a real army, state, economy, and engine of innovation to support it.

What makes Yamanism and bin Ladenism so unfortunate as strategies for Arab influence in the world is that they ignore the examples within Arab culture and civilization — when it was at its height — of discipline, hard work, knowledge, achievement, scientific inquiry, and pluralism. As Nayan Chanda, the editor of YaleGlobal Online, pointed out to me, it was the Arab-Muslim world that gave birth to algebra and algorithms, terms both derived from Arabic words. In other words, noted Chanda, "The entire modern information revolution, which is built to a large degree on algorithms, can trace its roots all the way back to Arab-Muslim civilization and the great learning centers of Baghdad and Alexandria," which first introduced these concepts, then transferred them to Europe through Muslim Spain. The Arab-Muslim peoples have an incredibly rich cultural tradition and civilization, with long periods of success and innovation to draw on for inspiration and example for their young people. They have all the resources necessary for modernization in their own cultural terms, if they want to summon them.

Unfortunately, there is huge resistance to such modernization from the authoritarian and religiously obscurantist forces within the Arab-Muslim world. That is why this part of the world will be liberated, and feel truly empowered, only if it goes through its own war of ideas — and the moderates there win. We had a civil war in America some 150 years ago over ideas — the ideas of tolerance, pluralism, human dignity, and equality. The best thing outsiders can do for the Arab-Muslim world today is try to collaborate with its progressive forces in every way possible — from trying to solve the Arab-Israeli conflict, to stabilizing Iraq, to signing free-trade agreements with as many Arab countries as possible — so as to foster a similar war of ideas within their civilization. There is no other way. Otherwise this part of the world has the potential to be a huge unflattening force. We have to wish the good people there well. But the battle will be one for them to fight and to win. No one can do it for them.

No one has expressed what is needed better than Abdel Rahman al-Rashed, the general manager of the London-based al-Arabiya news channel. One of the best-known and most respected Arab journalists working today, he wrote the following, in *Al-Sharq Al-Awsat* (September 6, 2004), after a series of violent incidents involving Muslim extremist groups from Chechnya to Saudi Arabia to Iraq: "Self-cure starts with self-realization and confession. We should then run after our terrorist sons, in the full knowledge that they are the sour grapes of a deformed culture . . . The mosque used to be a haven, and the voice of religion used to be that of peace and reconciliation. Religious sermons were warm behests for a moral order and an ethical life. Then came the neo-Muslims. An innocent and benevolent religion, whose verses prohibit the felling of trees in the absence of urgent necessity, that calls murder the most heinous of crimes, that says explicitly that if you kill one person you have killed humanity as a whole, has been turned into a global message of hate and a universal war cry . . . We cannot clear our names unless we own up to the shameful fact that terrorism has become an Islamic enterprise; an almost exclusive monopoly, implemented by Muslim men and women. We cannot redeem our extremist youth, who commit all these heinous crimes, without confronting the Sheikhs who thought it ennobling to reinvent themselves as revolutionary ideologues, sending other people's sons and daughters to certain death, while sending their own children to European and American schools and colleges."

Too Many Toyotas

The problems of the too sick, the too disempowered, and the too humiliated are all in their own ways keeping the world from becoming entirely flat. They may do so even more in the future, if they are not properly addressed. But another barrier to the flattening of the world is emerging, one that is not a human constraint but a natural resource constraint. If millions of people from India, China, Latin America, and the former Soviet Empire who were living largely outside the flat world all start to walk onto the flat world playing field at once — and all come with their own dream of owning a car, a house, a refrigerator, a microwave, and a toaster — we are going to experience either a serious energy shortage or, worse, wars over energy that would have a profoundly unflattening effect on the world.

As I mentioned earlier, I visited Beijing in the summer of 2004 with my wife and teenage daughter, Natalie. Before we left, I said to Natalie, "You're really going to like this city. They have these big bicycle lanes on all the main roads. Maybe when we get there we can rent bikes and just ride around Beijing. I did that last time I was there, and it was a lot of fun."

Silly Tom. I hadn't been to Beijing in three years, and just in that brief period of time the explosive growth there had wiped out many of those charming bicycle lanes. They had been either shrunken or eliminated to add another lane for automobiles and buses. The only biking I did there was on the stationary exercise bike in our hotel, which was a good antidote for having to spend so much time sitting in cars stuck in Beijing traffic jams. I was in Beijing to attend an international business conference, and while there I discovered why all the bikes had disappeared. According to one speaker at the conference, some thirty thousand new cars were being added to the roads in Beijing *every month* — one thousand new cars a day! I found that statistic so unbelievable that I asked Michael Zhao, a young researcher in the *Times*'s Beijing bureau, to double-check it, and he wrote me back the following e-mail:

Hi Tom, Hope this email finds you well. On your question about how many cars are added each day in Beijing, I did some research on the Internet and found that . . . car sales in [Beijing] for April 2004 were 43,000 — 24.1% more than same period last year. So that is 1,433 cars added [daily] to Beijing, but including second-hand car sales. New car sales this month were 30,000, or 1,000 cars each day added to the city. The total car sales from Jan. to April 2004 were 165,000, that is about 1,375 cars added each day to Beijing over this period. This data is from the Beijing Municipal Bureau of Commerce. The city's bureau of statistics has it that the total car sales in 2003 were 407,649, or 1,117 cars each day added. The new car sales last year were 292,858, or 802 new cars each day . . . The total number of cars in Beijing is 2.1 million . . . But the recent months seem to have witnessed surging sales. Also noteworthy is last year's SARS outbreak, during which period a lot of families bought cars, due to panic about public contact and a sort of doomsday-stimulated enjoy-life mentality. And many new car owners did enjoy their time driving, as the traffic in the city so much improved with a lot of people voluntarily caged at home, without daring to go out. Since then, coupled with dropping car prices due to China's commitment to reduce tariffs after joining the WTO, a large number of families have advanced their timetable of buying a car, although some others decided to wait for further drops of prices. All the best, Michael.

As Michael's note indicated, you can see China's middle class rising right before your eyes, and it is going to have enormous energy and environmental spillover. The Great Chinese Dream, like the Great Indian Dream, the Great Russian Dream, and the Great American Dream, is built around a high-energy, high-electricity, high-bent-metal lifestyle. To put it another way, the thirty thousand new cars a month in Beijing, and the cloud of haze that envelops the city on so many days, and the fact that the city's official Web site actually keeps track of "blue sky" days all testify to the environmental destruction that could arise from the triple convergence — if clean alternative renewable energies are not developed soon. Already, according to the World Bank, sixteen of the twenty most polluted cities in the world are in China, and that pollution and environmental degradation together cost China $170 billion a year (*The Economist*, August 21, 2004).

And we have not seen anything yet. China, with its own oil and gas reserves, was once a net exporter. Not anymore. In 2003 China surged ahead of Japan as the second largest importer of oil in the world, after the United States. Right now about 700 to 800 million of China's 1.3 billion people live in the countryside, but they are heading for the flat world, and roughly half are expected to try to migrate to the cities over the next two decades, if they can find work. This will spur a huge surge in demand for cars, houses, steel beams, power plants, school buildings, sewage plants, electricity grids — the energy implications of which are unprecedented in the history of Planet Earth, round or flat.

At the business conference I was attending in Beijing, I kept hearing references to the Strait of Malacca — the narrow passage between Malaysia and Indonesia that is patrolled by the U.S. Navy and controls all the oil tanker traffic from the Middle East to China and Japan. I hadn't heard anyone talking about the Strait of Malacca since the 1970s oil crises. But evidently Chinese strategic planners have begun to grow increasingly concerned that the United States could choke off China's economy at any time by just closing the Strait of Malacca, and this threat is now being increasingly and openly discussed in Chinese military circles. It is just a small hint of the potential struggle for power — energy power — that could ensue if the Great American Dream and the Great Chinese Dream and the Great Indian Dream and the Great Russian Dream come to be seen as mutually exclusive in energy terms.

China's foreign policy today consists of two things: preventing Taiwan from becoming independent and searching for oil. China is now obsessed with acquiring secure oil supplies from countries that would not retaliate against China if it invaded Taiwan, and this is driving China to get cozy with some of the worst regimes in the world. The Islamic fundamentalist government in Sudan now supplies China with 7 percent of its oil supplies and China has invested $3 billion in oil drilling infrastructure there.

In September 2004, China threatened to veto a move by the United Nations to impose sanctions on Sudan for the genocide that it is perpetrating in its Darfur province. China followed by opposing any move to refer Iran's obvious attempts to develop nuclear-weapons-grade fuel to the United Nations Security Council. Iran supplies 13 percent of China's oil supplies.

Meanwhile, as the *Daily Telegraph* reported (November 19, 2004), China has begun drilling for gas in the East China Sea, just west of the line that Japan regards as its border: "Japan protested, to no avail, that the project should be a joint one. The two are also set to clash over Russia's oil wealth. China is furious that Japan has outbid it in their battle to determine the route of the pipeline that Russia intends to build to the Far East." At the same time it was reported that a Chinese nuclear submarine had accidentally strayed into Japanese territorial waters. The Chinese government apologized for the "technical error." If you believe that, I have an oil well in Hawaii I would like to sell you . . .

In 2004, China began competing with the United States for oil exploration opportunities in Canada and Venezuela. If China has its way, it will stick a straw into Canada and Venezuela and suck out every drop of oil, which will have the side effect of making America more dependent on Saudi Arabia.

I interviewed the Japanese manager of a major U.S. multinational that was headquartered in Dalian, in northeastern China. "China is following the path of Japan and Korea," said the executive, on the condition that he and his company not be quoted by name, "and the big question is, Can the world afford to have 1.3 billion people following that path and driving the same cars and using the same amount of energy? So I see the flattening, but the challenge of the twenty-first century is, Are we going to hit another oil crisis? The oil crisis in the 1970s coincided with Japan and Europe rising. [There was a time] when the U.S. was the only big consumer of oil, but when Japan and Europe came in, OPEC got the power. But when China and India come into being the consumers, it will be a huge challenge that is an order of magnitude different. It is megapolitics. The limits of growth in the 1970s were overcome with technology. We got smarter than before, equipment became more efficient, and energy consumption per head was lower. But now [with China, India, and Russia all coming on strong] it is multiplied by a factor of ten. There is something we really need to be serious about. We cannot restrict China, [Russia,] and India. They will grow and they must grow."

One thing we will not be able to do is tell young Indians, Russians, Poles, or Chinese that just when they are arriving on the leveled playing field, they have to hold back and consume less for the greater global good. While giving a talk to students at the Beijing College of Foreign Affairs, I spoke about the most important issues that could threaten global stability, including the competition for oil and other energy resources that would naturally occur as China, India, and the former Soviet Union began to consume more oil. No sooner did I finish than a young Chinese woman student shot up her hand and asked basically the following question: "Why should China have to restrain its energy consumption and worry about the environment, when America and Europe got to consume all they energy they wanted when they were developing?" I did not have a good answer. China is a high-pride country. Telling China, India, and Russia to consume less could have the same geopolitical impact that the world's inability to accommodate a rising Japan and Germany had after World War I.

If current trends hold, China will go from importing 7 million barrels of oil today to 14 million a day by 2012. For the world to accommodate that increase it would have to find another Saudi Arabia. That is not likely, which doesn't leave many good options. "For geopolitical reasons, we cannot tell them no, we cannot tell China and India, it is not your turn," said Philip K. Verleger Jr., a leading oil economist. "And for moral reasons, we have lost the ability to lecture anyone." But if we do nothing, several things will likely result. First, gasoline prices will continue to trend higher and higher. Second, we will be strengthening the very worst political systems in the world — like Sudan, Iran, and Saudi Arabia. And third, the environment will be damaged more and more. Already, the newspaper headlines in China every day are about energy shortages, blackouts, and brownouts. U.S. officials estimate that twenty-four out of China's thirty-one provinces are now experiencing power shortages.

We are all stewards of the planet, and the test for our generation is whether we will pass on a planet in as good or better shape than we found it. The flattening process is going to challenge that responsibility. "Aldo Leopold, the father of wildlife ecology, once said: 'The first rule of intelligent tinkering is save all the pieces,' " remarked Glenn Prickett, senior vice president of Conservation International. "What if we don't? What if the 3 billion new entrants start gobbling up all the resources? Species and ecosystems can't adapt that fast, and we will lose a major portion of the earth's remaining biological diversity." Already, noted Prickett, if you look at what is happening in the Congo Basin, the Amazon, the rain forest of Indonesia — the last great wilderness areas — you find that they are being devoured by China's rising appetite. More and more palm oil is being extracted from Indonesia and Malaysia, soybeans out of Brazil, timber out of central Africa, and natural gas out of all of the above to serve China — and, as a result, threatening all sorts of natural habitats. If these trends go on unchecked, with all the natural habitats being converted to farmland and urban areas, and the globe getting warmer, many of the currently threatened species will be condemned to extinction.

The move to sharply reduce energy consumption has to come from within China, as the Chinese confront what the need for fuel is doing to their own environment and growth aspirations. The only thing — and the best thing — we in the United States and Western Europe can do to nudge China toward that understanding is set an example by changing our own consumption patterns. That would give us some credibility to lecture others. "Restoring our moral standing on energy is now a vital national security and environmental issue," said Verleger. That requires doing everything more seriously — more serious government funding for alternatives, a real push by the federal government to promote conservation, a gasoline tax that will drive more consumers to buy hybrid vehicles and smaller cars, legislation to force Detroit to make more fuel-efficient vehicles, and yes, more domestic exploration. Together, added Verleger, that could help stabilize the price at around $25 a barrel, "which seems to be the ideal range for sustainable global growth."

In sum, we in the West have a fundamental interest in keeping the American dream alive in Beijing and Boise and Bangalore. But we have to stop fooling ourselves that it can be done in a flat world with 3 billion potential new consumers — if we don't find a radical new approach to energy usage and conservation. If we fail to do so, we will be courting both an environmental and geopolitical whirlwind. If there was ever a time for some big collaboration, it is now, and the subject is energy. I would love to see a grand China–United States Manhattan Project, a crash program to jointly develop clean alternative energies, bringing together China's best scientists and its political ability to implement pilot projects, with America's best brains, technology, and money. It would be the ideal model and the ideal project for creating value horizontally, with each side contributing its strength. Said Scott Roberts, the Cambridge Energy Research Associates analyst in China, "When it comes to renewable technology and sustainable energy, China could be the laboratory of the world — not just the workshop of the world."

Why not?

TWELVE

The Dell Theory of Conflict Prevention

Old-Time Versus Just-in-Time

Free Trade is God's diplomacy. There is no other certain way of uniting people in the bonds of peace.
— British politician Richard Cobden, 1857

Before I share with you the subject of this chapter, I have to tell you a little bit about the computer that I wrote this book on. It's related to the theme I am about to discuss. This book was largely written on a Dell Inspiron 600m notebook, service tag number 9ZRJP41. As part of the research for this book, I visited with the management team at Dell near Austin, Texas. I shared with them the ideas in this book and in return I asked for one favor: I asked them to trace for me the entire global supply chain that produced my Dell notebook. Here is their report: My computer was conceived when I phoned Dell's 800 number on April 2,

2004, and was connected to sales representative Mujteba Naqvi, who immediately entered my order into Dell's order management system. He typed in both the type of notebook I ordered as well as the special features I wanted, along with my personal information, shipping address, billing address, and credit card information. My credit card was verified by Dell through its work flow connection with Visa, and my order was then released to Dell's production system. Dell has six factories around the world — in Limerick, Ireland; Xiamen, China; Eldorado do Sul, Brazil; Nashville, Tennesee; Austin, Texas; and Penang, Malaysia. My order went out by e-mail to the Dell notebook factory in Malaysia, where the parts for the computer were immediately ordered from the supplier logistics centers (SLCs) next to the Penang factory. Surrounding every Dell factory in the world are these supplier logistics centers, owned by the different suppliers of Dell parts. These SLCs are like staging areas. If you are a Dell supplier anywhere in the world, your job is to keep your SLC full of your specific parts so they can constantly be trucked over to the Dell factory for just-in-time manufacturing.

"In an average day, we sell 140,000 to 150,000 computers," explained Dick Hunter, one of Dell's three global production managers. "Those orders come in over Dell.com or over the telephone. As soon these orders come in, our suppliers know about it. They get a signal based on every component in the machine you ordered, so the supplier knows just what he has to deliver. If you are supplying power cords for desktops, you can see minute by minute how many power cords you are going to have to deliver." Every two hours, the Dell factory in Penang sends an e-mail to the various SLCs nearby, telling each one what parts and what quantities of those parts it wants delivered within the next ninety minutes — and not one minute later. Within ninety minutes, trucks from the various SLCs around Penang pull up to the Dell manufacturing plant and unload the parts needed for all those notebooks ordered in the last two hours. This goes on all day, every two hours. As soon as those parts arrive at the factory, it takes thirty minutes for Dell employees to unload the parts, register their bar codes, and put them into the bins for assembly. "We know where every part in every SLC is in the Dell system at all times," said Hunter.

So where did the parts for my notebook come from? I asked Hunter. To begin with, he said, the notebook was codesigned in Austin, Texas, and in Taiwan by a team of Dell engineers and a team of Taiwanese notebook designers. "The customer's needs, required technologies, and Dell's design innovations were all determined by Dell through our direct relationship with customers," he explained. "The basic design of the motherboard and case — the basic functionality of your machine — was designed to those specifications by an ODM [original design manufacturer] in Taiwan. We put our engineers in their facilities and they come to Austin and we actually codesign these systems. This global teamwork brings an added benefit — a globally distributed virtually twenty-four-hour-per-day development cycle. Our partners do the basic electronics and we help them design customer and reliability features that we know our customers want. We know the customers better than our suppliers and our competition, because we are dealing directly with them every day." Dell notebooks are completely redesigned roughly every twelve months, but new features are constantly added during the year — through the supply chain — as the hardware and software components advance.

It happened that when my notebook order hit the Dell factory in Penang, one part was not available — the wireless card — due to a quality control issue, so the assembly of the notebook was delayed for a few days. Then the truck full of good wireless cards arrived. On April 13, at 10:15 a.m., a Dell Malaysia worker pulled the order slip that automatically popped up once all my parts had arrived from the SLCs to the Penang factory. Another Dell Malaysia employee then took out a "traveler" — a special carrying tote designed to hold and protect parts — and started plucking all the parts that went into my notebook.

Where did those parts come from? Dell uses multiple suppliers for most of the thirty key components that go into its notebooks. That way if one supplier breaks down or cannot meet a surge in demand, Dell is not left in the lurch. So here are the key suppliers for my Inspiron 600m notebook: The Intel microprocessor came from an Intel factory either in the Philippines, Costa Rica, Malaysia, or China. The memory came from a Korean-owned factory in Korea (Samsung), a Taiwanese-owned factory in Taiwan (Nanya), a German-owned factory in Germany (Infineon), or a Japanese-owned factory in Japan (Elpida). My graphics card was shipped from either a Taiwanese-owned factory in China (MSI) or a Chinese-run factory in China (Foxconn). The cooling fan came from a Taiwanese-owned factory in Taiwan (CCI or Auras). The motherboard came from either a Korean-owned factory in Shanghai (Samsung), a Taiwanese-owned factory in Shanghai (Quanta), or a Taiwanese-owned factory in Taiwan (Compal or Wistron). The keyboard came from either a Japanese-owned company in Tianjin, China (Alps), a Taiwanese-owned factory in Shenzen, China (Sunrex), or a Taiwanese-owned factory in Suzhou, China (Darfon). The LCD display was made in either South Korea (Samsung or LG.Philips LCD), Japan (Toshiba or Sharp), or Taiwan (Chi Mei Optoelectronics, Hannstar Display, or AU Optronics). The wireless card came from either an American-owned factory in China (Agere) or Malaysia (Arrow), or a Taiwanese-owned factory in Taiwan (Askey or Gemtek) or China (USI). The modem was made by either a Taiwanese-owned company in China (Asustek or Liteon) or a Chinese-run company in China (Foxconn). The battery came from an American-owned factory in Malaysia (Motorola), a Japanese-owned factory in Mexico or Malaysia or China (Sanyo), or a South Korean or Taiwanese factory in either of those two countries (SDI or Simplo). The hard disk drive was made by an American-owned factory in Singapore (Seagate), a Japanese-owned company in Thailand (Hitachi or Fujitsu), or a Japanese-owned factory in the Philippines (Toshiba). The CD/DVD drive came from a South Korean–owned company with factories in Indonesia and the Philippines (Samsung); a Japanese-owned factory in China or Malaysia (NEC); a Japanese-owned factory in Indonesia, China, or Malaysia (Teac); or a Japanese-owned factory in China (Sony). The notebook carrying bag was made by either an Irish-owned company in China (Tenba) or an American-owned company in China (Targus, Samsonite, or Pacific Design). The power adapter was made by either a Thai-owned factory in Thailand (Delta) or a Taiwanese, Korean, or American-owned factory in China (Liteon, Samsung, or Mobility). The power cord was made by a British-owned company with factories in China, Malaysia, and India (Volex). The removable memory stick was made by either an Israeli-owned company in Israel (M-System) or an American-owned company with a factory in Malaysia (Smart Modular).

This supply chain symphony — from my order over the phone to production to delivery to my house — is one of the wonders of the flat world.

"We have to do a lot of collaborating," said Hunter. "Michael [Dell] personally knows the CEOs of these companies, and we are constantly working with them on process improvements and real-time demand/supply balancing." Demand shaping goes on constantly, said Hunter. What is "demand shaping"? It works like this: At 10 a.m. Austin time, Dell discovers that so many customers have ordered notebooks with 40-gigabyte hard drives since the morning that its supply chain will run short in two hours. That signal is automatically relayed to Dell's marketing department and to Dell.com and to all the Dell phone operators taking orders. If you happen to call to place your Dell order at 10:30 a.m., the Dell representative will say to you, "Tom, it's your lucky day! For the next hour we are offering 60-gigabyte hard drives with the notebook you want — for only $10 more than the 40-gig drive. And if you act now, Dell will throw in a carrying case along with your purchase, because we so value you as a customer." In an hour or two, using such promotions, Dell can re-shape the demand for any part of any notebook or desktop to correspond with the projected supply in its global supply chain. Today memory might be on sale, tomorrow it might be CD-ROMs.

Picking up the story of my notebook, on April 13, at 11:29 a.m., all the parts had been plucked from the just-in-time inventory bins in Penang, and the computer was assembled there by A. Sathini, a team member "who manually screwed together all of the parts from kitting as well as the labels needed for Tom's system," said Dell in their production report to me. "The system was then sent down the conveyor to go to burn, where Tom's specified software was downloaded." Dell has huge server banks stocked with the latest in Microsoft, Norton Utilities, and other popular software applications, which are downloaded into each new computer according to the specific tastes of the customer.

"By 2:45 p.m., Tom's software had been successfully downloaded, and [was] manually moved to the boxing line. By 4:05 p.m., Tom's system [was] placed in protective foam and a shuttle box, with a label, which contains his order number, tracking code, system type, and shipping code. By 6:04 p.m., Tom's system had been loaded on a pallet with a specified manifest, which gives the Merge facility visibility to when the system will arrive, what pallet it will be on (out of 75+ pallets with 152 systems per pallet), and to what address Tom's system will ship. By 6:26 p.m., Tom's system left [the Dell factory] to head to the Penang, Malaysia, airport."

Six days a week Dell charters a China Airlines 747 out of Taiwan and flies it from Penang to Nashville via Taipei. Each 747 leaves with twenty-five thousand Dell notebooks that weigh altogether 110,000 kilograms, or 50,000 pounds. It is the only 747 that ever lands in Nashville, except Air Force One, when the president visits. "By April 15, 2004, at 7:41 a.m., Tom's system arrived at [Nashville] with other Dell systems from Penang and Limerick. By 11:58 a.m., Tom's system [was] inserted into a larger box, which went down the boxing line to the specific external parts that Tom had ordered."

That was thirteen days after I'd ordered it. Had there not been a parts delay in Malaysia when my order first arrived, the time between when I phoned in my purchase, when the notebook was assembled in Penang, and its arrival in Nashville would have been only four days. Hunter said the total supply chain for my computer, including suppliers of suppliers, involved about four hundred companies in North America, Europe, and primarily Asia, but with thirty key players. Somehow, though, it all came together. As Dell reported: On April 15, 2004, at 12:59 p.m., "Tom's system had been shipped from [Nashville] and was tenured by UPS shipping LTL (3-5-day ground, specified by Tom), with UPS tracking number 1Z13WA374253514697. By April 19, 2004, at 6:41 p.m., Tom's system arrived in Bethesda, MD, and was signed for."

I am telling you the story of my notebook to tell a larger story of geopolitics in the flat world. To all the forces mentioned in the previous chapter that are still holding back the flattening of the world, or could actually reverse the process, one has to add a more traditional threat, and that is an outbreak of a good, old-fashioned, world-shaking, economy-destroying war. It could be China deciding once and for all to eliminate Taiwan as an independent state; or North Korea, out of fear or insanity, using one of its nuclear weapons against South Korea or Japan; or Israel and a soon-to-be-nuclear Iran going at each other; or India and Pakistan finally nuking it out. These and other classic geopolitical conflicts could erupt at any time and either slow the flattening of the world or seriously unflatten it.

The real subject of this chapter is how these classic geopolitical threats might be moderated or influenced by the new forms of collaboration fostered and demanded by the flat world — particularly supply-chaining. The flattening of the world is too young for us to draw any definitive conclusions. What is certain, though, is that as the world flattens, one of the most interesting dramas to watch in international relations will be the interplay between the traditional global threats and the newly emergent global supply chains. The interaction between old-time threats (like China *versus*

Taiwan) and just-in-time supply chains (like China *plus* Taiwan) will be a rich source of study for the field of international relations in the early twenty-first century.

In *The Lexus and the Olive Tree* I argued that to the extent that countries tied their economies and futures to global integration and trade, it would act as a restraint on going to war with their neighbors. I first started thinking about this in the late 1990s, when, during my travels, I noticed that no two countries that both had McDonald's had ever fought a war against each other since each got its McDonald's. (Border skirmishes and civil wars don't count, because McDonald's usually served both sides.) After confirming this with McDonald's, I offered what I called the Golden Arches Theory of Conflict Prevention. The Golden Arches Theory stipulated that when a country reached the level of economic development where it had a middle class big enough to support a network of McDonald's, it became a McDonald's country. And people in McDonald's countries didn't like to fight wars anymore. They preferred to wait in line for burgers. While this was offered slightly tongue in cheek, the serious point I was trying to make was that as countries got woven into the fabric of global trade and rising living standards, which having a network of Mc-

Donald's franchises had come to symbolize, the cost of war for victor and vanquished became prohibitively high.

This McDonald's theory has held up pretty well, but now that almost every country has acquired a McDonald's, except the worst rogues like North Korea, Iran, and Iraq under Saddam Hussein, it seemed to me that this theory needed updating for the flat world. In that spirit, and again with tongue slightly in cheek, I offer the Dell Theory of Conflict Prevention, the essence of which is that the advent and spread of just-in-time global supply chains in the flat world are an even greater restraint on geopolitical adventurism than the more general rising standard of living that McDonald's symbolized.

The Dell Theory stipulates: No two countries that are both part of a major global supply chain, like Dell's, will ever fight a war against each other as long as they are both part of the same global supply chain. Because people embedded in major global supply chains don't want to fight old-time wars anymore. They want to make just-in-time deliveries of goods and services — and enjoy the rising standards of living that come with that. One of the people with the best feel for the logic behind this theory is Michael Dell, the founder and chairman of Dell.

"These countries understand the risk premium that they have," said Dell of the countries in his Asian supply chain. "They are pretty careful to protect the equity that they have built up or tell us why we should not worry [about their doing anything adventurous]. My belief after visiting China is that the change that has occurred there is in the best interest of the world and China. Once people get a taste for whatever you want to call it — economic independence, a better lifestyle, and a better life for their child or children — they grab on to that and don't want to give it up."

Any sort of war or prolonged political upheaval in East Asia or China "would have a massive chilling effect on the investment there and on all the progress that has been made there," said Dell, who added that he believes the governments in that part of the world understand this very clearly. "We certainly make clear to them that stability is important to us. [Right now] it is not a day-to-day worry for us . . . I believe that as time and progress go on there, the chance for a really disruptive event goes down exponentially. I don't think our industry gets enough credit for the good we are doing in these areas. If you are making money and being productive and raising your standard of living, you're not sitting around thinking, Who did this to us? or Why is our life so bad?"

There is a lot of truth to this. Countries whose workers and industries are woven into a major global supply chain know that they cannot take an hour, a week, or a month off for war without disrupting industries and economies around the world and thereby risking the loss of their place in that supply chain for a long time, which could be extremely costly. For a country with no natural resources, being part of a global supply chain is like striking oil — oil that never runs out. And therefore, getting dropped from such a chain because you start a war is like having your oil wells go dry or having someone pour cement down them. They will not come back anytime soon.

"You are going to pay for it really dearly," said Glenn E. Neland, senior vice president for worldwide procurement at Dell, when I asked him what would happen to a major supply-chain member in Asia that decided to start fighting with its neighbor and disrupt the supply chain. "It will not only bring you to your knees [today], but you will pay for a long time — because you just won't have any credibility if you demonstrate you are going to go [off] the political deep end. And China is just now starting to develop a level of credibility in the business community that it is creating a business environment you can prosper in — with transparent and consistent rules." Neland said that suppliers regularly ask him whether he is worried about China and Taiwan, which have threatened to go to war at several points in the past half century, but his standard response is that he cannot imagine them "doing anything more than flexing muscles with each other." Neland said he can tell in his conversations and dealings with companies and governments in the Dell supply chain, particularly the Chinese, that "they recognize the opportunity and are really hungry to participate in the same things they have seen other countries in Asia do. They know there is a big economic pot at the end of the rainbow and they are really after it. We will spend about $35 billion producing parts this year, and 30 percent of that is [in] China."

If you follow the evolution of supply chains, added Neland, you see the prosperity and stability they promoted first in Japan, and then in Korea and Taiwan, and now in Malaysia, Singapore, the Philippines, Thailand, and Indonesia. Once countries get embedded in these global supply chains, "they feel part of something much bigger than their own businesses," he said. Osamu Watanabe, the CEO of the Japan External Trade Organization

(JETRO), was explaining to me one afternoon in Tokyo how Japanese companies were moving vast amounts of low- and middle-range technical work and manufacturing to China, doing the basic fabrication there, and then bringing it back to Japan for final assembly. Japan was doing this despite a bitter legacy of mistrust between the two countries, which was intensified by the Japanese invasion of China in the last century. Historically, he noted, a strong Japan and a strong China have had a hard time coexisting. But not today, at least not for the moment. Why not? I asked. The reason you can have a strong Japan and a strong China at the same time, he said, "is because of the supply chain." It is a win-win for both.

Obviously, since Iraq, Syria, south Lebanon, North Korea, Pakistan, Afghanistan, and Iran are not part of any major global supply chains, all of them remain hot spots that could explode at any time and slow or reverse the flattening of the world. As my own notebook story attests, the most important test case of the Dell Theory of Conflict Prevention is the situation between China and Taiwan — since both are deeply embedded in several of the world's most important computer, consumer electronics, and, increasingly, software supply chains. The vast majority of computer components for every major company comes from coastal China, Taiwan, and East Asia. In addition, Taiwan alone has more than $100 billion in investments in mainland China today, and Taiwanese experts run many of the cutting-edge Chinese high-tech manufacturing companies.

It is no wonder that Craig Addison, the former editor of *Electronic Business Asia* magazine, wrote an essay for the *International Herald Tribune* (September 29, 2000), headlined "A 'Silicon Shield' Protects Taiwan from China." He argued that "Silicon-based products, such as computers and networking systems, form the basis of the digital economies in the United States, Japan and other developed nations. In the past decade, Taiwan has become the third-largest information technology hardware producer after the United States and Japan. Military aggression by China against Taiwan would cut off a large portion of the world's supply of these products . . . Such a development would wipe trillions of dollars off the market value of technology companies listed in the United States, Japan and Europe." Even if China's leaders, like former president Jiang Zemin, who was once minister of electronics, lose sight of how integrated China and Taiwan are in the world's computer supply chain, they need only ask their kids for an update.

Jiang Zemin's son, Jiang Mianheng, wrote Addison, "is a partner in a wafer fabrication project in Shanghai with Winston Wang of Taiwan's Grace T.H.W. Group." And it is not just Taiwanese. Hundreds of big American tech companies now have R & D operations in China; a war that disrupted them could lead not only to the companies moving their plants elsewhere but also to a significant loss of R & D investment in China, which the Beijing government has been betting on to advance its development. Such a war could also, depending on how it started, trigger a widespread American boycott of Chinese goods — if China were to snuff out the Taiwanese democracy — which would lead to serious economic turmoil inside China.

The Dell Theory had its first real test in December 2004, when Taiwan held parliamentary elections. President Chen Shuibian's pro-independence Democratic Progressive Party was expected to win the legislative runoff over the main opposition Nationalist Party, which favored closer ties with Beijing. Chen framed the election as a popular referendum on his proposal to write a new constitution that would formally enshrine Taiwan's independence, ending the purposely ambiguous status quo. Had Chen won and moved ahead on his agenda to make Taiwan its own motherland, as opposed to maintaining the status quo fiction that it is a province of the mainland, it could have led to a Chinese military assault on Taiwan. Everyone in the region was holding his or her breath. And what happened? *Motherboards won over motherland.* A majority of Taiwanese voted against the pro-independence governing party legislative candidates, ensuring that the DPP would not have a majority in parliament. I believe the message Taiwanese voters were sending was not that they never want Taiwan to be independent. It was that they do not want to upset the status quo right now, which has been so beneficial to so many Taiwanese. The voters seemed to understand clearly how interwoven they had become with the mainland, and they wisely opted to maintain their de facto independence rather than force de jure independence, which might have triggered a Chinese invasion and a very uncertain future.

Warning: What I said when I put forth the McDonald's theory, I would repeat even more strenuously with the Dell Theory: It does not make wars obsolete. And it does not guarantee that governments will not engage in wars of choice, even governments that are part of major supply chains. To suggest so would be naïve. It guarantees only that governments whose countries are enmeshed in global supply chains will have to think three times, not just twice, about engaging in anything but a war of self-defense. And if they choose to go to war anyway, the price they will pay will be ten times higher than it was a decade ago and probably ten times higher than whatever the leaders of that country think. It is one thing to lose your McDonald's. It's quite another to fight a war that costs you your place in a twenty-first-century supply chain that may not come back around for a long time.

While the biggest test case of the Dell Theory is China versus Taiwan, the fact is that the Dell Theory has already proved itself to some degree in the case of India and Pakistan, the context in which I first started to think about it. I happened to be in India in 2002, when its just-in-time services supply chains ran into some very old-time geopolitics — and the supply chain won. In the case of India and Pakistan, the Dell Theory was working on only one party — India — but it still had a major impact. India is to the world's knowledge and service supply chain what China and Taiwan are to the manufacturing ones. By now readers of this book know all the highlights: General Electric's biggest research center outside the United States is in

Bangalore, with seventeen hundred Indian engineers, designers, and scientists. The brain chips for many brand-name cell phones are designed in Bangalore. Renting a car from Avis online? It's managed in Bangalore. Tracing your lost luggage on Delta or British Airways is done from Bangalore, and the backroom accounting and computer maintenance for scores of global firms are done from Bangalore, Mumbai, Chennai, and other major Indian cities.

Here's what happened: On May 31, 2002, State Department spokesman Richard Boucher issued a travel advisory saying, "We urge American citizens currently in India to depart the country," because the prospect of a nuclear exchange with Pakistan was becoming very real. Both nations were massing troops on their borders, intelligence reports were suggesting that they both might be dusting off their nuclear warheads, and CNN was flashing images of people flooding out of India. The global American firms that had moved their back rooms and R & D operations to Bangalore were deeply unnerved.

"I was actually surfing on the Web, and I saw a travel advisory come up on India on a Friday evening," said Vivek Paul, president of Wipro, which manages backroom operations from India of many American multinationals. "As soon as I saw that, I said, 'Oh my gosh, every customer that we have is going to have a million questions on this.' It was the Friday before a long weekend, so over the weekend we at Wipro developed a fail-safe business continuity plan for all of our customers." While Wipro's customers were pleased to see how on top of things the company was, many of them were nevertheless rattled. This was not in the plan when they decided to outsource mission-critical research and operations to India. Said Paul, "I had a CIO from one of our big American clients send me an e-mail saying, 'I am now spending a lot of time looking for alternative sources to India. I don't think you want me doing that, and I don't want to be doing it.' I immediately forwarded his message to the Indian ambassador in Washington and told him to get it to the right person." Paul would not tell me what company it was, but I have confirmed through diplomatic sources that it was United Technologies. And plenty of others, like American Express and General Electric, with back rooms in Bangalore, had to have been equally worried.

For many global companies, "the main heart of their business is now supported here," said N. Krishnakumar, president of MindTree, another leading Indian knowledge outsourcing firm based in Bangalore. "It can cause chaos if there is a disruption." While not trying to meddle in foreign affairs, he added, "What we explained to our government, through the Confederation of Indian Industry, is that providing a stable, predictable operating environment is now the key to India's development." This was a real education for India's elderly leaders in New Delhi, who had not fully absorbed how critical India had become to the world's knowledge supply chain. When you are managing vital backroom operations for American Express or General Electric or Avis, or are responsible for tracing all the lost luggage on British Airways or Delta, you cannot take a month, a week, or even a day off for war without causing major disruptions for those companies. Once those companies have made a commitment to outsource business operations or research to India, they expect it to stay there. That is a major commitment. And if geopolitics causes a serious disruption, they will leave, and they will not come back very easily. When you lose this kind of service trade, you can lose it for good.

"What ends up happening in the flat world you described," explained Paul, "is that you have only one opportunity to make it right if something [goes] wrong.

Because the disadvantage of being in a flat world is that despite all the nice engagements and stuff and the exit barriers that you have, every customer has multiple options, and so the sense of responsibility you have is not just out of a desire to do good by your customers, but also a desire for self-preservation."

The Indian government got the message. Was India's central place in the world's services supply chain the only factor in getting Prime Minister Vajpayee to tone down his rhetoric and step back from the brink? Of course not. There were other factors, to be sure — most notably the deterrent effect of Pakistan's own nuclear arsenal. But clearly, India's role in global services was an important additional source of restraint on its behavior, and it was taken into account by New Delhi. "I think it sobered a lot of people," said Jerry Rao, who, as noted earlier, heads the Indian high-tech trade association. "We engaged very seriously, and we tried to make the point that this was very bad for Indian business. It was very bad for the Indian economy . . . [Many people] didn't realize till then how suddenly we had become integrated into the rest of the world. We are now partners in a twenty-four by seven by three-sixty-five supply chain."

Vivek Kulkarni, then information technology secretary for Bangalore's regional government, told me back in 2002, "We don't get involved in politics, but we did bring to the government's attention the problems the Indian IT industry might face if there were a war." And this was an altogether new factor for New Delhi to take into consideration. "Ten years ago, [a lobby of IT ministers from different Indian states] never existed," said Kulkarni. Now it is one of the most important business lobbies in India and a coalition that no Indian government can ignore.

"With all due respect, the McDonald's [shutting] down doesn't hurt anything," said Vivek Paul, "but if Wipro had to shut down we would affect the day-to-day operations of many, many companies." No one would answer the phones in call centers. Many e-commerce sites that are supported from Bangalore would shut down. Many major companies that rely on India to maintain their key computer applications or handle their human resources departments or billings would seize up. And these companies did not want to find alternatives, said Paul. Switching is very difficult, because taking over mission-critical day-to-day backroom operations of a global company takes a great deal of training and experience. It's not like opening a fast-food restaurant. That was why, said Paul,

Wipro's clients were telling him, " 'I have made an investment in you. I need you to be very responsible with the trust I have reposed in you.' And I think that created an enormous amount of back pressure on us that said we have to act in a responsible fashion . . . All of a sudden it became even clearer that there's more to gain by economic gains than by geopolitical gains. [We had more to gain from building] a vibrant, richer middle class able to create an export industry than we possibly could by having an ego-satisfying war with Pakistan." The Indian government also looked around and realized that the vast majority of India's billion people were saying, "I want a better future, not more territory." Over and over again, when I asked young Indians working at call centers how they felt about Kashmir or a war with Pakistan, they waved me off with the same answer: "We have better things to do." And they do. America needs to keep this in mind as it weighs its overall approach to outsourcing. I would never advocate shipping some American's job overseas just so it will keep Indians and Pakistanis at peace with each other. But I would say that to the extent that this process happens, driven by its own internal economic logic, it will have a net positive geopolitical effect. It will absolutely make the world safer for American kids.

Each of the Indian business leaders I interviewed noted that in the event of some outrageous act of terrorism or aggression from Pakistan, India would do whatever it takes to defend itself, and they would be the first to support that — the Dell Theory be damned. Sometimes war is unavoidable. It is imposed on you by the reckless behavior of others, and you have to just pay the price. But the more India and, one hopes, soon Pakistan get enmeshed in global service supply chains, the greater disincentive they have to fight anything but a border skirmish or a war of words.

The example of the 2002 India-Pakistan nuclear crisis at least gives us some hope. That cease-fire was brought to us not by General Powell but by General Electric.

We bring good things to life.

Infosys Versus al-Qaeda

Unfortunately, even GE can do only so much. Because, alas, a new source for geopolitical instability has emerged only in recent years, for which even the updated Dell Theory can provide no restraint. It is the emergence of mutant global supply chains — that is, nonstate actors, be they criminals or terrorists, who learn to use all the elements of the flat world to advance a highly destabilizing, even nihilistic agenda. I first started thinking about this when Nandan Nilekani, the Infosys CEO, was giving me that tour I referred to in Chapter 1 of his company's global videoconferencing center at its Bangalore headquarters. As Nandan explained to me how Infosys could get its global supply chain together at once for a virtual conference in that room, a thought popped into my head: Who else uses open-sourcing and supply-chaining so imaginatively? The answer, of course, is al-Qaeda.

Al-Qaeda has learned to use many of the same instruments for global collaboration that Infosys uses, but instead of producing products and profits with them, it has produced mayhem and murder. This is a particularly difficult problem. In fact, it may be the most vexing geopolitical problem for flat-world countries that want to focus on the future. The flat world — unfortunately — is a friend of both Infosys and al-Qaeda. The Dell Theory will not work at all against these informal Islamo-Leninist terror networks, because they are not a state with a population that will hold its leaders accountable or with a domestic business lobby that might restrain them. These mutant global supply chains are formed for the purpose of destruction, not profit. They don't need investors, only recruits, donors, and victims. Yet these mobile, self-financing mutant supply chains use all the tools of collaboration offered by the flat world — open-sourcing to raise money, to recruit followers, and to stimulate and disseminate ideas; outsourcing to train recruits; and supply-chaining to distribute the tools and the suicide bombers to undertake operations. The U.S. Central Command has a name for this whole underground network: the Virtual Caliphate. And its leaders and innovators understand the flat world almost as well as Wal-Mart, Dell, and Infosys do.

In the previous chapter, I tried to explain that you cannot understand the rise of al-Qaeda emotionally and politically without reference to the flattening of the world. What I am arguing here is that you cannot understand the rise of al-Qaeda technically without reference to the flattening of the world, either. Globalization in general has been al-Qaeda's friend in that it has helped to solidify a revival of Muslim identity and solidarity, with Muslims in one country much better able to see and sympathize with the struggles of their brethren in another country — thanks to the Internet and satellite television. At the same time, as pointed out in the previous chapter, this flattening process has intensified the feelings of humiliation in some quarters of the Muslim world over the fact that civilizations to which the Muslim world once felt superior — Hindus, Jews, Christians, Chinese — are now all doing better than many Muslim countries, and everyone can see it. The flattening of the world has also led to more urbanization and large-scale immigration to the West of many of these young, unemployed, frustrated Arab-Muslim males, while simultaneously making it much easier for informal open-source networks of these young men to form, operate, and interconnect. This certainly has been a boon for underground extremist Muslim political groups. There has been a proliferation of these informal mutual supply chains throughout the Arab-Muslim world today — small networks of people who move money through *hawalas* (hand-to-hand financing networks), who recruit through alternative education systems like the madrassas, and who communicate through the Internet and other tools of the global information revolution. Think about it: A century ago, anarchists were limited in their ability to communicate and collaborate with one another, to find sympathizers, and to band together for an operation. Today, with the Internet, that is not a problem. Today even the Unabomber could find friends to join a consortium where his "strengths" could be magnified and reinforced by others who had just as warped a worldview as he did.

What we have witnessed in Iraq is an even more perverse mutation of this mutant supply chain — the suicide supply chain. Since the start of the U.S. invasion in March 2002, more than two hundred suicide bombers have been recruited from within Iraq and from across the Muslim world, brought to the Iraqi front by some underground railroad, connected with the bomb makers there, and then dispatched against U.S. and Iraqi targets according to whatever suits the daily tactical needs of the insurgent Islamist forces in Iraq. I can understand, but not accept, the notion that more than thirty-seven years of Israeli occupation of the West Bank might have driven some Palestinians into a suicidal rage. But the American occupation of Iraq was only a few months old before it started to get hit by this suicide supply chain. How do you recruit so many young men "off the shelf" who are ready to commit suicide in the cause of jihad, many of them apparently not even Iraqis? And they don't even identify themselves by name or want to get credit — at least in this world. The fact is that Western intelligence agencies have no clue how this underground suicide supply chain, which seems to have an infinite pool of recruits to draw on, works, and yet it has basically stymied the U.S. armed forces in Iraq. From what we do know, though, this Virtual Caliphate works just like the supply chains I described earlier. Just as you take an item off the shelf in a discount store in Birmingham and another one is immediately made in Beijing, so the retailers of suicide deploy a human bomber in Baghdad and another one is immediately recruited and indoctrinated in Beirut. To the extent that this tactic spreads, it will require a major rethinking of U.S. military doctrine.

The flat world has also been such a huge boon for al-Qaeda and its ilk because of the way it enables the small to act big, and the way it enables small acts — the killing of just a few people — to have big effects. The horrific video of the beheading of *Wall Street Journal* reporter Danny Pearl by Islamist militants in Pakistan was transmitted by the Internet all over the world. There is not a journalist anywhere who saw or even just read about that who was not terrified. But those same beheading videos are also used as tools of recruitment. The flat world makes it much easier for terrorists to transmit their terror. With the Internet they don't even have to go through Western or Arab news organizations but can broadcast right into your computer. It takes much less dynamite to transmit so much more anxiety. Just as the

U.S. Army had embedded journalists, so the suicide supply chain has embedded terrorists, in their own way, to tell us their side of the story. How many times have I gotten up in the morning, fired up the Internet, and been confronted by the video image of some masked gunman threatening to behead an American — all brought to me courtesy of AOL's home page? The Internet is an enormously useful tool for the dissemination of propaganda, conspiracy theories, and plain old untruths, because it combines a huge reach with a patina of technology that makes anything on the Internet somehow more believable. How many times have you heard someone say, "But I read it on the Internet," as if that should end the argument? In fact, the Internet can make things worse. It often leads to more people being exposed to crazy conspiracy theories.

"The new system of diffusion — the Internet — is more likely to transmit irrationality than rationality," said political theorist Yaron Ezrahi, who specializes in the interaction between media and politics. "Because irrationality is more emotionally loaded, it requires less knowledge, it explains more to more people, it goes down easier." That is why conspiracy theories are so rife in the Arab-Muslim world today — and unfortunately are becoming so in many quarters of the Western world, for that matter. Conspiracy theories are like a drug that goes right into your bloodstream, enabling you to see "the Light." And the Internet is the needle. Young people used to have to take LSD to escape. Now they just go online. Now you don't shoot up, you download. You download the precise point of view that speaks to all your own biases. And the flat world makes it all so much easier.

Gabriel Weimann, a professor of communication at Haifa University, Israel, did an incisive study of terrorists' use of the Internet and of what I call the flat world, which was published in March 2004 by the United States Institute of Peace and excerpted on YaleGlobal Online on April 26, 2004. He made the following points:

> While the danger that cyber-terrorism poses to the Internet is frequently debated, surprisingly little is known about the threat posed by terrorists' use of the Internet. A recent six-year-long study shows that terrorist organizations and their supporters have been using all of the tools that the Internet offers to recruit supporters, raise funds, and launch a worldwide campaign of fear. It is also clear that to combat terrorism effectively, mere suppression of their Internet tools is

not enough. Our scan of the Internet in 2003–04 revealed the existence of hundreds of websites serving terrorists in different, albeit sometimes overlapping, ways . . . There are countless examples of how [terrorists] use this uncensored medium to spread disinformation, to deliver threats intended to instill fear and helplessness, and to disseminate horrific images of recent actions. Since September 11, 2001, al-Qaeda has festooned its websites with a string of announcements of an impending "large attack" on US targets. These warnings have received considerable media coverage, which has helped to generate a widespread sense of dread and insecurity among audiences throughout the world and especially within the United States . . .

The Internet has significantly expanded the opportunities for terrorists to secure publicity. Until the advent of the Internet, terrorists' hopes of winning publicity for their causes and activities depended on attracting the attention of television, radio, or the print media. The fact that terrorists themselves have direct control over the content of their websites offers further opportunities to shape how they are perceived by different target audiences and to manipulate their image and the images of their enemies. Most terrorist sites do not celebrate their violent activities. Instead —

regardless of their nature, motives, or location — most terrorist sites emphasize two issues: the restrictions placed on freedom of expression; and the plight of their comrades who are now political prisoners. These issues resonate powerfully with their own supporters and are also calculated to elicit sympathy from Western audiences that cherish freedom of expression and frown on measures to silence political opposition . . .

Terrorists have proven not only skillful at online marketing but also adept at mining the data offered by the billion-some pages of the World Wide Web. They can learn from the Internet about the schedules and locations of targets such as transportation facilities, nuclear power plants, public buildings, airports and ports, and even counterterrorism measures. According to Secretary of Defense Donald Rumsfeld, an al-Qaeda training manual recovered in Afghanistan tells its readers, "Using public sources openly and without resorting to illegal means, it is possible to gather at least 80 percent of all information required about the enemy." One captured al-Qaeda computer contained engineering and structural architecture features of a dam, which had been downloaded from the Internet and which would enable al-Qaeda engineers and planners to simulate catastrophic failures. In other captured computers, U.S. investigators found evidence that al-Qaeda operators spent time on sites that offer software and programming instructions for the digital switches that run power, water, transportation, and communications grids.

Like many other political organizations, terrorist groups use the Internet to raise funds. Al-Qaeda, for instance, has always depended heavily on donations, and its global fundraising network is built upon a foundation of charities, nongovernmental organizations, and other financial institutions that use websites and Internet-based chat rooms and forums. The fighters in the Russian breakaway republic of Chechnya have likewise used the Internet to publicize the numbers of bank accounts to which sympathizers can contribute. And in December 2001, the U.S. government seized the assets of a Texas-based charity because of its ties to Hamas.

In addition to soliciting financial aid online, terrorists recruit converts by using the full panoply of website technologies (audio, digital video, etc.) to enhance the presentation of their message. And like commercial sites that track visitors to develop consumer profiles, terrorist organizations capture information about the users who browse their websites. Visitors who seem most interested in the organization's cause or well suited to carrying out its work are then contacted. Recruiters may also use more interactive Internet technology to roam online chat rooms and cyber cafes, looking for receptive members of the public, particularly young people. The SITE Institute, a Washington, D.C.–based terrorism research group that monitors al-Qaeda's Internet communications, has provided chilling details of a high-tech recruitment drive launched in 2003 to recruit fighters to travel to Iraq and attack U.S. and coalition forces there. The Internet also grants terrorists a cheap and efficient means of networking. Many terrorist groups, among them Hamas and al-Qaeda, have undergone a transformation from strictly hierarchical organizations with designated leaders to affiliations of semi-independent cells that have no single commanding hierarchy. Through the Internet, these loosely interconnected groups are able to maintain contact with one another — and with members of other terrorist groups. The Internet connects not only members of the same terrorist organizations but also members of different groups. For instance, dozens of sites supporting terrorism in the name of jihad permit terrorists in places as far-removed from one another as Chechnya and

Malaysia to exchange ideas and practical information about how to build bombs, establish terror cells, and carry out attacks . . . Al-Qaeda operatives relied heavily on the Internet in planning and coordinating the September 11 attacks.

For all of these reasons we are just at the beginning of understanding the geopolitical impact of the flattening of the world. On the one hand, failed states and failed regions are places we have every incentive to avoid today. They offer no economic opportunity and there is no Soviet Union out there competing with us for influence over such countries. On the other hand, there may be nothing more dangerous today than a failed state with broadband capability. That is, even failed states tend to have telecommunications systems and satellite links, and therefore if a terrorist group infiltrates a failed state, as al-Qaeda did with Afghanistan, it can amplify its power enormously. As much as big powers want to stay away from such states, they may feel compelled to get even more deeply embroiled in them. Think of America in Afghanistan and Iraq, Russia in Chechnya, Australia in East Timor.

In the flat world it is much more difficult to hide, but much easier to get connected. "Think of Mao at the beginning of the

Chinese communist revolution," remarked Michael Mandelbaum, the Johns Hopkins foreign policy specialist. "The Chinese Communists had to hide in caves in northwest China, but they could move around in whatever territory they were able to control. Bin Laden, by contrast, can't show his face, but he can reach every household in the world, thanks to the Internet." Bin Laden cannot capture any territory but he can capture the imagination of millions of people. And he has, broadcasting right into American living rooms on the eve of the 2004 presidential election.

Hell hath no fury like a terrorist with a satellite dish and an interactive Web site.

Too Personally Insecure

In the fall of 2004, I was invited to speak at a synagogue in Woodstock, New York, home of the famous Woodstock music festival. I asked my hosts how was it that they were able to get a synagogue in Woodstock, of all places, big enough to support a lecture series. Very simple, they said. Since 9/11, Jews, and others, have been moving from New York City to places like Woodstock, to get away from what they fear will be the next ground zero. Right now this trend is a trickle, but it would become a torrent if a nuclear device were detonated in any European or American city.

Since this threat is the mother of all unflatteners, this book would not be complete without a discussion of it. We can live with a lot. We lived through 9/11. But we cannot live with nuclear terrorism. That would unflatten the world permanently.

The only reason that Osama bin Laden did not use a nuclear device on 9/11 was not that he did not have the intention but that he did not have the capability. And since the Dell Theory offers no hope of restraining the suicide supply chains, the only strategy we have is to limit their worst capabilities. That means a much more serious global effort to stanch nuclear proliferation by limiting the supply — to buy up the fissile material that is already out there, particularly in the former Soviet Union, and prevent more states from going nuclear. Harvard University international affairs expert Graham Allison, in his book *Nuclear Terrorism: The Ultimate Preventable Catastrophe*, outlines just such a strategy for denying terrorists access to nuclear weapons and nuclear materials. It can be done, he insists. It is a challenge to our will and convictions, but *not to our capabilities*. Allison proposes a new American-led international security order to deal with this problem based on what he calls "a doctrine of the Three No's: No loose nukes, No new nascent nukes, and No new nuclear states." No loose nukes, says Allison, means locking down all nuclear weapons and all nuclear material from which bombs could be made — in a much more serious way than we have done up till now. "We don't lose gold from Fort Knox," says Allison. "Russia doesn't lose treasures from the Kremlin armory. So we both know how to prevent theft of those things that are super valuable to us if we are determined to do it." No new nascent nukes means recognizing that there is a group of actors out there who can and do produce highly enriched uranium or plutonium, which is nothing more than nuclear bombs just about to hatch. We need a much more credible, multilateral nonproliferation regime that soaks up this fissile material. Finally, no new nuclear states means "drawing a line under the current eight nuclear powers and determining that, however unfair and unreasonable it may be, that club will have no more members than those eight," says Allison, adding that these three steps might then buy us time to develop a more formal, sustainable, internationally approved regime.

It would be nice also to be able to deny the Internet to al-Qaeda and its ilk, but that, alas, is impossible — without undermining ourselves. That is why limiting their capabilities is necessary but not sufficient. We also have to find a way to get at their worst intentions. If we are not going to shut down the Internet and all the other creative and collaborative tools that have flattened the world, and if we can't restrict access to them, the only thing we can do is try to influence the imagination and intentions that people bring to them and draw from them. When I raised this issue, and the broad themes of this book, with my religious teacher, Rabbi Tzvi Marx from Holland, he surprised me by saying that the flat world I was describing reminded him of the story of the Tower of Babel.

How so? I asked. "The reason God banished all the people from the Tower of Babel and made them all speak different languages was not because he did not want them to collaborate per se," answered Rabbi Marx. "It was because he was enraged at what they were collaborating on — an effort to build a tower to the heavens so they could become God." This was a distortion of the human capacity, so God broke their union and their ability to communicate with one another. Now, all these years later, humankind has again created a new platform for more people from more places to communicate and collaborate with less friction and more ease than ever:

the Internet. Would God see the Internet as heresy?

"Absolutely not," said Marx. "The heresy is not that mankind works together — it is to what ends. It is essential that we use this new ability to communicate and collaborate for the right ends — for constructive human aims and not megalomaniacal ends. Building a tower was megalomaniacal. Bin Laden's insistence that he has the truth and can flatten anyone else's tower who doesn't heed him is megalomaniacal. Collaborating so mankind can achieve its full potential is God's hope."

How we promote more of that kind of collaboration is what the final chapter is all about.

CONCLUSION: IMAGINATION

THIRTEEN

11/9 Versus 9/11

Imagination is more important than knowledge.
> — Albert Einstein

On the Internet, nobody knows you're a dog.
> — Two dogs talking to each other, in a *New Yorker* cartoon by Peter Steiner, July 5, 1993

Reflecting on this past decade and a half, during which the world went flat, it strikes me that our lives have been powerfully shaped by two dates: 11/9 and 9/11. These two dates represent the two competing forms of imagination at work in the world today: the creative imagination of 11/9 and the destructive imagination of 9/11. One brought down a wall and opened the windows of the world — both the operating system and the kind we look through. It unlocked half the planet and made the citizens there our potential partners and competitors. Another brought down the World

Trade Center, closing its Windows on the World restaurant forever and putting up new invisible and concrete walls among people at a time when we thought 11/9 had erased them for good.

The dismantling of the Berlin Wall on 11/9 was brought about by people who dared to imagine a different, more open world — one where every human being would be free to realize his or her full potential — and who then summoned the courage to act on that imagination. Do you remember how it happened? It was so simple, really: In July 1989, hundreds of East Germans sought refuge at the West German embassy in Hungary. In September 1989, Hungary decided to remove its border restrictions with Austria. That meant that any East German who got into Hungary could pass through to Austria and the free world. Sure enough, more than thirteen thousand East Germans escaped through Hungary's back door. Pressure built up on the East German government. When in November it announced plans to ease travel restrictions, tens of thousands of East Germans converged on the Berlin Wall, where, on 11/9/89, border guards just opened the gates.

Someone there in Hungary, maybe it was the prime minister, maybe it was just a bureaucrat, must have said to himself or herself, "Imagine — imagine what might happen if we opened the border with Austria." Imagine if the Soviet Union were frozen in place. Imagine — imagine if East German citizens, young and old, men and women, were so emboldened by seeing their neighbors flee to the West that one day they just swarmed that Berlin Wall and started to tear it down? Some people must have had a conversation just like that, and because they did, millions of Eastern Europeans were able to walk out from behind the Iron Curtain and engage with a flattening world. It was a great era in which to be an American. We were the only superpower, and the world was our oyster. There were no walls. Young Americans could think about traveling, for a semester or a summer, to more countries than any American generation before them. Indeed, they could travel as far as their imagination and wallets could take them. They could also look around at their classmates and see people from more different countries and cultures than any other class before them.

Nine-eleven, of course, changed all that. It showed us the power of a very different kind of imagination. It showed us the power of a group of hateful men who spent several years imagining how to kill as many innocent people as they could. At some point bin Laden and his gang literally must have looked at one another and said, "Imagine if we actually could hit both towers of the World Trade Center at the exact right spot, between the ninety-fourth and ninety-eighth floors. And imagine if each tower were to come crashing down like a house of cards." Yes, I am sorry to say, some people had that conversation, too. And, as a result, the world that was our oyster seemed to close up like a shell.

There has never been a time in history when the character of human imagination wasn't important, but writing this book tells me that it has never been *more* important than now, because in a flat world so many of the inputs and tools of collaboration are becoming commodities available to everyone. They are all out there for anyone to grasp. There is one thing, though, that has not and can never be commoditized — and that is imagination.

When we lived in a more centralized, and more vertically organized, world — where states had a near total monopoly of power — individual imagination was a big problem when the leader of a superpower state — a Stalin, a Mao, or a Hitler — became warped. But today, when individuals can easily access all the tools of collaboration and superempower themselves, or their small cells, individuals do not need to control a country to threaten large numbers of other people. The small can act very big today and pose a serious danger to world order — without the instruments of a state.

Therefore, thinking about how we stimulate positive imaginations is of the utmost importance. As Irving Wladawsky-Berger, the IBM computer scientist, put it to me: We need to think more seriously than ever about how we encourage people to focus on productive outcomes that advance and unite civilization — peaceful imaginations that seek to "minimize alienation and celebrate interdependence rather than self-sufficiency, inclusion rather than exclusion," openness, opportunity, and hope rather than limits, suspicion, and grievance.

Let me try to illustrate this by example. In early 1999, two men started airlines from scratch, just a few weeks apart. Both men had a dream involving airplanes and the savvy to do something about it. One was named David Neeleman. In February 1999, he started JetBlue. He assembled $130 million in venture capital, bought a fleet of Airbus A-320 passenger jets, recruited pilots and signed them to seven-year contracts, and outsourced his reservation system to stay-at-home moms and retirees living around Salt Lake City, Utah, who booked passengers on their home computers.

The other person who started an airline was, as we now know from the 9/11 Commission Report, Osama bin Laden. At a meeting in Kandahar, Afghanistan, in March or April 1999, he accepted a proposal initially drawn up by Khalid Sheikh Mohammed, the Pakistan-born mechanical engineer who was the architect of the 9/11 plot. JetBlue's motto was "Same Altitude. Different Attitude." Al-Qaeda's motto was "Allahu Akbar," God is great. Both airlines were designed to fly into New York City — Neeleman's into JFK and bin Laden's into lower Manhattan.

Maybe it was because I read the 9/11 report while on a trip to Silicon Valley that I could not help but notice how much Khalid Sheikh Mohammed spoke and presented himself as just another eager engineer-entrepreneur, with his degree from North Carolina Agricultural and Technical State University, pitching his ideas to Osama bin Laden, who comes off as just another wealthy venture capitalist. But Mohammed, alas, was looking for *adventure capital*. As the 9/11 Commission Report put it, "No one exemplifies the model of the terrorist entrepreneur more clearly than Khalid Sheikh Mohammed (KSM), the principal architect of the 9/11 attacks . . . Highly educated and equally comfortable in a government office or a terrorist safe house, KSM applied his imagination, technical aptitude and managerial skills to hatching and planning an extraordinary array of terrorist schemes. These ideas included conventional car bombing, political assassination, aircraft bombing, hijacking, reservoir poisoning, and, ultimately, the use of aircraft as missiles guided by suicide operatives . . . KSM presents himself as an entrepreneur seeking venture capital and people . . . Bin Laden summoned KSM to Kandahar in March or April 1999 to tell him that al-Qaeda would support his proposal. The plot was now referred to within al-Qaeda as the 'planes operation.' "

From his corporate headquarters in Afghanistan, bin Laden proved to be a very deft supply chain manager. He assembled a virtual company just for this project — exactly like any global conglomerate would do in the flat world — finding just the right specialist for each task. He outsourced the overall design and blueprint for 9/11 to KSM and overall financial management to KSM's nephew, Ali Abdul Aziz Ali, who coordinated the dispersal of funds to the hijackers through wire transfers, cash, traveler's checks, and credit and debit cards from overseas bank accounts. Bin Laden recruited from the al-Qaeda roster just the right muscle guys from Asir Province, in Saudi Arabia, just the right pilots from Europe, just the right team leader from Hamburg, and just the right support staff from Pakistan. He outsourced the pilot training to flight schools in America. Bin Laden, who knew he needed only to "lease" the Boeing 757s, 767s, A320s, and possibly 747s for his operation, raised the necessary capital for training pilots on all these different aircraft from a syndicate of pro-al-Qaeda Islamic charities and other Muslim adventure capitalists ready to fund anti-American operations. In the case of 9/11, the total budget was around $400,000. Once the team was assembled, bin Laden focused on his own core competency — overall leadership and ideological inspiration of his suicide supply chain, with assistance from his deputies Mohammed Atef and Ayman Zawahiri.

You can get the full flavor of the bin Laden supply chain, and what an aggressive adopter of new technology al-Qaeda was, by reading just one entry from the December 2001 U.S. District Court for the Eastern District of Virginia's official indictment of Zacarias Moussaoui, the so-called nineteenth hijacker from 9/11. It reported the following: "In or about June 1999, in an interview with an Arabic-language television station, Osama bin Laden issued a . . . threat indicating that all American males should be killed." It then points out that throughout the year 2000, all of the hijackers, including Moussaoui, began either attending or inquiring about flight school courses in America: "On or about September 29, 2000, Zacarias Moussaoui contacted Airman Flight School in Norman, Oklahoma, using an e-mail account he set up on September 6 with an Internet service provider in Malaysia. In or about October 2000, Zacarias Moussaoui received letters from Infocus Tech, a Malaysian company, stating that Moussaoui was appointed Infocus Tech's marketing consultant in the United States, the United Kingdom and Europe, and that he would receive, among other things, an allowance of $2,500 per month . . . On or about December 11, 2000, Mohammed Atta purchased flight deck videos for the Boeing 767 Model 300ER and the Airbus A320 Model 200 from the Ohio Pilot Store . . . In or about June 2001, in Norman, Oklahoma, Zacarias Moussaoui made inquiries about starting a cropdusting company . . . On or about August 16, 2001, Zacarias Moussaoui, possessed, among other things: two knives; a pair of binoculars; flight manuals for the Boeing 747 Model 400; a flight simulator computer program; fighting gloves and shin guards; a piece of paper referring to a handheld Global Positioning System receiver and a camcorder; software that could be used to review pilot procedures for the Boeing 747 Model 400; letters indicating that Moussaoui is a marketing consultant in the United States for Infocus Tech; a computer disk containing information related to the aerial application of pesticides; and a hand-held aviation radio."

A devout Mormon, who grew up in Latin America where his father was a UPI correspondent, David Neeleman, by contrast, is one of those classic American entrepreneurs and a man of enormous integrity. He never went to college, but he has started two successful airlines, Morris Air and JetBlue, and played an important role in shaping a third, Southwest. He is the godfather of ticketless air travel, now known as e-ticketing. "I am a total optimist. I think my father is an optimist," he said to me, trying to explain where his innovative genes came from. "I grew up in a very happy home . . . JetBlue was created in my own mind before it was created on paper." Using his optimistic imagination and his ability also to quickly adopt all the latest technology because he had no legacy system to worry about, Neeleman started a highly profitable airline, creating jobs, low-cost travel, a unique onboard, satellite-supported entertainment system, and one of the most people-friendly places to work you can imagine. He also started a catastrophe relief fund in his company to help employee families who are faced with a sudden death or catastrophic illness of a loved one. Neeleman donates $1 of his salary for every $1 any employee puts in the fund. "I think it is important that people give a little," said Neeleman. "I believe that there are irrevocable laws of heaven that when you serve others you get this little buzz." In 2003, Neeleman, already a wealthy man from his JetBlue stock, donated about $120,000 of his $200,000 salary to the JetBlue employee catastrophe fund.

In the waiting room outside his New York City office, there is a color photo of a JetBlue Airbus flying over the World Trade Center. Neeleman was in his office on 9/11 and watched the Twin Towers burn, while his own JetBlue airliners were circling JFK in a holding pattern. When I explained to him the comparison/contrast I was going to make between him and bin Laden, he was both uncomfortable and curious. As I closed up my computer and prepared to leave following our interview, he said he had one question for me: "Do you think Osama actually believes there is a God up there who is happy with what he is doing?"

I told him I just didn't know. What I do know is this: There are two ways to flatten the world. One is to use your imagination to bring everyone up to the same level, and the other is to use your imagination to bring everyone down to the same level. David Neeleman used his optimistic imagination and the easily available technologies of the flat world to lift people up. He launched a surprising and successful new airline, some profits of which he turns over to a catastrophe relief fund for his employees. Osama bin Laden and his disciples used their twisted imagination, and many of the same tools, to launch a surprise attack, which brought two enormous symbols of American power down to their level. Worse, they raised their money and created this massive human catastrophe under the guise of religion.

"From the primordial swamps of globalization have emerged two genetic variants," observed Infosys CEO Nandan Nilekani — one is al-Qaeda and the other are companies like Infosys or JetBlue. "Our focus therefore has to be how we can encourage more of the good mutations and keep out the bad."

I could not agree more. Indeed, that effort may be the most important thing we learn to do in order to keep this planet in one piece.

I have no doubt that advances in technology — from iris scans to X-ray machines

— will help us to identify, expose, and capture those who are trying to use the easily available tools of the flat world to destroy it. But in the end, technology alone cannot keep us safe. We really do have to find ways to affect the imagination of those who would use the tools of collaboration to destroy the world that has invented those tools. But how does one go about nurturing a more hopeful, life-affirming, and tolerant imagination in others? Everyone has to ask himself or herself this question. I ask it as an American. I stress this last point because I think it starts first and foremost by America setting an example. Those of us who are fortunate to live in free and progressive societies have to set an example. We have to be the best global citizens we can be. We cannot retreat from the world. We have to make sure that we get the best of our own imaginations — and never let our imaginations get the best of us.

It is always hard to know when we have crossed the line between justified safety measures and letting our imaginations get the best of us and thereby paralyzing ourselves with precautions. I argued right after 9/11 that the reason our intelligence did not pick up the 9/11 plotters was "a failure of imagination." We just did not have enough people within our intelligence community with a sick enough imagination to match that of bin Laden and Khalid Sheikh Mohammed. We do need some people like that within our intelligence services. But we *all* don't need to go down that route. We all don't need to become so gripped by imagining the worst in everyone around us that we shrink into ourselves.

In 2003, my older daughter, Orly, was in her high school's symphonic orchestra. They spent all year practicing to take part in the national high school orchestra competition in New Orleans that March. When March rolled around, it appeared that we were heading for war in Iraq, so the Montgomery County School Board canceled all out-of-town trips by school groups — including the orchestra's attendance at New Orleans — fearing an outbreak of terrorism. I thought this was absolutely nuts. Even the evil imagination of 9/11 has its limits. At some point you do have to ask yourself whether Osama bin Laden and Ayman al-Zawahiri were really sitting around a cave in Afghanistan, with Ayman saying to Osama, "Say, Osama, d'you remember that annual high school orchestra competition in New Orleans? Well, it's coming up again next week. Let's really make a splash and go after it."

No, I don't think so. Let's leave the cave dwelling to bin Laden. We have to be the masters of our imaginations, not the prisoners. I had a friend in Beirut who used to joke that every time she flew on an airplane she packed a bomb in her suitcase, because the odds of two people carrying a bomb on the same plane were so much higher. Do whatever it takes, but get out the door.

Apropos of that, let me share the 9/11 story that touched me most from the *New York Times* series "Portraits of Grief," the little biographies of those who were killed. It was the story of Candace Lee Williams, the twenty-year-old business student at Northeastern University, who had worked from January to June of 2001 as a work-study intern at the Merrill Lynch office on the fourteenth floor of 1 World Trade Center. Both Candace's mother and colleagues described her to *The New York Times* as a young woman full of energy and ambition, who loved her internship. Indeed, Candace's colleagues at Merrill Lynch liked her so much they took her to dinner on her last day of work, sent her home in a limousine, and later wrote Northeastern to say, "Send us five more like Candace." A few weeks after finishing midterm exams — she was on a June–December academic schedule — Candace Lee Williams decided to meet her roommate at her home in California. Candace had recently made the dean's list. "They'd rented a convertible preparing for the occasion, and Candace wanted her picture taken with that Hollywood sign," her mother, Sherri, told the *Times*.

Unfortunately, Candace took the American Airlines Flight 11 that departed from Boston's Logan Airport on the morning of September 11, 2001, at 8:02 a.m. The plane was hijacked at 8:14 a.m. by five men, including Mohammed Atta, who was in seat 8D. With Atta at the controls, the Boeing 767-223ER was diverted to Manhattan and slammed Candace Lee Williams right back into the very same World Trade Center tower — between floors 94 and 98 — where she had worked as an intern.

Airline records show that she was seated next to an eighty-year-old grandmother — two people at opposites ends of life: one full of memories, one full of dreams.

What does this story say to me? It says this: When Candace Lee Williams boarded Flight 11 she could not have imagined how it would end. But in the wake of 9/11, none of us can now board an airplane *without* imagining how it could end — that what happened to Candace Lee Williams could also happen to us. We all are now so much more conscious that a person's life can be wiped out by the arbitrary will of a madman in a cave in Afghanistan. But the fact is, the chances of our plane being hi-

jacked by terrorists today are still infinites-
imal. We are more likely to be killed
hitting a deer with our car or being struck
by lightning. So even though we *can* now
imagine what could happen when we get
on an airplane, we have to get on the plane
anyway. Because the alternative to not getting on that plane is putting ourselves in
our own cave. Imagination can't just be
about reruns. It also has to be about
writing our own new script. From what I
read about Candace Lee Williams, she was
an optimist. I'd bet anything she'd still be
getting on planes today if she had the
chance. And so must we all.

America's role in the world, from its inception, has been to be the country that
looks forward, not back. One of the most
dangerous things that has happened to
America since 9/11, under the Bush administration, is that we have gone from exporting hope to exporting fear. We have
gone from trying to coax the best out of
the world to snarling at it way too often.
And when you export fear, you end up importing everyone else's fears. Yes, we need
people who can imagine the worst, because
the worst did happen on 9/11 and it could
happen again. But, as I said, there is a fine
line between precaution and paranoia, and
at times we have crossed it. Europeans and
others often love to make fun of American

optimism and naïveté — our crazy notion that every problem has a solution, that tomorrow can be better than yesterday, that the future can always bury the past. But I have always believed that deep down the rest of the world envies that American optimism and naïveté, it needs it. It is one of the things that help keep the world spinning on its axis. If we go dark as a society, if we stop being the world's "dream factory," we will make the world not only a darker place but also a poorer place.

Analysts have always tended to measure a society by classical economic and social statistics: its deficit-to-GDP ratio, or its unemployment rate, or the rate of literacy among its adult women. Such statistics are important and revealing. But there is another statistic, much harder to measure, that I think is even more important and revealing: Does your society have more memories than dreams or more dreams than memories?

By dreams I mean the positive, life-affirming variety. The business organization consultant Michael Hammer once remarked, "One thing that tells me a company is in trouble is when they tell me how good they were in the past. Same with countries. You don't want to forget your identity. I am glad you were great in the fourteenth century, but that was then and this is now. When memories exceed dreams, the end is near. The hallmark of a truly successful organization is the willingness to abandon what made it successful and start fresh."

In societies that have more memories than dreams, too many people are spending too many days looking backward. They see dignity, affirmation, and self-worth not by mining the present but by chewing on the past. And even that is usually not a real past but an imagined and adorned past. Indeed, such societies focus all their imagination on making that imagined past even more beautiful than it ever was, and then they cling to it like a rosary or a strand of worry beads, rather than imagining a better future and acting on that. It is dangerous enough when other countries go down that route; it would be disastrous for America to lose its bearings and move in that direction. I think my friend David Rothkopf, the former Commerce Department official and now a fellow at the Carnegie Endowment for International Peace, said it best: "The answer for us lies not in what has changed, but in recognizing what has not changed. Because only through this recognition will we begin to focus on the truly critical issues — an effective multilateral response to weapons of mass destruction proliferation, the creation of real stakeholders in globalization among the world's poor, the need for reform in the Arab world and a style of U.S. leadership that seeks to build our base of support worldwide by getting more people to voluntarily sign onto our values. We need to remember that those values are the real foundation for our security and the real source of our strength. And we need to recognize that our enemies can never defeat us. Only we can defeat ourselves, by throwing out the rule book that has worked for us for a long, long time."

I believe that history will make very clear that President Bush shamelessly exploited the emotions around 9/11 for political purposes. He used those 9/11 emotions to take a far-right Republican domestic agenda on taxes, the environment, and social issues from 9/10 — an agenda for which he had no popular mandate — and drive it into a 9/12 world. In doing so, Mr. Bush not only drove a wedge between Americans, and between Americans and the world, he drove a wedge between America and its own history and identity. His administration transformed the United States into "the United States of Fighting Terrorism." This is the real reason, in my view, that so many people in the world dislike President Bush so intensely. They feel that he has taken away something very dear to them — an America that exports hope, not fear.

We need our president to restore September 11 to its rightful place on the calendar — as the day after September 10 and before September 12. We must never let it become a day that defines us. Because ultimately September 11 is about *them* — the bad guys — not about us.

We're about the Fourth of July. We're about 11/9.

Beyond trying to retain the best of our own imaginations, what else can we do as Americans and as a global society to try to nurture the same in others? One has to approach this question with great humility. What leads one person to the joy of destruction and what leads another to the joy of creation, what leads one to imagine 11/9 and another to imagine 9/11, is surely one of the great mysteries of contemporary life. Moreover, while most of us might have some clue about how to nurture a more positive imagination for our own kids, and maybe — maybe — for our fellow citizens, it is presumptuous to think that we can do it for others, particularly those of a different culture, speaking different languages, and living half a world away. Yet 9/11, the flattening of the world, and the continuing threat of world-disrupting terrorism suggest that not thinking about this is its own kind of dangerous naïveté. So I insist on trying to do so, but I approach this issue with a keen awareness of the limits of what any outsider can know or do.

Generally speaking, imagination is the product of two shaping forces. One is the narratives that people are nurtured on — the stories and myths they and their religious and national leaders tell themselves — and how those narratives feed their imaginations one way or another. The other is the context in which people grow up, which has a huge impact on shaping how they see the world and others. Outsiders cannot get inside and adjust the Mexican or Arab or Chinese narrative any more than they can get inside the American one. Only they can reinterpret their narrative, make it more tolerant or forward looking, and adapt it to modernity. No one can do that for them or even with them. But one can think about how to collaborate with others to change their context — the context within which people grow up and live their daily lives — to help nurture more people with the imagination of 11/9 than 9/11.

Let me offer a few examples.

eBay

Meg Whitman, the CEO of eBay, once told me a wonderful story that went like this:

"We took eBay public in September 1998, in the middle of the dot-com boom. And in September and October our stock would go up eighty points and down fifty in a single day. I thought, 'This is insane.' Anyway, one day I am minding my own business, sitting in my own cubicle, and my secretary runs over and says to me, 'Meg, it's Arthur Levitt [chairman] of the SEC on the phone.' " The Securities and Exchange Commission oversees the stock market and is always concerned about issues of volatility in a stock and whether there is manipulation behind it. In those days, for a CEO to hear that "Arthur Levitt is on the line" was not a good way to start the day.

"So I called my general counsel," said Whitman, "who came over from his cubicle, and he was white like a sheet. We called Levitt back together and we put him on the speakerphone, and I said, 'Hi, it's Meg Whitman of eBay.' And he said, 'Hi, it's Arthur Levitt of the SEC. I don't know you and have never met you but I know that you just went public and I want to know: How did it go? Were we [the SEC] customer-friendly?' And so we breathed a sigh of relief, and we talked about that a little bit. And then [Levitt] said, 'Well, actually, another reason that I am calling is that I just got my tenth positive feedback on eBay and have earned my yellow star.

And I am so proud.' And then he said, 'I am actually a collector of Depression-era glass, post-1929, and so I have bought and sold on eBay and you get feedback as a buyer and seller. And I thought you would just like to know.' "

Every eBay user has a feedback profile made up of comments from other eBay users who have done transactions with him or her, relating to whether the goods bought or sold were as expected and the transaction went off smoothly. This constitutes your official "eBay reputation." You get +1 point for each positive comment, 0 points for each neutral comment, and –1 for each negative comment. A colored star icon is attached to your user ID on eBay for ten or more feedback points. My user ID on eBay might be TOMF (50) and a blue star, which means that I have received positive feedback comments from fifty other eBay users. Next to that is a box that will tell you whether the seller has had 100 percent positive feedback comments or less, and also give you the chance to click and read all the buyers' comments about that seller.

The point, said Whitman, is that "I think every human being, Arthur Levitt or the janitor or the waitress or the doctor or the professor, needs and craves validation and positive feedback." And the big misconception is to think that it has to be money. "It can be really small things," said Whitman, "telling someone, 'You did a really great job, you were recognized as doing a great history paper.' Our users say to us [about eBay's star system], 'Where else can you wake up in the morning and see how much people like you?' "

But what is so striking, said Whitman, is that the overwhelming majority of feedback on eBay is positive. That's interesting. People don't usually write Wal-Mart managers to compliment them on a fabulous purchase. But when you are part of a community that you feel ownership in, it is different. You have a stake. "The highest number of feedback we have is well over 250,000 positive comments, and you can see each one," said Whitman. "You can see the entire history of each buyer and seller, and we have introduced the ability to rebut . . . You cannot be anonymous on eBay. If you are not willing to say who you are, you should not be saying it. And it became the norm of the community really fast . . . We are not running an exchange — we are running a community." Indeed, with 105 million registered users from 190 countries trading more than $35 billion in products annually, eBay is actually a self-governing nation-state — the V.R.e., the Virtual Republic of eBay.

And how is it governed? EBay's philosophy, said Whitman, is, "Let's make a small number of rules, really enforce them, and then create an environment in which people can fulfill their own potential. There is something going on here besides buying and selling goods." Even allowing for corporate boosterism, Whitman's essential message is really worth contemplating: "People will say that 'eBay restored my faith in humanity' — contrary to the world where people are cheating and don't give people the benefit of the doubt. I hear that twice a week . . . EBay offers the little guy, who's disenfranchised, an opportunity to compete on a totally level playing field. We have a disproportionate share of wheelchairs and disabled and minorities, [because] on eBay people don't know who you are. You are only as good as your product and feedback."

Whitman recalled that one day she got an e-mail from a couple in Orlando who were coming to an "eBay Live" event at which she was speaking. These are big revival meeting–conventions of eBay sellers. They asked if they could come backstage to meet Whitman after her speech. "So after the keynote," she recalled, "they come back to my green room, and in comes mom and dad and a seventeen-year-old boy in a wheelchair — very disabled with cerebral palsy. They tell me, 'Kyle is very disabled and can't go to school, [but] he built an eBay business and last year my husband and I quit our jobs, and now we help him — we have made more money on eBay than we ever made on our jobs.' And then they added the most incredible thing. They said, 'On eBay, Kyle is not disabled.' "

Whitman told me that at another eBay Live event a young man came up to her, a big power seller on eBay, and said that thanks to his eBay business he had been able to buy a house and a car, hire people, and be his own boss. But the best part, said Whitman, was that the young man added, "I am so excited about eBay, because I did not graduate from college and was sort of disowned by my family, and I am now the hit of my family. I am a successful entrepreneur."

"It's this blend of economic opportunity and validation" that makes eBay tick, concluded Whitman. Those validated become transparent as good partners, because bad validation is an option for the whole community.

Bottom line: eBay didn't just create an online market. It created a self-governing community — *a context* — where anyone, from the severely handicapped to the head of the SEC, could come and achieve his or her potential and be validated as a good and trustworthy person by the whole community. That kind of self-esteem and validation is the best, most effective way of producing dehumiliation and redignification. To the extent that America can collaborate with regions like the Arab-Muslim world to produce contexts where young people can succeed, can achieve their full potential on a level playing field, can get validation and respect from achievements in this world — and not from martyrdom to get into the next world — we can help foster more young people with more dreams than memories.

India

If you want to see this same process at work in a less virtual community, study the second largest Muslim country in the world. The largest Muslim country in the world is Indonesia and the second largest is not Saudi Arabia, Iran, Egypt, or Pakistan. It is India. With some 150 million Muslims, India has more Muslims than Pakistan. But here is an interesting statistic from 9/11: There are no Indian Muslims that we know of in al-Qaeda and there are no Indian Muslims in America's Guantánamo Bay post-9/11 prison camp. And no Indian Muslims have been found fighting alongside the jihadists in Iraq. Why is that? Why do we not read about Indian Muslims, who are a minority in a vast Hindu-dominated land, blaming America for all their problems and wanting to fly airplanes into the Taj Mahal or the British embassy? Lord knows, Indian Muslims have their grievances about access to capital and political representation. And interreligious violence has occasionally flared up in India, with disastrous consequences. I am certain that out of 150 million Muslims in India, a few will one day find their way to al-Qaeda — if it can happen with some American Muslims, it can happen with Indian Muslims. But this is not the norm. Why?

The answer is context — and in particular the secular, free-market, democratic context of India, heavily influenced by a tradition of non-violence and Hindu tolerance. M. J. Akbar, the Muslim editor of the *Asian Age*, a national Indian English-language daily primarily funded by non-Muslim Indians, put it to me this way: "I'll give you a quiz question: Which is the only large Muslim community to enjoy sustained democracy for the last fifty years? The Muslims of India. I am not going to exaggerate Muslim good fortune in India. There are tensions, economic discrimination, and provocations, like the destruction of the mosque at Ayodhya [by Hindu nationalists in 1992]. But the fact is, the Indian Constitution is secular and provides a real opportunity for economic advancement of any community that can offer talent. That's why a growing Muslim middle class here is moving up and generally doesn't manifest the strands of deep anger you find in many nondemocratic Muslim states."

Where Islam is embedded in authoritarian societies, it tends to become the vehicle of angry protest — Egypt, Syria, Saudi Arabia, Pakistan. But where Islam is embedded in a pluralistic democratic society — Turkey or India, for instance — those with a more progressive outlook have a chance to get a better hearing for their interpretation and a democratic forum where they can fight for their ideas on a more equal footing. On November 15, 2003, the two main synagogues of Istanbul were hit by some fringe suicide bombers. I happened to be in Istanbul a few months later, when they were reopened. Several things struck me. To begin with, the chief rabbi appeared at the ceremony, hand in hand with the top Muslim cleric of Istanbul and the local mayor, while crowds in the street threw red carnations on them both. Second, the prime minister of Turkey, Recep Tayyip Erdogan, who comes from an Islamic party, paid a visit to the chief rabbi in his office — the first time a Turkish prime minister had ever called on the chief rabbi. Lastly, the father of one of the suicide bombers told the Turkish newspaper *Zaman,* "We cannot understand why this child had done the thing he had done . . . First let us meet with the chief rabbi of our Jewish brothers. Let me hug him. Let me kiss his hands and flowing robe. Let me apologize in the name of my son and offer my condolences for the deaths . . . We will be damned if we do not reconcile with them."

Different context, different narrative, different imagination.

I am keenly aware of the imperfections of Indian democracy, starting with the oppressive caste system. Nevertheless, to have sustained a functioning democracy with all its flaws for more than fifty years in a country of over 1 billion people, who speak scores of different languages, is something of a miracle and a great source of stability for the world. Two of India's presidents have been Muslims, and its current president, A. P. J. Abdul Kalam, is both a Muslim and the father of the Indian nuclear missile program. While a Muslim woman sits on India's Supreme Court, no Muslim woman is allowed even to drive a car in Saudi Arabia. Indian Muslims, including women, have been governors of many Indian states, and the wealthiest man in India today, high on the *Forbes* list of global billionaires, is an Indian Muslim:

Azim Premji, the chairman of Wipro, one of India's most important technology companies. I was in India shortly after the United States invaded Afghanistan in late 2001, when Indian television carried a debate between the country's leading female movie star and parliamentarian — Shabana Azmi, a Muslim woman — and the imam of New Delhi's biggest mosque. The imam had called on Indian Muslims to go to Afghanistan and join the jihad against America, and Azmi ripped into him, live on Indian TV, basically telling the cleric to go take a hike. She told *him* to go to Kandahar and join the Taliban and leave the rest of India's Muslims alone. How did she get away with that? Easy. As a Muslim woman she lived in a context that empowered and protected her to speak her mind — even to a leading cleric.

Different context, different narrative, different imagination.

This is not all that complicated: Give young people a context where they can translate a positive imagination into reality, give them a context in which someone with a grievance can have it adjudicated in a court of law without having to bribe the judge with a goat, give them a context in which they can pursue an entrepreneurial idea and become the richest or the most creative or most respected people in their own country, no matter what their background, give them a context in which any complaint or idea can be published in the newspaper, give them a context in which anyone can run for office — and guess what? They usually don't want to blow up the world. They usually want to be part of it.

A South Asian Muslim friend of mine once told me this story: His Indian Muslim family split in 1948, with half going to Pakistan and half staying in Mumbai. When he got older, he asked his father one day why the Indian half of the family seemed to be doing better than the Pakistani half. His father said to him, "Son, when a Muslim grows up in India and he sees a man living in a big mansion high on a hill, he says, 'Father, one day, I will be that man.' And when a Muslim grows up in Pakistan and sees a man living in a big mansion high on a hill, he says, 'Father, one day I will kill that man.' " When you have a pathway to be the Man or the Woman, you tend to focus on the path and on achieving your dreams. When you have no pathway, you tend to focus on your wrath and on nursing your memories.

India only twenty years ago, before the triple convergence, was known as a country of snake charmers, poor people, and Mother Teresa. Today its image has been recalibrated. Now it is also seen as a country of brainy people and computer wizards. Atul Vashistha, CEO of the outsourcing consulting firm NeoIT, often appears in the American media to defend outsourcing. He told me this story: "One day I had a problem with my HP printer — the printing was very slow. I was trying to figure out the problem. So I call HP tech support. This guy answers and takes all my personal information down. From his voice it is clear he is somewhere in India. So I start asking where he is and how the weather is. We're having a nice chat. So after he is helping me for about ten or fifteen minutes he says, 'Sir, do you mind if I say something to you?' I said, 'Sure.' I figured he was going to tell me something else I was doing wrong with my computer and was trying to be polite about it. And instead he says, 'Sir, I was very proud to hear you on Voice of America. You did a good job . . .' I had just been on a VOA show about the backlash against globalization and outsourcing. I was one of three invited guests. There was a union official, an economist, and myself. I defended outsourcing and this guy heard it."

Remember: In the flat world you don't get just your humiliation dished out to you fiber-optically. *You also get your pride dished out to you fiber-optically.* An Indian help-line operator suddenly knows, in real time, all about how one of his compatriots is repre-senting India half a world away, and it makes him feel better about himself.

The French Revolution, the American Revolution, the Indian democracy, and even eBay are all based on social contracts whose dominant feature is that authority comes from the bottom up, and people can and do feel self-empowered to improve their lot. People living in such contexts tend to spend their time focusing on what to do next, not on whom to blame next.

The Curse of Oil

Nothing has contributed more to retarding the emergence of a democratic context in places like Venezuela, Nigeria, Saudi Arabia, and Iran than the curse of oil. As long as the monarchs and dictators who run these oil states can get rich by drilling their nat-ural resources — as opposed to drilling the natural talents and energy of their people — they can stay in office forever. They can use oil money to monopolize all the instruments of power — army, police, and intelligence — and never have to introduce real trans-parency or power sharing. All they have to do is capture and hold the oil tap. They never have to tax their people, so the rela-tionship between ruler and ruled is highly distorted. *Without taxation, there is no representation.* The rulers don't really have to pay attention to the people or explain how they are spending their money — because they have not raised that money through taxes. That is why countries focused on tapping their oil wells always have weak or nonexistent institutions. Countries focused on tapping their people have to focus on developing real institutions, property rights, rule of law, independent courts, modern education, foreign trade, foreign investment, freedom of thought, and scientific enquiry to get the most out of their men and women. In an essay in *Foreign Affairs* called "Saving Iraq from Its Oil" (July–August 2004), development economists Nancy Birdsall and Arvind Subramanian point out that "34 less-developed countries now boast significant oil and natural gas resources that constitute at least 30 percent of their total export revenue. Despite their riches, however, 12 of these countries' annual per capita income remains below $1,500 . . . Moreover, two-thirds of the 34 countries are not democratic, and of those that are, only three score in the top half of Freedom House's world rankings of political freedom."

In other words, imagination is also a product of necessity — when the context you are living in simply does not allow you to indulge in certain escapist or radical fantasies, you don't. Look where the most creative innovation is happening in the Arab-Muslim world today. It is in the places with little or no oil. As I noted earlier, Bahrain was one of the first Arab Gulf states to discover oil and was *the* first Arab Gulf state to run out of oil. And today it is the first Arab Gulf state to develop comprehensive labor reform for developing the skills of its own workers, the first to sign a free-trade agreement with the United States, and the first to hold a free and fair election, in which women could both run and vote. And which countries in that same region are paralyzed or actually rolling back reforms? Saudi Arabia and Iran, which are awash in oil money. On December 9, 2004, at a time when crude oil prices had soared to near $50 a barrel, *The Economist* did a special report from Iran, in which it noted, "Without oil at its present sky-high price, Iran's economy would be in wretched straits. Oil provides about half the government's revenue and at least 80% of export earnings. But, once again under the influence of zealots in parliament, the oil cash is being spent on boosting wasteful subsidies rather than on much-needed development and new technology."

It is worthy of note that Jordan began upgrading its education system and privatizing, modernizing, and deregulating its economy starting in 1989 — precisely when oil prices were way down and it could no longer rely on handouts from the Gulf oil states. In 1999, when Jordan signed its free-trade agreement with the United States, its exports to America totaled $13 million. In 2004, Jordan exported over $1 billion of goods to America — things Jordanians made with their hands. The Jordanian government has also installed computers and broadband Internet in every school. Most important, in 2004, Jordan announced a reform of its education requirements for mosque prayer leaders. Traditionally, high school students in Jordan took an exam for college entrance, and those who did the best became doctors and engineers. Those who did the worst became mosque preachers. In 2004, Jordan decided to gradually phase in a new system. Henceforth, to become a mosque prayer leader, a young man will first have to get a B.A. in some other subject, and can study Islamic law only as a graduate degree — in order to encourage more young men of talent to go into the clergy and weed out those who were just "failing" into it. That is an important change in context that should pay dividends over time in the narratives that young Jordanians are nurtured upon in their mosques. "We had to go through a crisis to accept the need for reform," said Jordan's minister of planning, Bassem Awadallah.

There is no mother of invention like necessity, and only when falling oil prices force the leaders in the Middle East to change their contexts will they reform. People don't change when you tell them they should. They change when they tell themselves they must. Or as Johns Hopkins foreign affairs professor Michael Mandelbaum puts it, "People don't change when you tell them there is a better option. They change when they conclude that they have no other option." Give me $10-a-barrel oil, and I will give you political and economic reform from Moscow to Riyadh to Iran. If America and its allies will not collaborate in bringing down the price of crude oil, their aspirations for reform in all these areas will be stillborn.

There is another factor to consider here. When you have to make things with your hands and then trade with others in order to flourish, not just dig an oil well in your own backyard, it inevitably broadens imagination and increases tolerance and trust. It is no accident that Muslim countries make up 20 percent of the world's population but account for only 4 percent of world trade. When countries don't make things anyone else wants, they trade less, and less trade means less exchange of ideas and openness to the world. The most open, tolerant cities in the Muslim world today are its trading centers — Beirut, Istanbul, Jakarta, Dubai, Bahrain. The most open, tolerant cities in China are Hong Kong and Shanghai. The most closed cities in the world are in central Saudi Arabia, where no Christians, Hindus, Jews, or other non-Muslims are allowed to express their religions in public or build a house of worship, and, in the case of Mecca, even enter. Religions are the smelters and founders of imagination. The more any religion's imagination — Hindu, Christian, Jewish, Muslim, Buddhist — is shaped in an isolated bubble, or in a dark cave, the more its imagination is likely to sail off in dangerous directions. People who are connected to the world and exposed to different cultures and perspectives are far more likely to develop the imagination of 11/9. People who are feeling disconnected, for whom personal freedom and fulfillment are a utopian fantasy, are more likely to develop the imagination of 9/11.

Just One Good Example

Stanley Fischer, the former deputy managing director of the IMF, once remarked to me, "One good example is worth a thousand theories." I believe that is true. Indeed, people do not change only when they must: They also change when they see that others — *like themselves* — have changed and flourished. Or as Michael Mandelbaum also points out, "People change as a result of what they notice, not just what they are told" — especially when what they notice is someone just like them doing well. As I pointed out in Chapter 10, there is only one Arab company that developed a world-class business strong enough to get itself listed on the Nasdaq, and that was Aramex. Every Jordanian, every Arab, should know and take pride in the Aramex story, the way every American knows the Apple and Microsoft and Dell stories. It is the example that is worth a thousand theories. It should be the role model of a self-empowered Arab company, run by Arab brainpower and entrepreneurship, succeeding on the world stage and enriching its own workers at the same time.

When Fadi Ghandour took Aramex public again in 2005, this time in Dubai, some four hundred Aramex employees from all over the Arab world who had stock options divided $14 million. I will never forget Fadi telling me how proud these employees were — some of them managers, some of them just delivery drivers. This windfall was going to enable them to buy homes or send their kids to better schools. Imagine the dignity that these people feel when they come back to their families and neighborhoods and tell everyone that they are going to build a new house because the world-class *Arab* company they work for has gone public. Imagine how much dignity they feel when they see themselves getting ahead by succeeding in the flat world — not in the traditional Middle Eastern way by inheritance, by selling land, or by getting a government contract — but by working for a real company, an Arab company. Just as it is no accident that there are no Indian Muslims in al-Qaeda, it is no accident that the three thousand Arab employees of Aramex want to deliver only packages that help economies grow and Arab people flourish — not suicide bombs.

Speaking of the Aramex employees with stock options, Ghandour said, "They all feel like owners. A lot of them came up to me and said, 'Thank you, but I want to invest my options back in the company and be an investor in the new IPO.'"

Give me just one hundred more examples like Aramex, and I will start to give you a different context — and narrative.

From Untouchables to Untouchables

And while you are at it, give me one hundred Abraham Georges as well — individuals who step out of their context and set a different example can have such a huge impact on the imagination of so many others. One day in February 2004, I was resting in my hotel room in Bangalore, when the phone rang. It was a young Indian woman who said she was attending a private journalism school on the outskirts of the city and wanted to know if I would come by and meet with her class. I've learned over the years that these sorts of accidental invitations often lead to interesting encounters, so I said, "What the heck, sure. I'll come." Two days later I drove ninety minutes from downtown Bangalore to an open field in which stood a lonely journalism school and dormitory. I was met at the door by a handsome, middle-aged Indian man named Abraham George. Born in Kerala, George served in the Indian Army, while his mother immigrated to the United States and went to work for NASA. George followed her, went on to study at NYU, started a software firm that specialized in international finance, sold it in 1998, and decided to come back to India and use his American-made fortune to try to change India from the bottom — the absolute bottom — up.

One thing George learned from his time in the United States was that without more responsible Indian newspapers and journalists, the country could never improve its governance. So he started a journalism school. As we sat in his office sipping juice, it quickly became apparent to me, though, that as proud as he was of his little journalism school, he was even more proud of the elementary school he had started in a village outside Bangalore populated by India's lowest caste, the untouchables, who are not supposed even to get near Indians of a higher caste for fear that they will pollute the very air they breathe. George wanted to prove that if you gave these untouchable children access to the same technologies and solid education that have enabled other pockets of India to plug in and play with the flat world, they could do the same. The more he talked about the school, the more I wanted to see it and not talk journalism. So as soon as I finished speaking to his journalism students, we hopped into his jeep, along with his principal, Lalita Law, and set out on a two-hour drive to the Shanti Bhavan school, which, as I explained in Chapter 11, was located about ten miles and ten centuries from the outskirts of Bangalore. The word "wretched" does not even begin to describe the living conditions in the villages around the school.

When we eventually reached the school complex, though, we found neatly painted buildings, surrounded by some grass and flowers, a total contrast to the nearby hamlets. The first classroom we walked into had twenty untouchable kids at computers working on Excel and Microsoft Word. Next door, another class was practicing typing on a computer typing program. I loudly asked the teacher who was the fastest typist in the class. She pointed to an eight-year-old girl with a smile that could have melted a glacier.

"I want to race you," I said to her. All her classmates gathered round. I crunched myself into a tiny seat in the computer stall next to her, and we each proceeded to type the same phrase over and over, seeing who could do more in a minute. "Who's winning?" I shouted. Her classmates shouted her name back and cheered her on. I quickly surrendered to her gleeful laugh.

The selection process to get into Shanti Bhavan is based on whether a child is below the poverty line and the parents are willing to send him or her to a boarding school. Shortly before I arrived, the students had taken the California Achievement Tests. "We are giving them English education so they can go anywhere in India and anywhere in the world for higher education," said Law. "Our goal is to give them a world-class education so they can aspire to careers and professions that would have been totally beyond their reach and have been so for generations . . . Around here, their names will always give them away as untouchables. But if they go somewhere else, and if they are really polished, with proper education and social graces, they can break this barrier."

Then they can become *my* kind of untouchables — young people who one day can be special or specialized or adaptable.

Looking at these kids, George said, "When we talk about the poor, so often it is talk about getting them off the streets or getting them a job, so they don't starve. But we never talk about getting excellence for the poor. My thought was that we can deal with the issue of inequality, if they could break out of all the barriers imposed upon them. If one is successful, they will carry one thousand with them."

After listening to George, my mind drifted back to only four months earlier, in the fall of 2003, when I had been in the West Bank filming another documentary about the Arab-Israeli conflict. As a part of that project, I went to Ramallah and interviewed three young Palestinian militants who were members of Yasser Arafat's paramilitary Tanzim organization. What was so striking about the interview were the mood swings of these young men from suicidal despair to dreamy aspirations. When I asked one of the three, Mohammed Motev, what was the worst thing about living in the context of Israeli occupation, he said the checkpoints. "When a soldier asks me to take off my clothes in front of the girls. It's a great humiliation to me . . . to take off my shirt and my pants and turn around and all the girls are standing there." It is one reason, he said, that all Palestinian young people today are just suicide bombers in waiting. He called them "martyrs in waiting," while his two friends nodded in assent. They warned me that if Israel tried to kill Yasser Arafat, who was then still alive (and was a leader who knew how to stimulate only memories, not dreams), they would turn the whole area into a living "hell." To underscore this point, Motev took out his wallet and showed me a picture of Arafat. But what caught my eye was the picture of a young girl next to it.

"Who's that?" I asked. That was his girlfriend, he explained, slightly red-faced. So there was his wallet — Yasser Arafat on one page, whom he was ready to die for, and his girlfriend on the other, whom he wanted to live for. A few minutes later, one of his colleagues, Anas Assaf, became emotional. He was the only one in college, an engineering student at Bir Zeit University near Ramallah. After breathing fire about also being willing to die for Arafat, he began waxing eloquent about how much he wanted to go to the University of Memphis, where his uncle lived, "to study engineering." Unfortunately, he said, he could not get a visa into the United States now. Like his colleague, Assaf was ready to die for Yasser Arafat, but he wanted to live for the University of Memphis.

These were good young men, not terrorists. But their role models were all angry men, and these young men spent a lot of their time imagining how to unleash their anger, not realizing their potential. Abraham George, by contrast, produced a different context and a different set of teacher role models for those untouchable children in his school, and together they planted in his students the seeds of a very different imagination. We must have more Abraham Georges — everywhere — by the thousands: people who gaze upon a classroom of untouchable kids and not only see the greatness in each of them but, more important, get them to see the greatness in themselves while endowing them with the tools to bring that out.

After our little typing race at the Shanti Bhavan school, I went around the classroom and asked all the children — most of whom had been in school, and out of a life of open sewers, for only three years — what they wanted to be when they grew up. These were eight-year-old Indian kids whose parents were untouchables. It was one of the most moving experiences of my life. Their answers were as follows: "an astronaut," "a doctor," "a pediatrician," "a poetess," "physics and chemistry," "a scientist and an astronaut," "a surgeon," "a detective," "an author."

All dreamers in action — not martyrs in waiting.

Let me close with one last point. My own daughter went off to college in the fall of 2004, and my wife and I dropped her off on a warm September day. The sun was shining. Our daughter was full of excitement. But I can honestly say it was one of the saddest days of my life. And it wasn't just the dad-and-mom-dropping-their-eldest-child-off-at-school thing. No, something else bothered me. It was the sense that I was dropping my daughter off into a world that was so much more dangerous than the one she had been born into. I felt like I could still promise my daughter her bedroom back, but I couldn't promise her the world — not in the carefree way that I had explored it when I was her age. That really bothered me. Still does.

The flattening of the world, as I have tried to demonstrate in this book, has presented us with new opportunities, new challenges, new partners but also, alas, new dangers, particularly as Americans. It is imperative that we find the right balance among all of these. It is imperative that we be the best global citizens that we can be — because in a flat world, if you don't visit a bad neighborhood, it might visit you. And it is imperative that while we remain vigilant to the new threats, we do not let them paralyze us. Most of all, though, it is imperative that we nurture more people with the imaginations of Abraham George and Fadi Ghandour. The more people with the imagination of 11/9, the better chance we have of staving off another 9/11. I refuse to settle for a world that gets smaller in the wrong sense, in the sense that there are fewer and fewer places an American can go without a second thought and fewer and fewer foreigners feeling comfortable about coming to America.

To put it another way, the two greatest dangers we Americans face are an excess of protectionism — excessive fears of another 9/11 that prompt us to wall ourselves in, in search of personal security — and excessive fears of competing in a world of 11/9 that prompt us to wall ourselves off, in search of economic security. Both would be a disaster for us and for the world. Yes, economic competition in the flat world will be more equal and more intense. We Americans will have to work harder, run faster, and become smarter to make sure we get our share. But let us not underestimate our strengths or the innovation that could explode from the flat world when we really do connect all of the knowledge centers together. On such a flat earth, the most important attribute you can have is creative imagination — the ability to be the first on your block to figure out how all these enabling tools can be put together in new and exciting ways to create products, communities, opportunities, and profits. That has always been America's strength, because America was, and for now still is, the world's greatest dream machine.

I cannot tell any other society or culture what to say to its own children, but I can tell you what I say to my own: The world is being flattened. I didn't start it and you can't stop it, except at a great cost to human development and your own future. But we can manage it, for better or for worse. If it is to be for better, not for worse, then you and your generation must not live in fear of either the terrorists or of tomorrow, of either al-Qaeda or of Infosys. You can flourish in this flat world, but it does take the right imagination and the right motivation. While your lives have been powerfully shaped by 9/11, the world needs you to be forever the generation of 11/9 — the generation of strategic optimists, the generation with more dreams than memories, the generation that wakes up each morning and not only imagines that things can be better but also acts on that imagination every day.

ACKNOWLEDGMENTS

In 1999 I published a book on globalization called *The Lexus and the Olive Tree*. The phenomenon we call globalization was just taking off then, and *The Lexus and the Olive Tree* was one of the early attempts to put a frame around it. This book is not meant to replace *The Lexus and the Olive Tree*, but rather to build on it and push the arguments forward as the world has evolved.

I am deeply grateful to the publisher of *The New York Times* and chairman of the New York Times Company, Arthur Sulzberger Jr., for granting me a leave of absence to be able to undertake this book, and to Gail Collins, editorial page editor of *The New York Times*, for supporting that leave and this whole project. It is a privilege to work for such a great newspaper. It was Arthur and Gail who pushed me to try my hand at documentaries for the Discovery Times Channel, which took me to India and stimulated this whole book. Thanks in that regard also go to Billy Campbell of the Discovery Channel for his enthusiastic backing of that Indian documentary, and to Ken Levis, Ann Derry, and Stephen Reverand for helping to bring it off. Without Discovery the show would not have happened.

I never could have written this book, though, without some wonderful tutors from the worlds of technology, business, and politics. A few individuals must be singled out for particular thanks. I never would have broken the code of the flat world without the help of Nandan Nilekani, CEO of the Indian technology company Infosys, who was the first to point out to me how the playing field was being leveled. Vivek Paul, president of the Indian technology company Wipro, really took me inside the business of the flat world and deciphered it all for me — time and time again. Joel Cawley, the head of IBM's strategic planning team, helped me connect so many of the dots between technology and business and politics on Planet Flat — connections I never would have made without him. Craig Mundie, chief technology officer of Microsoft, walked me through the technological evolutions that made the flat world possible and helped ensure that in writing about them I would not fall flat on my face. He was a tireless and demanding tutor. Paul Romer, the Stanford University economist who has done so much good work on the new economy, took the time to read the book in draft and brought both his humanity and his intellect to several chapters. Marc Andreessen, one of the cofounders of Netscape; Michael Dell of Dell Inc.; Sir John Rose, chairman of Rolls-Royce; and Bill Gates of Microsoft were very generous in commenting on certain sections. My inventor friend Dan Simpkins was enormously helpful in walking this novice through his complex universe. Michael Sandel's always challenging questions stimulated me to write a whole chapter — "The Great Sorting Out." And Yaron Ezrahi, for the fourth book in a row, let me bounce countless ideas off his razor-sharp mind. The same was true for David Rothkopf. None of them is responsible for any mistakes, only for insights. I am truly in their debt.

So many other people shared with me their valuable time and commented on different parts of this book. I want to thank in particular Allen Adamson, Graham Allison, Alex and Jocelyn Attal, Jim Barksdale, Craig Barrett, Brian Behlendorf, Katie Belding, Jagdish Bhagwati, Sergey Brin, Brill Brody, Mitchell Caplan, Bill Carrico, John Chambers, Nayan Chanda, Alan Cohen, Maureen Conway, Lamees El-Hadidy, Rahm Emanuel, Mike Eskew, Judy Estrin, Diana Farrell, Joel Finkelstein, Carly Fiorina, Frank Fukuyama, Jeff Garten, Fadi Ghandour, Bill Greer, Jill

Greer, Ken Greer, Promod Haque, Steve Holmes, Dan Honig, Scott Hyten, Shirley Ann Jackson, P. V. Kannan, Alan Kotz, Gary and Laura Lauder, Robert Lawrence, Jerry Lehrman, Rick Levin, Joshua Levine, Will Marshall, Walt Mossberg, Moisés Naím, David Neeleman, Larry Page, Jim Perkowski, Thomas Pickering, Jamie Popkin, Clyde Prestowitz, Glenn Prickett, Saritha Rai, Jerry Rao, Rajesh Rao, Amartya Sen, Eric Schmidt, Terry Semel, H. Lee Scott Jr., Dinakar Singh, Larry Summers, Jeff Uhlin, Atul Vashistha, Philip Verleger Jr., William Wertz, Meg Whitman, Irving Wladawsky-Berger, Bob Wright, Jerry Yang, and Ernesto Zedillo.

And special thanks to my soul mates and constant intellectual companions Michael Mandelbaum and Stephen P. Cohen. Sharing ideas with them is one of the joys of my life. A special thanks too to John Doerr and Herbert Allen Jr., who each gave me the opportunity to road test this book on some of their very demanding and critical colleagues.

As always, my wife, Ann, was my first editor, critic, and all-around supporter. Without her help and intellectual input this book never would have happened. I am so lucky to have her as my partner. And thanks too to my daughters Orly and Natalie for putting up with another year of

Dad closeted away in his office for long hours, and to my dear mother, Margaret Friedman, for asking every day when my book would be done. Max and Eli Bucksbaum provided valuable encouragement in the early hours of the morning in Aspen. And my sisters Shelley and Jane have always been in my corner.

I am blessed to have had the same literary agent, Esther Newberg, and publisher, Jonathan Galassi, for four books, and the same line editor, Paul Elie, for the last three. They are simply the best in the business. I am also blessed to have the most talented and loyal assistant, Maya Gorman.

This book is dedicated to three very special people in my life: My mother- and father-in-law, Matt and Kay Bucksbaum, and my oldest childhood friend, Ron Soskin.

About the Author

THOMAS L. FRIEDMAN has won the Pulitzer Prize three times for his work at *The New York Times*, where he serves as the foreign affairs columnist. He is the author of three bestselling books: *From Beirut to Jerusalem* (FSG, 1989), winner of the National Book Award for nonfiction and still considered the definitive work on the Middle East; *The Lexus and the Olive Tree: Understanding Globalization* (FSG, 1999); and *Longitudes and Attitudes: Exploring the World After September 11* (FSG, 2002). He lives in Bethesda, Maryland, with his family.